MotoMysteries Collection
Books One to Three

SHERRI KUKLA

MOTOMYSTERIES Collection: Books One to Three
© 2021 Sherri Kukla
Published by S&S Publishing
www.sherrikukla.com

ISBN: 978-1-7349484-7-9

All rights reserved.
No part of this book may be reproduced in any form or by any electronic or mechanical means, including information storage and retrieval systems, without written permission from the author, except for the use of brief quotations in a book review.

Trust in the LORD with all your heart
And do not lean on your own understanding.
Proverbs 3:5

In loving honor of my greatest
prayer warrior and champion
My Mother
Juanita Noah, Servant of God
12/17/34 - 7/12/19

The Skeleton and the Lantern

MotoMysteries

Book 1

For my granddaughter Summer
She encouraged me not to give up.
If not for her, the book would never have been completed.

Prologue

How could I be dying already? I'm not done living.

"I know I'm only ten, but I'm serious, Dad. Someday I'm going to help boys, like that man in the movie did!" Was it really 60 years ago I said that?

My dad was right. He said the dream was too big.

It's not that I mind dying. It's my dream dying with me that hurts.

"Grandpa?"

Max, I wish I could talk to you.

"Grandpa, you're crying!" I hear the sadness.

"Grandpa . . ."

His voice is fading. Where is he going?

But wait, maybe it's not him leaving. It's me. I'm the one leaving.

"Don't forget the dream, Max." I try to get the words out, but my mouth won't work.

"Dad!" Max sounded excited. "Come in here! Grandpa talked to me!"

"No, son. Grandpa hasn't talked in days."

"He did, Dad. He said, 'Don't forget the dream, Max.'"

I wanted to jump for joy. God let me talk one last time. The dream won't die with me.

I can go now. Suddenly, I am jumping for joy.

The angels are taking me home.

Chapter 1

Jeremiah

Thirty years later

"Stop the car, Dad! There's a man hanging off the power station!"

Even though we were flying along the highway, I expected my dad to slam the brakes on right away so we could hop out and help that poor man. But my dad took his time on the narrow two-lane road. It seemed like forever before he found a safe spot to pull over.

I jumped out of the car before it came to a complete stop and ran over the rocky hills to get to the power station. We've seen it a billion times driving to the desert, but I never imagined we'd be rescuing a man in danger there some day.

Dad caught up with me just as I got close enough to realize my mistake. My very big mistake.

"Jeremiah! You risked our safety for a prank."

"Sorry, Dad. It looked like a real man as we whizzed by."

I watched the dummy flopping around in the breeze. Oops.

Back at the car we heard a horn honking. A white-haired guy in an old truck blew by us, missing our truck only by inches.

"Where did that idiot come from?" I knew that shook my dad up because normally he wouldn't call someone a name. At least not in front of me.

"I saw a motorcycle in his truck." It wouldn't help, but it was all I could think of.

"Well, I sure hope we don't run into him down there." Dad shook his head. "I doubt he is any safer in the dirt than on the pavement."

We were on our way to the desert to ride our dirt bikes and check out some land my parents planned to buy. "Hey, Dad, I hope that guy wasn't in a big hurry because he wants our land! He better not ruin it for us!"

Our long-time family dream was about to happen. Not dirt bike riding, but buying land out here. Riding motorcycles has been going on in my family for generations. Well, if you count me, my dad, his dad and his dad before that.

"Not likely." Dad checked the mirrors as he pulled back onto the road.

We had driven this way many times in my life because camping in Dry Brook – that's what they called the town we loved – was our number one, favorite family activity. Usually my mom and sister came too. We would bring our big toy hauler trailer. They call it that because there's room for the off-road toys and for sleeping. But this time we were doing a guys-only trip and roughing it.

"Minnesota!" I shouted, distracting my dad which isn't a good idea on a narrow winding road with an idiot ahead of us.

"What are you talking about?" He kept his eyes on the road and sighed like he just wanted to get there with no more surprises.

"That's where the idiot was from!"

"Jeremiah, don't call people names. I shouldn't have said that."

"Oh, okay." We went through this conversation every time an idiot, oops, I mean bad driver, passed us on the road. Dad would get upset, yell at the driver, then tell me later he was setting a bad example for me and that I shouldn't call people names.

"So how do you know?"

"Know what?" He confused me, because I had been thinking about Dad's habit of calling people names and then telling me not to call names. I thought he meant how did I know about that habit.

"How do you know he's from Minnesota?"

"I saw his license plate as he passed."

"Well, he's heading in the right direction. I hope he keeps driving and makes it there in one piece."

I never thought about this little highway leading to Minnesota. But I suppose if you headed east long enough, you could get almost anywhere from California.

We weren't expecting to see many people in Dry Brook on

this camping trip. The weekends were the crowded times in the off-road park.

I was home schooled so I could go motorcycle riding anytime. Sometimes I brought my schoolwork with me. This time I did extra work for a week to have fun on our trip without schoolwork to worry about.

I couldn't wait to live down here. I'd be able to ride every day. But I'm getting ahead of myself.

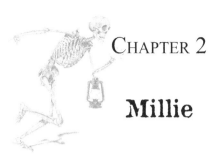

Chapter 2

Millie

"Millicent! What kind of name is that?" Millie stormed through the house, banging the bathroom door shut behind her. She always went there to hide.

"Millie, please." Her mother's soft voice called out as she followed her and knocked on the door. "Let's talk."

"There's nothing to talk about." Millie yelled from inside. "It isn't fair! Dad took Jeremiah and not me and it's because you guys never wanted a girl, anyway. That's why Jeremiah gets to have all the fun!"

The ranting gave way to sniffling and then tears.

"Millie, please come out so we can talk."

Mom waited until the door opened but Millie wouldn't look her in the eyes. Her head hung low and long hair covered her face. She was still holding the crumpled up envelope with the court paperwork.

This time when Mom held her arms out Millie didn't pull away. She hugged her mother, burying her head in her mom's chest, letting the tears flow.

"This isn't about Jeremiah, is it?"

"Huh-uh." Her voice sounded muffled.

Mom led her into the kitchen where the smell of homemade chocolate chip cookies wafted from the oven. "Milk, tea or ginger ale?" Mom asked as she removed the cookies.

While Millie munched on a cookie and drank ice cold soda, Mom picked up the envelope and removed the paper. "You wouldn't even have seen this if you had been doing your schoolwork instead of going through my mail."

Millie ignored the kind reprimand and mimicked "In the matter of Millicent C. Reginald, a ward of the State blah blah blah." She talked around a mouthful of cookie. "Millicent! Yuck and double yuck!"

Mom hugged her. "You're our daughter now and all this legal stuff isn't your concern. Next time stay out of my mail and save yourself some grief."

"Why is it taking so long to finish my adoption? There is no reason they should keep listening to that woman!" She picked up a cookie but then put it down again, hanging her head, then slamming her fist on the table. "She obviously doesn't want to be a mother. She never did one thing they told her to in six years."

Mom patted her shoulder. "And none of that is news to you. Why is it hitting you so hard today?"

"Because I wanted to go riding with Dad instead of doing stupid Social Studies!"

"Don't you think Jeremiah would have rather gone to the movies yesterday with you and Dad than doing schoolwork?" Mom stood and cleared the table. "Besides Dad left a surprise for you."

"Really?"

"As soon as your schoolwork is complete, you can go through the box he left for you. He said you've been asking about it."

The box! Millie couldn't believe she would finally get to look through it.

"Let me at that schoolwork!" She jumped up and disappeared from the kitchen.

CHAPTER 3

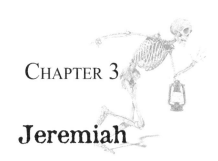

Jeremiah

We arrived at our destination without any more problems or unexpected stops. We were unloading the motorcycles when I heard a truck roaring along the dirt road nearby.

Oh, no! It was our friend from the highway. The idiot.

My dad seemed totally unaware. He was adjusting the motorcycle chain and getting his bike ready to ride. I don't know if it's what the adults call denial or if he just didn't realize the guy was heading right for us.

Sure enough, the guy pulled up next to us. Before my dad looked up, the guy shouted, "Holy buckets! I can't believe anyone else is out here today!"

I would have loved to see the look on my dad's face, but I was standing behind him.

Even if I hadn't seen the guy's license plate, I knew by that greeting he wasn't from around here.

"I'm Mike!" He shouted again. I don't know why he was so loud because he was standing right by us when he got out of his truck. "Minnesota Mike they call me!" He had a huge smile, like he just discovered something wonderful.

And then I discovered that he had just discovered something wonderful. Us.

"Man, am I glad to see you guys! Hey, mind if I set up camp right here alongside you?"

Oh, if only I could be inside my dad's head to hear what he was thinking.

I couldn't resist. I knew I'd pay for it, but I just couldn't resist. Stepping closer to my dad, I said, "Hey, Dad, isn't that the..."

"Jeremiah!" My dad's volume was only a little lower than Minnesota Mike's.

I struggled not to laugh. Minnesota Mike didn't even notice. He just seemed super happy.

"I'll tell you, man." He even talked with a big smile. "I'm glad I ran into you folks, because I haven't liked camping out here by myself, doncha know, ever since I found out about the skeleton. He shows up some dark nights, they say, wandering around these parts with that lantern in his belly."

He looked up into the sky. "I don't even think there's going to be a moon out tonight. Yikes!"

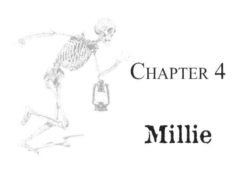

Chapter 4

Millie

Millie sat on the floor in the living room surrounded by pictures from decades ago. She was in heaven. She'd been begging her dad for weeks to let her go through this box, ever since she discovered it in a large drawer in the garage.

Millie held up a black and white 8x10 photo of motorcycle racers standing next to their bikes. The photo was over 60 years old. Names scrawled in pencil were hard to read, but there was no doubt about the rider on the far left. Thomas Anderson. Her great grandfather. Her dad's grandfather. She never met him. He only became her great grandfather once she joined the Anderson family two years ago.

Which still wasn't a done deal, she grumbled to herself as she thought about the letter. Then her eyes wandered to the photos surrounding her. History, decades old motorcycle racing photos, that warmed her soul. She had taken to the motorcycles as if she were born with the passion to ride. Now she was a part of the fourth generation of motorcycle riders. It gave her such a sense of belonging. Finally. She had waited all her life to feel like she belonged somewhere.

She heard the phone ringing and could tell by her mom's voice it was business. It sure wasn't her dad calling to let them know how the trip was going.

She was just about to move closer to the door to eavesdrop when a newspaper clipping caught her eye. The 1897 date intrigued her, and she forgot her love of eavesdropping and focused on the headline. "Charley Arizona going to the Arctic."

What a weird thing to keep with a bunch of motorcycle pictures. She skimmed the article about this old character and his cohorts leaving the wild west to head for a new adventure in the

Arctic. Okay, so what's the big deal? Why would Great Grandpa save a hundred-year-old article with his motorcycle photos?

"First discovered by an old prospector named Charley Arizona, the eight-foot skeleton rattled around the hills for years..." Millie read, then jumped up to go show her mom.

"Ha! This is a hoot!" She headed into the next room.

"Hey, Mom!" She walked with her head down, still reading what she could make out on the weathered clipping. Her laughter died when she rounded the corner to see her mom still on the phone and sounding way too serious.

"What new development?" Her mother demanded an answer from the person on the other end. Her back was to Millie. "She's already been our daughter for two years and nothing will change that!"

Millie's heart sank. She knew that letter meant trouble.

Chapter 5

Jeremiah

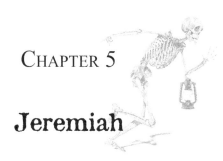

"So Mike, I'm guessing you're from Minnesota?"
I know this trick. Dad doesn't want to listen to some harebrained story about a skeleton, so before the guy can get one more word out, he's redirecting him. I think that's something Dad learned about working with kids. Which he needs to know. Which is why we're buying the land. But I'm too focused on Minnesota Mike and the skeleton to even think about our plans.
"Well, I was from Minnesota at one point." He smiled bigger than ever. "But I ain't even been to Minnesota in years! I mean ye-e-e-e-ars!"
"Ah." Dad rubbed his ear and scratched his head. Definite signs of being annoyed. This desert trip wasn't going like we planned. I think Dad was working on another question, but Mike wasn't one to give a person long to do their part in a conversation.
"I was born and raised there and I lived there well into my adulthood, doncha know. Back when I retired, which was a little younger than most people, I decided to leave Minnesota. I'm not going back until I hit every state in the good ol' US of A at least once, maybe even twice!"
Now I saw a genuine smile cross Dad's face. So the guy wasn't sticking around? And this guy may say he retired young, but that must have been a couple decades ago. With that white beard and long white hair he could have passed for Santa. He might even be that old. Funny, he was still riding a motorcycle.
"I just decided to run down here for a quick ride. Then I'll head back west to do some surfing before I head north."
Now Dad was even happier. This guy was just planning on taking one little ride and then leaving. Maybe when he said camp with us, he just meant park with us while he went riding.

Dad rummaged through his gear bag. "Well, you take it nice and safe on your ride." Clear sign of dismissal on Dad's part.

Minnesota Mike was not catching on.

"Where did you folks want to ride to, anyway? I'm game for anywhere!"

If it weren't for the good manners my parents have been drilling into me since they met me — I know, that's a strange way to put it. But, anyway, if it weren't for those manners I would have let out the biggest, hugest, loudest, noisiest groan you ever heard.

This guy was planning on riding with us! No way! Dad had to stop this.

I needed to watch, listen and take notes. If ever I met up with a Minnesota Mike later in life, then I would know how to ditch the guy without hurting his feelings.

Chapter 6

Millie

Mom hit the off button but held onto the phone, staring into space.

"What did that call mean?" She jumped at the sound of Millie's voice and turned to face her.

"Millicent! What are you doing eavesdropping?"

"What did that mean? There is a problem with my adoption, isn't there? They're going to make me leave, aren't they?" Questions tumbled out of her mouth. "I knew it was too good to be true. That this would be my home. That I would finally have a real family!"

Millie stormed off toward the bathroom.

Before she could get out of the room, her mom grabbed her by the shoulders.

"Now you stop right this minute, young lady!" Surprised by how stern she sounded, Millie stopped and faced her. But the tears, those she couldn't stop.

"Millie, challenges and difficulties are a part of life." She wiped at Millie's tears with a tissue. "So none of this is surprising, but what is surprising is you reading my mail and listening in on conversations."

"It's about me! I have a right to know!"

"Later, yes. But some things are so complicated. All it does is get you worried and fearful. How does that benefit you?"

She had no response, just her sniffles while she fiddled with the newspaper clipping.

"You trust us, don't you Millie?"

She nodded.

"Then let us handle all the legal stuff involved in making this adoption final. You just worry about getting your schoolwork done and beating Jeremiah on your motorcycle." She reached out for the paper Millie was holding.

"What have you got there?"

Millie sniffed and pushed her hair out of her eyes. "This is what I was coming to show you." She held it up. "It was with the old racing photos."

"There was a light in the skeleton's rib cage according to Charley Arizona," Mom read aloud and then chuckled. "I remember this." She held the paper up and waved it in the air. "It's been years since I thought of this."

"Tell me about it, Mom!"

"I remember a silly story the family used to tell about this mysterious skeleton."

"Have you heard the whole story?" Millie's curiosity kicked into high gear.

"Well, let me give it some thought and see if I can't piece it together the way I first heard it."

"I hope you can remember the story, it's sounds exciting."

"You finish going through that box and we'll chat about it later."

Chapter 7

Jeremiah

So much for the note-taking, I thought later as the three of us rode east on a well-traveled dirt road called Dry Brook Highway. My dad and I had a pattern to our riding. He led, I followed and every once in a long while he hung back and let me take the lead.

We weren't sure what Minnesota Mike would do and I'm not sure he did either. He was all over that road. Sometimes in the lead and sometimes in the middle of us. Sometimes he dropped back, back, back till we thought he had taken another trail for a solo ride. Next thing you know, there'd he be again, riding alongside, nearly running into one of us.

About five miles into the ride, the gas stop and ice cream store came into view. Right next to it was the real estate office where Dad's appointment was. He was meeting a man about the property we wanted to buy. I wondered what Dad would do now, because he's always Mr. Super Secret Agent with his business. No way was he going to say anything about it with Minnesota Mike hanging around, putting his two cents worth in. Which generally ended up being more like 92 cents.

We pulled to a stop outside the store. It felt good to get my helmet off and let the breeze blow through my hair. I watched Minnesota Mike out of the corner of my eye. Wonder if Dad could ditch him here?

"Hey man, how'd you know I felt for something cold to eat?"

Dad smiled. "Well, just a hunch," he mumbled, as he smoothed down his hair and hung his helmet on the end of his handlebars.

"Say, Mike." Dad was using his best trying-to-distract-someone voice. "While you're getting ice cream, I'm going to step in the office next door and say hello to a friend."

"Hey, no problemo, man. Try to get word on that big parcel.

19

The one that just went up for sale. That old geezer's owned it for years. I've been real interested in it myself. Maybe I'll even come along and ask the guy myself..."

"Well, I hoped you would take Jeremiah in for some ice cream too." Dad opened his fanny pack and pulled out some money.

Whew, that was close. It sounded like the land Mike was talking about, was the exact piece of property we've had our eye on.

"Yeah, okay. Besides, there's a story about gold being found on that land. Some major problem cropped up with the sale. Maybe can't even sell it now!"

Minnesota Mike stared off across the desert as if contemplating a big decision.

"You know, man, I think I'll just skip me that ice cream, save my money and see what the real scoop is on that desert land for sale." He was tossing his quarter up into the air and catching it. As if a quarter would buy anything to eat.

Dad's jaw hardened, and I saw him clenching his teeth.

A golden opportunity just presented itself and I sure wasn't going to let it pass by.

Chapter 8

Millie

"So what's this skeleton story all about?" Millie talked around a mouthful of pizza. "And why did he keep a newspaper clipping about it? Was he into ghost stories?"

"Don't talk with your mouth full, Millie."

"I can't help it." She still chewed and talked. "I've been waiting all day to hear the story."

"Grandpa Tom had some buddies he used to camp with..."

"In the desert where Dad and Jeremiah went?"

"I never thought about where, but I imagine it was. Your dad first went with his dad when he was a boy and maybe that's how he knew about it." Mom stopped talking while she took a bite of pizza and chewed it about a hundred times. It drove Millie crazy waiting for the rest of the story.

"They would sit around the campfire," Mom continued "and share the craziest stories. The skeleton story was the favorite."

"Were you there, Mom?"

"Oh, goodness, no. I never came along until Grandpa Tom was long gone. He handed the stories down to his son and grandson. So I heard them second and third-hand."

"Who told you?" Millie shoved another piece of pizza into her mouth.

Millie's mom frowned at the bad manners. "Was it Dad? Or did you know his dad well enough that he told you stories? How old were you, anyway, when you met Dad?"

"I was 19, and it was your dad who told me the story. We were on our way to the desert, and he was reminiscing about listening to his grandpa around the campfire."

"Wow, so Dad got to hear the ghost stories? Cool!"

"According to the legend, no one could remember where the lost desert mine was. Lost so long people doubted whether it was real. Soon people called it the Phantom Mine. The legend said the skeleton..."

The phone sang out dad's ring tone, interrupting the story.

"Ah mom, you'll be on there forever and I want to hear the story about the skeleton." Millie groaned, hoping she'd take the call later.

Her mom's face beamed when she heard her dad's voice.

"Tell me all about your trip so far." She ignored another loud groan coming from her daughter.

CHAPTER 9

Jeremiah

"Hey, Mike. I was hoping to hear more about that skeleton while we ate!"

Boy did that press the right button with old Minnesota. His face lit up and a grin the size of the Grand Canyon told me I was in for a whopper of a tale while we munched down the ice cream.

Last I saw of my dad, he was shaking his head and heading toward his appointment.

"Old Charley Arizona, was the first to spot that skeleton." Minnesota Mike jumped into the story after we got situated on a picnic bench outside. Me with an extra large milk shake while he slurped on a cone that was dripping all over his fingers. My mom would have had a cow if she could see the way he was licking his fingers.

"I hear tell he up and told people..." and at this point Mike hunched his shoulders and hunkered down. He stared me right in the eyes, his voice got lower, kinda spooky-like, as if he was Charley Arizona himself. "I could hear his old bones a'rattlin'!" Then, bam! He stood up and bellowed. "Was pert near eight, maybe even nine feet tall!"

This got embarrassing. The lady from the store rushed out to see what the commotion was. I like hearing a ghost story same as the next kid, but I didn't want to die of embarrassment in a town I hoped would soon be my hometown.

"You ain't telling that old wives tale, are ya?" She chomped on her gum while she stared at Minnesota. It popped and snapped as she waved her hand in dismissal at the crazy old man. The screen door slammed when she went back inside.

"What does she know?" Minnesota was kinda secretive like. "She must not a'heard the recent talk of gold around here."

23

At the mention of gold, he forgot all about telling me the scary story. "I gotta go see about that property. I mean if what they said is true about the hidden gold mine, this might be just the time to use up that old nest egg. Git me some land and settle down."

Before I could stop him, he was up and heading next door at a faster clip than I thought an old guy could go.

Chapter 10

Millie

"Did you make the offer?" Mom's voice sang with excitement, but legal stuff Millie didn't find interesting. She headed to the garage.

Millie had just started to clean her motorcycle when her mom showed up. She stopped what she was doing and looked up. "That was quick."

"Your dad couldn't talk, he was at the realtor's office. He wasn't able to put the offer in. There are complications."

"I don't understand any of that, but it doesn't sound good."

"When you want to buy a house, you submit an offer saying what you're willing to pay."

"Don't you just pay the price they say?" Millie squirted soapy water on the motorcycle plastics and rubbed them with a cloth while she listened.

"No, it's a little more complicated. Do you want me to explain to you how the offer works?"

"Boring!" Millie kept cleaning her bike. "Can we get back to the skeleton?"

Mom's blank stare told Millie she hadn't heard a word.

"Earth to Mom!" Millie waved her hands around, trying to get her mom's attention. "Remember the skeleton?"

"I was just thinking about the legend and your great grandpa and the property we want to buy."

"You've lost me there." Millie swung a leg over her bike and plopped down on the seat. She polished the handlebars with a different rag.

"Buying this property is a three generation dream," Mom said. "It started with your great grandpa. He loved the desert, and the tall tales, and he loved kids. He had a dream of one day starting a boys ranch."

25

"Were the boys going to ride motorcycles on this ranch?"

"Yes. Motorcycles were his passion, and he planned to use them as a rehabilitation tool for boys who'd been in trouble. But he never had the money. An amazing thing about him though. He never let go of the dream."

"How do you know that?" Millie wished she could have known him.

"After he died, the family found a notebook with handwritten notes about his plans. He dated all the pages, and he had written ideas down just a few months before he passed away."

"That's sad he never got to make his dream happen." Millie stopped polishing and found herself lost in thought like her mom, wondering about this man with the big dreams.

"His dreams kept him going." Mom nodded as she spoke. "Just because he didn't live to see it, doesn't mean his dreams won't happen."

"How could that be?"

"Like King David in the Bible." She stepped toward the door. "For all the years he planned to build the temple, he didn't get to be the one to fulfill that dream." Then, looking like she had a million things on her mind, she walked out.

Not real sure how we went from skeletons to lessons on how to sell land and then to King David, Millie thought. She probably wouldn't hear another word about the skeleton tonight.

Chapter 11

Jeremiah

Dad almost ran into Minnesota Mike when he came barreling out of the office next door.

"Hey there, doncha know, you're scurrying like you jist discovered gold and got to git there before the next feller!"

Dad apologized and chuckled politely. I could tell it was politely and not because he thought it was funny. He was probably tired of hearing about gold and skeletons and pretty much anything else old Minnesota had to say.

"Lunch back at camp is what I want to discover. Do you want us to wait for you?"

"No, I'm thinking I'll just hang around these parts for a while, I need to get some info from your pal here." He motioned with his thumb at the realtor's office. "You all head on back. I might catch up with you later."

I almost burst out laughing at the look of relief on my dad's face. But me, I was disappointed, because now I wouldn't get to hear the rest of the skeleton story, and why did this guy keep talking about gold?

"Mm-mmm! This is delicious!" Dad was on his second bite already of our ready-made lunch before I even got mine open. "I love your mom's sandwiches!" The fact we were eating in peace, just the two of us, made the meal even tastier. I have to admit as interesting as his stories sounded, I was also enjoying a break from our newfound friend.

Maybe when he showed back up, I'd be able to hear the rest of the story and make some sense of his ramblings about skeletons, lanterns and gold. Even if it was made up, I liked the stories.

"Push our bikes over there in the truck's shade," Dad said when I finished eating my sandwich.

"Are we going to ride over and check out our new property?" I sat back down with a cold soda and a big bag of pretzels.

"Well, Son," he sounded disappointed. "It may not become our property." He shook his head and looked at the ground. "At least not any time soon."

"What happened? I thought you went there to sign papers and give the guy some money."

"Yeah, I thought so too." Dad looked up, shaking his head again. "There are complications. The land isn't for sale."

"That makes no sense! Did someone else buy it?"

"No, he didn't say that's what happened," Dad took a long drink from his iced tea. "Your mom sure makes good iced tea!"

"What did he say about it being for sale two weeks ago?"

"Said he jumped the gun putting the for sale sign up. He doesn't have a signed contract yet."

"Oh." I was disappointed but still hopeful. "Well, at least it didn't get sold to someone else."

"Yeah. If that's really the story."

Uh-oh. That didn't sound good.

"What do you mean?" I jumped up in frustration, knocking over my drink and spilling the pretzels. Which was okay because pretzels weren't my favorite. I wanted Flamin' Hot Cheetos, but my mom didn't pack those.

"I just feel like something is up, but I can't put my finger on it." Dad stared across the desert.

"That's not fair!" I yelled. "What about all our plans? What about our kids ranch? What about me riding my motorcycle every day? It isn't fair!"

I knocked over the lawn chair and kicked my soda can. "We might as well go home, at least everything is okay there."

Dad picked up my lawn chair and the soda can and even the pretzel bag. "Well, not everything."

Chapter 12

Millie

"Hey, Mom!" Millie ran into the house searching for her. "Hey, Mom!" she called out again just as she rounded the corner into her mom's office.

"Millie! You scared me!" Mom clutched her chest. "Is something wrong?"

"No, I just had this great idea!"

Mom took her glasses off and rubbed her eyes. It looked like she had been staring at her laptop. Millie stepped around the desk to see what was so interesting. As usual, Mom had a bazillion tabs open on her browser. She clicked out of them when Millie got to where she could see the screen.

Forgetting what she came running in for, Millie's curiosity grew, knowing her mom was looking up something she didn't want her to see.

"What were you studying?"

Mom waved her hand in the air as if to dismiss her research as nothing of importance. "Oh, you know how I get Millie, just following a rabbit trail through the internet. Jumping from one thing to the next."

"But why did you click from the browser to your email as soon as I stepped around?"

"Oh Millie, really!" she put her glasses back on and snapped her laptop shut. "You know how far behind I get on my emails."

"Yeah, but you only got interested in your email when I came around to this side of your desk."

"Millie, you sound like a detective on a hot lead." Mom laughed and reached over to hug her. "So what did you want when you came running in, practically scaring me to death?" A forced laugh. Millie could tell.

"Maybe I am a detective." She refused to give up. "I know you didn't decide to answer emails at the exact moment I came in. I know you're reading about stuff you're hiding from me. Probably something about that letter or phone call. What was that phone call about?"

"Millie, please..."

"You keep saying that! Stop saying that!" Her voice rose louder than she meant.

Mom stared right at her. "Honestly!" She opened the laptop and clicked the mouse on one of the open tabs. Millie noticed it wasn't the last tab she was on and was just about to ask her why she didn't click on the one she was hiding until she caught sight of the topic.

"Legend of the skeleton in the desert!"

"Does that look like secret social worker research?"

"Oh." Now she forced a laugh. "I thought you were keeping something from me. Something bad."

Now Mom's laugh was genuine. "Maybe I was keeping something from you. I didn't want you to know I was curious about that silly old legend about the skeleton!"

While they laughed together, Mom closed the laptop. "What did you come running in for?"

"Oh yeah," Millie pushed her hair behind her ears and plopped down on the edge of Mom's desk. "I had the most awesome idea. Can I read the notebook Great Grandpa had about the boys ranch idea? Do you think Dad would let me read the journal?"

Mom's smile vanished. "That is a sad memory for your dad."

"Why?"

"Because the journal burned in a fire."

"Fire? Did someone's house burn down?"

"No. Someone threw it into a fire."

"Who would do that?"

"Millie, I'm sorry, but I can't talk about that without asking your dad. I shouldn't have mentioned the journal."

"But Mom! You can't leave me just hanging like this! First the skeleton story you haven't finished and now a mystery that involves my own family. Pleeease!!"

She could tell by the look on her mom's face no amount of begging would help. She wished she could get onto her mom's laptop to check the browsing history. Millie knew her mom was hiding more than the skeleton website.

Chapter 13

Jeremiah

"What do you mean everything isn't okay at home?"

Wouldn't you know it? Right when I needed to have a serious conversation with my dad, out of nowhere a motorcycle comes roaring in and slides to a stop in a cloud of dust.

"Hey there, hey now!" Minnesota Mike ripped his helmet off so fast it looked like his head would come off with it.

"What's happening here? You're not loading up and heading home, are you? You're not leaving, are you?"

Wow, this guy could talk. It was hard to get a word in.

"We've had a change in plans." Dad packed his jersey and riding pants into his gear bag.

"Doncha know, I got some news for you!" Minnesota popped open a soda can. "Let me down this pop first, I'm dying of thirst." He guzzled the soft drink we call soda. Dad kept packing, but Minnesota Mike just wasn't having it.

"Hey now, you gotta hear what I have to say and I think you'll change your mind about leaving." He followed that with a loud burp that would have sent my mom into orbit. "Whew! That hit the spot!" He patted his protruding stomach. Not sure the guy's heard of manners. But it was pretty funny. It almost made me forget about whatever was going on at home. Almost, but not quite.

"Come on, guys. Pull up a chair." He pulled his out of the back of his pickup truck. "You gotta hear what I learnt about that property for sale."

I saw Dad look at him. But I know how my dad thinks. He won't want this guy to think he's interested or to know how important that property is to us.

"I could use a rest and a cold drink before we hit the road."

31

Okay, now I knew for sure my dad wanted to hear what Minnesota Mike had to say. We had both just finished eating lunch and Dad just downed a big glass of iced tea.

"What's your hurry to git out of this place? Ya looked like you were all set to stay a few days."

Dad ignored the question and dropped into a chair with a cold water. I grabbed a bottle too and sat next to him.

"I never tip my hand what I know about things," Minnesota Mike said, "but I just wandered in all nonchalant-like and asked the guy what properties did he have for sale. He talked about every property this side of the moon but never mentioned THE property. You know, the big parcel that's got my interest and maybe yours, too."

How did he know that? I wondered. We didn't say anything about it.

"Least wise," Minnesota Mike continued, "that's what the guy in the office said when I told him the parcel that got my interest."

"What's that?" Dad's ears perked up when he realized the realtor was talking about him.

"Yeah, the guy said it was strange he'd get two people right in a row asking about the same parcel of land that ain't even for sale."

"What parcel is that?" I never knew Dad was so good at acting like he didn't know stuff. It's not actually lying, but it sure isn't admitting the truth.

Minnesota looked at him kinda strange, maybe wondering why Dad pretended he didn't just ask that guy about the land. Then he went back to his rambling.

"It's the gold! I know it's the gold. That's why..."

"Why do you keep talking about gold?" I interrupted. Dad gave me a look for butting in, but I think he was as curious as I was.

"Sure! The word is out there's gold on that land and now they're rethinking selling."

"Why do you think there's gold on land for sale out here?" Dad still didn't admit he knew what land it was.

Minnesota looked a little ashamed. "Well, I'll tell ya." He stared into the sky, then got up and took another can out of the ice chest in his truck. He popped it open, but just sipped on it. I don't even think he was thirsty, it's like he was stalling. Trying to decide what to tell us.

Dad was patient. I was not. But I didn't push my luck and ask. I just kept staring at him, waiting for the answer.

"Yeah, I'll tell ya." He was still looking up in the sky, then around the desert. Then back at my dad. "I'm not real proud about this, but there's a reason I know about the gold."

It seemed like he would never tell us.

He sat back down in his chair and stared at the ground for so long it was like he had forgotten what we were talking about. Forgot about his soda too. It tipped over in the dirt and the brown liquid oozing out made a mud puddle around the can.

Dad was growing impatient. He stood up and crushed his empty water bottle. "Sounds like nothing more than a legend." Dad returned to packing.

"I admit," Minnesota came to life. "It sounds far-fetched, but I got it on good authority."

Dad turned to look at him again, and me, well, I never stopped looking at him. I wanted to shake the story out of him, but I was too polite.

"Tell ya what though." Minnesota Mike stood and rubbed his chin. "You're good folks and I... Well, I just can't bring myself to tell ya how I know."

Chapter 14

Millie

Millie crept down the hallway and listened outside her mom's door. She could hear the shower water, so she hurried to the office.

Lifting the laptop open, her heart beat hard as she touched the mouse to bring the screen to life. She had to see what her mom was hiding. But she was taking a big risk. Both she and Jeremiah knew their mom's work laptop was off limits.

Clicking through the open tabs, she stopped when she saw a website about birth parents and adoption. She knew it was something about her adoption. Before skimming through the huge amount of text, she clicked another tab and saw a public records search for someone named Boyd Colston. Who was Boyd Colston? Why would Mom be researching him? That sure wasn't her biological dad's name. Maybe he was a new client.

That didn't seem likely as she read over the results of the public records search. Quite a criminal history this Boyd character had. Did not sound like someone who would hire a virtual assistant like Mom.

Mom had paid for the background info, so whoever this character was, he was worth $59.95 for her to learn about.

Millie jumped at the sound of her Mom's bedroom door opening. Breathing fast and with a pounding heart, she clicked back to the email and shut the laptop.

"Millie?" The voice floated down the hall.

She jumped out of the office chair and hurried to the hallway. "Did you need me Mom?"

The door cracked open a few inches. She saw her mom's dripping wet hair and part of her face.

"Yes, I'm sure you know why!" She didn't sound happy.

How could she have known? Millie wondered. Did she have secret cameras at her desk? Was her web cam synced with her phone? "I'm dead!" Millie moaned to herself.

"My conditioner!" Mom sounded annoyed.

Millie wanted to laugh out loud with relief but she knew that was the wrong response.

"I'm sorry Mom! I'm so sorry." She ran to the bathroom she and Jeremiah shared, grabbed her Mom's hair conditioner and hurried back down the hall with it.

Before her Mom could say anything else, she blurted out, "I know you've told me a hundred times not to take it without permission. I'm so sorry I inconvenienced you."

Mom was silent. Did she go overboard on that apology? Millie wondered. She wanted to get on her mom's good side. The guilt for touching the laptop was overwhelming.

"Thank you." Mom closed the bedroom door and Millie realized she still had a little more time.

Standing in the office doorway, she knew there were answers waiting there for her. If only she dared take another look.

She had to know what was going on. But what if she got caught? Would it be worth it?

CHAPTER 15

Jeremiah

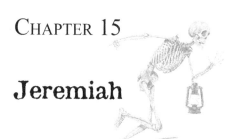

That was all it took. My dad was done listening to Minnesota Mike's ramblings about skeletons and property for sale and gold. He worked faster than ever cleaning up the area and moving the bikes in place to load into the truck.

"Now wait jist a minute. You folks aren't leaving, are you?" Minnesota Mike was whining now. "Thought you was staying all night, doncha know?"

"We thought about it," Dad didn't look at Minnesota, but moved even faster, if that was possible. The tailgate dropped open with a loud thump, very unlike Dad. He was super careful with all his stuff. I guess between running into this guy, getting the bad news about the property and now bad news from home, it was all too much.

"Well?" Minnesota prompted. "Ya sure didn't consider it for long then?"

"Something came up at home." Dad's voice sounded strained as he pushed his bike up the ramp onto the tailgate. I was so stunned at what was taking place I had forgotten to help push. But the look he gave - that look that says I'm going to die if I don't get over there and help him - lit a fire under me. Soon we had his bike in the truck bed. I hurried to the side and handed him the tie straps to cinch it down.

Then, because it was just that kind of day where you need nothing else to go wrong, I hurried over to my bike and rolled it to the edge of the ramp.

"Well, I'm right disappointed." Minnesota Mike's head hung down. You'd think we were old friends. "I was hoping to jaw with you about that property we're both so interested in."

"Look!" Dad's voice raised. "Why do you keep saying we're both interested in that property?"

"Well that feller, the real estate guy, told me you were asking about it."

"Well, so what if I was?" Dad said, as we pushed my bike up the ramp.

"It's because I wouldn't tell you how I knowed about the gold, ain't it? That's why you're leaving!"

Dad stopped so fast the bike rolled back down the ramp a few inches. I held on to it in mid-climb while he stared down Minnesota. "I don't mean to be rude here, Mike, but you're trying my patience and I've had about enough of your talk about gold and skeletons and properties for sale."

"Well now..." Minnesota Mike said.

"You don't need to fill my boy's head full of ghost stories and frankly, I've had some bad news from home and just need to get loaded up and hit the road."

Next thing I knew, Minnesota was behind my bike helping push it so Dad could pull it up into the truck bed where he was standing. "Man, am I sorry to hear that. I'll help any way I can. You won't hear no more of me going on about all I've discovered, when you got more important things on your mind."

He didn't seem offended. He also didn't seem to let go of the idea he had valuable info we might want to know.

Within minutes, we were back out on the two-lane highway heading west, chasing the sun that would soon dip past the mountains we had to cross. It was almost dusk when I saw the strangest thing in the distance.

Maybe I'd heard too much about the skeleton today, but there was something weird hovering just above the ground. I blinked my eyes and turned my head farther to my left, trying to see around my dad's head.

It couldn't be? Or could it? It sure is tall enough to be the skeleton Minnesota Mike had been rambling about. But it looks more like a ghost. Not that I've ever seen a ghost.

I shook my head and looked again. Nothing there. Even turning around and looking out the back window, I couldn't see it.

"Son, what on earth are you doing?"

"Oh, heh, heh." Wow, even I thought my laugh sounded phony. "Just saying goodbye to the desert I thought I was camping in tonight."

"Well, turn back around. You're distracting me with all that moving around."

Dad definitely had something on his mind. I knew he was as disappointed as I was about not getting the property deal started. That was the whole reason we had come out today.

"Dad, what's the bad news from home?"

I don't think he even heard me. He gets like that sometimes. Like he's lost in his own mind, concentrating on things so hard he doesn't know anyone is talking to him.

"Dad!" He looked my way, then back at the highway. I found that always works. Get his attention first, then ask.

"What's the bad news from home?"

"Oh that." He chuckled. Was that a pretend chuckle? "I just said the first thing I could think of to get him to stop pestering me."

"But before he pulled up, you said something was wrong at home."

"I did?" He stared at the road. He was a bad liar. Not enough practice, I guess.

"Yes, you did!"

"Oh, I don't even remember now. That guy has me so frustrated, I can't think."

Sure. Secrets in the desert. Secrets at home. What was going on?

Chapter 16

Millie

"Yes," Millie whispered. It would be worth it, even if she got caught.

She sat down in her mom's chair and opened the laptop again, clicking to the third tab from the left.

"Summary of criminal charges," the heading read. She scanned the list. Identity theft, robbery, fraud.

Millie tensed as she heard the faint chirping of her mom's phone. Maybe if she got into a long conversation, this would give her more time. The phone continued to chirp. Her mom must still be in the shower. Silence.

She couldn't waste any more time. The list went on. Boyd must have been a career criminal. There was something about dishonorable discharge from military service, whatever that meant. Still not what she was looking for.

The phone was chirping again. The ringtone wasn't familiar.

"Hello?" She could hear the muffled sound of her mom taking the call. "Yes, this is Norah Anderson."

She was out of the shower. Not much time left.

Millie stared back at the screen, scrolling to page two of the criminal summary. At the top was a new heading. This was the one she was expecting to see.

"Child Protective Services," she whispered. Bingo! This was the information she needed to find out what was going on in her life. Single space typing with scattered black marks across the page hid random words. Names of children, she guessed.

"Millie!" the voice carried down the hall. She hadn't even heard the bedroom door open.

"Yeah, Mom?" Millie yelled to cover the sound of the laptop clicking shut. She jumped out of the chair and ran to her mom's bedroom. Thankfully, her mom was just peeking out the door again.

"Millie! You will not believe it! It's so wonderful!" Mom squealed.

Millie shook from the close call. She did her best to sound interested, but her mind was back on the browser and the secrets it held.

"What's up, Mom?" She took a deep breath to stop the quiver in her voice.

"Pack your bags! We're going to the desert!"

This made no sense. "Are we driving out to meet Dad?"

"No!" Mom was laughing. This was getting weirder. "Hold on! I need to get dressed and I'll tell you all about it. But get your bag packed! I'll be right out."

Millie sat in the middle of her room staring at the overnight bag. The words "Child Protective Services" floated in front of her. The bag was still empty when Mom rushed through the door minutes later.

"It's so wonderful, your dad will be thrilled." She didn't even notice Millie hadn't packed a thing. "That was the realtor on the phone, the property is for sale!" Mom clapped her hands. "Your Dad just won't believe it. It was a mix-up on the parcel numbers in the system. There is another man interested, but he's giving us first chance if we can get back there tonight."

"You mean the dream still might happen?" She jumped up and embraced her mom, who noticed the empty bag.

"Yes, now come on goofball, you gotta get packing. Your dad will be home soon and I want to be ready! This time we're going with him."

"What do you mean, Dad won't believe it? Doesn't he know?"

"He sure doesn't." Mom floated out of the room on a cloud. "The man couldn't get a hold of him. Lots of dead areas on the drive home."

She could hear her mom going through drawers in the next room as she packed her own bag.

"But why was he driving home? They were supposed to stay the night!" She followed her mom into her bedroom.

"Oh Millie, so many questions!" Mom said. "They changed their plans. Now pack, girl! They'll be here soon."

Chapter 17

Jeremiah

The only thing I wanted to do when we got home was eat, shower and hit the sack. This had been a long disappointing day. I looked over at Dad and could tell he felt the same way.

Making the last turn onto our street, I couldn't believe my eyes. My mom and sister were out on the front porch. It looked like every light in the house was on. What was going on?

"What in the world?" Dad said.

He pulled into the driveway and Mom and Millie ran out and surrounded us when we stepped out of the truck.

"We're getting the property!" Millie told the entire neighborhood.

Mom shushed her, but then let out her own shriek at the surprised look on Dad's face. "It's true, Max!" she jumped up and down. This couldn't be my mom, could it?

Dad came to life and threw his arms around Mom. Then stepped back, looking into her face. "But how? Why?"

Mom tugged on both of us to come inside, "Hurry, we have to get ready to head back!"

She set out leftovers from last night's dinner and filled us in on the details while we ate.

This was unbelievably great. Just when I lost all hope, we come home and find hope waiting for us.

"I don't know who or what he's talking about," Mom said as we were finishing our food. "But he said some other guy wants the property too."

I groaned. "Oh no, he does want it!"

"Who? Who!" Millie sounded like a barn owl.

"Some crazy guy we met down in the desert, calls himself Minnesota Mike."

Mom looked at Dad.

He chuckled and nodded his head. "Yes, Norah, I'm afraid it's true. It's been quite a day."

"Well, let's quit talking and get on the road," Millie urged.

Mom and Millie had the SUV loaded with their overnight bags. We took ours out of the truck and put them in the back of the car with theirs. Dad pulled the truck into the garage so we didn't have to take time to unload our bikes.

"Next time we'll have the trailer and all the bikes. We'll make it a celebration trip for a week!" Dad said as he backed out of the driveway.

"What's the story on this Minnesota Mike character?" Mom looked over at Dad as he pulled onto the freeway and hit the cruise control.

"Just some nutty guy." Dad took a long drink of the iced tea Mom brought along for him.

"Yeah," I chimed in, "just some nutty guy talking about gold and skeletons and..."

"Skeletons!" Millie shouted.

"Yes, skeletons. What's the big deal?" I said, as if we talked about skeletons every day.

"We've been talking about skeleton stories around here today, too!"

"Are you kidding me?"

"No, you can ask Mom."

Before I could get my question out Mom turned to look at her. "Not now, Millie."

She wasn't easily discouraged once she got an idea into her head. She didn't look like she was going to accept Mom putting the conversation off.

"Is that the bad news that happened around here today?" I jumped in before Millie could stay on the skeleton subject.

Mom looked over at Dad. "You told him?"

I could see Dad looking at me in the mirror. Guess I shouldn't have opened my mouth. Before I could wonder any more about what was going on, Millie spoke up.

"No, the skeleton wasn't the bad news." She did not look happy. "Boyd Colston was!"

Mom's head turned toward the back seat so fast it scared me. By the look on Millie's face she knew she had said something she shouldn't have.

"Where did you hear that name?" Mom demanded.

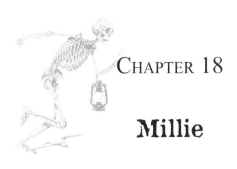

Chapter 18

Millie

Millie froze as her mom glared at her.

"Millicent! I asked you a question!"

Millie hated that name. "I don't know!" she yelled. She could see Jeremiah looking stunned. Yelling at parents was a big no-no in this family.

Her dad glanced at her in the mirror.

"You didn't just pull that name out of thin air." Mom stared without blinking. "I'm waiting."

Millie sat in silence, turning her head to stare out the side window.

"Millie," her dad's voice was quiet. "Answer your mother."

She hated it when he talked like that. It was much easier for parents to yell, because then you could just yell back and figure they deserved it.

"I don't know," she repeated, this time in a softer voice. Then she shrugged. "I heard you say it today."

Mom wasn't buying it. "No, I did not mention that name today."

"Sure you did, when you were on the phone talking and I walked in." It sounded convincing to her, but still no sale.

"You were on my laptop, weren't you?"

The car slowed and the loud click-click of the blinker echoed in the silence. Her mom turned to see what Dad was doing.

"Max?"

"We need a little break." He pulled onto the off ramp that led to a traveler's rest stop.

The car rolled to a stop under a bright street light, far away from the 18-wheeled trucks parked at the other end of the lot.

Dad motioned Mom to get out of the car. Before her door clicked shut Millie heard her angry words. "Max, you know the kids aren't allowed to touch my laptop."

Dad put his arm around her and they walked away from the car.

"I can't believe you did that!" Jeremiah whispered.

"Did what?" Millie squeaked out as tears fell.

"You know what. You used Mom's laptop. Otherwise you wouldn't have given her such lame answers."

"So what if I did?"

"Who is the guy, anyway?"

"I don't know! But I think it has something to do with why my adoption is dragging out. How long did it take for your adoption to be completed?"

"I don't know, Millie! I never paid attention to that. I was their son from the day I moved in. That's all I know."

"Oh, come on, Jeremiah!" Millie wiped her tears on the bottom of her shirt. "You know it's not safe until the adoption is final. I also know yours didn't take as long as mine."

"So, what if it is taking longer?"

"It's because something is going wrong with my adoption. I think it has something to do with that Boyd dude."

Millie saw her parents heading back to the car. Now she would get it. They had time to plot together and figure out what awful punishment they figured she deserved.

The door opened and her parents got back in.

"You know what we forgot to do before we left home?" Dad said. No one responded.

"We forgot to pray." He took his hat off and reached out for her mom's hand. Mom turned in her seat, but this time instead of looking angry, she smiled at Millie and took her hand.

Millie could feel tears begin again. Now her nose was running too, as she listened to the soothing sound of her Dad's voice, talking to God about their trip, asking Him to bless their plans. He asked for safety as they traveled and for renewed joy in their family.

"And God, protect our daughter Millie and please finish up her adoption soon! Amen."

The tears fell faster than ever now. Right when she thought she was in big trouble, they're praying for her. Who could figure out parents? Especially these parents. Mom dug around in her purse and handed a tissue back to Millie. She smiled and winked at her.

    Dad pulled the car back onto the highway. As he got up to speed in the darkness, he glanced in the mirror again, a sparkle in his eye.

    "Say," he looked over at Jeremiah, too. "Did I ever tell you kids about the desert skeleton story my grandpa used to tell me?"

Chapter 19

Jeremiah

"Are you kidding me, Dad? Now you're sounding like Minnesota Mike!"

Dad glanced at me in the mirror. He was in a much better frame of mind tonight. Earlier in the day there was nothing about old Minnesota that would have made Dad laugh.

"Yes, I guess I kind of do," he admitted, chuckling.

"Who is this Minnesota Mike guy?" Millie asked.

"Yes, I'd like to know too." Mom looked at Dad.

"Well, make up your minds. I can't tell two stories at once. What'll it be, Minnesota Mike or the skeleton in the desert?"

The car filled with loud chatter as we all gave our opinions. We settled on our friend in the desert, saving the skeleton story for later.

"Where to start?" Dad sounded like we had known the guy a hundred years.

"Let me start, Dad!" I jumped in. I loved a good story, and I knew I'd tell it more colorfully than Dad.

"It all started when this idiot," and I emphasized the word idiot, "blew by us on that little winding desert highway..."

"Jeremiah! That wasn't necessary."

"No, but it sure was fun!"

After the laughter died down, we filled Mom and Millie in on everything the two of us could remember about Minnesota Mike.

"I wonder if we'll ever see him again?" I said.

"Hopefully not in this lifetime!" Dad smiled at me in the mirror.

"Aw, he wasn't that bad."

"No, that's just why it took the whole drive to the desert to cover everything about our day with him," Dad said.

"I can't believe we're almost there," Mom said. "That was quite a story to pass the time." She reached into the small cooler at her feet and popped open a diet soda can. "Anyone want something to drink?"

"Do you think he was right about the gold story?" Millie honed in on the most intriguing part, not even hearing Mom's question. "Do you think he was talking about our property?"

"It sounded like he knew what he was talking about," I said.

"Now Jeremiah, he didn't sound like he knew what he was talking about regarding anything he said."

"Well, he knew about the property for sale, didn't he?"

"That's a no-brainer. There are for sale signs scattered throughout the desert.

"He knew you were interested in the property." I wasn't ready to give up on the idea that there was some truth to the gold story.

"I wasn't too happy with that realtor tipping him off that I was interested. That should have been private. Most likely the guy was using it to generate interest in the parcel."

"Why would he do that, though, if he was saying it wasn't for sale?"

"Is that what the guy told you, Dad?" Millie said. "Did he tell you right to your face the property wasn't for sale?"

"Yes and it was disappointing hearing it. But like he told your Mom, it was a mix-up with the parcel numbers."

"Maybe it was and maybe it wasn't." My mind churned out a dozen mysterious scenarios.

"What do you mean by that, Jeremiah?" Mom looked over her shoulder at me.

"Well, maybe it's true there is gold on the property and the realtor man wants to buy it himself. So he just tells anyone who asks that it isn't for sale anymore. How about that?"

"Yeah." Millie got caught up in the story line. "And maybe later in the day he learned that the gold is on the property next door to ours and decided he could sell it after all."

"You kids read too many mysteries," Dad said.

Millie wasn't giving up. "Did Minnesota Mike say how he knew about the gold?"

"He said someone told him. Isn't that right, Dad?"

"He was vague about it." Dad slowed the car while clicking on his blinker. "He said he had it on good authority, but he wouldn't tell us more." He pulled the car up next to the realtor's office. Bright lights shone through the windows. The gas station and ice cream store were dark.

"I remember now!" I wasn't ready to get out till we convinced Dad there might be gold. "He said we were good folks, and that's why he didn't want to tell us how he knew."

Mom was looking in the visor mirror, brushing her hair and putting gunk on her lips. "Sounds like he's just making excuses for his made-up story." She looked at Dad. "Ready to go sign up for the next adventure in our lives?" She had the biggest smile as she grabbed the door handle.

Dad and Mom were greeting the guy by the time we got out of the car. He stood on the porch motioning for us to come in.

Just before I stepped up onto the weather beaten wood planks, Millie grabbed my arm.

"Jeremiah!" she screeched. "Look over there!"

Chapter 20

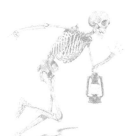

Millie

"It's the skeleton!" Millie took off running into the darkness before Jeremiah could respond.

Off in the distance she saw a ghostly-looking figure floating above the ground. She couldn't make it out for sure, but it looked a lot like a giant skeleton. Coming from inside him, or wait, maybe it was at his side, a dim light. "It's the lantern! Just like the legend!"

"Millie, come back here!" Jeremiah ran to catch up with her.

She ignored him and kept going, "It's the skeleton! I know it!" She turned back to look at Jeremiah, but lost her footing and fell onto the asphalt. She put out her hands and saved herself from a face plant into the black gravel. Dad taught her to do that when she first started riding motorcycles and was crashing so much. Jeremiah caught up to her as she scrambled to get up. She looked back at the skeleton, but it had disappeared over the ridge.

"It was him!" she yelled into Jeremiah's face as he took hold of her shoulders and tried to quiet her.

"Stop! Mom and Dad will hear you and think we're crazy."

"I know I saw him, didn't you see him, Jeremiah? You were right behind me!"

"No, I didn't." He helped her brush the gravel off her knees. "Well, I don't think I did." He hesitated. "Maybe I did see something, but I couldn't say it was a skeleton."

"Well, it sure wasn't human." Millie was insistent. "It was floating in the air."

"I don't know, Millie." Jeremiah shook his head.

"You saw something." She stared into his eyes. "It sure wasn't walking on land, was it?"

"I was too busy staring at my lame brain sister. I knew you would fall the way you were charging ahead."

They both breathed hard as they headed back to the office.

"Well, at least we know Minnesota Mike isn't crazy."

"Ha!" Jeremiah howled. "More like, you're just as crazy as he is." He laughed as they made their way over to the lighted parking area. But Millie noticed his laugh was stilted. She wondered why. He probably saw it, but didn't want to encourage her. He was too level-headed to believe something like that existed. Even with the evidence right in front of them.

They were almost to the building when Millie grabbed his arm again.

"Jeremiah!" she screeched. "Look over there! He's back!"

CHAPTER 21

Jeremiah

That girl scared me half to death. She gripped my arm so tight with one hand I thought her nails would dig into my skin right through my jacket. She pointed into the darkness.

I could see movement at the other end of the parking lot and a faint flicker of light.

"It's him, Jeremiah! It's the skeleton with the lantern. I told you I saw him!" She was still screeching, but now it was a whispery weird kind of screech, like someone losing their voice.

I could see Mom and Dad sitting in the office and they seemed to have forgotten about us. I figured it was okay to investigate before we went in.

As I took a few steps toward the creature, Millie grabbed the back of my jacket. "No! It's not safe!"

"Well, you weren't scared before." I tried to yank my jacket away from her.

"He wasn't coming in our direction before!"

The outline of a man took shape. He was heading toward us, swinging a lantern.

"Millie, you have skeletons on the brain. That's just a man. Look! Skin, clothes, hair. I don't see any bones sticking out, do you?"

"Why is he wandering around in the dark?" She was so jumpy.

"I don't know, maybe he lives here."

As he got closer, we could see a white beard and wispy hair sticking out under a beanie cap. "Hey, that must be your M&M guy!" she whispered in my ear, still hanging onto my jacket.

"M&M guy? What are you talking about?"

"You know, that mountain man or mountain Mike or

whatever you called him." She stared across the parking lot.

I almost laughed out loud. "Minnesota Mike, and that is way easier to say." I stepped up on the porch. "Yeah, I like that!"

"Where are you going?"

"Inside, to hear what's going on." I opened the door and turned back to her. "And no, that's not our M&M guy."

"Oh." Millie sounded disappointed we hadn't discovered the living breathing skeleton legend and not even M&M.

"There you are!" Mom looked up as we walked into the office, shielding our eyes, as they adjusted to the bright light. "What were you doing out there?"

"Just watching a guy across the parking lot," I said.

"That's Gus, my maintenance man," Mr. Property Seller Guy said, without looking up from the paperwork he had spread across his desk. "He likes to take a walk by lantern light every evening before bed."

"Oh, I thought it was the..."

I jumped in before Millie could mention the skeleton. "He startled us. We thought we were the only crazy people out here at this time of night." I laughed like I had just made a big joke. The adults ignored us and continued signing thousands of pieces of paper. Or maybe not quite that many.

Millie shot me a dirty look for interrupting and I shot her one back for being stupid enough to mention the skeleton legend in front of this guy.

It seemed they would never be done signing papers. I looked over and saw Millie studying a brochure on the table next to where she was sitting.

"What's that?" I said, as I sat in the chair next to her.

She held it up. "The History of Dry Brook," I read. "Hey, that looks interesting."

"You kids are welcome to take one of those."

I looked over at the realtor.

"I have lots of those." He reached into his desk drawer and pulled out a stack of brochures. "They didn't prove to be as popular as I thought. You can each take one."

"Amos, thank you very much for letting us come down this late." Dad stood up to leave several minutes later.

"I'll call you as soon as we get a response from the seller."

I stared at the guy, listening to the sound of his voice, trying to decide if he was honest. What was going on with this property? I wasn't sure I believed the story about the gold discovery. I didn't know much. In fact, nothing, about buying land. But something did not seem right. The property was for sale, then it wasn't for sale, then it was for sale.

"Who was the other guy who wanted to buy it?" I asked, remembering what Mom told us back at the house.

"Jeremiah," Dad scolded. "That isn't appropriate for you to ask."

Amos chuckled. "It's all right, Mr. Anderson. I remember what it was like to be a curious youngster." He turned in my direction. "An older gentleman. Not from around here. He came in after your dad did. Had a strange name."

He looked back at Dad and Mom. "But you had inquired first, so I wanted to give you first crack at it."

"Minnesota Mike?" Everyone looked at Millie. Mom's eyes said volumes as she stared at her but she didn't speak.

"Yes, young lady. That was his name. He said he would be camping in the area and was eager to put in an offer."

"Well, we appreciate you giving us first chance," Mom said.

"How long before we'll have an answer from the seller?"

"Oh, didn't I tell you?" Before Amos could tell us whatever it was he forgot to tell us, his phone rang. He looked down at the caller ID. "I'm sorry. I need to get this." He shook my dad's hand, signaling the end of the unfinished conversation.

Chapter 22

Millie

Millie noticed a car speeding toward them as they pulled out of the parking lot, seconds before impact, not in enough time to warn her dad.

The car hit the front driver's side of the SUV with such force they spun around facing back into the parking lot they had just pulled out of. Millie's body jerked forward, but the seatbelt held her rigid, biting into her neck. The harsh sound of metal on metal echoed in her ears. A man's grinning face staring at them, before he sped off into the night, embedded itself in her mind.

"Keep your belts on," Dad said. He spun the steering wheel around, giving the car so much gas the wheels screeched on the pavement. "We'll catch that guy!"

"Max, slow down!" Mom said.

A quarter mile away, the front tire blew, and they skidded to a stop.

"Drat!" Dad slammed both hands on the steering wheel. "I wanted his license plate number."

"Dad!" Millie sobbed. "That man swerved for us!"

"He sure did, Dad, he came in our lane on purpose."

Millie looked out the window and saw Gus the maintenance man running along the highway, his lantern swinging at his side.

Dad didn't respond to them, just punched 911 into his phone. "Need to report a hit and run."

Millie and Jeremiah hopped out of the car as Gus reached them. Mom joined them, putting her arm around Millie, hugging her to her side. "Thank God, we're okay."

The broken driver's side headlight left a trail of scattered glass on the asphalt road. Steam spewed out of the radiator where the grill pushed through it.

"I've got 911 on the line!" Amos, the realtor man, shouted as he caught up to the group.

"My dad's talking with them now," Jeremiah said.

Millie's teeth chattered. She couldn't get a single word out, when her mom asked if she was okay. She nodded and swiped at tears.

"Your dad must not have seen him, when he pulled out," Amos said.

"That guy aimed for us!" Millie blurted out. The minute he implied her dad might have been at fault, she forgot she was cold and scared. "He laughed when he hit us!" She stared at the realtor, as if he caused the crash.

"Millie, Millie. It's okay." Her mom led her to the other side of the car where her dad stood outside the door.

"I meant nothing by it, Mrs. Anderson."

"Yeah, sure!" Millie said under her breath. Her mom squeezed her tight.

"Did you see the accident happen, Gus?" Jeremiah discussed the wreck with the maintenance man on the other side of the SUV, but she wanted to listen to her dad.

"What did they say, Max?"

"They took the information, but won't send anyone out tonight, since no one is hurt. There's only one deputy on duty so we'll hear from him tomorrow."

"Good! I have something to tell him. I think Mr. Know-Everything Realtor Guy caused this."

Mom looked stunned. "Millie! What makes you think he's involved?" Dad looked as if he also wanted an answer.

"When you went to the car, I ran back into his office because I left my jacket on the chair."

Dad looked at her. "And?"

"It's what I overheard while he was on the phone." She looked at her dad. "I'm sure he's involved!"

Chapter 23

Jeremiah

The tow truck arrived as I was trying to break away from Gus. It sounded like Millie's conversation was way more interesting.

I was too late for the good stuff.

"We'll discuss this later." Dad motioned us to move away from the highway as the tow truck maneuvered into place. The reality of our wrecked car hit me. What are we supposed to do now? Hang out with Gus and Amos? Maybe even a skeleton?

It seemed like ages ago we were having fun talking about a silly ghost story. Now we were stuck in the desert with a not-so-honest salesman, a maintenance man who was a dead ringer for M&M and who knew what other weird creatures. My stomach growled, and I was cold and tired, too.

"Jeremiah!" Dad's voice penetrated my foggy brain. I don't know how many times he called me. No wonder he kept getting louder and louder.

I hurried over in his direction.

"Get our bags from the back. Millie!" He turned his attention away from me. "Check the back seat for jackets, backpacks and anything else. Grab whatever you find."

Mom rifled through the front seat, gathering things she and Dad brought.

"Do you need me to give you a lift anywhere?" Amos called out to Dad. "I can drive you anywhere you need to go."

"Yeah, you should be helping." Millie muttered as I slammed the back doors shut. I set the bags where Dad told me and hurried over to the side door.

"What's that about, Millie? Why are you mad at the realtor?"

She glanced over her shoulder before answering. "He told the person on the phone, 'they're leaving now, they'll be pulling out any minute.'"

She stared right into my eyes, her own eyes as big as a giant squid's. "So there! What does that mean? Kinda strange, not long after I overhear his comment, a car comes out of nowhere and crashes into us."

Before I answered, Dad said, "Hurry, you two. Get clear of the car. He's ready to load it."

Dad sat up front with the driver and the three of us had plenty of room in the large backseat compartment. Millie obsessed over our wrecked car out the back window, while I, on the other hand, stared in awe at the digital map and radios mounted to the dash. The large roadmap glowed an eerie green in the dark night and a red blip of a light blinked our course along the highway.

Thirty minutes later the tow truck approached the Ridge Riders Lodge. The loud click-click of the blinker sounded, as I caught sight of a figure out the driver's side passenger window. Even though it was off in the distance, the hazy figure looked tall and appeared to float above the ground. I gasped and wished I hadn't when my sister snapped her head around in my direction.

"What?"

"Nothing. I realized we're here already."

"That isn't why, Jeremiah," Millie whispered. "It was the skeleton. You were looking out the window."

"Hush, you two," Mom scolded as the tow truck pulled up in front of the plush lodge.

Saved by mom's interference, I breathed a sigh of relief as one by one we climbed out of the big rig.

Dad told the driver where to deliver the car, while Mom and I carried our bags to the covered entry way near the office.

"Cool! I've always wanted to stay here. Hey, Millie!" I wanted to take her mind off our conversation inside the truck. "Check out the pool. I wish we brought swim suits." She didn't care. She didn't even pester me further about what caught my eye.

That girl could squeeze the joy out of any moment by dwelling on everything wrong. But even I had to admit there was plenty wrong tonight. Like our car riding off on the big flat bed tow truck pulling out onto the highway.

As we gathered near the doorway, a light came on inside the office. Through the glass-paned door, we watched a scruffy looking man fiddling with the lock.

He got the door unlocked and greeted us with a smile, which was nice since we most likely got him out of bed. He hadn't even run a comb through his hair.

"I've been expecting you." He smiled and picked up two of our bags, carrying them inside. Dad and Mom followed him.

"What did that mean?" I whispered to Millie. She was crying when I looked at her.

Chapter 24

Millie

"Let's get some ice cream," Jeremiah said. He pointed to the bright neon ice cream sign flashing in the darkness.

She shrugged. "I don't want any. I'm too upset about everything. I still want to know who Boyd Colston is and why he's messing up my adoption."

"Oh man, Millie, you don't let a single discouraging thing out of that brain of yours." Jeremiah tugged on her arm. "Come on, Mom and Dad are in there getting a room and I see a big ice cream display over in the corner."

Millie didn't budge. She plopped down on a picnic bench close to the door. Who cares what Jeremiah wants, she thought. He has nothing to be worried about like I do. His adoption is final. No one can take him away. He looked like he was giving up on her as he reached for the handle to the door.

Millie wiped at more tears. She was exhausted and just wanted to sleep. Maybe forever. She dropped her head to rest on the table when she heard a sudden shout from Jeremiah. "Millie!" Her head jolted back up in alarm.

"What?" she grumbled.

"They have mint chocolate chip ice cream!" He had a big silly grin. "Mint chocolate chip, Millie. You've never in your life passed up mint chocolate chip."

She had to admit, that sounded good right now. He was right. She never could turn down her favorite flavor.

"I see a smile." Jeremiah teased. He came closer, like he was planning on dragging her into the store if she didn't get up on her own power.

Later Millie reveled in the sweet creamy taste of the light green ice cream. She crunched on the extra large chocolate bits while enjoying the plushness of the bed and pillows she leaned back on. "I can't believe a lodge in the middle of nowhere has such luxurious rooms."

They all nodded as they each enjoyed their own favorite flavors. "The store is awesome. So many kinds of ice cream."

"Obviously," Mom said, in between bites, "whoever is in charge, is a big fan of ice cream."

"I knew we should have come here a long time ago." Jeremiah scraped the bottom of his container and licked the last bite off the spoon.

"Well, we're here now." Dad looked rested and content as he stretched out his long legs in the reclining chair.

Mom sat straight up and looked at her. "Millie, I just remembered what you said earlier about hearing the realtor say something on the phone."

Dad swallowed the last bite of his rocky road and looked over at her. "What made you so suspicious of him?"

Millie set her ice cream container down and threw herself into repeating what she'd already told Jeremiah.

"Hmm," her Dad said. "I agree that sounds strange, but I just can't imagine he would risk causing an accident."

"Yes," Mom added. "If what you suspected was true, he could be in trouble with the law and lose his real estate license."

"I just know what I heard." Millie resumed eating her ice cream.

"Well, thank you for sharing it with us," Dad said. "We'll keep it in mind, if other unusual things come up with this property purchase."

The room grew quiet as they finished their snacks and lost themselves in contemplating the day's events.

Millie glanced at the clock on the nightstand when Dad's phone squawked out a text notification. Why would someone from his office be texting him after one in the morning? That reminded her, why did the guy downstairs say he had been expecting them?

Before she could pepper Dad with questions, he started laughing and said "Fantastic!"

"What is it, Max?"

"Just that we'll be driving home in style tomorrow. None of you will believe it!" He looked over at Millie with a smile that just wouldn't quit.

How could he be so happy and wide awake this late? She

stifled a yawn. It made her happy seeing her dad so happy.

"Spill the beans, Dad." Jeremiah got off the roll-away bed and tossed his ice cream container in the trash.

"That was Naomi." Dad looked over at Mom. "Lucky, she's a night owl!"

"She and Harrison will drive out tomorrow and bring us a car to borrow." Dad had this smile that just wouldn't quit.

He looked at Millie again and then over at Jeremiah. "How would you two like to go for a drive in a cobalt blue Lamborghini SUV?"

"Max! I didn't even know Lamborghini made SUV's!"

Millie was off the bed, jumping up and down, hugging her dad and laughing. "Wow, Dad, just wow!"

"Valued at close to a quarter of a million dollars," Dad added.

"Cobalt blue. I suddenly am in love with that color! And I don't even know what color that is!" Millie fell back on her bed and stared at the ceiling. She loved this life and never wanted it to end.

"Did they pick up that car today, Max?"

"They did. I wasn't sure they would make that happen, but it looks like it all worked out."

"Did who pick up the car?" Millie sat up in the bed and stared at her parents, as if they were speaking a foreign language. "Where is this car coming from? Are we buying it?"

"Whoa there!" Dad said. "This is temporary, while our car is being repaired."

He bent over to take off his shoes while Mom pulled the covers back on their bed. "But it will be fun to drive for a few days. Don't you think, Millie?"

She nodded with half-closed eyes. She had so many more questions, but sleep was overtaking her. The clock looked blurry as she leaned back on the pillow. It looked like 2 a.m.

So many questions. The guy downstairs knowing they were coming, the Boyd dude lurking in her mind, and where did this car really come from?

Dad never answered when she asked. She drifted off to a fitful sleep, wondering if her dad was a part of the nationwide car theft ring she'd heard about in the news.

CHAPTER 25

Jeremiah

The roar worked it's way into my dream. It sounded louder than any motorcycle I'd ever ridden. It revved up once, twice, then again. This wasn't a dream. This was The Car.

I leaped out of bed, ran to the window and saw nearly everyone at the lodge crowding around the magnificent vehicle. The Lamborghini was here.

I heard Dad and Mom stirring across the room. So dead tired when they dropped off to sleep a few hours ago, they didn't even hear the engine's roar.

Slipping over to Dad's side of the bed, I whispered, "Dad, it's here!"

Millie, in the next bed, was sleeping with the blankets over her head and the world blocked out. Mom rolled over and yanked the covers higher over her shoulder. Dad looked at me with groggy eyes. "What time is it?" He grabbed the alarm clock on the nightstand.

"Seven o'clock? We haven't even been asleep five hour." He groaned.

"Yeah, I guess your night owl friend is also an early bird."

"What? Is the car here?"

"It sure is. I'm surprised you didn't hear it. That exhaust sounds like cannon fire." I rubbed my hands together in anticipation.

He jumped up and grabbed clothes, heading to the bathroom. I was too tired to change before dropping off to sleep a few hours ago, so I woke up in the clothes I went to sleep in.

I ran a comb through my hair, threw on my shoes and hat and paced the floor waiting for Dad.

"Sleepy-head finally decided to get up?" A man greeted Dad with a loud voice when we got down to the car. I circled it a dozen times before Dad could get my attention.

"Son, these are my co-workers, Harrison and his wife Naomi. This is my son Jeremiah. He's just a little excited about our loaner car."

We shook hands. "What are you doing here so early?" Dad asked them. "You working 24-hour shifts these days?"

Naomi had a soft voice that contrasted with her loud husband. "We went into work at 10 last night. The timing of your text message was uncanny. We had just gotten back to the warehouse with the car."

"The client hadn't even been told yet that we had the car," Naomi said. "So when we were texting, we also mentioned you were stranded in the desert and needed a vehicle."

"He was more than happy for us to bring it to you." Harrison patted the car like it was a living creature. "Said you've done more than enough for him."

Dad circled the car for the first time, just as Mom and Millie arrived. Millie's mouth dropped open. "Watch it kid," I said, "you'll be catching flies."

Millie slapped me on the arm and we got into a playful tussle a ways from the car. But not so far that we didn't hear dad mention something about gunshots.

"Did you hear that?" Millie said.

"Yeah." I pointed to the car. "They're all staring at the back window." I edged my way toward them, not wanting to draw attention.

"Had some trouble here?" Dad sounded concerned.

Harrison shrugged. "Just a few shots."

Dad ran his hand over a couple spots on the back window. "Bulletproof?"

"That's what the spec sheet said."

"Glad you got away."

"Some slick driving and plenty of power were our tickets to freedom." Naomi patted her husband on the back.

"Not to mention, we knew the area better than they did. An alley here, a shortcut there, and we lost them no problem." Harrison added to the get-away story.

"That's why we're here so early," Naomi said. "Rather than risk them finding the warehouse, this remote location was better."

I turned to look at Millie. "Did you hear that?" I mouthed the words.

Her eyes were bulging. I'm guessing she heard.

Harrison dropped keys into Dad's hands. An old Cadillac was parked next to the Lamborghini. "Our shift is over, so we'll be going." They hopped into the other car and took off.

Dad put his arm around Mom's shoulders. "I'm starving. Let's take this car for a spin!"

As Mom and Dad headed for the stairway Millie appeared at my side. "Do you think that is a stolen car?" she whispered.

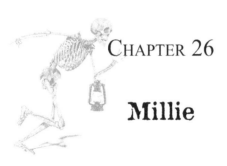

Chapter 26

Millie

"Millie! Why would you say something like that?"

"Don't you listen to the news?" she asked him. "Auto theft is a big thing. It's suspicious this expensive car with bullet holes just shows up." She glared at him. "Figure it out. The pieces add up."

Jeremiah shook his head. "No, the pieces don't add up. Especially one big piece you're leaving out."

"And what is that, Mr. Know-it-All?"

"Our dad is not a car thief."

But how do we really know? Millie thought. She didn't say more though. Jeremiah already thought she was a worrywart, and he didn't even know half the things going on inside her head. Sometimes she couldn't believe these parents were as good as they seemed. She had lived with families where stolen cars would have been no big deal. In fact her own family, not that she remembered much about them, but she'd heard stories from social workers and foster families. They supported themselves by stealing anything they could find. That and selling drugs.

"Well, I didn't say he stole the car, but he could be involved with people who did."

"Let's go eat breakfast. We're tired, yesterday was rough. Later we'll get some answers from Dad that will put your mind at ease." He tugged on her arm and headed toward the stairs.

"You better not tell him what I said."

"I'm not that stupid. Now come on!"

The Lamborghini was beyond luxurious and Millie couldn't help but sink into the plush back seat, while she looked around in awe at the rest of the interior. The sound system was out of this world and her favorite Christian music permeated the air so thoroughly she couldn't tell where the speakers were. "Funny how Christian music would come on in a stolen car," she whispered to Jeremiah. Then she thought, maybe God does stuff like that to make criminals feel guilty.

"You're a goofball." Jeremiah said.

Millie looked over at him, but he was looking out the side window.

"Dad! Check out the license plate on that truck."

They all looked where he pointed and Millie read, "Minnesota... Hey!"

Dad and Jeremiah burst out laughing.

"I don't believe it." Dad smacked his forehead. "It's our good buddy."

"Well, I guess if his truck is still here when we get back, we'll pay him a visit." Dad pulled the luxury car onto the two-lane highway.

"I'm looking forward to that." Mom smiled at Jeremiah. "You've told such wonderful tales, I just have to meet this man."

"I want to hear what he has to say about the skeleton and the gold," Millie said. "Let's hurry and get back!"

The car filled with laughter as they covered the 40 miles between the lodge and the restaurant.

At the restaurant Millie wanted answers but found it difficult to ask her dad anything. And she sure didn't want to let on to her mom she had seen Boyd's name on the laptop. She started with something safe.

"Mom." She cut her French toast and slathered it with syrup while she talked. "Why did that guy say he was expecting us last night when we got there?"

"Yeah," Jeremiah joined in. "That was weird, like someone was telling him about us."

Mom smiled. "Someone was," she said and took a sip of her orange juice.

"See, Jeremiah." Millie thumped his arm with the back of her hand. "I told you weird things were going on."

Jeremiah looked like he finally believed her.

"Oh Millie, honey, there's been too much talk of desert legends and far too little sleep. You're seeing mysteries everywhere."

"What do you mean? You said someone was talking to the man about us."

"I'm sorry, honey I shouldn't have teased you. What I meant was, we talked with the man."

Millie still looked confused. "Earlier in the day," Mom said. "After I got the call from the realtor, I made the reservations."

Even Jeremiah looked a little sheepish for believing something strange was happening. Millie was relieved, but she still had so many other questions.

They resumed eating quietly until Millie broke the silence. "But what about the car?"

Dad looked up over the edge of the iced tea he was drinking. "What do you want to know about the car?" he said as he set his glass down.

"Why does it have bullet holes and where did it come from?"

CHAPTER 27

Jeremiah

I just about spit my apple juice out when I heard the questions that rushed out of my sister's mouth.

Dad smiled at her. "Well, you don't want to know much, do you?"

Oh, if you only knew, Dad, I was thinking, but I didn't want to get Millie started on anything else.

"Well?" Millie said.

"You might say it's a company car we're borrowing."

If he was hoping to put Millie off with a vague answer like that, well, as the saying goes, he had another think coming.

"What do you mean. 'you might say?'"

Dad took a deep breath and looked at Mom. "It's up to you," she said.

"Actually Millie, it would be easier to explain the skeleton in the desert to you than to get into the details about the company car."

"Well, I want to know that story too. But I'm curious about the car. And I want to know about the company too."

My sister looked over at me. "Do you even know what Dad does when he goes to work?"

Hmm. "Now that you mention it, I guess I don't." I realized right then and there, I am no way as curious about every detail in life as Millie is. "I know he works for RPM something or other." Maybe I would score some points with my vast knowledge and big smile.

"Works for or owns the company?" she asked.

I looked across the table at Dad and Mom who seemed to enjoy this, then back at my sister. "Well, I guess I never thought of it."

"That's the problem with you, Jeremiah. You never wonder about anything."

"Oh. I didn't know that was a problem. And may I point out one of your problems?" Without waiting for her answer, I said "You not only wonder about every little detail in the world, you also worry about it. Constantly!" I stared at her for emphasis.

"He's right, you know." Mom reached across the table and patted her hand.

"It's good to want to know what's going on," Dad said. "But we need to help you put a stop to the worry."

Millie hung her head. If I had to guess, I would say she was torn between admitting they were right and wanting to get back to the question that started this whole conversation.

She looked up at Dad. "Okay. If I promise to stop worrying so much, will you tell me about the car we 'might say' is a company car?"

As he was about to respond, his phone vibrated on the table. He glanced at the caller ID then back at us. "Excuse me." He stood and stepped away from the table. "I need to take this. It's the sheriff's office."

Millie and I stared at each other as Dad walked out of the restaurant.

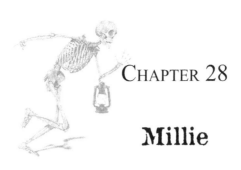

CHAPTER 28

Millie

Millie could feel her insides shaking. She fidgeted and fretted so much on the drive back to the lodge she couldn't enjoy the surround sound and plush upholstery.

"I won't know what to say, Dad. I'm too scared."

"You sound like Moses in the Bible," Jeremiah said.

"Be quiet." She glared at him. "You're not the one who has to talk to the deputy."

"This is one time where your attention to every little detail is good. And bad."

"Why do you say that?" She looked at her brother.

"Because you know what that guy looks like, so that's good. And it's bad for you because you're the one the deputy wants to talk to."

She frowned.

"Take me for instance, I didn't notice anything during the wreck, so they don't need me."

"Well, I wish I was you," Millie held her stomach and rocked forward and back. It had been a long time since she had done that. She had a vague memory of rocking and rocking when she was a little girl scared and... no, she wouldn't go there. Mom interrupted her thoughts.

"Millie, you'll be fine, and Jeremiah is right, you noticing all the details is very helpful. They might catch the guy who ran into us."

The deputy was standing next to his patrol car talking on the radio when they pulled into the nearest parking space.

"Hi, I'm Deputy Black. Mr. Anderson?"

"Yes, good morning." Dad extended his hand. "Thank you for coming out."

Millie could see people in the office looking out, which made her more nervous. She looked around and spotted the truck from Minnesota and wished they were discussing tales of skeletons and gold instead of answering questions.

"My daughter's a little nervous." Dad put his arm around her.

"Millie, the only one who should be nervous is the creep who wrecked your car and endangered your family." The deputy smiled at her, then pulled his phone out and scrolled to a picture of a dented up car.

"That's it!" Millie blurted out, startling even herself. "I know that car, it's the one that ran into us last night."

"Where did you find it?" Mom asked.

"About 15 miles west of here, abandoned on the side of the highway." He put his phone away and pulled out a small notepad and pen. "It appears he ran out of gas, but how he got out of the area, we don't know."

"Can't you get his name from the car registration?" Jeremiah asked.

"The car was stolen."

Millie's eyes grew wide, and she rolled them to the side to see Jeremiah without turning her head. She hoped this proved to him she knew what she was talking about when she said there was a rash of car thefts.

She just hoped her dad's company wasn't involved. It seemed risky to have the deputy so close to the Lamborghini with the bullet holes. Thankfully, he wasn't paying attention to it.

After she described the man, and her parents answered questions, he shook hands with them. "We'll have the report ready in a few days." He handed her dad a business card. "Just check with my office and you can get a copy for your insurance company."

None of them noticed Minnesota Mike standing nearby. When the deputy turned to approach his car, M&M cleared his throat and said, "Well, howdy folks, doncha know, I was hoping we would run into each other again, real soon like!"

Wow, his voice was just as loud as Jeremiah said it was. Millie choked back laughter.

Before the deputy could get into his car, M&M turned his attention from Dad and said "Excuse me there, Deputy. I was hoping to ask you a question."

"Sure, what can I do for you?"

"Well, er, well." He seemed like he didn't know how to get started. "It's kind of a silly question, and I'm not from around here. But can you tell me if there's any truth to the stories I been hearing about a skeleton wandering around at night with a lantern in his belly?"

Jeremiah burst out laughing, attracting everyone's attention. Especially Dad, who did not look happy about his reaction.

The deputy chuckled and said, "You know, ordinarily, I would say that is a silly question, but..." He stopped talking and flipped through the pages on his spiral notepad.

Time seemed to stand still as they all stood speechless at the deputy's reaction.

He found what he was looking for. "Sure enough," he said, reading his notes. "Last week, we got a call from one of the off roaders camping in the area. He claimed while he was out on a night run in his buggy he saw something that looked like a tall skeleton carrying a lantern."

The deputy looked up from his notes. "We chalked it up to a little too much to drink at the local tavern." He looked right at Minnesota Mike. "So, have you seen this skeleton yourself?"

M&M bounced back and forth from one foot to the other and seemed to be searching for an answer. "Well, now, I ain't saying I saw it myself for sure."

The deputy closed his notepad, slipping it back into his top pocket. "Okay, big fellow, well, you keep an eye out and if you ever see it, just let me know."

He got into his patrol car and the engine roared to life. Before driving off, he rolled the window down and said to M&M, "You be careful about driving after you've been to the tavern, you hear?"

CHAPTER 29

Jeremiah

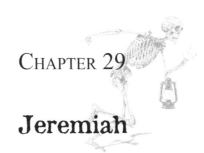

Minnesota Mike let out a loud belly laugh as the deputy drove off. When he could catch his breath, he turned to Dad. "He must think I'm a drinker to believe a story like that."

Dad smiled. "Well, it is far-fetched to think an old desert legend has come to life in modern times."

"Oh, I don't doubt what you're saying." Minnesota looked in my direction. "But I betcha Jeremiah wouldn't think so if he coulda seen what I saw late last night after I checked in here." He motioned over his shoulder with his thumb.

"What did you see?" Millie butted into the conversation before I could respond.

"Just like I told the deputy..."

"Wait a minute," Millie interrupted. "You told the deputy you didn't see anything." She pointed her finger right at him and squinted her eyes. "Were you lying?"

That girl will be an investigator or maybe even a judge someday. She doesn't stop till she gets to the truth.

"Millie, Jeremiah," Dad inserted himself into the conversation. "We're meeting someone in town this afternoon, so we need to get packed." He looked in M&M's direction. "It was nice seeing you again."

Dad motioned for both of us to follow him. Mom smiled in Minnesota's direction. "Maybe we can visit another time." She turned and headed for the stairway.

"Oh, sure, yeah, okay," Minnesota waved. "Don't let me hold you up. By the way, that's a right nice ride you got there. Sure is a step up from the truck you was in yesterday."

"Thank you," Dad said, "it's borrowed from a friend."

"Oh, okay." M&M smiled. "Well, I know some tricks to repair auto glass if you want me to help you with those bullet holes in the back."

I could see Dad gritting his teeth. This guy had such a way of getting under Dad's skin, but he played it cool. "I'll mention that to my friend," he said and walked away.

"Well, now hold on there, just one more second." M&M hurried after us while digging around in his pocket. He pulled out a crumpled looking business card. "Lookie here. Keep this with you in case your friend wants help. It's got my number scribbled on the back."

He gave me the card since I was closest to him. I read "Amos Lee, Realtor".

"Oh, that ain't me." Minnesota saw me reading the card. "I got that from that realtor guy down the road. I put my number on the back for you folks, then forgot to give it to you yesterday."

"Okay, thank you." Dad motioned to me. "Come on, Jeremiah."

I felt bad shutting Minnesota down like that. He was a nice guy, even if he had some strange ideas.

"Say, I heard you put your offer in on that property," he yelled as we started up the stairs.

No secrets in this town.

Dad kept going.

"You might want to hear to what I have to say, before you sign any agreement to buy."

I wanted to stay and hear the story but knew I better not, so I waved and hurried to catch up with the rest of the family. It surprised me Millie was so content to just walk away from this gold mine of information.

What was up with her?

It didn't take long to find out.

Chapter 30

Millie

Millie was crying so hard she couldn't talk. Her dad and mom were both trying to comfort her when Jeremiah walked in. "Whoa! What is going on?"

She looked at her brother, but couldn't stop crying.

Mom brought over a wet washcloth and wiped her face.

"Millie, honey, please. Try to be calm and tell us what is wrong."

"Take deep breaths, Millie." Her dad rubbed her back. That always helped when she was like this.

She was so grateful for these parents. She didn't know what she would have done if they hadn't come into her life. That caused the tears to flow harder, as she thought about the problems with her adoption.

"Deep breaths, Millie," Dad said. "You were doing good for a minute."

Mom took the cloth. "Let me run this under cold water again."

She wiped Millie's face when she came back. "Honey, what's wrong? Did something happen downstairs to upset you?"

The tears subsided as she continued to inhale and breathe out like her dad said. "Well," she started.

"It was probably Minnesota Mike carrying on," Jeremiah said. "He's enough to make any of us cry."

"It was when he talked about the bullet holes." Her tears started again. Why is it so hard to talk when you're crying? She looked over at Jeremiah. "You tell him," she squeaked.

Her parents looked surprised. "Me? Why me? I'm not even the one wondering about the car."

"Jeremiah?" Dad looked his way. "Do you know what's bothering her?"

"Yes." He took a deep breath. "She thinks the Lamborghini is stolen."

"Stolen!" Mom jumped to her feet. "Why on earth would you think it's stolen, Millie?"

Dad put his arm around her shoulders and hugged her to his side. She still couldn't talk and stared in Jeremiah's direction.

"Millie doesn't know what your job is, and she thinks it's strange that an expensive car shows up with bullet holes in it. She's been hearing in the news about car theft rings." Jeremiah let out a sigh of relief when he finished.

"Thank you," she whispered.

"Max, tell them about your job." Mom put her hand on their dad's shoulder.

"You know, it's funny." Dad shook his head a little. "You think you're protecting your kids by keeping some things from them, but instead you're making them more worried."

Yeah, like what's going on with my adoption? Millie wondered, but decided that could wait for another time.

"When people buy expensive cars, they borrow money from a lender to pay for it," Dad said.

"What does that have to do with bullet holes in the car?" Millie interrupted.

Dad smiled. "I'm getting to that."

He took a drink from the cold water bottle Mom handed him.

"Can I have one too, Mom?" Millie said.

"The borrower makes payments every month. But if they don't, the lender will repossess their vehicle."

"What does that mean?"

"It means it's getting taken away from them," Jeremiah said.

"Is that right, Dad?"

"Yes it is. When that happens, some borrowers are cooperative, but others aren't. They'll hide the car to keep the lender from taking it back."

"And, somehow, this is getting us to the bullet holes?" Millie asked in between gulps of water.

"Yes. And that's why I don't talk about my work at home. It can be dangerous. The items we specialize in are very expensive. Yachts, airplanes, luxury vehicles. Sometimes people go to great lengths to stop us from taking the vehicles."

Millie opened her mouth to speak, but Dad shushed her with his hand held up. "Let me finish."

"Someone shot at my coworkers last night when they were recovering the Lamborghini for our client."

Jeremiah and Millie gasped. "Dad! That could have been you," Millie said.

"Not anymore. I don't work in the field any longer. I haven't for quite some time."

"What if that guy who hit our car knew who you were? What if he was following you to hurt you?"

She saw her Dad glance over at her mom.

"Millie," Dad said. "You're jumping to conclusions. Let's stick with what we know."

Millie looked at her mom, who was still staring at her dad. It looked like she thought there was something to the idea about the man hunting for Dad.

"How did your coworkers keep from getting hurt when the people shot at them?" Jeremiah asked.

"It's bulletproof glass. The bullets never pierced the window. We knew about that safety feature, because it was in the paperwork we got from our client."

Millie jumped up and threw her arms around her dad, hugging him. "Oh Dad! I'm so glad you're not a car thief!"

"Oh brother, Millie!" Jeremiah shook his head. "Crying because you're upset. Crying because you're happy."

"But what about Mom? Did she know about all this?" She turned to her mom. "Did you, Mom?"

"Yes, honey. I also work for your Dad's company."

"What do you do?"

"She does the research on people we're hunting for. To find out as much as we can about them."

Jeremiah stared over at Millie and then turned to their Mom. "You mean like background checks on people?"

"That is some of the research I do."

Without looking at him, Millie could feel Jeremiah's eyes boring a hole into her. She knew just what he was thinking.

Chapter 31

Jeremiah

"Hey, Dad, how soon are we leaving? Is it okay for us to look around the lodge first?"

I couldn't wait to talk to Millie away from our parents. I wanted to make sure she would stop worrying about that Boyd guy now.

"Sure, son. In fact, I'm going to cancel that appointment this afternoon. I think we'll stay another day."

"Oh, cool!" Millie jumped up. "Let's go."

As we got to the door, Dad said, "If you see good old M&M, tell him we'd like to have lunch with him later in the cafe here."

"Wow. Really, Dad?" I couldn't believe my ears.

"Yes, I feel kind of bad for the way I've been giving him the brush off." He looked over at Mom. "Besides your mom told me I had to."

That sounded like something Mom would make him do.

"When you get back up here," Mom added, "we'll drive over to the realtor's office to see if he has any word on our offer."

"Wow, double wow! What a great day this is turning out to be."

"We'll be back soon," Millie said, as we headed out the door.

We almost tripped over each other rushing down the stairs. There was so much I wanted to see here, but I was also looking forward to news from the realtor.

"How about we just check out the pool, then find M&M, and get right back after that?"

"That's the same thing I was thinking," Millie agreed. "There's plenty of time to explore later, and if we get that property, we'll have the rest of our lives to explore."

At the pool, two men stormed through the wooden gate, almost running into us. They were arguing. They were talking too quietly to make out the words, but you could tell it was an argument by the tone of their voices and hand gestures. They didn't even notice us.

"What do you think that was about?" Millie whispered.

"I don't know, but they sure were mad." I followed her into the pool area.

"Check out those rooms, Millie." I pointed across the patio area. "They have sliding glass doors leading right out to the pool."

"That would be cool to stay in. We should ask Dad if we can do that the next time we come here."

The sound of motorcycles racing around in the desert nearby made me wish we had brought ours. An old dune buggy with two people in it chugged along the dirt road by the pool heading toward the open desert. Maybe we'd get a buggy when we moved into our new desert home. That way the whole family could go out together.

I was just about to tell Millie my idea when she motioned me to follow her around the large patio area. As we got to the other side of the pool, the angry voices we'd heard earlier sounded close. This time they weren't so quiet.

"I think they're in one of those rooms," Millie whispered.

"Yeah, I think you're right."

She sat on a cushioned recliner at the pool's edge. One that was closest to the room with the loud voices. Millie stretched out like a sunbather who would be here for a while.

"What are you doing? I thought we were in a hurry to find Mike and get back to Dad and Mom?"

"Shh." She held her finger to her lips. Then in a louder voice, "Come on, Jeremiah, let's enjoy the sun." She patted the reclining lounge next to her.

I was just about to tell her no when we heard a loud noise, like someone knocking over a table. Then yelling. "I told you that idiot would talk about the gold!"

I plopped down so fast on the lounge next to her, I almost tipped over. She laughed.

"Shush! We don't want them to hear us."

There was more yelling but not loud enough to make out the words.

Something crashed against one of the glass doors. It surprised me the window didn't shatter. "And that's just what I'll do to that old geezer if I hear one more time he's blabbing about that property."

Silence. We strained our ears to listen, but they had either left the room or quit talking.

"Millie, did you hear that?"

"Yes!" Her whisper was louder than mine. "You think they're talking about M&M?"

"I bet they are and I bet they're talking about our property."

"Who are they?" she said "And I wonder where M&M is now."

"He sure didn't seem to be in the room the way they were talking about him."

"No, it wasn't like they were talking to him, just about him," she said.

"It almost seems like there is something to that gold story he's been talking about, for as mad as those guys were."

"Do you think Mike is in danger?" Millie looked scared. I hoped she wouldn't cry again.

"I don't know, but I think we should tell Mom and Dad what we heard."

"No, Jeremiah. Let's wait till we find out more. We've had enough trouble today."

"Oh yeah." I remembered what I came outside to talk to her about. "Speaking of trouble, you can quit worrying about that Boyd guy now. Did you hear what Dad said about Mom's background checks for his company?"

Millie looked sheepish, and so she should. Once again she was making a mountain out of a molehill. To use my Dad's words.

"Yes, you're right. I worry too much."

"Yeah, so now you can cross Boyd off your worry list."

"Okay. I'll cross Boyd off and add Minnesota Mike's name. He might be in some kind of trouble."

I had the same bad feeling.

Chapter 32

Millie

"Let's go ask in the office what room M&M is in," Millie said as they left the pool area.

"No! It's probably the room those men were in."

"Yeah, I guess you could be right. Let's at least wander around the store. We might overhear something while we're in there."

"It pays to hang out with the master eavesdropper when we need information." Jeremiah smiled at his sister.

She pushed the door open and the desk clerk greeted them. They hadn't seen her before.

"Hi there, what can I do for you?" She was friendly, young and tan. Like she spent every waking moment out by the swimming pool when she wasn't working. You could do that out here in the desert. The sun was shining 360 days a year, Millie thought.

"We thought we'd check out all your cool items," Jeremiah said while Millie stared at her. "We're in room 201."

"Oh, you're the Lamborghini. Awesome car!" She gave two thumbs up.

"Yeah, no kidding," Jeremiah said. "It's a loaner since ours got wrecked last night."

"Wow, you guys made out on that deal!"

"How old are you?" Millie could tell that annoyed Jeremiah. Someday maybe she'd stop being so blunt, but right now it was the only way she knew to get information.

"Fifteen in six more months." The girl smiled. She didn't seem to mind being questioned.

"How come you're not in school?"

"Millie, do you have to interrogate her?"

"I don't think two questions is an interrogation."

The counter girl laughed at the brother and sister bickering. "It's okay, I know how it is, I've got a little brother, and someone is always annoyed with someone else in our house." Then she answered Millie's question. "Homeschool."

"Awesome!" both Jeremiah and Millie responded.

"Same here," Millie said.

"By the way, my name is Paisley." She held her hand across the counter and shook their hands.

"So what are you guys doing out here? You don't have a truck or trailer, so I doubt you're doing any riding."

"Not this trip," Jeremiah said. "Hopefully we'll be back in a week or two with the bikes."

"Yeah, we're just here with our parents to..."

Jeremiah cut her off. "We just went for a desert drive, got in a wreck and ended up staying all night."

Millie gave him a puzzled look, but decided he must have a good reason for stopping her.

"That's cool you got the loaner car delivered to you." Paisley stared out the window at the Lamborghini. "Must have some great connections."

"I guess." Jeremiah stared out the window.

"Say," Millie jumped in to redirect the conversation. "Have you seen the guy around that goes by the name of Minnesota Mike?"

"That old guy?" Paisley chuckled. "Happiest guy I've ever seen, except..."

"Except what?" Millie interrupted.

"I haven't seen him today. But his truck is parked in the same spot."

"We saw him not too long ago," Jeremiah said.

"I haven't seen him since I came on duty an hour ago." Paisley tapped on the keyboard, staring at the screen as she scrolled through several pages. "He's scheduled to check out today, but he's already missed the check-out time."

Jeremiah and Millie looked at each other as Paisley punched numbers into her phone. "Excuse me. I need to check with my dad."

She waited a minute or two, then it sounded like she was leaving a message. "Can you check on Room 110? He should have checked out an hour ago, but I haven't seen him."

"Is he a friend of yours?" Paisley continued looking at the computer.

"Well, not really. More like an acquaintance. My dad and brother met him yesterday."

"Same here." Paisley still didn't look up from the computer screen while she talked. "He checked in late yesterday afternoon while I was on duty. I was doing my schoolwork since it was slow and he kept popping in and out of the store all afternoon and evening. Asked me a thousand questions about school and then told me a thousand stories about wandering around the country."

"He's a character, all right," Jeremiah agreed. "But as you said, a friendly one."

"You got that right." Paisley picked up the phone again as if hoping it would ring.

"My dad and I went for a ride with him yesterday. He must have checked into his room after we left for home."

Paisley looked up when he said that. "Wait a minute, you left for home yesterday but then you checked in here late last night." She glanced back at the computer, scrolling through the info, then looked back at them. "Actually, early this morning. You must have done a lot of driving yesterday."

Jeremiah and Millie laughed. "Yeah, long story."

Before Paisley could ask any more questions, the phone rang. "Saved by the bell," Millie whispered as the girl took the call. It sounded like her dad by the one-sided conversation.

"She asks as many questions as you do," Jeremiah whispered.

"Yeah, how annoying."

"What, Dad?" her voice raised, "Are you sure? Did you call 9-1-1?"

She punched the off button on her phone and stared at Jeremiah and Millie. "My dad said he's on his floor, unconscious." Her voice was quivering.

They heard the siren before they saw the fire truck.

As the three of them rushed outside, Millie saw the man who had checked them in last night, signaling the driver where to go.

"Millie! Jeremiah!" Their parents were outside. "We were afraid something happened to you." Her mom put an arm around Millie's shoulders. "What is it, honey?"

"It's Minnesota Mike, Mom. Something terrible happened."

83

Chapter 33

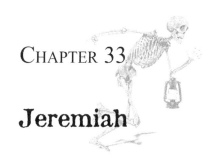

Jeremiah

Dad put an arm around both of us. "Let's step over here and pray for Mike."

We moved away from the small crowd that was growing. An ambulance pulled in and parked next to the fire truck.

"Lord, we don't know what is going on with our new friend Mike, but You do. Please touch Him with your healing hand and breathe health and life into his body. Please give the paramedics wisdom to know what to do. Show us how we can be a blessing to Mike and all those involved."

When I looked up, I saw them wheeling an awake and talking Minnesota Mike out of his hotel room. Millie and I rushed over. "Hey there." M&M reached out a feeble hand for mine. He was talking all right, but not with the exuberance of yesterday.

"What kind of trouble are you causing everyone?" I walked along as they rolled him over to the ambulance. "You get beat up by some friends?" I was only half kidding and looked around to see if the two men were in the crowd that had formed.

Minnesota looked up at me with what I would call a startled look. I could tell by his reaction there was something to that argument we heard earlier.

He shook his head and smiled. "Not today. Too much pop and not enough water, I guess."

"Really?" Millie said.

"Dehydration," he said. Mike's strength was gone. But he held onto my hand.

"Are you folks family?" The attendant looked at my dad who stood next to us.

"Friends." It was amazing how much had changed since we first saw Mike on the highway yesterday morning. "Is he going to be okay?"

"Well, I'm only supposed to be talking to family…"

"Oh go on, you young whippersnapper." M&M summoned the strength to scold the attendant who was young enough to be his grandson. "Tell my good friends here the whole story. They're the only ones I got to trust and help me right now."

Mike winked at me as he talked, his voice trailing off to a whisper.

"He is severely dehydrated. His blood pressure had dropped too. Apparently he stood up too fast and passed out, then hit his head on a table when he fell. We're not sure how long he was out when we got the call."

"We saw him not more than an hour ago," Mom said.

"It's a good thing we got to him so soon."

They loaded him into the ambulance and Mike called out, "You make sure my friends know where you're taking me, you hear? I need them there." He looked me right in the eye. "I got somethin' important I need to discuss with you, Jeremiah."

I noticed a key hanging on a chain around his neck. Mike saw me and moved his hand up to his chest. He took hold of the key. "Yep, something mighty important I need to discuss with you."

He closed his eyes and drifted off as they shut the ambulance doors.

I turned to Millie, but the sight of the men we had seen arguing, standing off in the distance, made me forget what I was going to say.

Chapter 34

Millie

"Drive faster, Dad!" Millie urged as the ambulance pulled away from them on the highway. "We may not find the hospital if we're not right behind them!"

"In this car?" her Dad said. "Doubt that." He pointed to the GPS tracking map on the dash. "Mom has already put in the hospital's name."

"Besides, getting stopped for speeding would take us even longer," Jeremiah said.

"This looks like the way to the restaurant." Millie watched the hard-packed desert racing past their side windows. An occasional group of motorcycles or quads ripping along the washes and jumping the hills in the distance made her wish they were on their dirt bikes having fun. Not dealing with so many problems.

"Yes, it is," Dad said. "The hospital is about 10 miles past the town where we ate."

"That seems like so long ago." Millie stared out the window, rubbing her chin and worrying. It was her specialty.

Dad checked in at the front desk. The waiting room was noisy and crowded with most of the chairs full. Millie thought sure she could hear M&M talking each time the door opened to admit someone to the emergency room. He must be feeling stronger already.

"They said it will be a few minutes." Dad looked at Mom. "This is kind of unusual, but Mike only wants Millie and Jeremiah to visit."

"Max!" Mom sounded like she didn't agree.

"The doctor said that could help calm him." Dad looked over at Millie and Jeremiah, then back to Mom. "They're concerned he will escalate to an anxiety attack on top of the dehydration.

They noticed his heart rate going up when the doctor said adults only."

Jeremiah looked at Millie and leaned close. "The plot thickens."

She had to hold back laughter.

"Let's take a seat while we wait." Mom motioned to a row of chairs.

Millie paced the floor, thinking about the information Mike had for them. Maybe he'd tell them where the gold was. Or if the skeleton was real. Or who those men were.

As she paced, she noticed an older woman in a wheelchair watching her. Every time she walked one way, her gray head turned and followed her. When she walked back, the woman's head turned that way. Millie stopped in front of her.

"This is Miss Nita."

The voice startled Millie. She saw a woman sitting next to the wheelchair. "Is she sick?"

"She has dementia." The woman looked sad. "It's where your mind stops working." She touched Miss Nita's cheek. "She's my mother. I'm Ivy."

Millie knelt down and looked into Miss Nita's eyes. "Hi, there!" she said.

"Oh my goodness!" Ivy said when Miss Nita smiled. "I haven't seen her smile in weeks!"

"She's sweet." Millie took hold of Miss Nita's hand. It was clenched shut. She held Miss Nita's fist. "What's wrong with her hand?"

"She holds it like that." Ivy placed her hand on top of Millie's. "Sometimes I pry her hand open to trim her fingernails."

"Does she let you?"

Ivy laughed. "You wouldn't believe how strong she is. She fights me, but I win."

"Visitors for Mike Bailey." A nurse stood by the emergency room door.

"I'll see you later, Miss Nita." Millie said.

Before Millie and Jeremiah crossed the waiting room, the men from the hotel stepped over to the nurse. "That would be us."

The nurse looked at the chart. "I don't think so." She looked back at them. "You're not Millie and Jeremiah."

"Hey, Mike is our brother!" one of them barked out. "Family before strangers."

"Take that up with the front desk."

"Do you think they are brothers?" Millie whispered to Jeremiah as they followed the nurse past a lot of beds with curtains around them.

"Beats me," Jeremiah said, "but we're about to find out!"

Chapter 35

Jeremiah

"Well, lookie here, if it ain't my best buddies on the planet." Minnesota Mike's voice was weak. Tubes taped to his hand were connected to machines near his bed.

"Well, I'll be." The nurse was looking at a monitor by the bed. "You really are good for him, his heartbeat slowed."

I took Mike's hand and pointed in Millie's direction. "Not sure you met my mouthy sister." I felt a sharp jab in my ribs as I was about to introduce the source of that jab.

"Hey! Don't call me mouthy."

"Well, little lady. Iff'n the shoe fits, as they say." He chuckled and I joined in.

"Anyway, this is Millie."

"Just a few minutes now." The nurse pulled the curtain shut and left.

"Come in here, close-like." M&M motioned for them to lean down. "I got to get this key to you real fast before our time runs out."

I looked at the key still hanging around his chest. He fumbled with it and Millie reached over to help with the clasp.

"You take this and hang onto it for me. I can't afford to lose it and these hospital people keep trying to take it off me. Says it's in their way."

Millie slipped it into the pocket of her jeans. "What's the key for?"

"I can't go into that now, but I can tell you there's a couple guys who want it bad."

Millie's eyes grew wide as she looked away from M&M and over at me.

"I think I know what guys you're talking about," I said. "We heard them arguing at the lodge."

"Oh, you heard that, did ya?"

"Is that why you're in here?" Millie butted in.

M&M looked at me. "She don't mince words none, now does she?"

"Well, is it?" Millie ignored the comment.

"Actually, Mike, I'm kind of wondering that myself."

"Well if ya can keep a secret, I'll tell you."

We both nodded.

"They took me by surprise and got into my room when I was heading back from talking with you and that deputy."

"What did they want?" I prodded.

"I don't want to go into all that, but I knowed for sure they want this key. They was searching my room."

"What were you talking about when you told my dad I'd be interested in what you saw last night?"

"Oh, that," M&M waved his hand in the air. "That's not as important as what I got to talk to you about now."

The nurse popped her head in through the curtains, "Five minutes and then we're taking him to x-ray."

"Thank you." Millie answered for all of us.

"Anyways, they ended up shoving me a little too hard and when I fell, I guess I hit my head on a table and got knocked out. They must'a high-tailed it outta there. But they didn't get my key."

"What should we do with it?" Millie asked the question we both were wondering.

"Well, you jist hang onto it for me. You got my number in case I don't get out before you all leave the lodge. I know we'll see each other again soon, I just feel it in my bones. But whatever you do, ya gotta protect that key."

"Can't you give us a hint what it's for?" I said.

"Nah, it's just too dang long of a story."

He rested his head back against the pillow and closed his eyes. His breathing was steady and deep.

We heard the curtains rustling. A different attendant stepped in and checked the wires and tubes.

M&M opened his eyes at the sound and winked at both of us. "There's danger out there. Don't lose that key," he whispered.

We stepped aside and watched as the attendant wheeled him away in his bed.

Minutes later we pushed open the door to the waiting room and came face-to-face with the angry men.

"Did he give you that key?" The loud demanding voice attracted the attention of everyone in the waiting room.

Chapter 36

Millie

Millie looked past the two men, relieved to see Miss Nita and Ivy still waiting their turn. She knew what to do.

Before she or Jeremiah could respond, her Dad intervened. "Don't talk to my kids that way!" Wow, she had never heard him sound so angry.

Millie edged away as the armed security guard joined her dad.

She could hear the rumble of their voices, as she hurried across the waiting room and knelt in front of Miss Nita.

"Are you okay, dear?" Ivy said to her.

Millie nodded and stared up into Miss Nita's eyes. "Hi there!"

Miss Nita's face lit up, and she shocked Millie when she spoke in a husky, monotone, "Hi."

"Wow!" Millie looked over at Miss Nita's daughter. "Did you hear that?"

"You are a gift from heaven." She hugged Millie. "She hasn't spoken in weeks." Ivy wiped tears away.

Millie didn't see her approach, but now Mom joined in the hug. As the two women talked, Millie eased her way out of the embrace. She rubbed Miss Nita's clenched fist.

The ladies, and the men still arguing across the room, were so engrossed in their conversations no one noticed Millie slip a key into the elderly fingers she pried open. When she let go, they snapped back into the tight fist, hiding the treasure Mike had entrusted to them.

The voices were dying down across the room and Millie stood up to see what would happen. As she turned, she saw Jeremiah looking her way. He moved next to her. "Well played, sister," he whispered.

She smiled. "Oh, you saw that?"

He nodded, just as the two of them became the center of attention.

"Let's all step outside to talk." Her Dad motioned, as the two men and the security guard watched them. The men headed for the automatic doors at the waiting room entrance.

Millie turned to offer a quick goodbye to Miss Nita. "I have to go talk to my dad, but I'll be right back." She hurried to catch up to her family.

"Your kids have something that belongs to us and we want it right now." The taller man glared at them.

Dad turned to them, "Millie, Jeremiah, these men believe that Mike gave you something of theirs."

Millie looked at her brother, then back to her dad. She shrugged her shoulders. "He didn't give us anything."

"That's not true." The shorter one insisted.

"I don't know how you would know what went on in there," Dad said.

"It's a key, it would be easy for them to hide it."

"Millie," Dad sounded exasperated. "Do you have a key from Mike?"

"Search her! She won't tell. He probably told her what it was for."

"What is it for?" Now Dad looked interested.

"Never mind! Just check her pockets."

"Millie, they have no right to ask, but to keep peace, can you empty your pockets?"

"I'll pull my pockets out and show you they're empty."

She reached in and yanked out both pockets. The only thing they produced were bits of lint.

Before the men could ask, Jeremiah did the same. His pockets were filled with gum and candy wrappers, bullet casings and a couple rubber bands.

"What are you doing with all that junk?" Millie helped him pick up all the trash.

He shrugged. "It's a handy little wastebasket."

The men stormed off. Millie could hear them muttering. "I'm sure he gave those kids that key!"

Dad looked at Mom. "What was that all about?"

Mom chuckled. "I don't know, but it goes right along with how our week is going."

Dad put his arm around her shoulder and looked toward the kids, "How about we head back and check in with the realtor?"

"Wait a sec, Dad." Millie turned toward the door. "I promised Miss Nita I'd tell her goodbye."

"I'll bring the car around." Dad headed to the parking lot.

"Oh, no!" Millie stood near the empty chair where she last saw Ivy. There was no sign of her or Miss Nita in her wheelchair.

"What do I do now?" She moaned and plopped down into the empty chair.

Chapter 37

Jeremiah

"Jeremiah, go see what's keeping your sister." Mom watched Dad pull the car to the nearby curb.

I hurried through the automatic doors and at first didn't even see Millie. Then I took a second look around the waiting room.

"Millie! What are you doing just sitting there?"

She lifted her head from her hands and looked up at me. "I've lost the key, Jeremiah." She whimpered and dropped her gaze back to the floor.

This girl! How was I ever going to survive till she got through this emotional time of her life? Or maybe girls never get through it. Who knew?

"Did you drop it?"

"No." She whimpered more. "The ladies weren't here." She looked at me. "I asked at the front desk if I could talk to Ivy and they said no."

"No? That's it, they just said 'no' with no reason?"

"I don't remember, I was too upset."

This girl needed to learn a little more about perseverance and a lot less about giving up and crying. As I crossed the waiting room floor in the direction of the check-in window, the door to the emergency room opened. Ivy walked through. My dopey sister didn't even see her because she was too busy moping.

"My sister's over there, if you're looking for her."

"Millie, what is wrong?" Ivy said.

Millie's face lit up. "Ivy! I thought I'd never see you again."

"I didn't know I was so important to you already." She held out her hand, palm up. "Maybe this is what you thought you'd never see again."

Millie let out a gasp, but before she could take the key, I grabbed it. "I'll take that, since you already lost it once."

"Imagine my surprise when a key fell out of my mother's hand during the examination."

Talk about embarrassing. But it kept us from losing the key to the bad guys.

"Sorry," Millie said, "it's a long story."

Ivy handed me a business card. "If you two are around again, my mother would love a visit."

My sister hugged her.

"Millie, Jeremiah! Hurry, your dad is waiting." Mom was standing inside the door.

"Be right there, Mom," I said.

She turned and headed back out the door. I stuffed the key in my pocket.

It should be safe there.

Chapter 38

Millie

"Dad," Millie said "have you noticed that blue car back there?"

He looked in the mirror.

"What about it?" He resumed watching the roadway in front.

"Earlier they were alongside us and I'm sure it was those men from the hospital."

"How did they go from being next to us to that far behind?" He looked in the mirror again.

"When we were at that last light they were one car behind in the other lane. Then they moved into our lane. I've been watching them for a while."

"That's why you had your little mirror out," Jeremiah said. "All this time I thought you were staring at yourself."

"It's just one of my detective tricks. Some dodo like you thinks I'm a vain female, when really, I'm spying on everyone behind me." She focused the mirror on Jeremiah. "Or some dodo right beside me."

"Max." Mom was looking in her side mirror. "He's right behind us now. Those other two cars turned off."

"I'm keeping an eye on them. You're right Millie, it is them."

"I wonder what they're up to," Mom said.

"Well, we're about to find out. They're flashing their lights and tailgating.

"Jeremiah!" Millie poked her brother in the arm. "Don't turn and look, they'll see you."

"Well, give me your little spy thing then, I'm the only one who can't see what's going on."

"Everyone got your seat belts on tight?" Dad said. "We might be in for a wild ride here soon."

Their mom looked over at him. "Max?"

"Just sit tight, Norah."

Millie's head bounced back as the car surged forward. She held her mirror up and saw the blue car keeping the same pace. Their headlights flashing, now the driver was waving his arm out the window.

They cruised at the faster speed for several miles. "Okay, everybody listen up," Dad said. "I'll make these guys think I'm pulling over for them, but sit tight. No talking and no turning around to look."

Dad let off the gas and Millie could hear the blinker clicking. She saw a bridge up ahead. The car slowed enough to pull over and stop just before the bridge. She was dying to look in her mirror. What if they had a gun?

The car shook every time a car whizzed by them going the full highway speed. She thought she heard car doors open behind them, but before she could be sure, Dad hit the gas and jerked the steering wheel to the right. All four tires squealed as they left the pavement and hit the dirt.

"Max! What about the fence?" Mom pointed to the fencing running along the highway.

The car bounced along the edge of the roadway and then dropped downhill. "Fence has been down for years by this bridge," he said, concentrating on losing the bad guys.
Dad stayed on the gas. Dirt was flying as he whipped the steering wheel to the left and they flew under the bridge, dodging rocks and debris from flash flood waters earlier in the year. Some places the back end slid so far to the right and then the left, Millie thought the car would spin all the way around.

"Hang on everyone." Dad worked the steering wheel like a pro racer, keeping them headed in the right direction. "We're taking the fun way back to Dry Brook. Hopefully, we've lost our tailgater."

"Wow, Dad, that was awesome!" Jeremiah said.

"Max, we haven't done that in years." Even Mom was smiling.

"What do you mean, Mom?" Millie said.

"When we were first dating, he scared me every time he took me out. Every bit of dirt or sand he saw, whether it was scattered on the asphalt or out in the desert, he was slipping and sliding the truck around. I was always hanging on for dear life."

Her voice was shaky and breaking up as she tried to talk over all the bumps and ruts they were flying over.

Millie and Jeremiah looked behind them but couldn't see through the dust the tires were kicking up. "I think you lost them, Dad!" Millie said.

He kept his foot on the gas, "I'm not counting on it, so we'll stay on it. Might be in for some rough spots ahead."

"Do you know how to find our way back going this way?"

"Do I know how to find our way back?" Dad mimicked her. "I was practically raised in this desert."

"Maybe we'll get some air." Jeremiah no sooner had the words out of his mouth than the car careened off a dirt ledge and soared through the air.

"Hold on!" Dad yelled, as they crashed to the ground.

"Great suspension, Dad!" Jeremiah shouted.

Dad kept the pedal to the floor, and they continued dodging ruts, rocks and bushes. The desert flew by them and in the distance they could see the realtor's office.

"Wow, that came up fast," Millie said.

"Nice little shortcut." Dad slowed the car way down as the parking lot came up fast. "Now that was a ride. Let's catch our breath so we can go into the office calmly as if it's just a normal day."

"Well, this seems to be our new normal, doesn't it Dad?" Millie said, and they all laughed together.

When they stepped out of the car, they saw Amos Lee standing on his porch.

"I'm glad you folks are here. I've got some news for you."

By the look on his face, it wasn't good.

CHAPTER 39

Jeremiah

Dad took two big steps and was face to face with the man. "What's the problem?"

"The seller is in ICU, we're not sure for how long. We don't even know if he'll live."

I let out a loud groan before Dad could respond.

"I knew it!" Millie said. "It was all too good to be true."

"Isn't this rather sudden? He lists the property and now he's in the hospital not expected to live."

Mr. Lee stammered and moved around from foot to foot. "Well, yes, it came on suddenly. But you know how heart problems can be."

"Is that what it is?" Dad pushed for info. "Was it a heart attack?"

Mr. Lee looked away. "Well, I can't say for sure." Then he looked back at Dad. "I'm not at liberty to give out that personal information."

Dad turned to talk with Mom. Mr. Lee interrupted them. "He didn't just suddenly list it. The seller accepted two other offers before yours."

"What? How can that be?"

"Well, the buyers backed out when they heard the talk about the property."

"What talk?" Millie asked. I wondered what took her so long to insert herself into the conversation.

"Millie." Mom gave her that look. The one that says shut up and let us handle this.

I looked to see how she would respond. She kept her mouth shut.

Dad followed up on Millie's question. "Can you explain what talk they heard?"

Mr. Lee hemmed and hawed. Then he chuckled, but it seemed forced. "It's just a rumor, but they claimed the property is haunted."

"Haunted?" Mom blurted out. She sounded more like Millie than herself.

"It's just a silly story, but word has been going around there is a skeleton roaming at night and people claim to have seen him at this property."

I did not trust this guy and as I looked over at Dad, I knew he was feeling the same way.

"What hospital is he in? I want to check on him."

"I'm sorry Mr. Anderson, that's confidential." Mr. Lee was wagging his head back and forth like a little kid denying he broke the cookie jar. "I can't give out that information."

"It's a matter of public record who the owner is. If you won't help us, we'll move forward ourselves."

He pulled his keys out, but before he turned toward the car he said, "I'm wondering if you have a signed listing agreement at all, Amos."

The realtor looked stunned and his eyes widened. He just stood on the porch with his mouth open.

I sure hoped there wasn't any law enforcement out on the road, because Dad was flying down the highway back toward the lodge. I could tell by the intense look on his face he had a dozen thoughts going through his head. Even Mom wasn't asking questions. I was shocked by my sister's silence.

I looked over at her. Her eyes were closed but her lips were moving. No sound came out. Maybe she's learning to think before she speaks.

"We'll pack up as soon as we get back to our room," Dad said. "I have a plan."

He hit the brakes hard when the driveway for the lodge came up. The tires slid as we hit the dirt road heading back into the Ridge Riders. After a few awesome slides, Dad got the Lambo straightened out and slowed down to the posted 10 mph speed limit.

We cruised into the parking lot just in time to see a tow truck backing up to Minnesota Mike's truck.

"What are they doing to his truck?" I yelled.

Chapter 40
Millie

Millie's silent praying got interrupted by the wild ride into the lodge parking lot and her brother's loud voice.

She opened her eyes to see a tow truck driver hooking chains up to M&M's truck.

"Dad?" Millie said, as everyone hopped out of the car.

She hurried over to Paisley, standing outside the office door. "Where are they taking Mike's truck?"

Paisley smiled. "It's okay, Millie. My dad is having it moved to the back lot, since he doesn't know when Mike will return."

Paisley motioned for her to step inside the office.

"Can you keep a secret?" Paisley whispered, when they got inside.

Millie's face lit up. "You bet I can. Oh wait, can I tell my brother?"

"Can he keep a secret?"

"Better than I can." At the doubting look on Paisley's face, Millie added, "I promise! I'll keep your secret."

"There were some men here earlier looking for Mike. My dad wants his truck hidden, so if they come back they'll think he's checked out." She looked around as she whispered.

"I know who you're talking about!"

"Shh!" Paisley hushed her.

"They were at the hospital trying to see Mike."

"You're kidding? I'll tell my dad. If that's okay with you?"

"Yes, I think there are weird things going on with them. I don't trust them."

Their conversation ended when Millie's dad stepped in the office.

"Hello, young lady."

"This is Paisley, Dad," Millie said. "She's my friend."

"Well, now, that was some fast friendship."

Both girls laughed.

"Say Millie, can you head on up to our room and pack?" He turned to Paisley, "We're checking out sooner than we thought."

"Oh that's sad," Paisley said. "I was hoping to get to know Millie better."

"We'll be back soon. Won't we, Dad?"

He smiled and looked at Paisley. "Yes, we'll be back. So let me settle up our bill." Millie waved good bye and hurried up to the room.

She couldn't believe what she heard her Dad say as the car headed west on the road home.

"We're coming back? Tomorrow?" Millie said. "Then why are we going home at all?"

"You and your dad and brother are coming back with the trailer and the bikes," Mom said. "I'm staying home to work."

She saw the look her Mom and Dad shared and knew there was more to it than that. She shivered from the memory of seeing Boyd Colston's name on her mom's laptop. Jeremiah looked at her.

"What's up with you?" he whispered.

She shook her head, giving him the message to be quiet. Then she mouthed "That guy."

"What?" he said out loud.

Oh brother, Millie thought, this guy was impossible when it came to secret communication. Her mom and dad were deep in a quiet conversation up front, so she whispered to Jeremiah.

"That guy I told you about, Boyd, who is messing up my adoption."

"No." Jeremiah shook his head. "He had something to do with this car."

Millie pondered that. "I don't know, I've been thinking and I'm not sure that's the reason."

"What kind of work do you have to do, Mom?" Millie asked. "Is this for Dad's company?"

"Not exactly, Millie," Mom said, and then Dad chimed in.

"You sure are the curious one, little missy." He smiled at her in the mirror, but Millie could tell something was wrong.

She felt it. There was a lot more to them heading home early than her parents were telling her.

And for once, she just didn't have the energy to question them.

Chapter 41

Jeremiah

I couldn't believe I slept all the way home. Considering we'd only had a few hours sleep the night before though, it was no wonder.

My sister was still asleep, slumped over with her face planted in her knees. I never understood how she could sleep like that. Even the sudden quiet when the roar of the Lambo engine shut off in the driveway didn't wake her.

"Millie." I could hear Mom whispering, as I hopped out of the car.

"Jeremiah, can you get the mail?" Dad opened the back of the car and took out two of our bags.

"Sure." Our mailbox stood in a barrel of fresh flowers at the edge of the yard. Neighbors said we had the prettiest mailbox on the street. That was all Mom's doing.

Glancing through the mail, I sauntered back up the driveway. A white envelope addressed to my sister stopped me cold. I couldn't believe it. She was right about that guy. The return address said Boyd Colston. The man she had been fretting about for two days.

Now, what to do? Give the letter right to Millie, or show it to Mom and Dad first? Why did I have to be the one to see this first? No matter what decision I made, I'd betray someone.

"What do you have there, Jeremiah?" I jumped at the sound of my mom's voice. She reached over and took the envelope from me, her eyes focusing on the return address.

"Mom." I touched her hands when she opened the edge of the envelope.

"What?" She looked up at me.

"It's addressed to Millie."

She glanced back at the envelope, then sighed and looked over at the car. Millie was standing outside the car and picked that moment to look our way.

"Jeremiah," Mom whispered. "Please keep this to yourself for right now."

I handed Mom the rest of the mail and agreed, against my will.

"Can you grab my bag too?" she said, this time in a loud voice. Oh brother, Mom, I thought, could you be any more obvious that you were trying to keep something a secret?

I avoided looking at my sister, but just as I bent down to grab my bag and Mom's, Millie was right there. I could feel her staring at me.

"What are you supposed to keep to yourself, Jeremiah?" Millie demanded. "What was in the mail?"

Chapter 42

Millie

Millie gave her brother about half a second to answer, then stormed into the house.

"Mom!" She rushed through the entryway and headed for her mom's office. "Mom!" She jumped when both her Mom and Dad stepped out of the dining room across the hall.

"Millie, let's go in here and talk." Dad turned. "Norah, will you pour me an iced tea and get something for Millie, too?"

"I don't want anything but answers!"

Dad put his arm around her as they entered the dining room. She saw him nod to her mom and knew that was his way of saying "get her something, anyway."

An envelope on the table caught her eye. She gasped when she saw the return address. Maybe she would get some answers.

Millie slumped into the chair and welcomed the cold root beer her Mom set on the table. Now she was afraid to hear the answers she'd been begging for.

"Millie." Mom sat down next to her. Dad sat at the end of the table in his usual chair. "Have you ever heard of someone named Boyd Colston?"

Millie cringed. She wanted to say no, but her mom most likely already knew. "Only when I saw him on the public records search on your computer." She looked right at her mom. "I'm so sorry. I know I'm not supposed to touch it, but I was desperate to find out what's going on with my adoption."

Mom reached over and put her hand on top of Millie's to calm her as she fidgeted.

"Okay, so you heard no one discussing that person being related to you?" she said.

Millie could feel her face forming into a snarl. "No way!" She gave in to her thirst and took a long drink of the root beer. "Thank you, Mom. This is scrumptious."

Mom took a deep breath. "Millie, what is happening, is that your birth mother is grasping for a way to hold on to her parental rights. Once those are terminated, we can complete the adoption."

"I thought she was in prison," Millie said.

"She is," her dad said, "but she can still communicate with the social worker. She also may use someone else to help her."

"Is that who this Boyd man is?" Millie looked from one parent to the other.

"It appears so," Mom said. "She is claiming that a man named Boyd is your real birth father. She says that the man named on the birth certificate, who had his rights terminated, is not your real father."

"This way she is hoping to hold open the case while they search for Boyd to do a DNA test and give her more time to fight for her rights to be retained," Dad said.

"Well, she sure wasn't interested in keeping her rights all those years ago when I first got taken away." Millie took a deep breath and looked at the only people who had been real parents to her. "She never came for one visit, and I can remember, I was five years old, and I can still remember. The foster home kept saying I would have a visit soon. But it never happened. Not when I was five. Not when I was six and by the time I was seven, I never even asked anymore when she was going to visit."

Millie's eyes were dry as she talked. She had long ago stopped crying about her birth mother. She just wanted that woman out of her life so she could be a part of this family permanently.

"Mom, they won't take me away, will they?" Now tears formed.

Dad took hold of her hands. "You're our daughter, Millie. We will fight this and win."

"Is that what Mom will work on while we're gone?"

"Yes. She'll continue her research on Boyd and also find out what's going on with the desert property."

As Millie sipped her drink, she could feel herself calming down. It made a big difference knowing what was going on, instead of wondering and worrying that the worst was about to happen.

Mom picked up the envelope and tapped it on the table. "He addressed the letter to you, but Dad and I prefer that you not open it. At least not now. We want to read it and I'll do more research."

Millie let out a sigh of relief. "That's fine with me. There's nothing anyone connected to my birth mom has to say I want to hear."

"Okay." Mom stood up and pushed her chair in. "Let's get some dinner. I'm sure we're all hungry."

"I'm starved! Did we even eat lunch today?" Millie said, as the doorbell echoed through the house. She headed to the kitchen for a root beer refill when she heard Jeremiah call out.

"Dad, you better come here."

Chapter 43

Jeremiah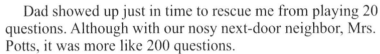

Dad showed up just in time to rescue me from playing 20 questions. Although with our nosy next-door neighbor, Mrs. Potts, it was more like 200 questions.

"Hello, Irma." Dad reached out to shake her hand.

She put her hands behind her back, "Oh no, Max, I don't want to spread my germs. I'm getting over a cold."

I backed away from the door, around the corner leading to the hallway. While I didn't want to be a part of the conversation, I also didn't want to miss anything. I was curious how Dad would answer the questions I stumbled through.

"I'm sorry to hear you've been sick." I could clearly hear Dad from where I was standing. "What can I do for you?"

"Well, Max. I noticed a strange car in your driveway and dear me, but those look like bullet holes or something in the back window. Is everything okay with you and your family?"

"You're very observant, Irma. Thank you for your concern. Yes, we're all well." He was trying to dismiss her. I know that technique of his.

"But, Max, the bullet holes? The fancy car?" She wasn't easily dismissed. I almost laughed out loud, but that would have given away my hiding place.

"Your son says you've been out of town."

"Yes, we were away on a short business trip. We're getting ready to go out of town again, so I must get packing."

"But, Max? Why are there bullet holes in that car window? I'm scared I might be in danger."

"Nothing to worry about, Irma." How Dad could be so polite, I had no clue. "The car belongs to one of my client's and he didn't explain how they got there. Our company will repair the damage."

"Oh, I see," she said, in a voice that said she clearly did not see. "And what is it your company does, Max? All these years of being neighbors and I don't think I've ever asked you that."

I had to put my hand over my mouth to hold the laughter in. I couldn't imagine there wasn't a question she hadn't asked, and not just once, but a dozen times.

"We're in the automotive business, Irma. Thank you for your concern. I've got to get going. So much to do before we leave and I don't want to let the kids down."

"Oh, okay, well, I wanted to tell you about the man I saw..." her voice trailed off.

"Where did you see a man?" Dad's voice changed. I hoped Mrs. Potts didn't notice or she might get scared again.

"It was earlier today, right after the mailman came. It looked like he put something in your mailbox. Was there anything strange in your mailbox when you got home?"

Out of the corner of my eye, I could see my sister heading my way. I didn't look at her. She would know I was listening in and if I looked at her, she'd know it was something that concerned her. No way did I want to give her one more thing to worry about.

I was trying to remember, did that envelope with Millie's name have a stamp on it? What if that creepy Boyd guy had been to our house just before we got home? Now I was feeling a little like Mrs. Potts. Scared.

CHAPTER 44

Millie

"Mom, I'm so glad you're coming with us." Millie carried her bags to the trailer the next morning.

Mom was tucking her laptop away in the front cabinet. "I am too, honey! Dad and I realized that I can work while you three are out riding."

Millie heard a car pull up and voices out front. "Oh no, who is that?" she said to her Mom, who was rearranging the food in the cabinets. "I hope this won't ruin our trip."

"Don't worry about it, honey, it's one of your Dad's coworkers. Dad wants him to house sit while we're gone. He'll also take the Lamborghini back to their headquarters."

"We've never had someone house sit before." Millie stared at her mom. "What is going on?"

She noticed her mom kept busy rearranging food she had just put away. "Oh honey, please don't find something else to worry about." Mom still didn't look at her. "We didn't want to leave an expensive car here unattended, while we're gone."

Millie tapped her mom on the shoulder. When she turned around, she stared into her eyes. "Are you sure you're not hiding something else from me?"

Mom hugged her. "Millie, please. Make sure you have all your riding gear packed, you don't want to get out there without your helmet again."

Millie groaned. "Mom! That was only once." But she hurried out of the trailer to get her gear from the garage.

A few hours later Millie straddled her motorcycle, waiting for her dad and brother to finish getting ready. She couldn't believe they were already back in Dry Brook.

"Are we really staying for a whole week?" she said, loud enough for her Mom to hear her voice from under the helmet.

"We sure are!" Mom looked as happy as Millie felt.

"Thanks for that delicious lunch, Mom. I'm glad you came with us!" When she saw her Dad and brother kick over their bikes she pulled her start lever out and kicked it several times. The engine roared to life.

Mom stepped over to Dad's bike and patted him on the back. "You guys have a fun ride."

"We'll ride over to the lodge and see if there is any word on Mike." Dad yelled over the rumble of the engines.

Mom gave him two thumbs up and took a few steps backward as the three of them rode off.

Millie kept the throttle twisted hard as she tried to keep up with her Dad and Jeremiah. She could see them in the distance but kept her eyes on the ground not far in front of her. She glanced up every few minutes to see which direction they were going.

"Ya-hooo!" She screamed inside her helmet as she launched off a small ledge and slammed down in the sand wash. The suspension in her motorcycle absorbed the drop easily. She felt the back end slip a little, but stayed on the gas and the bike straightened out. She kept following the trails left by her dad and brother.

Millie loved the power that surged under her when she twisted the throttle harder. Even though she wasn't going as fast as they were, there was nothing like racing through the desert, hanging on and maneuvering through the sandy washes that twisted and turned. Just when she almost lost sight of them, she saw Jeremiah doubling back to check on her. When he saw her she gave him a quick thumbs up. He motioned that Dad was ahead waiting, then turned and sped away from her, leaving a plume of dust to follow.

She'd get lost riding in the desert by herself, but her Dad had grown up out here. He seemed to know where every trail led over the thousands of acres they had to ride on.

That reminded her. Maybe tonight around the campfire she could get him to tell her the story of the skeleton.

She shivered as she turned her head from side to side taking in the vast desert. She was sure what she had seen the other night could have been the skeleton Mike was talking about. But that was crazy. A skeleton walking around the desert? It sure looked real, though.

Maybe they would get to see it while they were camping. Her

thoughts were interrupted as she rounded a bend on the trail and saw they were almost to the Ridge Riders Lodge.

    There was Jeremiah, but where was Dad? She raised her hand questioningly in Jeremiah's direction. He pointed up and Millie laughed. Sure enough, there was Dad riding the ridge of the steep mud hill to the north of where Jeremiah was waiting. Dad was brave. Even Jeremiah wouldn't follow him up on the ridges.

    Suddenly their Dad disappeared over the back of the steep hill and Millie's laughter died.

Chapter 45

Jeremiah

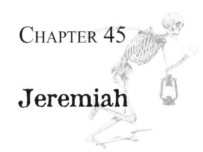

I laughed at the look of horror on my sister's face when Dad dropped off the back side of the mud hill.

"Oh Millie!" I took my helmet off to get some air. "You worry about everything."

"Well, what if he fell off the back side of the hill? Shouldn't we ride around and see?"

"Nah, he's fine. Dad rides those ridges all the time, he never comes down the same way he goes up." I hung my helmet on the handlebar and pulled two cold waters out of my fanny pack.

"Here have a drink." I handed a bottle to her. "You'll see. He'll show up any minute."

Millie took her helmet off and was sipping the cool water when her dad rode up and grabbed the water bottle.

"Hey, that looks good." He tipped his helmet back, pouring the water into his mouth through the helmet.

"Hey Dad, I've been thinking about the gold Minnesota Mike said was on our property," Jeremiah said after their Dad pulled his helmet off.

Dad shook his head. "Jeremiah, you can't put any stock in his rambling."

"But Dad," Millie chimed in. "Do you think gold has ever been found around here?"

"Yeah, and if it was, then why couldn't it be again?" I said.

Millie agreed. "And why couldn't we be the ones to discover it?"

"Yeah!" I loved that idea.

"Well, there was a story I remember my grandpa telling me."

"About a gold mine?"

My pushy sister interrupted again. "Just let Dad finish."

"Yes, oh impatient one." Dad smiled at her. "About a gold mine."

He took a few more swigs of the cold water. I could see the frustration building in Millie.

"It was back in the 1800s. There was a discharged soldier..."

"What's a discharged soldier?"

"Millie! Let him talk!"

"Well, I don't know what he's talking about!"

"He was a soldier in the Army, but then he got out. He went in search of a lost gold mine around here. He found some small nuggets on top of a steep hill he climbed. The legend talked about three buttes being near the missing gold mine. A butte is a steep hill that sticks straight up with a small flat area on top."

"Dad, can we skip the geography lesson and just hear about the gold?"

"Millie, don't you want to know why the soldier climbed the steep hill?" Dad said.

"No, because if he found the gold mine, then it isn't even missing anymore."

"That's just it," Dad said. "No one knows if he found it. He went to a big town to have the nuggets checked, and sure enough they were gold."

"Really?" Millie said.

"He got a group of his friends to go back with him to hunt for the mine. But no one ever heard from them again."

"And that's the end of the story? That's lame."

"No it isn't, Millie," I said. "That means the mine is still out there waiting for us to find it."

"Dad, could that mine be on our property?"

Dad laughed. "Well, Millie, my guess would be no. But, you never know."

"What do you mean, Dad?"

"Well, the legend says the gold mine could be in Dry Brook somewhere."

"I can't wait till we can explore every bit of that land," Millie said. "Maybe there's a butte thingee somewhere on the property and we'll find the gold."

Dad pulled his helmet back on. "You just never know, Millie. You just never know!"

Chapter 46
Millie

When they pulled up to the Ridge Riders Lodge, Minnesota Mike was sitting out front, like he had been expecting them.

"Now lookie who it is, come to welcome me home!" he shouted as the three of them dismounted and took their helmets off. Even Paisley came out of the office to greet them like they were old friends.

It will be great living down here in the desert, Millie thought. She couldn't wait. Well, if it really happens.

A loud bell rang on the outside wall. "Excuse me, I've got to get the phone." Paisley ran back inside as Dad was shaking hands with M&M.

Millie took that opportunity to whisper to her brother. "Did you bring that key with you?"

"It's back in the trailer in my bag."

"Wonder if he'll ask for it back?"

"I hope not, I want to find out what it's for," Jeremiah said.

"Maybe it unlocks the door to the skeleton's house," Millie whispered.

The two laughed out loud, causing their dad and Mike to look their direction. "Well, if it ain't my favorite two people in the world," M&M said. "You two act like you're discussing big business over there!"

"We sure are." Millie moved closer to her dad and Mike. "We're discussing where to ride when we leave here!"

"Oh," she added. "And we might have been wondering how you're doing."

"Is that so, young lady?" M&M let out a belly laugh.

"You're looking a lot better than the last time we saw you." Jeremiah sat next to him on the bench. "How are you feeling?"

"I'm back to my old self. They pumped me full of liquids all night. This morning I was good as new. The good folks here sent someone over to fetch me. I was jist sittin' here deciding where I should head to for my next adventure, when what do you suppose happened?"

"What?" Millie said at the same time as her brother.

"Well, doncha know?" He looked back and forth between them. "My next adventure up and found me!"

"Say Mike," their dad said. "If you're feeling up to it, why don't you have dinner with us at our camp?"

"Are you kidding me now?" He rubbed his belly. "That's an offer I'd take you up on even if I wasn't feeling up to it."

"That's great. We're camped over off Coyote Pack Trail. We're the only camp there, about a half mile off the highway," Dad said. "About 5:30 sound good to you?"

"Whatever time you say pardner and I'm there!"

"Finally," Millie chimed in. "I'll be able to hear first-hand right from you about the skeleton and the gold."

"Gold?" He looked puzzled. "Not sure where you got an idea like that, little missy." He glanced around as he answered.

"What do you mean you don't know where we got the gold idea? You..." Millie stopped in mid-sentence at the look on her dad's face.

He motioned for them to stand. "That's just fine, Mike. We'll finish our ride and head back and let my wife know we're having company for dinner."

Minnesota stood up with them, looking a little uneasy. "I'm going to take me a little snooze right now. Then I'll be fresh as a daisy when it comes time to meet you and your Mrs. for dinner." He motioned to Millie and Jeremiah. "And these young'uns too."

He turned and headed into the office without even saying goodbye.

"Dad," Millie whispered when M&M was out of earshot. "Why did you stop me about the gold? You told me yourself he kept talking about it over and over."

Her dad glanced around the parking lot and up into the balcony of the lodge before he answered. "It was clear he didn't want to talk about it, Millie."

"Maybe it's those two guys," Jeremiah said.

Millie shivered at the memory. Was someone watching them right now?

Chapter 47

Jeremiah

I poked a stick in the fire and watched the end flare up, then fizzle out when I held it in the air. My sister fiddled with the bag of marshmallows. It looked like she was trying to put about ten of them on the metal rod she held in her hand.

There was so much to talk about, but it wasn't safe with Mom and Dad in hearing range. After Minnesota Mike left, they said we could sit around the campfire awhile longer.

I was torn. I wanted to bounce a bunch of things off Millie, but I also wanted to hear what Mom and Dad were talking about. This had been a strange night.

"Don't be out too late kids," Mom said, before she clicked the door shut.

"Whew!" Millie let out a breath. "I thought they'd never go in."

"Me too. But I'd sure love to hear what they're talking about."

"Yeah, what was up with Mike tonight?" She scooted her chair closer to mine while she set her marshmallows on fire.

"I think he's scared," I said. "I'm telling you the other day when we were here, all he wanted to talk about was the skeleton sightings and some story about gold connected to our property."

"I wish I was as positive as you."

"What do you mean?"

"You're already calling it our property." She moaned. "It doesn't seem like that will ever happen. There are roadblocks and car wrecks everywhere we turn."

"As usual, you're exaggerating. There's only been one car wreck and look what came of that. We got to ride around in a Lamborghini!" My joke did nothing to cheer her up.

"It's just that it doesn't seem like the property deal will go through, and I don't know what's going on with my adoption."

She tossed her metal rod into the fire and we watched the marshmallows sizzle and pop as the black goo dripped off the end. "Who knows? Even if we get the property, I might not even be part of this family by then."

"Come on, Millie." I hit her on the arm. "No way I'm lucky enough to get rid of you that easy."

Okay, that was the wrong thing to say. She put her head down and it sounded like she was crying. Oh man. I hate it when she cries. I was trying to make her laugh.

"Hey, now," I whispered, "I was just kidding, stop worrying. It doesn't help."

She sniffed and rubbed her nose on her sleeve. "Did you see that letter that came in the mail for me? I bet that's what you and Mom were talking about when we got home."

"Yeah," I admitted. "Did Mom give it to you?"

"They told me what's going on and said they'd rather open the letter themselves."

"What did you say?"

"I said fine." She looked right at me. "I don't know about you, but I don't want anything to do with the people I was born to. They couldn't bother to take care of me or try to get me back. Why do they have to ruin my life now when I finally have a good family?"

A look of anger replaced her tears.

"Yeah, that's a bad deal." I reached for another stick to poke around in the fire, "But look, Mom and Dad will handle it, so quit dwelling on your fears." I handed her the stick. "Here poke the fire. That's always fun."

It surprised me when she laughed at my lame joke. She took the stick.

"Besides we've got a mystery to solve," I reminded her. "Did you hear what Mike said about us being good people?"

"Yeah. What did he mean by that?"

"I'm not sure, but he said that the other day when he was trying to convince Dad the gold story was true."

"Did he tell you what he meant?"

"No. Dad was in a hurry to pack and kept shutting Mike down when he was talking about that stuff. Mike said, 'I know for certain the gold story is true but I can't tell you how I know because you're good people,' or something like that."

"Maybe he's been in some kind of trouble."

"That would make sense," I said. "Maybe he's been in jail and heard something about gold."

"Yeah! That would explain those creeps who knocked him out. They looked like criminals."

"You're right, Millie, and that's why he won't talk about the gold anymore. Remember what we heard those guys saying in the room yesterday?"

"Something about not trusting someone with information about the gold. I bet they were talking about Mike."

"And saying the old geezer needed to stop talking about the property."

"It's our property they're talking about." Millie finished my thought.

"Did you hear what you just said, Millie? You called it our property!"

Her eyes lit up. "You're right! See, I'm already more positive."

"Just don't you forget that five minutes from now! So what are we going to do about this mystery that keeps growing?"

Millie didn't answer. She was staring over my shoulder off in the distance.

"Jeremiah, look!"

Chapter 48
Millie

Millie couldn't take her eyes off the apparition, so she didn't know if her brother turned around to look. She held her breath as she watched a giant skeleton with a light glowing from the middle. It floated near the top of the mud hill, a little way, from the camp.

She stood up to get a better look and saw Jeremiah heading toward the skeleton.

"Jeremiah! Don't go over there."

He continued on. When she took her eyes off Jeremiah and looked back to the ghostly figure, she saw it moving farther away and fading. Then there was nothing there at all.

Jeremiah turned and looked at her. "Can you believe it was that close to us, Millie?" He headed back to the fire.

Millie looked over at the trailer. Her parents must not have seen it.

"Wow!" was all she could say.

"Was that what we think it was?" her brother said.

Millie sat down and stared at the fire. How could this be? Ghosts aren't real. Are they?

She looked at her brother, "Ghosts aren't real. Not even skeleton ghosts."

He didn't respond.

"Well, are they?" she insisted.

"Hush!" he whispered. "We don't need Mom and Dad coming out. We need to figure out what's going on."

"You didn't answer my question. Are ghosts real? You've been in this family longer than I have." Millie begged her brother for information. "I never even went to church before I moved in."

Jeremiah looked back over where they had seen the strange sight, then back to Millie.

"The answer is yes, and no," he finally said.

"Oh, you're a lot of help." She picked up the stick and poked it back into the fire.

"So was that a ghost? Should we get Mom and Dad?"

"I can't say for sure about the first question," Jeremiah said. "But the second one, definitely not. They'll think we've been paying too much attention to Mike and besides they'll make us come inside."

"Well, that's not a bad idea." Millie shivered. "I'm not sure I like a ghost lurking around. And what do you mean by that lame answer, yes and no?" She stared at him. "I need some answers."

"Well..." He was off to a slow start.

"Tell me the 'no' part first," Millie said. "And keep your eyes peeled behind me in case whatever that thing is shows up again." Her eyes were scanning the desert hills in the direction where they had spotted the strange vision.

"Well, I'm no expert," Jeremiah said. "But once at a church sleepover some kids were telling ghost stories, and the leader tried to explain it to us."

"Explain what?" Millie pushed for immediate answers.

"That's what I'm getting to," Jeremiah said. "But I gotta try to remember."

Millie sighed. "Okay, I'm waiting."

"Yeah, but not very patiently."

Their Dad cut his answer off when he opened the trailer door. "Hey kids, can you come in now? We're going for an early morning ride. You need to get to sleep."

Millie glared at her brother.

"It's not my fault."

She knew that. But she needed someone to blame for their conversation being interrupted.

"Come on, kids," Dad said.

Chapter 49

Jeremiah

Getting our conversation interrupted last night seemed worth it now. We rolled to a stop on top of a hill overlooking our property.

Dad wasn't kidding when he said early. We hit the trail before sunrise which kept the sun from blinding us as we rode east.

This was the perfect place to stop. We had a spectacular view of the sunrise in one direction. Turning our heads a little to the right gave us a bird's-eye view of the property.

"How many acres is it, Dad?" I said as we dismounted. Dad reached into his backpack and pulled out the breakfast burritos and drinks Mom had packed.

"This is an amazing view!" Millie's gaze roamed the vast property. "Oh, Dad, we just have to get this place!"

Dad smiled as he handed the food to us. "It's 1,023 acres, Jeremiah."

"Wow!"

After Dad offered a prayer of thanks, we sat in the dirt near our bikes and devoured the egg and cheese filled tortillas.

"I wish I could have seen inside the house when you and Mom toured it," Millie said. "Don't you, Jeremiah?"

"Who cares about the inside? It's all the land to ride on I care about. We can make our own tracks. And what about the shop building? Have you been inside there, Dad?"

Before he could answer, Millie interrupted, "What are those little buildings there? That one just looks like a bunch of cement blocks with no way to get in."

Dad nodded his head, "That's what it is, Millie."

"What's it for?" I asked.

"Well, the original owners of the property didn't understand that you can't build a well house until they drill the well. They got overanxious and built that block structure."

"What's a well house?" Millie interrupted. That girl could be exasperating.

"When you don't live in a city, you have to have your own well to get water out of the ground. The little building over there, about 100 feet from the block structure, is the well house. It protects the water tank and well pump from the weather. See the door on that one?"

We both nodded.

"That way you can get inside to check on the well and do maintenance."

"I wonder why they didn't just tear that other one down?" I asked.

"I don't know," Dad said. "That's what I would have done."

"I doubt it, Dad."

"Why did you say that?" Millie looked at me like I was rude.

"Because Dad never would have built it. He always checks things out to make sure he's doing the right thing."

"Good point," Millie said.

Dad yawned and pulled a ball cap out of his backpack, then laid down in the dirt. "I'll just take a little rest here." He covered his face with the cap.

"Look at those big metal containers near the well house," I whispered to Millie.

"Hold on just a sec." She dug around in her backpack and pulled out a pair of binoculars. "Let's inspect."

"Do you see locks on them?" I said, as she stared down there.

"Yes. And are you thinking what I'm thinking?"

"The key," I whispered. "I wonder if it's to one of those containers."

"But how could that be?" Millie said, "Why would Mike have a key to something on property he doesn't even own?"

"Beats me," I said. "But there is a lot of weird stuff going on."

"Yeah. Almost like someone - or something - is trying to keep us from getting this house and land."

"But why?"

"Maybe there is a gold mine and someone else wants it," Millie said.

"Then why didn't they just put an offer in to buy it?" I said. "It makes no sense."

"Well, I can't wait to ride our bikes on every inch of the land to find those butte thingees Dad was talking about and discover gold," Millie said.

I stood up and turned in a full circle to take in the desert land that surrounded us. Not too far away something moving caught my eye.

"By the way," Millie said, "when are you going to answer my question about ghosts being real or..."

Now it was my turn to interrupt.

"Hey, Millie," I said. "Look over there!"

Chapter 50

Millie

"That is weird. He's so close, and I didn't even hear his engine."

"Look he's still moving, but you can't hear anything," Jeremiah pointed.

"That's because that side-by-side has an electric motor. They're quiet."

They both jumped at the sound of Dad's voice.

"Dad!" Millie said, "You scared me! I thought you were asleep."

"No, I woke up just when the conversation was getting good." He smiled when she turned and looked at him.

Millie felt her heart beating hard. She wondered what he meant. What if he heard them talking about the key?

"What do you mean by that?" She hoped her voice sounded normal.

"Well, let's see." He sat up and put his hat on. "There was talk about gold and ghosts."

He stood up and brushed dirt off the back of his riding pants. "I almost thought Minnesota Mike had caught up with us." He looked over at them and smiled.

"Well, you have to admit, the stuff he was talking about can get your imagination going." Jeremiah piped up, which was a relief to Millie. She didn't want her dad to know about the key or the skeleton they saw last night.

It wasn't like they had done something wrong, but she knew her parents would want to know about both those facts.

"I was telling Millie a story around the campfire last night, about our youth leader talking about ghosts."

Millie would be forever indebted to her brother for digging her out of this hole. Well maybe not forever, but at least until he made her mad.

"How did that topic come up?" Dad said.

"It was at that guy's only sleepover, last summer at the church."

"Oh yeah," Dad said.

"Millie wanted to know what he told us, but I couldn't remember how he explained it."

"Yeah." Millie regained her ability to speak. "All he said when I asked if ghosts were real was yes and no. A big lot of help, huh, Dad?"

"Well, I can see why he'd say that. I might have answered the same way."

They both looked surprised at his answer.

He reached into his backpack and pulled out a water bottle. After taking a few sips, he sat back in the dirt and patted the ground next to him. "We're not in any hurry. Let's talk about your question now, Millie."

"Dad, I sure prefer the sound of an engine," Jeremiah watched the electric side-by-side drive down a hill and out of sight.

Dad laughed. "I have to agree with you there, Jeremiah, but some people love innovation."

"Okay Dad, what about ghosts?" Millie settled in next to him.

"First, Millie," Dad looked straight into her eyes, "I want you to remember, when you have questions about anything, you can come to us. It doesn't matter what it's about."

"Are you saying this, because of that man, Boyd?"

"Well, like the ghost question, that would be a yes and no answer."

"Oh, brother," Millie said laughing.

"What I meant is, you have a very inquisitive mind, and the tendency to worry. We want you to ask us questions rather than struggling."

Millie reached her arm as far as she could around her Dad's shoulders and squeezed him. "Thank you Dad."

"You're welcome." He patted her knee.

"Now what about the ghosts?" she demanded.

"Direct and to the point, here we go," Dad said. "If you're talking about a ghost that is the spirit of someone who died, the answer is no. But if you're talking about someone encountering an apparition, or maybe a voice that claims to be someone who has died, then yes."

Millie gasped. "Yes?" Her voice wobbled

"Demons can impersonate the dead, that's why someone might believe they're communicating with a family member or friend who has died."

"Demons!" Millie repeated. "You mean like from the devil? How do you know this stuff, Dad?"

"That's Bible truth, Millie," he said, "In a number of places it talks about deceitful spirits and demons."

"Are you kidding me, Dad? That stuff is in the Bible?"

"Sure it is," he said. "Ephesians, Corinthians, Revelation, Leviticus. It's throughout the Bible. We'll make a study of that together one day soon."

She stared at the ground without talking. Then she realized what that could mean.

"Wait a minute!" she said. "So that means if someone sees something that looks like a ghost, it might be a demon?"

She looked at Jeremiah. "That means..."

Jeremiah interrupted. "That means Dad answered the question way better than I did."

"Millie, you look like you've just seen a ghost." Dad laughed. "To use a corny old phrase."

Before Millie could answer, they heard the notification of Mom sending a text.

Dad jumped up to get his phone out of his backpack.

"That's weird," Millie whispered to her brother. "She said she'd only text if it was something urgent."

Chapter 51

Jeremiah

Back at camp, Dad dropped the ramp door and loaded the bikes in the trailer to keep them safe. Then he unhitched the truck from the trailer.

Mom offered to stay at camp, so we could ride the motorcycles over to Ridge Riders Lodge to meet Deputy Black, but Dad wanted her to be there. Millie seemed scared about seeing him again to talk about our wreck. I was glad Mom would be there to help if Millie got weird on us.

Minnesota Mike was out front on the same bench as before. He waved.

"Hey there!" I took a seat next to him.

"What brings you folks over this way?"

"Millie has to identify a photo for the deputy. They think they caught the man who wrecked our car."

"So they's meeting you here again?"

"Yeah, Dad told them it would be easier than coming to our campsite."

I watched to see what Dad, Mom and Millie were doing. They took their sweet time getting out of the truck. I needed to talk to Mike, but didn't want my parents to hear.

"Looks like that sis of yours ain't too keen on getting out." M&M stared at the truck.

"I'm glad my mom came along to talk her out of the truck when the deputy gets here."

I looked around to make sure no one was close by, then lowered my voice. "Say Mike, what am I supposed to do with that key?"

"What key you talking about?" M&M said.

"You know what key I'm talking about." I didn't have much time, so I wasn't happy about him joking around.

"No, sonny boy." He stared into my eyes. "I don't know what you're talking about."

The guy was nutty, I admit, but now he was making me mad. "The key you gave us when we visited you at the hospital."

He kept staring at me. "I can't rightly say I remember that."

"Come on, Mike. You had it on a chain around your neck and said we needed to hang onto it."

M&M got fidgety and kept glancing over his shoulders. "I think you got me mistook for some other feller."

"Oh sure," I whispered as I saw the patrol car pull into the parking lot. "Just like I'm confused about the gold story."

My parents and Millie were out of the truck and heading toward Deputy Black.

I didn't want to miss out on what they were talking about, but to do that I'd have to quit trying to get the truth out of Mike. I decided to make one last attempt.

"Does that key unlock something on the property we're buying?"

"Sonny boy!" Mike startled me with his sternness. "You just don't seem to take a hint now, do you?"

He stood and shuffled off toward his room.

Chapter 52

Millie

Millie got out of the truck and headed toward the patrol car. The deputy was out of his car by the time she and her parents got there. She saw Jeremiah talking to Minnesota Mike and wished she could be over there.

"Afternoon, Millie."

He shook hands with her dad. "Thanks for coming here to meet me, Mr. Anderson."

"We're glad to. Thank you for tracking this guy down."

"We ran into a bit of luck," Deputy Black said. "We got some prints off the car and he did us a favor by getting picked up on an unrelated charge last night."

"What did he do now?" Millie said, anger replaced her fear.

"Millie!" Mom scolded. "That's not our business."

"Your mom's right," the deputy said and then grinned. "I'm not at liberty to talk about the drug deal they busted him on last night."

Millie decided this guy wasn't so scary. She could get through this. No problem.

"So, Millie." He pulled his phone from his pocket. "Let me know if any of these guys look familiar to you." He scrolled through the screen, tapped on it a couple times and showed her a photo, then scrolled to the next one.

She was disappointed and shook her head. "Sorry, but that isn't him."

"Neither of them?" the deputy said.

"Nope." The rat got away with it, she thought. They hadn't caught him.

Deputy Black scrolled again, bringing up another photo. Before he turned it all the way around to show her, she yelled, "That's him! I'd know that guy anywhere. That's him!"

Deputy Black smiled. "Bingo!"

"You're kidding? Is he the one who matches the prints?" Millie said.

"Sure is!"

"Mom! I did it."

"You sure did," Mom said, wrapping an arm around Millie's shoulders and giving her a squeeze.

"You deserve an ice cream," Dad said. "Great observation! All the rest of us missed seeing who was driving the car."

Deputy Black put his phone away and shook their hands. "I'll be in touch if we need anything else on this case. But looks like this guy won't be free any time soon. He had a couple other warrants out for him."

"Busy guy," Millie laughed. "What's his name, anyway? Al Capone?"

Deputy Black looked surprised. "Aren't you a little young to know about Capone?"

"Hey, what can I say?" Millie was still laughing. "I like old movies."

Her parents chuckled along with her until the deputy stunned them with his answer.

"No," he said. "This guy's name is Boyd Colston."

Chapter 53

Jeremiah

I couldn't believe what I heard when I joined my family by the patrol car. I hadn't heard everything, but I clearly heard the name of the driver who crashed into us.

Deputy Black was writing on the notepad he carried. He hadn't noticed the look on everyone's face.

"Did you say Boyd Colston?" It was hard not to notice Millie's strained voice.

The deputy looked at her. "Yes, that's his name." He looked from one to the other. "Does that name mean something to you all?"

"Boy, I'll say!" I couldn't believe I was the first to respond. That's loud mouth Millie's job.

"It's a long story," our Dad said. "But yes, this man has caused some problems for our family in recent days."

Deputy Black got his notepad back out. "Maybe you better tell me about it." He jotted on the pad while Dad talked. "Sounds like it wasn't a coincidence he was out here the same time as you folks."

Later we all sat around a picnic table outside the store eating ice cream. It was a rare moment when we were all quiet at the same time.

I knew what I was thinking. Maybe my worry-wart sister wasn't so wrong about everything that was happening. Something didn't seem right with this character following us around, then showing up at our house and leaving a letter in the mailbox.

"Mom? Did you guys ever read the letter that guy sent?"

Millie looked up from her ice cream. I'm surprised she hadn't thought to ask.

"No, Son," Dad said. "We haven't opened it yet."

"Aren't you curious to know what it says?" I prodded. "Did you bring it with you?"

"Yeah," Millie said, "maybe we need to see what it says."

"Now Millie." Mom reached across the table to touch her hand. "We agreed you'd let Dad and I handle this."

"Yeah, but that was before we found out the guy is tracking us down like a bloodhound." She spit the words out like they tasted bad.

"No kidding, even coming to our house," I joined in. At the sudden jerk of Millie's head in my direction, I realized I shouldn't have said that.

"What do you mean by that?" She stared at me, then turned to glare at my parents. She jumped up from the picnic bench, knocking her ice cream over. "You're all keeping secrets from me!"

Next thing I knew, I was chasing a crying shrieking Millie through the parking lot of the Ridge Riders Lodge. Oh brother, I thought, I hope Paisley isn't watching this. She'll think our family is nuts.

Too late.

"Millie?" I heard a girl's voice call out as Paisley stepped out of the maintenance building my sister ran by.

CHAPTER 54

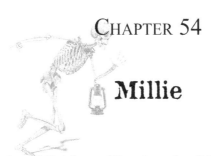

Millie

Millie heard Paisley calling, but she didn't want to talk to anyone. Not even her new friend. She would have kept running, for who knows how long, if she hadn't tripped over a rock in the parking lot that sent her sprawling.

She heard her brother calling her name, but Paisley got to her first. All she could do was bury her face in her hands and cry.

"Millie." Paisley's voice was kind, as she knelt next to her and put her arm around Millie's shoulders. "What's going on?"

Millie couldn't talk for the sobbing. By now she heard Jeremiah's voice on the other side of her. She knew her parents were probably right behind him.

The news about Boyd still upset her, but the embarrassment of sitting in the middle of the parking lot crying got her moving. Millie stood up and wiped her eyes. "I'm fine!" She threw out her hands to push Paisley and Jeremiah away. "I'm fine!" she said again. "Leave me alone."

She hadn't counted on her mom being so close.

"Millie." That was her scolding voice. "They care about you. Don't shove them away."

Millie groaned. She hoped someday she would get control of her emotions. Not only was she angry and embarrassed, but now ashamed, too.

"Do you want to talk?" Paisley whispered into her ear.

Millie took a deep breath and forced a smile. "Thank you, but not yet. I'm sure I'm just overreacting, as usual."

Dad caught up to them and gave her a hug. "We'll work through this."

She opened her mouth to respond, but Dad shushed her with his index finger tapping her lips.

"Listen, how would you two like to go for a cruise around the desert with Paisley in their dune buggy?"

"Wow! Are you kidding me, Dad?" The question stunned Millie.

Jeremiah whooped with excitement.

"Max? Is that safe?" Oh no, hopefully Mom wouldn't put the brakes on.

"It will be fine, Norah. They'll have a long-range walkie talkie to reach the lodge if they have trouble. Eric says it's more reliable than a cell phone."

"Dad loves his walkie talkies," Paisley said.

Dad helped brush dirt off her pant legs and checked the palms of her hands like she was a little kid who fell on the playground. It felt good to let him take care of her. Crashing onto the asphalt wasn't high on her list of fun things to do. It was the second time in two days she'd done it.

"Paisley's dad came up with the idea," Dad said. "When he saw how upsetting this day has been for Millie, he offered."

"Awesome!" Paisley said. Millie wondered if the plan surprised even her.

"Eric said Paisley's been working hard, and he and Amelia are excited about new kids moving into the neighborhood. He wants the kids to get to know each other."

"That's hilarious!" Jeremiah said. "I never thought of 100,000 acres of off-road land as a neighborhood."

Paisley laughed too. "Well, there are a few humans living here and there. Just not 10 feet apart like you're used to in the city."

"Boy, am I looking forward to living in this neighborhood," her brother said.

If it happened, Millie thought. She didn't want to jinx the plan by acting like it was a for sure thing. She knew her parents and Jeremiah didn't believe in jinxing things, but she wasn't taking any chances.

"Come on," Paisley said. "Let's head over to the barn where Dad keeps the off-road toys. We've got helmets you can borrow."

"Let's meet back here by the store in about an hour," Dad said.

"Sure thing!" Millie ran to catch up with Paisley and Jeremiah.

As they drove off the lodge property, the silent little side-by-side they had seen early that morning drove into the parking lot.

"Hey." Jeremiah tapped her shoulder from the back seat. "There's that guy we saw this morning."

Millie turned around. Before she could respond, Paisley stopped the buggy and stared at the electric vehicle. "I've been watching that guy."

Why did she sound suspicious? Millie wondered.

Chapter 55

Jeremiah

"Why? What's up with that guy?" I tried to ask, but my words vanished in the wind as Paisley floored the buggy and tore out into the open desert.

We jostled around, as we sped along the desert sand washes. I was glad to hear Millie screaming and laughing. This was a great idea to take her mind off everything.

Landmarks were looking familiar and soon I was screaming with excitement just like my nutty sister. Paisley was taking us to the property. This would be my chance to sneak over the fence and try out those locks. Man, was I glad I tucked that key into my pocket before we left the trailer earlier.

The buggy roared up to the gated property and slid sideways to a halt. She obviously didn't believe in hitting the brakes until she got where she wanted to stop.

"That was awesome!" Millie climbed out and took her helmet off. I was right behind her doing the same thing.

"Here hold my helmet." I thrust it into her stomach without giving her a chance to answer. She shoved it back.

"Hold it yourself! I'm not your slave."

I tossed it into the back seat and checked my pocket for the key. "Be right back," I called over my shoulder as I climbed the fence and ran for the big metal containers. They were a lot harder to see from ground level than from the hilltop this morning. I figured if I kept running up the pathway, I would get to them.

"What are you doing?" The girls yelled at me. I kept going. I was on a mission and was about to get some questions answered as soon as I slipped this key into one of those locks.

"Jeremiah!" Millie called out. "Wait for us."

I thought about it, but if they wanted to see what I was doing, they could catch up with me. I wished I had brought a water bottle. Dad said this property was over a thousand acres, but the containers couldn't be that far from the entrance, could they?

"Jeremiah!" Millie's cries sounded more intense now. "Jeremiah!" she screamed out again.

Now Paisley's voice joined hers. "Jeremiah!"

Good grief, I thought. Why can't they just wait till they catch up with me, instead of announcing to the world I was here?

"Come see what we found!" Both voices together this time.

That got my attention.

Chapter 56
Millie

Millie and Paisley sat on the ground leaning against the container door, laughing, while they waited for Jeremiah.

They heard him breathing hard before they saw him. "I can't believe you ran right by these," Millie said when he appeared and dropped on the ground beside them.

"I feel like an idiot. What was I going to do? Run the whole thousand acres?"

He sat on the ground panting. "I didn't realize they were behind these big bushes. I never even looked over this way."

"What's this all about, anyway?" Paisley looked at Millie.

"Uh," Millie hesitated. She didn't know her well yet and wasn't sure how much she should say. Would Paisley think they were nuts for believing the skeleton and the gold story? She just realized, this was the first time she admitted to herself that she believed them. Or at least wanted them to be true.

"We saw these big storage containers from up on the hill this morning and I told my sister I wanted to see them up close." Jeremiah saved her from answering.

"So you run yourself ragged just to see what containers look like?"

"My brother's kinda nutty sometimes."

"Yeah, it helps me to get along with my sister."

Millie jumped up and dusted off the back of her pants. "We better get back out to the buggy, so we have time to cruise around before meeting Dad and Mom." Paisley got up too, but Jeremiah still leaned against the container. Millie could see him eyeing the padlock right next to his arm.

"I'll catch up with you guys." His panting seemed a little faked, but Millie knew what he was doing.

"Okay." She walked away, hoping Paisley would follow her lead. "But if you don't hurry, we might leave you."

"Come on Paisley! Race you!" Millie took off running. She was eager for Jeremiah to try those keys. He seemed to be feeling the same need to be cautious around Paisley.

Just as they hopped the fence and were getting their helmets back on, Millie saw the electric side-by-side driving on a dirt road intersecting the one they were on.

"Hey look." She nudged Paisley. "There's that little car again."

Paisley looked in the direction she pointed and frowned.

"Why does that bother you?"

"I don't know why. I've been seeing it a lot. He drives through the lodge property but never stops at the store or the cafe."

Millie watched as the silent little car drove onto a small fenced property and parked near a mesquite tree. The driver got out and disappeared out of their line of sight. "Maybe he's new in the area," Millie said. "Do you think he might own that property he's parked on?"

Paisley took a few steps away from her buggy to get a better view. "He might," she said. "My dad said there were some small parcels for sale over here near the big one your family is buying."

"You mean, the big one we hope we're buying."

Paisley looked surprised. "Why do you say that? My dad said your parents made an offer on it."

"I don't know what's going on with it. The realtor keeps changing the story about the property. Now he says the owner is in the hospital and might not even live."

"That is weird. I'm sure my dad would have heard something about that if it's true."

"You mean the realtor might be lying?"

"Well, I didn't mean that," Paisley paused. "I don't know, maybe I did mean that."

The girls were standing in the road laughing, when Millie saw Jeremiah heading their direction.

Chapter 57

Jeremiah

That was awesome how Millie picked up I didn't want to try the key in front of Paisley. She's nice enough, but right now it seems like we should keep it top secret.

I watched while they headed all the way back to the gate. You never know about ditzy girls. Sometimes they'll say they're doing something and then change their mind and do the opposite.

When they were out of sight, I dug around in my pocket for the key. Once I got it out, my hands were shaking so much from excitement, I dropped it in the dirt.

Two padlocks, one on each container. This key had to work in at least one. It had to. I was so excited I could hardly think. I'd been curious about the mystery brewing since the first day we met Minnesota Mike and heard his stories about the skeleton and the gold. The stories he claims now, he knows nothing about.

That is weird. Why is he doing that? Is he just a nutty old man getting old timer's disease? Or is there another reason he won't talk?

I struggled to get the key in the lock. The padlock was so low, my head was almost touching the ground trying to see where to insert the key. Finally, it slipped in.

Yes! I almost yelled out, but didn't want to alert the girls. So close I could feel it. The answer to the mystery was just on the other side of this big door. I hoped it didn't squeak when I opened it because Paisley might hear it from the road.

"Okay, here goes." I turned the key. Or at least tried to. No luck. Maybe the other way. "Rats!" I yanked the key out. Must be the other container.

The key slipped in. But that was as far as I got.

It would not turn either way. I wanted to kick the side of the container and bellow out my frustration, but I knew I better stay quiet. Especially since we shouldn't even be on this property. Who knew if anyone was nearby?

I stuffed the key in my pocket and jogged back to the road.

Millie caught my eye as I was hopping over the gate. She looked as disappointed as I felt.

She bounced back quicker than I did from the disappointment and surprised me by what she turned and said to Paisley. So much for top secret.

Chapter 58

Millie

"So, have you seen the skeleton people are talking about?" Paisley laughed as she pulled on her helmet. "No, not yet. Have you?"

"As a matter of fact, we have."

Paisley pulled her helmet back off and stared bug eyed at Millie, then looked over at Jeremiah. He shrugged.

Thanks a lot, Millie thought, now she won't believe me.

"Where and when did this happen?"

"The most recent time was at our camp last night." Jeremiah answered before Millie could. She didn't mind, because now her story sounded believable.

"Did your parents see it?"

"No," Millie said, "they were in the trailer."

"Did you tell them about it?"

"No."

"Are you going to?"

Millie looked at her brother. "What do you think?"

He seemed to mull the idea over.

"We haven't had a chance to talk about it," she said when Jeremiah didn't respond.

"Yeah. Right after we saw it they called us to come in. Then, it's just been one thing after another."

"This is the first time Jeremiah and I have been alone to talk since we saw it."

"I can't believe this," Paisley said, but she didn't seem to doubt their story. "What did it look like?"

"Tall!" Millie shouted.

"Yeah," Jeremiah said, "and it was carrying a lantern."

"You think it was carrying the lantern, Jeremiah?" Millie looked at him. "I thought it was inside of him."

"Now that you mention it, I guess I didn't see him carrying it." He tilted his head and stared off in the distance like he was trying to remember what he saw. "But how could it just be inside of him?"

The girls laughed out loud. Jeremiah stared from one to the other. "What?"

"It's funny, because how could there even be a skeleton walking around?" Millie said.

"Yeah and if a skeleton can walk around, I guess he can have a lantern inside of him, if he wanted," Paisley said.

"It's all pretty ridiculous." Jeremiah agreed.

"Hey," Millie said, "we better get back. Mom and Dad said an hour, I bet it's been at least that."

They slipped their helmets on and climbed in. Before Paisley started the buggy, she looked over at Millie and then in the back at Jeremiah. "We have to get together again. I have to hear more about this."

Millie gave her a thumbs up and they sped off toward the lodge.

Chapter 59

Jeremiah

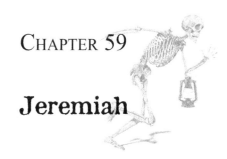

Paisley got her wish about getting together again sooner than we expected.

"Hey kids," Dad walked over to us as we were climbing out of the buggy. "Paisley's parents have invited us to dinner."

"Cool! Do we get to stay?" Millie, as usual, answered first. This would be the perfect opportunity to talk with Paisley.

"You bet," Dad said.

"We'll run back to camp to check on everything and leave a light on in the trailer," Mom said. "Do you want to go or stay here?"

That was a no-brainer.

"We'll stay here, if that's okay with Paisley," I said. The big smile on her face confirmed what we were all thinking.

"I'll ask my Dad if it's okay to take you on a tour of the lodge grounds," Paisley said as our parents drove away.

"How much do you think we should tell her?" I whispered when Paisley disappeared into the office.

"I think it's okay to talk about seeing the skeleton."

"Yeah, but let's keep quiet about the gold and the key and Mike."

"Good idea," Millie whispered, just as Paisley ran out the door of the office. She was carrying popsicles.

"The benefits of your parents owning the store?" I tore the wrapper off the cherry-pineapple Big Stick. "These are my favorite popsicles in the world!"

Paisley laughed. "It is a benefit, but I have to keep a log so it doesn't mess up the inventory," she took a big lick from her popsicle. "Now let's get going, I want to hear about that skeleton!"

"What scares me most," Millie said as we walked, "is that maybe what we saw last night was a demon!" She shivered when she said it and I don't think it was because the popsicle was cold.

"Demon?" Paisley squealed. "How did we go from skeletons to demons? That sounds super scary."

I filled her in on what our Dad had told us about ghosts.

"So you guys both saw something?"

"Yes!" we said, at the same time.

"Did you say this wasn't the first time you had seen it?"

"Well, Millie said she saw it the night we were at the realtor's office, but I didn't."

"Yeah, and I know you saw something later when the tow truck was bringing us here, but you wouldn't admit it."

"It's true. I didn't see it as well as what we saw last night though."

"Wow, this is so strange." Paisley had finished her popsicle and was gnawing on the stick. "I thought the old guy was just nutty."

"What old guy?" I played dumb. "You mean the one who went to the hospital?" Millie looked over at me like I violated our oath not to talk about M&M.

"No, not him."

That was a relief, I didn't want to talk about Minnesota Mike and his part of this strange story.

"We had a guy stop in to buy ice a couple weeks ago. He was camping in the area, not too far from your property." She tossed her popsicle stick in a trash container we were passing. "He said he saw a 12-foot tall skeleton floating on top of a hill the night before."

"Did you ask him anything about it?" Millie said.

"No, I just thought he had been drinking and imagined it. He's the only person I'd heard mention a skeleton."

"Did you tell your dad what he said?" I felt a sliver of wood prick my tongue. I had chomped on my popsicle stick till it was splintering apart.

"No, it didn't seem important." Paisley looked over at me. "Didn't your dad wonder why you were asking about ghosts?"

Before I could answer, a loud gong echoed from back at the store area.

"Dinner time," Paisley said. "Let's go! Mom is a stickler for being on time."

Chapter 60

Millie

Even with their parents sitting around the campfire, Millie kept scanning the surroundings expecting the skeleton to show up again. She tried to do it without her parents noticing. No such luck.

"Millie, what's got you so interested over on that hillside?" her dad said.

Her mom and dad both looked over their shoulders in the direction she had been staring. Wouldn't that be something if he appeared right then?

"Nothing." She changed the subject. "Hey Mom, do you think you can track down the owner of the property now that Paisley's dad gave you his name?"

"Yeah, what was his name again?" Jeremiah said.

"George Smith," Dad said.

"Oh, that ought to be an easy one to search, huh Mom?" Millie tossed a stick into the fire.

"Sure." Mom chuckled. "Just have to narrow it down from 600,000 name matches."

"If anyone can do it, your mom can."

"With the address of the property and his name, we should know something tomorrow, after I get some time on-line."

"That's good," Jeremiah said. "I can't wait to learn the real story about that guy."

"Moving right along," Millie looked at her dad. "Can we talk about the journal your grandpa had for his boys' ranch dream?"

"That's a specific topic," Dad looked over at their mom. "Sounds like someone has been sharing private information with you." He didn't seem too pleased.

Millie held her breath. She didn't want to cause problems for her parents. But she wanted to know what happened to that journal.

"I'm sorry, Max. Millie and I got carried away talking about a newspaper clipping she found in that box, and one topic led to another."

"What newspaper clipping?"

"The one about the prospector and the skeleton."

Dad nodded his head while staring into the desert night. "I forgot that was in there."

He looked back at all of them sitting around the campfire. "That brings back memories. I was the same age as the kids, maybe younger, when my dad and grandpa sat around the campfire with me. Maybe even this very spot."

"Is that when they told you the skeleton story, Dad?"

"It sure is, Millie."

"Did you ever see the skeleton?"

"Nah, it's just a legend, Millie. The stuff of late night campfire stories."

"Well, we..." Millie started.

"We love stories like that!" Jeremiah interrupted and shot Millie a warning look.

She had been about to say they saw a skeleton, but obviously her brother didn't want her to talk about it, yet.

"What about the journal, Dad? Mom said it wasn't up to her to tell me about it."

"What journal are you talking about?" Jeremiah asked her.

Millie looked at her dad and then her mom, trying to decide if it was safe to keep going with this topic.

Her dad sighed. Jeremiah looked confused.

She was guessing her mom wished she had never told her anything. But the story was out now. At least some of it.

"It's a difficult story to tell, Jeremiah. I shouldn't have told Millie anything without okaying it with your dad."

"Go ahead and tell them, Norah." Dad stood and moved toward Mom. "It's okay." He patted her on the shoulder and headed for the trailer.

Chapter 61

Jeremiah

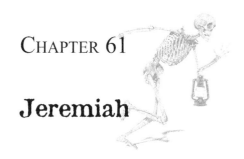

"Some things you just don't want to remember," Mom said as she watched Dad close the trailer door behind him.

"I have no clue what's going on," I said.

Millie surprised me. She looked at Mom. "You can tell him better than I can."

"The desert property dream started with your dad's grandpa. When he was 10 years old, he saw a movie called Boys Town."

"Hey," Millie interrupted. "I never heard this part."

"No, Millie, I guess I didn't get into all this."

"Let her finish," I said, when I saw Millie open her mouth to say more. It surprised me when she closed it.

"The movie was about a man who took care of orphaned boys. He started with five boys but eventually there were so many he bought a farm to have plenty of room. Later he named the farm Boys Town."

"What does that have to do with great-grandpa's dream?" Millie said.

"I'm getting to that," Mom shushed her. "That movie inspired your great-grandpa. He felt bad thinking about boys who didn't have a family like he did."

"You mean he got this idea when he was only 10 years old?" I thought that was amazing.

"That's where it started. It was all written in his journal." Mom stared off into the night sky for so long I wondered if the skeleton had shown up again. I looked over but saw nothing.

"Long story short," she continued. "He kept that dream his whole life, he made notes in his journal about ideas he had for someday when he had enough money to buy the land."

"Did you read the journal?" Millie asked her.

Mom smiled. "Yes, several times. Especially after your dad told me he wanted to do something about his grandpa's dream."

"Is the journal still around?" I was looking forward to reading it.

"No."

"And that's what I want to know," Millie said. "Who threw it in the fire?"

"Some years ago, before either of you were born, your dad and I spent time with kids who came from difficult situations."

Wow that was news to me. I always assumed Millie and I were the only kids in their lives.

"We'd take them to church, they'd hang out with your dad in the garage, learning about motorcycles. And a few of them we even took on desert trips."

"No kidding?" I couldn't help myself. I knew my parents had a life before we came along, but I didn't know there were kids involved.

"One boy in particular, Judson, was very difficult. We made the mistake of taking him on an overnight trip to the desert."

"What happened?" Millie said. "Is that when the journal got burned?"

Mom nodded her head. "Yes," she stared at the hillside so long it was as if she was replaying the scene in her head like a movie. "He disobeyed everything we said from the moment we got here. That night, after Judson drifted off to sleep, your dad sat by the fire reading his grandpa's journal."

Mom paused. Millie looked over at me and seemed to be thinking the same thing I was. Here it comes.

"The next morning when we woke up, Judson and one of the motorcycles were missing. It was a chilly morning, so while your dad was looking for him, I lit the fire. I didn't notice that your dad had left the journal in the chair where he'd been sitting.

"When they got back, Judson was angry because your dad scolded him and told him we were going home. As Dad cleaned up the campsite getting ready to load up, Judson must have spotted the journal on the chair."

"Did he know what it was?" Millie interrupted. Which was okay by me, because I wondered the same thing.

"Yes, he knew. Your dad mentioned the dream to some of the kids and they'd all say, 'when you do that we want to live with you.'"

"When we weren't looking, Judson picked up the journal and threw it in the fire. We didn't notice until he called out to Dad, 'There goes your old journal, you don't know nothin' about taking care of kids, anyway!'"

"What did Dad do?" I said, before Millie could get in a word. I couldn't believe a kid would do that. How could he treat my dad that way? Who was that kid? I wanted to beat him up.

"It took a few minutes for us to realize what he was talking about. I don't think either of us remembered the journal had been in the chair. By then it was too far gone to save."

"What happened next?" Millie's voice was softer than I'd ever heard it.

"Honestly, the rest of that day and the whole trip home is a blur."

"Oh, Mom." Millie got out of her chair and put her arms around Mom. "That's so sad." She knelt in the dirt next to Mom's chair and rested her head on Mom's shoulder.

I had no idea what to say or do.

Chapter 62

Millie

Paisley was outside watching for them as soon as they got to the lodge the next morning. Millie was the first one out of the truck, eager to see what was on the mind of her new friend. She hadn't known her long, but she could just tell she had something to say. And by that smile that wouldn't quit, she knew it was something good.

Paisley grabbed her by the hand and led her away. Millie turned to wave at her brother and Dad, "Be right back."

"Girl talk!" Paisley called out.

"Who needs it?" Jeremiah yelled back. "I'm going with Dad to see that old truck."

"You won't believe what happened here last night," Paisley whispered as the girls walked along. She looked around as she talked. Millie was still reeling from what they had learned last night at their camp, but that wasn't something she wanted to share.

"What? Tell me!"

They sat on a bench under a shade tree. Even though it was still early, she could tell this would be a hot day in the desert.

"You know that quiet little side-by-side we saw a couple times the other day?"

"Yeah," Millie whispered back to her, not sure why they were whispering. "Did you see it again?"

"I saw that and a lot more." Paisley squealed with excitement.

"The skeleton?"

"Yes! I was taking the trash to the dumpster. It was up there, hovering right above that hill."

"That's just how it was when we saw it at camp," Millie said. "On top of a hill."

"Were you scared when you saw it?"

"Well, not really scared," Millie said. "More startled. Then my brother ran toward it and that scared me. Then it vanished."

"I know!" Paisley said, "And you wonder if you imagined it."

"Exactly! What about you? Were you scared?"

"It seems like I should have been, especially since your dad said it could be a demon. But it happened so fast, I didn't have time to be. I was just standing there holding two big trash bags staring at the hill."

The girls laughed at the thought of what she must have looked like.

"It would seem like if it was a demon, we would feel terrified."

"Yeah, so if it wasn't a demon, what was it?" Paisley said.

"Is someone playing a trick?" Millie hadn't thought of that idea before.

"I saw the side-by-side twice last night."

"Hmm," Millie said. "Was it before or after you saw the skeleton?"

"Both!"

Millie gasped. "Are you thinking what I'm thinking?"

Before Paisley could answer they heard Jeremiah, "Hey, girls, get over here. Dad needs to tell us something."

Chapter 63

Jeremiah

"What were you girls talking about?" They looked like they'd just solved the crime of the century.

"Jeremiah!" Millie whispered. "We think we know the source of the skeleton."

"This I gotta hear!"

"Jeremiah, Millie," Dad stood near the office door. "Would you two be fine with staying here all day?"

Would we? It's the best thing I could imagine happening right now. This would give us the perfect opportunity to discuss the skeleton and maybe search for it.

"Sure Dad," I said. "What are you and Mom doing?"

"Your mom has a lead on where we can find George Smith. We're heading into the city to pay him a visit."

"Oh Dad, that's awesome," Millie said. "Maybe we can find out what's going on."

"That's what we're hoping. Paisley's parents said it's fine for the two of you to hang around here. They'll even feed you."

"You can't beat a deal like that!" I couldn't wait for Dad to drive away.

"So what's this all about?" I said to both girls as they led me over to the bench where they'd been sitting. It was far enough away from the hotel and campground no one would overhear.

"Paisley, tell him what you told me."

"Last night I saw the skeleton!"

"No kidding?"

"Yes, and just before I saw it and just after, what do you think I saw?"

Oh, brother! Girls! Why can't they just tell you something without the guessing games?

"I don't know. What?" I never play guessing games.

"That silent little side-by-side that's been driving around."

"You think that's connected to the skeleton?" I wasn't following her line of thinking. But if her thought processes worked like my sister's, that's understandable.

"I do."

"Why is that?" Millie asked.

"Because first he drove in through here just like he did the other day. He drove down this road and toward that hill over there."

We looked in the direction she was pointing, at the mid-size mud hill on the far side of the lodge property.

"I didn't think much of it, so I didn't keep my eye on him," Paisley said. "Plus I was struggling to get the bag out of this trash can here."

Now we looked at the big trash can next to the bench. We must have looked funny to anyone watching. Every time she mentioned a landmark, our heads turned in that direction.

"So I got the bag and was heading down the road to the dumpster and that's when I saw the skeleton appear on the hill."

"Were you scared?"

Millie laughed. "That's the same thing I asked her."

"No," Paisley said, "more startled, I think. And by the time I realized what I was seeing, it faded away. I stood there for a few minutes holding both my trash bags."

"Where did the other bag come from?" Millie said.

"Oh, come on, Millie!" I said, "like that matters."

Paisley chuckled. "It was the one from outside the store."

She looked right at me. "Look, girls like to get all the details."

I shook my head and waited impatiently for the important details. Forget that stuff that doesn't matter.

"After I dumped the trash and headed back to the store, I noticed that little side-by-side again and this time it was coming over that hill. He drove back through here and right by me."

"Did you get a look at the driver?" I said.

"No. He had a helmet on with a black face shield. I don't even know how he could see, since it was already dark outside."

"Does that guy live out here or is he just camping in the area?" I was thinking out loud and didn't expect them to have an answer, but they surprised me.

"We think we know," Millie said.

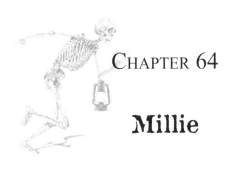

CHAPTER 64

Millie

"Well, now, lookie here, who I jist ran into."
Millie jumped when she heard the familiar voice. Paisley and Jeremiah looked just as startled.
Minnesota Mike was standing not two feet away from them. They had been so engrossed in the conversation, they hadn't seen him approach.
I wonder how much he heard? Millie thought. But then she realized it wouldn't matter, since he was the first one who told them about the skeleton. And the gold. Which he won't talk about now and they hadn't told Paisley about.
She would use this opportunity to get more info.
"Hey there, M&M!"
"M&M! I like that. I like that a lot." He patted Millie on the shoulder. "You're all right in my book."
That was enough small talk. "Hey, have you seen that quiet little side-by-side that's been driving around the desert?"
A flicker of recognition crossed his face before he jumped in with his cover-up story. At least that's what Millie figured it was. "No, I can't say as I have." Minnesota was stroking his beard and looking up in the sky as if he was deep in thought. "No, nothing like that has crossed my path."
Why won't he tell us anything? Millie wondered. She looked at her brother and could tell he didn't believe him either.
"So are you checking out today, sir?" Paisley filled in the awkward silence that hung between them. That silence when everyone knows what someone has said isn't true, but no one knows how to proceed.
"You know," he said, "I keep saying I'm only staying one more day, and doncha know, I'm gonna have to say that again

today. It's a right pleasant place you folks got here, and I think I'll stick around at least until tomorrow."

"Well, that's okay with us." Paisley must have been great at her job.

"I was just thinking on buying some ice cream for my good buddies here." He smiled and looked in Millie's direction. "You like ice cream, don't you?"

"Boy do I! And they have my favorite flavor here." She hopped up from the bench. "Let's go!"

Jeremiah and Paisley followed and as the group headed toward the store, Paisley veered off toward the shop. "You guys go ahead, I'm going to find my dad and ask if we can take the buggy out again."

That gleam in her eye told Millie just what she wanted to know. They would get to hunt for the skeleton man.

She gave two thumbs up to Paisley, and licked her lips at the thought of the mint chocolate chip ice cream waiting for her.

Chapter 65

Jeremiah

Paisley did a perfect job of getting us just close enough to where she and Millie had seen the guy pull in. Yet, not close enough that anyone would hear the buggy engine.

She pulled over near a large tree and shut off the walkie-talkie so it wouldn't make any noise and give us away. We all climbed out and stashed our helmets on the floor.

"Are you two ready?" I said. The plan was to hike around the edge of the fence line until we could find a good place to climb over or under. Luckily, this place had lots of bushes and trees, plenty of things to hide behind, in case we saw anyone.

The sand was thick from so many off-road vehicles racing along the road, so it made walking slow going. Millie charged on ahead. Paisley lagged behind.

Within minutes, Millie darted back. "Come on, you guys, I found a spot where the barbed wire is down. We can get through. It's right by a bushy tree to cover us."

We wandered around on the property heading in the direction where the girls had seen the side-by-side pull in. "Look here." I pointed to tire tracks.

"Let's follow them," Paisley said.

"Millie, you keep an eye out for people, I'll keep my eyes on the tracks and lead both of you."

After about 10 minutes of trudging through the stickers and bushes and stumbling into rodent holes, our efforts paid off.

"Look at that!" I said.

We all stared at the storage container in front of us. Tire tracks led up to it and disappeared. Someone had driven right into the container.

"There's no lock on the doors." I glanced over at the girls.

"Let's open it!"

"Fine by me," Paisley agreed with Millie. "Be careful though, sometimes these doors are really loud when you pull them open."

"I'll go slow." I was already grabbing hold of the big handle and pulling it up, to free it from the latch.

Millie hopped from one foot to the other, "I'm so excited I can't stand it."

Paisley was right. The door was loud, but her idea to open it slowly worked great. The suspense was killing us.

"It's dark in there," Millie whispered.

Once the door was open, we waited for our eyes to adjust to the darkness. The little car was parked just inside the doors. The container extended probably 25 feet past the car. It was filled with junk that looked like it would be fun to explore.

"Jeremiah!" Millie said. "Look way back in there, what's hanging from the ceiling?"

We peered in, still without stepping inside, trying to make out what was in the rear. We all figured it out at once. "The skeleton!" we whisper-yelled.

"But how could that be?" I said. "That thing can't be what we've been seeing."

"Yeah," Millie said. "How would it just appear and then disappear?"

"But it has something to do with what we've been seeing," Paisley said. "It's too much of a coincidence."

"I'm checking it out. You girls stand guard and tell me if you see anyone coming."

Before they agreed and before Millie tried to push her way in, I scrambled around the car and stepped over tools and boxes, on my way to the back. Instead of watching where I was going I stared at the skeleton hanging from the ceiling. Big mistake. I tripped over a metal box and crashed down on the other side.

Cardboard boxes stacked on the floor toppled on me, as I went down. I could feel my shin throbbing.

As I was struggling to get unburied from the boxes, I heard the girls' frantic voices.

"Jeremiah! Someone's coming."

I could already hear a car approaching.

"Shut the door. I'll hide in here till they're gone," I called back. "Then run!"

Chapter 66

Millie

Millie was shaking as she and Paisley peered out from the bushy tree they were hiding in. The sharp twigs were poking into her skin and she wished she had worn long sleeves.

They could see two men staring at the dirt on the ground, in front of the container doors.

"They see our footprints," she whispered to Paisley, who was nodding.

"Maybe we should get farther away from here," Paisley said, "what if they follow our footprints and find us?"

Millie couldn't decide. She wanted to watch what they were doing, but it would be terrible to get caught. It was bad enough with Jeremiah inside the container.

"Come on," Paisley urged.

"I don't know. What if they hear the bushes rattling?"

"We're too far away for that."

"Even if we run farther, they might keep following the prints," Millie said. "I don't know what to do." She wanted to cry. That seemed to be her solution for every problem. Not that it ever solved anything. So it was out of the question now.

"Okay." She finally agreed.

The girls shoved their way through to the back side of the prickly bush and crouched down as they broke free of the covering. They ran, half bent over, as fast as they could, to the place where they came through the fence.

Millie stopped to catch her breath once they were on the other side.

"Come on, Millie." Paisley grabbed her arm. "Let's get back to the buggy and we can get away."

"But what about Jeremiah?"

"Just for now. We'll be back for him."

Ten minutes later, the girls stared down from a plateau on a nearby hill. They watched the men back the side-by-side out of the container. Millie focused her gaze on the car parked to the side of the container. She gasped.

"I know that car!"

Paisley looked in Millie's direction. "How can you know a car?"

"Those are the men from the hospital. The ones who chased us on the way home."

"What?" Paisley yelled. "You never told me about any of that!"

"As soon as we get Jeremiah out of there, we need to talk."

The girls watched as one of the men slammed the container doors shut and latched them.

"He's spending a long time with that latch," Paisley said.

"I noticed that. What do you think he's doing?"

"I don't know for sure, but I have a bad feeling." Paisley looked over at her, fear in her eyes.

"Same here." Millie's eyes mirrored that fear. "I bet he's locking it."

Chapter 67

Jeremiah

While the girls were shutting the doors, I fumbled my way through the darkness trying to get as far away from the front as possible. I half crawled, half crouch-walked until I was at the far end, right under the dangling skeleton. My eyes had adjusted to the dark and I could see it was a big plastic skeleton. Sure enough, there was a lantern mounted inside his rib cage.

I heard muffled voices outside the container and the sound of someone lifting the latch. Kneeling down on the floor, I found a pile of rags and some dirty blankets. I crawled to the far corner and covered myself. Any other time I'd have thought that was disgusting, but right now the alternative was much worse.

"Someone's been poking around this place," a man was saying over the sound of the squeaking door banging open. "Did you see all those footprints?"

"Yeah!" The other voice sounded gruff, familiar and angry. Where had I heard that voice?

"I told you we shoulda locked it. It's a good thing they didn't get inside."

"How do you know they didn't?" Gruff Voice said.

"Well, look around here. Nothing looks different. If anyone broke in, there would be evidence."

They stopped talking, and it sounded like they were moving things around. I was just getting ready to sneak a peak, when I saw a flashlight beam glowing through the blankets. I held my breath, prayed and wondered how far away the girls were. They must have gotten away. The men didn't say anything about them.

"Okay, everything's okay," the first man said.

"The laptop's there?" Gruff Voice said.

Some words were muffled. It sounded like they were moving around while they talked, sometimes facing away from my direction. I needed to hear what these guys were saying, but did I dare move enough to stick my ear out from under the blanket? Something was strange about a laptop being in a storage container full of junk.

"Yeah, it's all good. We need to go charge the battery on it before tonight," the first man said.

"Okay, grab it and let's get out of here. We don't have much time left before dark." That was Gruff Voice.

Then more from Gruff Voice. "You go in the car to find somewhere to charge it. I'll follow you. That will save time."

"And put that lock on this time!" One final word from Gruff Voice.

I heard the doors slam shut.

Now, how was I going to get out?

CHAPTER 68

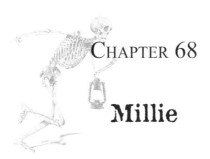

Millie

Millie watched as both cars drove off the property and down the dirt road. "Come on Paisley. We've got to get down there and figure out what to do."

"Do you think it's safe to drive right up to the container now?"

"We might as well. They're gone and besides, if they come back, we can get away faster if the buggy is close by."

"Jeremiah might think it's them coming back," Paisley said.

"No, he'll recognize us." Millie had to yell over the sound of the buggy speeding up. They shot down off the hill and headed toward the container to rescue Jeremiah.

Minutes later Paisley shut the engine off as they coasted to a stop, hidden in some bushes behind the container.

"Jeremiah!" Millie yelled, as she hopped out. "Leave your helmet on, Paisley, in case we have to make a quick get away."

"Jeremiah!" Paisley joined in.

"I'm here." His voice sounded muffled. It was coming from the rear.

Millie moved toward him. "Jeremiah, can you hear me?"

"Yes." His voice was louder. He must have come out from whatever he was hiding under.

"It's locked, Jeremiah," Millie said. "Do you have the key with you?"

"What key?" Paisley said.

"I'll tell you later," Millie whispered to her. "Jeremiah! Did you hear me?"

"Yes. I have it, but what good does that do, if I'm in here with it? I've got to get out of here."

"Hold on," Millie said. "We'll look around to see if there are any vents you can push the key through."

165

"You think you have a key for this lock?" Paisley was persistent.

"I don't know. But it's worth a try." Millie circled the container.

"I found one!" she screamed out. "Jeremiah, come toward my voice. There is a vent down near the floor."

"Okay." She could hear him moving junk around.

"I'm here, I see it."

"Okay, shove the key through. I'll let you know when I see it."

Within a few seconds the girls could see the tip of a key. "Yahoo!" Paisley screamed. "We see it!"

"You girls need to be quiet! Someone might hear you."

"Okay," Millie said, in a quieter voice. "I've got the key. Hold on while I try it."

"Oh man," Paisley said, "this has to work, this has to work, this has to work."

"Hush!" Millie said. "You're making me nervous. I'm shaking so much, I can hardly get the key in."

"Does it work?" Jeremiah's voice called from the other side of the container wall. "What's taking so long?"

"Millie's hands are shaking, she's having trouble getting it in the lock."

"Well, hurry!"

Millie's stomach flipped, when she tried turning the key. It wouldn't turn. Maybe the other way, she thought, but knew in her heart that wouldn't work either.

"Well?" Jeremiah yelled from inside.

"It doesn't work, Jeremiah."

"What do we do now?" Paisley looked over at Millie.

"Got any ideas, Jeremiah?"

"Does your dad have any bolt cutters, Paisley?"

"Yeah, but if we go back there without you, how are we going to explain that?"

"Let me think for a minute," Jeremiah said.

"We could just tell her dad the truth and ask him to help us," Millie said to her brother.

"No!" Paisley said.

"Why? Don't you think he would help?" Her answer startled Millie.

"Well sure he would help, but then he wouldn't trust us to go out in the buggy alone again. It's only been since you guys have been here, he's been letting me go."

"I've got an idea," Jeremiah said. "Millie, look around and see if you can find a bigger vent. We can kick it out, so I can crawl through."

"You take this side, Paisley, I'll check the other." Millie ran to the other side and within seconds shouted. "I found one! I found one!"

Paisley showed up at the same time Jeremiah's voice sounded close to her.

"Can you see it, Jeremiah?" Millie said.

"Hold on, I need to move a bunch of junk off the bottom shelf."

The girls could hear him shoving things and a few grunts and groans. It must have been heavy stuff.

"Okay, yeah, I see it," he said. "Stand back, I'll lay on my back and kick it."

Millie stepped back a few feet, just as the vent bulged out with Jeremiah's first kick.

"Millie, look over there!" Paisley whispered. "Someone's coming!"

Chapter 69

Jeremiah

I couldn't tell what was going on out there, but something didn't sound right.

"Jeremiah," Millie whispered. "Hide!"

I didn't stop to ask why, just shoved all the boxes back on the shelf and ran back to my hiding spot. Once again, I tripped and stumbled on the way.

I don't know how long I'd been in the container, but it felt like hours. Paisley's parents were sure to get suspicious, and I sure hoped Mom and Dad hadn't called to check in.

My heart beat hard as I crawled back under the smelly dirty blankets. I pulled them over my head, just in the nick of time.

The large metal doors screeched as the dry hinges rubbed against each other. I never heard the buggy start up, but since no one was yelling at them, I guessed they were safe. They must have hidden the buggy, too.

It sounded like someone was overturning boxes and kicking things around. Then Gruff Voice. "That stupid idiot! Can't believe he forgot the charger."

More sounds of things being tossed and kicked around. "Where the heck does he keep that thing?"

I held my breath as long as I could and then let it out before taking another deep one. I didn't want to take any chances. As mad as this guy sounded, this would be a super bad time to get caught.

"Finally!" Gruff Voice yelled. Then the sound of the doors slamming shut.

I waited for the girls to give me the all-clear sign. I was eager to get back to kicking the vent. We had to get back soon or we would all be in trouble. If we weren't already.

The minutes ticked by and I wondered just how far away they ran. But I wasn't about to come out of my hiding place. We'd already had two close calls.

Finally. "Jeremiah," Millie's whispered voice behind the container. "Can you hear me?"

I popped my head out from under the blankets. "Yes. Are they gone?"

"We think so, we'll go check. We've been hiding behind the container."

A couple of minutes passed when I heard the doors opening again. I yanked the blankets back over my head.

Oh man, they're back again, I mumbled to myself. I hope the girls got away.

"Jeremiah!" Millie's voice was clear. And loud. I couldn't believe it. She was inside.

"Jeremiah! Where are you?" Paisley said.

I threw off the dirty blankets. I never thought I'd be so happy to see my sister. "How did you get in?"

"That guy was in such a hurry, he left the lock open," Millie said.

I jumped over some debris and shoved my way around other stuff. "Come on, let's get out of here!"

"The buggy is around back, go get your helmet on," Millie grabbed hold of the big door. "We'll shut this and catch up with you."

"Oh man," I yelled out, as the buggy sailed down the dirt road and away from that property. "That is the most scared I've ever been in my life!"

"Us too!" Millie shouted over her shoulder.

I leaned forward so they could both hear me. "You won't believe what I learned though. It was worth getting trapped in there."

Paisley glanced back over her shoulder. "Yeah, you can say that now, when you're safe!"

Chapter 70

Millie

Millie wanted Paisley to pull over so they could hear what her brother had learned. But she knew they had to get back.

They'd been gone almost two hours.

Paisley's dad was waiting for them as the buggy pulled into the barn.

Have to act normal, Millie told herself, as they hopped out and pulled off their helmets.

"That was so much fun, Mr. Morgan," Millie gushed, hoping she wasn't overdoing it. "Thank you for letting Paisley take us out again."

"Yeah," Jeremiah said. "It was a blast!"

Paisley's dad smiled, then looked at his daughter. "That was a little longer than I expected. I couldn't reach you on the walkie."

"Oh Dad, I'm sorry," Paisley looked over at Millie with a sick look, then back at her dad. "I guess I forgot to turn it on."

"We got carried away, Mr. Morgan," Jeremiah said. "We stopped to do some exploring."

"Yeah," Millie said. "I love rocks, I can never get enough."

"That's fine, Millie. Did you bring some back?"

"Bring what back?" Millie saw her brother stare at her, like she was an idiot.

"Rocks." Mr. Morgan said.

"Oh, that," Millie tried to recover from the goof-up. "I had nothing to carry them in. And I didn't want them sliding around on the floor."

She wanted to change the subject. This lie was growing.

Mr. Morgan saved her by changing the topic. "Your parents called." He looked from Millie to Jeremiah. "They said they have good news. They're on their way back."

Millie hugged Paisley and then Jeremiah. "Yippee!" she shouted and danced around.

"I'm excited too!" Paisley said, "I can't wait for you guys to move here. I've had so much fun the last couple days."

"Me too," Millie said. "I feel like for the first time in my life, I've made a real friend."

Paisley gave her double thumbs up. "Hey Dad. How long till their parents get here?"

"Not more than an hour."

"Can we walk around and empty the trash cans while we're waiting?"

"Great idea, Paisley." He looked over at Millie and Jeremiah. "You two don't mind, do you?"

"We'd be glad to," Millie spoke up while Jeremiah nodded in agreement.

They weren't far from the store when Paisley whispered, "How did you like that for getting us a chance to talk?"

"That was awesome," Jeremiah said.

"Jeremiah, if you want to grab the bag from that can by our bench, Millie and I will get the one from the pool area. We'll meet you down the road near the dumpster." She turned back to look in her dad's direction. He was still there. "We'll be out of sight when we get close to the dumpster. There's another shade tree with a bench down that way."

Moments later, the girls listened as Jeremiah related what he'd heard the men talking about in the container.

"But what is it with the laptop?" Millie asked. "I don't get it."

"I do. It's obvious."

"Holograms!" Paisley squealed.

"Bingo!" Jeremiah pointed at her.

"Holograms?" Millie was still in the dark.

"That's how they make the skeleton appear."

"Did you hear them say that?" Millie was unconvinced.

"No, but why else do they keep the laptop in there, and they needed it charged before tonight."

"That silent little side-by-side is perfect for the job," Paisley snapped her fingers at the realization. "They can drive around, and no one hears them."

"Yes," Jeremiah continued. "They're out of sight, behind a hill like the one over there, where Paisley saw it."

"And then they project the image up on the hill." Paisley added.

"Really? They can do that with a laptop?"

"You bet!" Jeremiah nodded his head. "I've been reading about the apps you can download to do that."

"And that's why they had the skeleton in the container," Paisley said. "They photographed it to create the hologram." They finally convinced her. "Wow!" She looked from Paisley to Jeremiah and back again. "Wow."

"Yeah, that's what I say too," Paisley's eyes were big.

"But, why would they do that?"

"That we still have to figure out," Jeremiah said.

"And what does all this have to do with our property?"

"Why do you think it has something to do with the property?" Paisley asked her.

"Because when Minnesota Mike gave us that key, he also said he had something he had to tell our dad before he bought the property." Jeremiah answered for her.

"Plus, Amos said two other buyers were scared away by the place being haunted," Millie told Paisley.

"You never told me the whole story about the key." Paisley stood up and grabbed her bag of trash. "Come on, we better finish up. Let's dump these. We have three more cans to get to."

"Yeah," Jeremiah said, "and I need some time to think through all this. I know, somehow, it all connects."

They were each lost in their own thoughts as they headed to the dumpster. They dropped the bags in the trash and turned around, in time to see the car heading in their direction.

Chapter 71

Jeremiah

"Come on, let's hide," I said as the car creeped along the dirt road. It looked like they were searching for something. Or someone.

"Follow me." Paisley took off through some trees that led to what looked like an RV park. She pointed to a tree with a ladder attached to it.

I looked up to see wooden planks hidden among the branches.

She climbed up and looked down at us from the platform.

I looked at Millie. "You want to go first?"

"Sure, this looks fun!"

"Look," Paisley said once we were all up there. "We can watch the car from here and they'll never see us."

"This is awesome," I said, "a perfect spy tower."

"Yeah, I don't think that's what my dad had in mind when he built it, but I love to come here and watch people. It's good entertainment."

"Are they looking for us?" Millie said.

"I doubt it," I said, "they don't know we were the ones at the container. I bet they're looking for Minnesota Mike."

Millie turned to Paisley. "Have you seen him today? Or did he check out?"

"He was still here when we left in the buggy."

"I hope they don't find him." I said. "Is his truck still parked in the back?"

"Yes. When my dad told him where it was, he seemed happy to leave it there."

"I know something's up with him." I peered out through the tree branches to watch the car. "Those guys must be looking for him."

"And it has something to do with that key." Millie was right by my side.

"Will you guys tell me what this key business is about?"

Just as we finished filling Paisley in on the key and chase story, we heard the loud gong.

I looked at Paisley.

"Seems too early for dinner time. Maybe your parents are back."

Millie moved to the edge of the planks near the ladder.

"Wait a minute," I said. "Are we going to say anything to our parents about the skeleton discovery?"

"No!" Paisley said.

"Oh, that's right. Can't risk not getting to go out in the buggy."

"Maybe we can tell them later," Millie said.

"Let's get going." Paisley was already halfway down the ladder.

As we climbed down, I hoped like crazy we wouldn't run into the little car stalking the place.

Chapter 72

Millie

"Dad! Mom!" Millie ran screaming to her parents when they got back to the office.

She tried to embrace them both at once and Jeremiah joined in. "Group hug!" they heard Paisley calling out.

"What's the good news? What is it?" Millie burst out.

"Yeah," Jeremiah joined in. "We can't wait to hear."

"We sure can't!" Even Paisley was excited.

"Well." Dad smiled at Mom. "It's a long story, but it looks like we'll get the property."

"Yippee!" Millie jumped up and down, surprised to see Jeremiah doing the same.

"So you found the man?" Jeremiah said.

"We sure did," Mom said. "He's a wonderful older gentleman, who's been through some hard times."

"Tell us all about it," Millie said.

"Hey, how about letting your parents catch their breath?"

All three kids looked over, as Mr. Morgan approached. He shook hands with her parents and said, "Dinner will be ready in 30 minutes. Why don't you join us?"

"Absolutely," Dad said. "We're famished. We haven't eaten a bite since we left this morning."

"And then you can tell us all your news." Paisley said.

"Paisley." Her dad reprimanded. "That isn't our business."

"Actually," Mom said, "we'd love to share the story if you want to hear it."

"I want to hear it!" We looked over as Mrs. Morgan joined us.

"Mom! Millie's going to move out here. She's the best friend we've been praying for!"

Mrs. Morgan hugged Millie. "I believe you are."

175

Millie could feel little tingles up and down her neck. No one had ever called her their best friend before. She almost wanted to cry, but knew she needed to get over that crybaby stuff. She made the mistake though, of looking at her mom who was wiping tears from her own eyes. That was all it took.

Millie sniffed and wiped her nose on her sleeve.

"Oh good grief!" Jeremiah said. "What are you crying about now!"

Paisley jumped to her defense. "Those are tears of joy, at the thought of having me for a best friend!"

Millie was laughing and crying and nodding her head in agreement.

CHAPTER 73

Jeremiah

Mrs. Morgan was a fantastic cook, but I barely tasted the grilled chicken and mashed potatoes. All I could think about was what Mom and Dad would tell us. They were gushing about the delicious food and how kind the Morgans were for letting us stay there. I just wanted to yell out "Come on! Get to the good stuff." But I know better.

Finally.

Dad looked over at Mom. "I think it's time to share our news."

Mom looked at me and then around the table. If the way I felt was any sign, she saw a lot of eager faces staring back at her. Hungry for information.

"First, Mr. Smith is not in the hospital and never has been. He is a delightful 82-year-old man who lost his wife about a year and a half ago. They'd been married 61 years." Mom looked around the table as she spoke.

I groaned and looked at my sister. She looked as frustrated as I felt. Please no history, just tell us the good news. Are we getting the property, for sure, I wondered.

"Besides coping with the loss of his wife," Dad said. "He has dealt with the heartbreak of a wayward son for many years."

"What's wayward?" Millie interrupted. I swear, that girl knows nothing, which makes stories take a lot longer.

"He does bad things," I said, hoping to prevent one of my mom's teachable moments, where she takes forever to explain one word.

"Okay, keep going," Millie said. Good. She was learning.

"The son stole Mr. Smith's phone, so he never knew we had made an offer," Dad said.

"When we told him, he asked us to have the realtor mail him the paperwork," Mom said. "But we contacted Amos and convinced him to drive into town tomorrow, and get Mr. Smith's acceptance or counter-offer, right away."

"Remember, that's where he asks for a different price than Mom and Dad offered." I directed my comment to Millie hoping to prevent a real estate lesson from Mom.

"How do you know so much?" Millie grumbled. I heard snickers around the table.

"I read. I listen. You should try it."

The snickers turned into outright laughter. Even Mom and Dad got a kick out of that.

"Do you think he will accept?" Mr. Morgan said.

"We feel good about it," Dad said. "He wanted us to stay and visit, and was curious about what we planned to do with the property."

"Mr. Smith was interested in our idea about using it to help kids from troubled backgrounds," Mom said.

"He showed us a photo of his son, when he was about 14," Dad said. "'This is the last good memory I have of my son,' he told us."

"What happened?" I asked.

"How old is his son now?"

"He's 42." Mom looked in Millie's direction.

"About the time his boy turned 15, he met up with a rough group of kids and started skipping school, stealing, drinking," Dad continued. "When he was 18, Mr. Smith made him join the military. He thought that would help straighten him out."

"He was hoping the strict discipline he'd learn would change his life." Mom added.

"But, he continued his downward spiral there. He got hooked up with other troublemakers."

I looked around the table and saw that everyone was as fascinated with the story as I was. Well, everyone but Millie.

"What does all that have to do with him selling us the property?" My sister interrupted.

"That's why he was so interested in us wanting to help kids. He said it would be the best thing to happen to that place, if it could help kids," Mom said.

"So the military didn't help?" I thought that would have made a difference.

"No. The son and his friends continued to cause trouble and were kicked out." Dad looked sad and it wasn't even his son.

"Dishonorably discharged," Mr. Morgan said.

"I've heard those words before!" My sister looked puzzled. "Where was that?"

That surprised me, because I hadn't, and she was the one who never knew anything.

"Where have you heard it?"

Dad and Mom were looking over at her, too.

"Oh, now I remember." The guilty look on her face made me think she wished she hadn't mentioned it.

Chapter 74

Millie

Millie felt her cheeks burning as everyone at the table stared.

"Millie?" Mom stared at her from across the table. "Is there a problem?"

"Well," she hesitated. "Just that, it was when I was doing something I shouldn't have."

"Maybe we should all leave," Mrs. Morgan suggested. "We're finished eating. The kids can help me in the kitchen."

"Thank you." Dad looked her way. "And we'll go take a walk."

Millie was relieved she wouldn't have to admit to snooping in front of so many people. She had hoped Mom would just forget about what she did, but here it was coming up again.

"Let's walk out by the hill where Paisley saw the skeleton." Jeremiah headed that way when they got outside. Millie shot him a warning glance, but it was too late.

"She saw what?" Mom asked, as we walked.

Millie looked over at her brother. She had enough on her hands with the dishonorable discharge. She would let him handle this.

"Well, it's kind of crazy, but she said she saw that skeleton people have been talking about. Last night. On that hill over there."

Mom looked at Dad. "That surprises me, she seems sensible enough. Why would she tell the kids that?"

"Maybe Paisley did see something." Her dad's response surprised her. This might make them forget about the whole discharge thingee.

Mom shook her head. "So much to digest here." Then she dashed Millie's hopes. "Let's get back to where Millie heard the dishonorable discharge phrase."

Millie stopped walking and sat down on what was becoming her favorite bench at the lodge. Her mom sat next to her.

"Remember, I told you I was reading about Boyd Colston on your computer?"

"Yes, I remember." So far so good. Mom didn't come unglued. Maybe she would get off with no punishment.

"Well, that was listed in his criminal background. It said dishonorably discharged from the United States Army. I didn't know what that meant."

Mom's mouth dropped open, and she looked at Dad. "You don't suppose they discharged him with Mr. Smith's son, do you?"

"It wouldn't surprise me," Dad said. "Didn't you say this Boyd character was in his 40's. They're about the same age. They both have ties to the area."

"Dad, why would the son steal his phone?" Jeremiah asked. Millie breathed a sigh of relief, with the focus off of her.

"The son was angry his father was selling the property. He thought he would inherit it someday. So he's been doing things to stop anyone from buying it."

"Like making a phony skeleton to scare people away?" Millie said. Jeremiah signaled with his eyes to keep her mouth shut.

"Like Amos told us the other day?" Millie added, to clue her brother in she wasn't giving anything away.

"He did say something like that." Dad looked over at her. "Do you remember that, Norah?"

"No. What did he say?"

"That two other buyers backed out, because the property was haunted," Jeremiah reminded his mom.

"It was when we saw him right after those guys chased us." Millie squealed.

"I remember now," Mom looked at Dad. "And he mentioned skeletons, didn't he? This is all so strange."

"That's also when Amos told us the owner was in ICU and may not live. I think Amos Lee is a liar. Maybe he is working with the son."

"No, Millie, I don't think so." Dad shook his head. "When I talked to him today, I asked who told him Mr. Smith was in the hospital. He confirmed it was the son."

"So, the son still does bad things, Mom?"

"Yes, Millie. He has been in and out of jail since his Army days."

"But Mom! What would Boyd Colston have to do with my adoption if he's mixed up with Mr. Smith's son?"

"That's a good question, Millie." Mom looked over at Dad and nodded.

"Millie, honey, we don't know. But we did something today that should get us some answers soon."

Millie could feel a tingling in her stomach. She didn't know whether it was fear or joy. But whatever it was, she couldn't talk. Jeremiah was probably happy about that.

"What did you guys do?" Jeremiah asked for her.

"We're having our attorney do a DNA test to compare Millie's DNA with Boyd Colston's," Mom said. "Then we'll know if he's telling the truth."

"But how did you get my DNA?"

"Well, once again, you forgot both your hairbrush and your toothbrush at home," Mom pretended to scold.

"Oops."

"We went home to find something of yours and those items were perfect. The attorney said Boyd's DNA is on file because of his felony arrests," Dad said.

Mom hugged Millie. "We'll have a definite answer in just a few days. Then we'll know how to proceed."

"We've hired the attorney to help us complete the adoption." Dad smiled at her.

Millie buried her face in her mom's shoulders and cried.

Chapter 75

Jeremiah

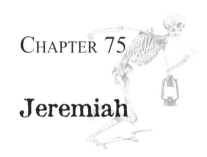

Millie and I had our eyes glued to the top of the hill near our campsite late that night.

"Do you think Mom and Dad would notice if we snuck up there?" I whispered.

My back was to the trailer, but Millie could see it by looking over my shoulder. "It looks like there is only one light on. I bet they fell asleep already."

"I'm sure they're tired after driving all day."

"What's the worst that can happen? They don't see us out here and they yell for us?"

"Yeah, but I hate to scare them." I struggled with the decision. "They might worry if they don't see us at the campfire."

Millie stood. "I'll tiptoe over and see if I can hear them talking."

At the trailer, she looked like she was trying to keep from laughing. She came back to the fire.

"They're asleep all right. I can hear Dad snoring."

"What about Mom?"

"Couldn't tell for sure. But I'll bet she is too."

I stood. "Let's crawl up, so no one can see us."

We no sooner reached the top than we could see, in the distance, the stealthy little side-by-side bouncing along the desert toward our hill.

"They know where we're camping, don't they?" Millie whispered.

I nodded and tried to flatten myself into the dirt. We had climbed the hill at the opposite end of where the skeleton appeared the last time. Hopefully, they would go to the same spot, or they'd find us for sure.

"They're driving with their lights off." Millie scooted closer to me. "Maybe they'll crash into a ditch."

"I hope not." I watched as they got closer. "I want to catch them in the act."

"You won't confront them, will you?" Millie sounded scared.

"No, I just mean I want to see how they do it. Then we can tell Mom and Dad and this way we're not getting Paisley in trouble."

"Yeah and not just Paisley," Millie cringed. "I don't think Dad would be too happy about us breaking into that container."

"Shh, they're almost here." I could feel Millie settling farther down into the dirt. We must have looked like snakes, slithering back and forth to move the dirt and get as low as we could. There was no moon out yet, so we were protected by darkness.

I bumped Millie with my elbow as the side-by-side came to a stop about ten feet from the back of the hill. Was that gruff voice or regular voice driving? He reached into the passenger seat and grabbed the laptop. Then he leaned down into the floor area and brought up another small device.

"What's that?" Millie mouthed as she looked in my direction.

"A projector," I whispered.

Within minutes an eerie green glow came out of the projector and the skeleton hovered just above the hillside about 50 feet from where we were.

Not squealing right then was the hardest thing either of us have ever done. I wished I had a video camera to record all this for solid proof, but I knew neither of us would ever forget what we were seeing.

"Jeremiah! Millie!" Mom's voice drifted in our direction. We turned to see her standing by the campfire. I looked back at the skeleton, but it had vanished and the side-by-side was heading back in the direction it came. Gruff Voice must have been scared away by Mom calling us.

"Come on, Millie!" I jumped up and she followed, as we ran down the hill to the campsite.

"Mom!" I yelled. "We're right here!"

We were both panting when we got back to the fire.

She didn't even ask where we had been. Her eyes were big as she stared at us. "You won't believe what I just saw!"

Chapter 76

Millie

"A skeleton?" Dad stared at Mom early the next morning while they ate breakfast in the trailer. "Are you sure you weren't walking in your sleep, Norah?"

"Tell him what you saw, kids!"

"She's right, Dad!" Millie verified. "She saw a skeleton. But it was a hologram."

"A hologram? That's just as unbelievable."

Millie told her dad what she and Jeremiah had seen the night before. Dad nodded his head as he listened.

"What made you two go up the hill?" Dad asked.

"Well," Millie looked over at Jeremiah to see if she should say more.

He jumped in. "We saw the skeleton the other night when we were sitting out there by ourselves."

"What?" Mom raised her voice. "And you never told us?"

"Well, it sounds unbelievable, doesn't it Mom?" Millie said.

"Besides Norah. If they had told us, would you have let them sit outside by themselves again?"

Dad was great, he remembered what it was like to be a kid.

"So after you guys fell asleep we went up there, in case it came back again." Millie looked at her brother for help with the story.

"Yeah," he agreed. "Even though we had seen something, it just didn't seem real."

"Ghostly images aren't real," Mom said.

"Actually, Norah," Dad looked over at her. "The kids and I had a good conversation recently about the fact that demons can impersonate dead people."

He looked back at the kids. "So that's why you two were discussing ghosts the other morning on the trail."

Millie and Jeremiah nodded. "And that's the thing, Dad," Millie said. "This didn't have the feeling of something demonic."

"What do you mean?" Mom interrupted.

"I don't know how to explain it, but I feel like, as Christians, we would sense an evil presence or something. It didn't feel that way at all."

Mom stepped over and hugged Millie. "You've come a long way in your faith, honey."

Millie hugged her back. She loved this family so much. She wished she could have the faith to believe she would really get to stay with them forever.

"So you two set out to solve the mystery?" Dad's voice brought her back to the present.

"I'm sure glad you didn't get into any more trouble than just climbing a dirt hill in your pursuit of truth." Mom squeezed her shoulders.

Millie's stomach did a flip flop. She was afraid to look at Jeremiah.

"I've got a great idea."

"What's that, Dad?" Millie was eager to change topics.

"Let's go for a ride this morning. We probably won't hear from Amos till this afternoon."

"Hey, Dad," Jeremiah said. "Can we ride over to the property again and look around?"

"And dream?" Millie added.

An hour later they rolled up to the gate. The roar of their motorcycles quieted as they hit the kill switches and climbed off the bikes.

They took their helmets off and watched Dad walk around staring at the ground. Millie could see him also looking past the gate, at the ground inside the property.

"What do you see, Dad?"

"Someone has been here."

"What do you mean?" Jeremiah stepped over to his side.

"Look at all the footprints," Dad pointed. "They start out here and then they must have climbed over the gate. They continue on the path as far as I can see."

Millie looked over at Jeremiah. He was looking right back at her. "We're dead!" she mouthed to him.

"Look at the tracks that pull up and stop here," he said. "Looks like a buggy parked here."

Who knew their dad was a tracker? No wonder he could find hidden vehicles in his job.

He looked at Millie, then over at Jeremiah. "What do you two know about these tracks?"

Chapter 77

Jeremiah

My heart sank into my stomach. I forgot about this lie. I was so busy feeling guilty for getting locked in the container; I forgot we came onto this property too. And without telling Dad. What now? I wondered. What should we say? And how much? Dad doesn't know about the key either. Do we tell him?

I wondered what was going through Millie's mind. Probably double what I was thinking, the way her mind worked.

"Well?" Dad stared at both of them. "Your silence tells me a lot."

I looked over at Millie and then back at Dad.

I wanted to confess. Just not to everything. Not yet anyway. How much to confess, was the big question?

"Dad, we were so excited about the property," Millie saved me from deciding. "We asked Paisley to drive us over here and then before we knew it we climbed the gate and wandered around."

"You know this isn't our property yet," Dad said. "All three of you were trespassing."

"I'm sorry, Dad," I could barely look him in the eyes.

It didn't help that we were standing by a "No Trespassing" sign nailed to the fence post we had climbed over.

"Thank you for admitting it."

That really made me feel guilty. Because we only admitted to a tiny bit of what we had done. I needed to talk to Paisley about telling the truth. Even if it meant we all lost the privilege of going out in the buggy.

"Dad, can we stand on the gate so we can look over?" Millie asked. "That's not trespassing, is it?"

What a dork she could be sometimes.

Dad reached over and rubbed the top of her head which sure didn't help her helmet hair. "I guess we can, Millie. I'm excited myself. Who knows? Maybe by the end of the day the property will be ours."

From our view looking over the gate, we could see the fake well house, but not the containers that the key wouldn't open.

"Dad, what's that big building just beyond the phony well house?"

"That will be our shop," Dad put his arm around my shoulders. "I can't wait to get all my tools and equipment moved in there. We'll have more room than we know what to do with."

"No more bumping into each other and the bikes, like in our garage when we're trying to do stuff," Millie said.

"I'm looking forward to filling that shop with even more motorcycles." I loved working with my dad in the shop. And if there was anything Dad loved besides family, it was motorcycles.

"That sounds like a worthy goal," he agreed.

"Hey Dad," Millie jumped off the gate. "What's the first thing you'll do once we get the key to this place and it becomes ours?"

"I'd tear down that stupid looking phony well house, if it was me," I answered before Dad could get a word in.

"Well, you're welcome to do that."

"Can I help him, Dad? I love tearing things apart. Then I could make something with the broken concrete blocks."

"What in the world are you going to make with smashed up concrete?" Only my sister could get excited about broken cement blocks.

"I don't know, maybe a statue or something."

"How about a bird bath?" Dad suggested.

"Or how about a dry creek bed?" I surprised everyone with my landscaping knowledge.

Millie looked at me like I was crazy. "What are you talking about?"

"I saw it on a landscaping channel."

"Well, if I do, I'll call mine a dry brook bed, after our new home town, Dry Brook," Millie said. "But, the first thing I want to do, is hunt for the lost gold mine."

"The first thing, Millie?" Dad said. "That might take a while."

"Yeah, like a hundred years." What I really meant was never, but didn't want to upset her.

"You wanted to search for it, too."

"But not first thing, there's too much other stuff to do."

"Dad, can't I spend at least the first day searching, then move on to other stuff?"

"Tell you what. You two need to be together for either of those ideas. We'll toss a coin and see which comes first, scouting for gold or demolition work."

"I better win. Hunting for the goldmine is a lost cause. It's just an old legend, Millie."

"Didn't you read what it said in the History of Dry Brook, that Amos gave us?"

Before I could answer, the muffled ringtone for Mom sounded from Dad's backpack.

We jumped off the gate and I hurried to unzip his pack and get the phone out for him.

"Hey, Norah?"

There was a long silence. Then, "We'll be right there."

"What's up, Dad?" I looked in Millie's direction. This didn't sound good.

He was already putting his helmet on. We did the same.

"I'm not sure."

"Well, is it good news or bad news?" Millie asked.

"It doesn't sound good. Amos said Mr. Smith didn't accept our offer."

Chapter 78

Millie

Millie and Jeremiah waited on the porch step while their parents met Mr. Lee.

"What do you think will happen?" Millie turned to her brother.

Jeremiah hung his head, staring at the gravel strewn asphalt between his boots. He looked up and shook his head. "I don't know. This has been the most messed up land deal I've ever heard of."

Millie chuckled.

"What's so funny?"

"I was just wondering how many land deals you have been a part of."

Jeremiah smiled. "I guess you're right. Just this one."

Millie stood up to peek in the office window. She was dying of curiosity.

"Jeremiah! Look!"

He stood and looked in the window with her.

Their parents were hugging each other. It looked like Mom was crying.   Was the news they got that bad? Millie wondered.

"The end of a dream." Jeremiah sat back down and scuffed his boots in the gravel.

Millie kept watching. "I am not giving up on Great-Grandpa's dream! He never did and neither will I!"

Then laughter came from inside the office. The door opened and their dad called out.

"Jeremiah! Millie. Come hear the good news."

"Is Mr. Smith going to sell us the property?" Millie stepped into the office first.

"No." Mom looked over at Dad. "He's not selling us the property." They had the biggest, silliest grins. But why?

Millie didn't see anything funny and she could tell by the look on Jeremiah's face, he didn't either.

Dad reached out and hugged them both. "Mr. Smith is giving us the property!"

Millie wasn't sure she heard right, but Mom continued the story. "He believes in Great-Grandpa's dream so much, that he wanted to help. So he's giving us the land."

Dad held up a set of keys. "It's ours! Right now!"

"Right now?" Millie looked at both of them and then at Mr. Lee. "Just like that? Don't you even have to sign something?"

"The detective's mind at work," Mom said to Dad.

"Sure, there is still paperwork to do. Mr. Smith is having his attorney draw up the papers. We'll meet at his office in a couple of weeks." Dad said.

"He told Mr. Lee to give us the keys today," Mom pointed at the keys in Dad's hand.

Amos stood behind his desk with a smile that matched Mom and Dad's. Maybe he wasn't such a bad guy after all. But Millie had to know one thing before she would believe it.

"Who did you talk to on the phone the night we got hit?"

"Millie!" Mom scolded. "That's not your place to ask."

"It's okay, Mrs. Anderson," Amos Lee said. "I knew your daughter seemed suspicious of me that night and I couldn't figure out why."

He looked over at Millie. "But now I understand, knowing what we do about Mr. Smith's son."

"What do you mean?" Millie asked.

"That's who called," Mr. Lee said. "Mr. Smith's son had been communicating with me regarding the sale. He called to see if you put in an offer and wanted to know if you had left yet."

"So it was Mr. Smith's son who told that guy to wreck our car," Jeremiah said. "They were already trying to scare us away."

Millie no sooner got one question answered than another one popped up in its place. But she didn't want to discuss this one in front of Amos.

"You know folks," Mr. Lee said, "Mr. Smith was not only generous to your family, but he still paid us the full commission on the property, since we lost the sale, due to his giving it to you."

"He's a very special man, indeed," Dad said. "We can never repay him."

"I have an idea how you could try," Mr. Lee said. "Mr. Smith told me today how much he misses the desert. I think he would love to come for a visit. And not just to see the desert, but to see your family settling in and enjoying the gift."

"We'll do just that," Mom shook hands with Amos. "Thank you for the idea."

Millie was growing fond of this man. She was sorry she had mistrusted him.

But she had to know how the man claiming to be her father was also involved with the desert property. What was in that letter?

Chapter 79

Jeremiah

"Paisley!" I yelled as soon as we got out of the truck in front of the lodge.

She looked startled to see us and came right over to where Millie and I were standing.

Her parents came out to greet ours. We pulled Paisley aside while all the parents were talking.

"We've got to tell our parents about breaking into the container," Millie blurted, before I could get the words out.

Paisley nodded her head.

"Really?" I didn't expect that response. "You're okay with that?"

"I've been feeling so guilty. My dad complimented me last night on being trustworthy with the family buggy. I felt so guilty."

Millie and I groaned. "Almost the same thing here," I said, "but wait till you hear…"

"Hey kids," Mom motioned to us to join them. "Let's head on in, they have dinner on the table waiting."

After Mr. Morgan prayed, he looked right at Mom and Dad. "Do you have news for us?"

"Boy, do we!" Millie didn't even wait for our parents to respond.

"Well, let's hear it!" Paisley poured gravy on her potatoes and passed the dish to Millie.

"Where do we start?" Mom's smile was the biggest I'd ever seen.

"How about start with the house news?" Mr. Morgan suggested. "Did you get the house?"

"Boy did we ever!" Mom said.

"I'm guessing you got a good price, then?"

Dad looked over at Mom, "You tell them."

"The seller, Mr. Smith, refused our offer," she started.

Mr. and Mrs. Morgan gasped.

"The reason he refused, is because he's not selling the property to us. He is giving it to us!"

"Amazing news, simply amazing!" Mr. Morgan stood and came around the table, patting dad on the back, then shaking his hand.

"And thank you for coming right over to share it with us," Mrs. Morgan hugged Mom. "We feel honored and can't wait to have you as neighbors."

"There's more," I said as Mr. and Mrs. Morgan returned to their seats. All eyes were on me, including Millie's and Paisley's. I'm sure they were content to let me be the one to tell.

"There sure is." Mom caught me off guard when she interrupted. "I saw the skeleton last night, and the kids saw how it was made."

I looked over at Paisley and took a deep breath. "It's now or never."

"What's that you said, Son?" Dad cut his ham into bite-size pieces while he talked.

"Last night was not when we discovered the skeleton was a hologram."

"How can that be?" Mom put her fork down and stared at me.

"I can answer that question." All of our parents looked surprised as they turned in Paisley's direction.

"Paisley? How do you know about the hologram?" Mr. Morgan stared at his daughter.

I was so glad to get that confession behind us. The girls and I headed off to what had become our bench. We were quiet as we walked.

I stood and stared at the hill where Paisley had seen the skeleton. "I sure am glad we got that out in the open." Millie breathed a sigh of relief.

"What do you think they will do?" Paisley looked back and forth between the two of us.

Our parents were still sitting around the dinner table. They said they needed to discuss what the consequences would be. But I thought they secretly looked proud of how we handled the situation.

"We probably won't be going out in the buggy for a long time."

I looked over at Paisley. "Well, we won't have time for a while, anyway. We're going home in the morning to unload the bikes and load up furniture."

"That's so awesome you're moving in right away. I can't wait."

"I can't either," Millie looked over at her. "You're the first real friend I've ever had."

Paisley leaned over and hugged Millie. And once again my dopey sister was getting ready to cry.

"Come on! We're starting a new adventure in our lives and all you can do is cry."

"Who's crying about a new adventure?" The deep voice surprised us.

We looked up to see Minnesota Mike heading our way.

"What's this I hear about a new adventure?"

"It's us!" Millie jumped up and hugged the old guy. That surprised me. But he was growing on us.

"What adventure might that be?"

"We're moving to the desert," I told him. "We got the property."

"You don't say?" M&M looked pretty happy to hear the news. "So you folks didn't let that skeleton scare you away?"

"Ha!" Millie said. "You mean the hologram!"

Minnesota let out a chuckle. "So you figgered it out, did ya?"

"Wait a minute." This guy had me so confused. "What do you mean we figured it out? You knew all along, didn't you?"

He looked around before he answered. "Well, I jist didn't figger there could be a real live skeleton walking around. 'Specially since skeletons is dead, doncha know." He threw his head back and laughed.

Millie and Paisley enjoyed the joke, but I was too busy trying to figure out how to get him to talk. He knew a lot more than he was saying.

"What is it you wanted to talk to my dad about?" I probed. "You said it was mighty important the day the deputy was here."

M&M looked over his shoulder again and then up and down the road. Then up in the sky. Stalling for time, no doubt.

"Well, it ain't my place to say anything," he said. "Besides, it will all come out in due time."

Chapter 80

Millie

Millie watched her dad swing the sledgehammer and hit the top of the cinderblock wall. Thankfully, whoever built this thing never went up higher than about six feet. Dad stood on a stepladder to tackle the demolition.

The block crumbled under the weight of the hammer. He swung again and again until the top row of blocks fell to the ground. Some fell on the outside and others landed on the inside.

"Dad, take a break and have some water." Millie held out a cold bottle of water when he stopped swinging and wiped the sweat off his face with his bandana.

He stepped down from the ladder and removed his safety goggles.

"Hey Dad," Jeremiah called from the other side of the fake well house. "Look at these blocks over here."

Millie stepped around to see what he was talking about.

"What is it?" She saw nothing different. The wall on the other side looked the same to her.

"I see what you mean." Dad ran his hands along the wall. "These blocks look newer than the other three walls."

"Look at the cement between the blocks," Jeremiah pointed. "It's a different shade of gray than on the other walls."

They heard a motorcycle approaching as they were studying the blocks and turned to see who was coming.

The white beard flowing out from the helmet gave it away. Soon, Minnesota Mike was pulling up next to them.

"Well, now, you don't let no moss grow under yer feet, doncha know!" M&M pulled off his helmet and hung it on the handlebars.

Dad stepped over to shake his hand. Millie reached into the ice chest and pulled out a cold water bottle for him.

"Boy you read my mind there, little missy." Mike took a long drink.

He circled the concrete structure and saw the broken bricks. "So you're taking this useless thing down, are ya'?"

"Well, for some reason the kids thought this looked like a fun project. I'm just helping them get started," Dad said.

"Yeah, but he made us work like dogs for three days first. Moving furniture and making about a million trips back and forth to the city," Jeremiah said.

"And we're only tearing it down today because I lost the stupid coin toss!"

M&M looked over at Millie. "What stupid coin toss is that, little missy?"

"I wanted to spend the day searching for the lost gold mine on our property. I read about it in the Dry Brook history. But I lost the coin toss."

"A lost gold mine," M&M looked intrigued. "Now that sounds like a worthy activity. I might want to be in on that, if you don't mind sharing some of the gold we find with an old codger like me."

"You're welcome to join them," Dad picked up the sledgehammer again. "I told them if they get this down today, they can have tomorrow to search for the gold."

"Now that's an adventure I'm looking forward to. I always suspected there was gold here!"

"That will be fun having you along on the hunt," Jeremiah crushed his water bottle and picked up his safety goggles.

"Shouldn't be a problem finishing this today." M&M chuckled as he peered over the edge of the broken blocks. "Looks like the people who built this thing made it easy for ya."

"They sure did," Dad agreed.

Millie had no clue what they were talking about.

"What'd they do? Just stack the blocks and cement them together?"

"Crazy, huh?" Dad looked over at M&M. "No rebar."

"What's rebar?" Millie asked.

"Metal rods running through the blocks," Jeremiah said.

Millie scowled. She was asking her dad. "Let me guess, you read that in a book?"

"Yeah." He grinned. "You should try it sometime."

"Hey Dad, can we knock them down ourselves now?"

"I'll do one more row, Jeremiah. Then you two can take over. Make sure you both wear your safety goggles."

"Mike, do you want to stay for lunch?" Millie noticed him heading back over to his motorcycle.

"Well, little missy, maybe I'll jist do that some other day. Right now I got me something I got to git done."

"Dad is that a concrete floor on the bottom?" Millie asked from up on the ladder as she stared down inside. "And why didn't they put a roof on this thing?"

"How is Dad supposed to know all that? He wasn't here when they built it."

"Because Dad knows everything."

Dad looked over the wall. "I'm not sure what that is. I'm guessing someone put some plywood down and then spread concrete over it. They probably didn't bother with a roof once they realized it wouldn't be needed."

"I can't wait to build my dry brook. I hope we can get this done this afternoon."

"I'm planning on knocking this wall to the ground before lunch time." Jeremiah put on his goggles and picked up the sledgehammer.

"Thanks for helping, Dad." Millie looked in his direction. "I know you can't wait to organize your shop."

"That's where I'm headed. You kids be careful. Let me know if you need me."

Millie followed her Dad to the shop. She could hear the sledgehammer crashing into the concrete blocks as she walked away. "Hey Dad, is the wheelbarrow around somewhere?"

"Sure is. Check around the back. Are you going to load up your treasures while Jeremiah knocks them down?" Dad disappeared into his shop before she answered. He was like a kid at Christmas. He loved his tools and equipment.

"Millie," Jeremiah shouted, as she was heading back. "Run back and get the pickax."

"What for?" All she wanted to do was gather up the broken blocks.

"I want to break up the floor," Jeremiah yelled.

A few minutes later she was back with the wheelbarrow and the pickax. "Who cares about the floor? Those chunks won't be big enough to use."

"Because I told Dad we'd take this down to the dirt."
Jeremiah swigged a long drink of cold water.
It surprised Millie at how much progress he had made. The other three walls looked shaky with this one almost gone. They'd probably come down easy. She was glad whoever built it hadn't used those metal thingees Dad was talking about.

Millie had the wheelbarrow full, when Jeremiah started tearing into the floor.

"Dad was right," he said. "This is just a thin layer of concrete, with wood underneath."

"Hope those same people didn't build the house," Just as she spoke Millie heard the axe hit something that sounded like metal.

Jeremiah looked over at her. "Did you hear that?"

Chapter 81

Jeremiah

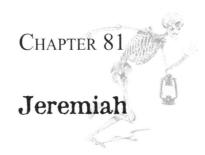

My whole body shook with the sudden stop of the axe. The first two times I swung, it dug right through the thin concrete, into the plywood and hit dirt. This time was different.

Millie appeared at my side as I dropped to my knees. "Jeremiah! What do you think it is?"

I choked way up on the axe and dug out the splintered wood and concrete to expose a large metal box. We scraped with our hands until the dirt got too hard, then used the axe to chisel dirt from around the box.

"Jeremiah! Look at that lock!"

"The key!"

"Do you still have it?" Millie's eyes were big as she stared at me.

I stood and reached into my pocket. "Are you kidding? I carry this thing everywhere."

I dropped back down on my knees and fumbled with the lock until the key slipped in easily and turned.

"Oh, Jeremiah! I'm so excited I can hardly stand it!"

She reached over and pulled off the lock. I opened the box to reveal what looked like solid gold bars. I had never seen a bar of gold, but if I had to guess, I'd say that's exactly what these were. There were numbers stamped on each one.

Millie gasped. I reached in to pick one up but it didn't budge. "Millie, these things are heavy!"

She reached in with both hands and struggled to get one out. "Feel like it weighs a hundred pounds!" Millie said.

"Twenty-five pounds. Now put it down and get your hands up!" The gruff voice came from the side us.

Millie dropped the gold bar, almost hitting my foot. We both jumped up and turned around. Neither of us had seen the little side-by-side drive onto the property.

We stared into the faces of the two men we'd been running from for days.

"You can't get away with this!" Millie yelled. I wished she would just shut her mouth as I stared down the barrel of their pistol.

"You just watch us," Gruff Voice did all the talking. "Now step aside, if you know what's good for you."

He looked over to his partner, "I told you that old coot gave the key to these brats."

Millie might have talked tough, but when I glanced over at her, I saw tears. Honestly, I felt like crying myself.

"Hold it right there!" a loud voice called from behind the men. "Put that gun down and get your hands up!"

I didn't dare take my eyes off Gruff Voice and his buddy yet. But once they put the gun on the ground, I looked beyond them.

There was Dad, approaching with a shotgun pointed right at the two men. Wow! I wanted to laugh with relief, but knew this was not the time.

Dad tossed his phone to me. "Call 9-1-1, Jeremiah!" He kept his eyes and the shotgun focused on the men.

"Jeremiah! Look!" Millie pointed down the dirt road. "They're already coming!"

Two deputy cars with lights flashing were flying up the dirt road. The white truck of Minnesota Mike followed them, bumping and bouncing along on the washboard road.

Chapter 82

Millie

"Dad would you have really shot those guys if they hadn't put the gun down?" Millie still sounded scared, as they gathered around the table for lunch a couple hours later.

"That sure made my day," Minnesota Mike howled. "When I pulled up there and saw you pointing that shotgun at those two fellers!" He let out one of the belly laughs he was famous for.

"Well, that would have been hard to do. The gun was empty." Dad joined in laughing. "I was getting ready to clean my shotgun, when I heard Millie shouting. I ran outside still holding it."

Millie had a million more questions but held off until Dad prayed for lunch. Minnesota Mike started gobbling down his sandwich and potato salad like he hadn't eaten in days. Millie knew she couldn't eat a bite till she got some answers.

"Where did you get that key?" she looked right at Mike. "And how did you know about them robbing that armored car and why did they bury the gold instead of spending it and why did you talk about there being gold on the property to my brother and then you stopped talking about the gold on the property and..."

"Hold it right there, little missy, now hold it one darn minute!" Minnesota Mike put his sandwich down and looked at Millie. "Can't a guy eat a decent meal, in peace, before we solve the problems of the world?"

"Not with my sister around," Jeremiah said in between bites of his sandwich.

Millie looked over at her brother. "How can you eat when there are so many unknowns?"

"Because I'm starving. Do you know how many times I swung that heavy sledgehammer. And getting a gun pointed at me took it out of me, too." He took another bite. "Besides, I have more patience than you do."

"Yes, Millie," Dad smiled at her. "Let Mike finish eating and then he can answer your questions." Dad looked over at Mike. "I don't mind saying, I'm curious about all those same things."

Millie gave in to her own hunger. She gulped her sandwich down, finishing just as Minnesota Mike pushed himself back from the table.

"Okay, listen up now, missy, because I don't want to go through this story more than once, doncha know. I'm mighty glad to be puttin' this whole sordid mess behind me. I haven't liked being involved one little bit, doncha know."

Dad and Mom were listening intently as M&M answered every question she asked, and more.

"Remember when I was tellin' you all, I had it on good authority, but I didn't want to tell you where I heard it?"

Millie breathed a sigh of relief. He really was going to tell everything.

Dad and Jeremiah nodded.

"Well, I used to drink me a bit of liquor, a little too often. There was this bar I got to hanging out in ever night, oh, about 50 miles from here.

"Well, that's where I met up with the two creeps the cops jist hauled away. And fer good, I hope.

"You know some people who are hidin' big secrets shouldn't oughta drink too much because then they start spoutin' their mouths off."

"Ohhh!" Millie interrupted. "That's how you found out!"

"Now you're catching on, little missy." M&M looked in her direction. "The one feller – what's that you called him, Jeremiah? Old gruff voice, heh-heh, that's a good one – well he's the one who took part in the hold-up four to five years ago. He was the lucky one what got away with the gold. His partner is in prison somewheres for who knows how long. These two fellers hatched up this plan way back when they was in the Army together, but they took years to get up the nerve."

"How did the gold get buried on our property?" Millie asked.

M&M laughed. "Well now missy, it warn't your property when it got buried there."

"No, but it sure is now!"

"Well, old Gruff Voice is the son of the feller who owned this place before you folks."

Dad and Mom gasped.

"He musta not known that some day his old pops would up and sell this place. When they buried the gold and added the last wall of blocks that sealed it off, he musta figured this would all be his some day."

"So's that's why he was doing all he could to scare away anyone wantin' to buy this place."

"Dad, that's why those blocks looked different on one wall." Jeremiah turned back to Mike, "How long was he going to keep the gold hidden?"

"Well, now, he had ta keep it buried until his partner got out of prison, so's they could share it."

"I didn't think criminals were that honest with each other."

"Well, now, you got a good point there, little missy." Mike looked her way again. "They ain't."

"Then why didn't the son cash it in and spend it?"

"Well, for one thing, it's got all those serial numbers on it, which is how the detectives can know where it come from. That guy jist ain't smart enough, on his own, to know how to git around that sort of thing.

"And for another, his partner in prison had another guy spying on him. If he ever did something with the gold his partner would rat him out and they'd be sharing a cell."

"Was the spy the other guy with him all the time?"

"It sure were, little missy." He held his palm up toward Millie. "But before you go firing more questions at me, the reason the spy couldn't git the gold hisself is, he didn't know where it was."

"But you did, didn't you?" Jeremiah said. "That's why you got the deputy when you saw us tearing down the concrete blocks."

"I sure did," Minnesota said. "That's one of those things that just spilled out of gruff guy's mouth when he was a'drinking."

"How did you get the key?" Millie asked.

"Well, I don't know why, but the dang fool always kept that key on a little chain clipped to his belt loop. Even boasted about it and showed me. Any smart person woulda kept the key locked away somewheres safe. One night he had so much to drink, he jist passed out there, with his head on the table. There was that key dangling down off his belt loop, jist beggin' me to take it."

He looked around at everyone at the table and smiled. "So's I took it."

"But why..." Millie started.

"Hold on there, I may be old but I knowed what you asked me earlier, jist let me finish this story.

"To tell you the truth, I wasn't so sure the story was all the way true and that's when I was talking about it myself to other people, like you folks. But the day came they busted into my room and knocked me unconscious, well then I knowed. And before they knocked me out, they let me know if I wanted to keep breathing, I better not mention another word.

"And seeing as how I enjoy breathing, and they were following me around, I made sure I never talked about it again no how, nowhere, to no one."

"Wow," Millie and Jeremiah said at the same time. Finally, Millie seemed satisfied she had heard all he knew.

"I can't believe I missed all this excitement," Mom stood and began clearing the table. "And all before lunch. What do you all have planned for this afternoon?"

Chapter 83

Jeremiah

I stood on the front porch looking out over our new desert property, enjoying the blue sky dotted with white puffy clouds. This was a perfect morning. A perfect life. "Thank you, God!" I shouted out to the world. Oh no, I was being as loud as my sister.

"What did you say?" I heard Millie, but I couldn't see her.

I stepped off the porch and walked toward her voice.

She was behind a big tree, about a hundred feet away, on the ground arranging her concrete chunks.

"I'm working on my dry brook." She looked up and smiled. Her face was smudged with dirt and her hair looked like she hadn't brushed it since we were tearing down the block wall yesterday. But at least she looked happy and wasn't crying.

"I thought we were going to search for the gold mine today."

She smiled. "No need. We found our gold."

"Yeah, but it's not ours to spend."

She rearranged the blocks while she talked. "I know, but that's the gold Mike was talking about all along. He didn't really believe there was a lost gold mine here. Besides, I'm too happy right now to worry about any more old legends."

"So you finally got all your answers." I plopped down on the ground next to her.

"Not all." She stopped moving chunks around and looked over at me. "Boyd."

I had forgotten about him. "It's strange, Mike never mentioned him when he was telling us everything."

"He wouldn't know anything about my adoption."

"Yeah, but even Mr. Lee said he had something to do with the property, because the crash happened after the son knew we were leaving."

207

"Oh, yeah, that's right," Millie moved a few more chunks around. "I don't get how he was involved in both things."

"I can tell you how." Dad's voice sounded close. We hadn't even noticed he was working on the sprinklers on the other side of the tree.

Dad sat next to us and wiped the sweat off his forehead with his sleeve. He reached over and grabbed the water bottle Millie had next to her and finished it.

"How did you find out?" Millie asked.

"Your mom got a call from the attorney this morning."

"Did he get the DNA results?" Millie interrupted.

"Didn't need to do the test," Dad said. "He went to the jail and had a talk with Boyd. He told him if he cooperated and answered all his questions, that he would represent him, at no charge, and get him a lighter sentence."

"Wow," Millie said, "what a nice guy."

"Well, let me rephrase that. At no charge to Boyd. We'll be paying for it."

"Dad!" Millie gave him a dirty, sweaty hug. "You're amazing."

"Now do you believe you can trust Mom and I to handle the hard stuff?"

I cringed. Any minute now I expected her to cry again. But she surprised me. "Yes Dad! Yes! Yes! Yes!" No tears. What a relief.

"So did he spill the beans?" I asked.

"Oh boy, did he! And there will be two people paying a heavy price for the stuff he confessed to."

"Who?" Millie asked.

"The armored car robber and your birth mom."

"How..." Millie started.

Dad laughed. "Now I know how Mike felt. Let me finish and I will answer all your questions, including what the letter said."

"You opened it?" I had almost forgotten about the letter.

"Yes, and we should have opened it a long time ago, it was good for a laugh."

"Did he say he was my dad?"

"It said, and I quote, 'I'm your real dad. Me and your mom love you. Tell those people don't buy the desert property.'"

"Are you kidding me?" Millie burst out laughing. "That's all it said."

"That's it, no 'Dear Millie' or 'Love Dad' or anything else."

"That's crazy," I said.

"Turns out that Boyd was accessing information on the dark web, posted by prisoners, looking for people on the outside to do jobs."

"Wait a minute." I was really confused. "How can a prisoner advertise online?"

"Same thing Mom asked our attorney. They have smart phones in prison."

"That's allowed?" Millie said.

"Nope but somehow they get them. That's why I said the birth mom and the robber will be in more trouble.

"It was just a coincidence that Boyd was working for both of them. The fact that the jobs involved the same people – us – made it easier for him."

"This is so unbelievable," Millie said.

"Ha! I wonder if he ever got paid?"

"And before you even ask the next question," Dad looked at Millie. "Based on this recent news, the attorney has sent a letter to the social services department demanding an immediate conclusion to your adoption. He threatened to sue them, on your behalf, for excessive delay in providing you with a permanent home, if they don't get right on it."

Millie burst into tears.

Even I felt a little teary eyed.

"Come on, Millie. That's good news, it's nothing to cry about."

She smiled over at me, tears still flowing.

"I'll tell you what you can cry about."

"What?" she mumbled.

"Mom says we've had a long enough break from school with all that's been going on. We have to get back to our schoolwork starting Monday."

"You're right," she wiped her tears and started laughing. "That is something to cry about."

CHAPTER 84
Millie

Millie stood barefoot in the kitchen, about ready to get a cold drink, when she heard a car approach. Hurrying over to the window, she saw the deputy they'd become friends with. Someone else was in the car with him.

Her dad opened the front door as she was slipping on her shoes. "Norah, Millie. Deputy Black has news for us."

When they got outside, Millie saw a little boy. He stared at the ground, kicking the dirt with the toe of his left foot. His shoelaces were raggedy and untied.

"Millie and Jeremiah, congratulations on solving the armored car theft." Deputy Black shook their hands. "There will be a formal ceremony next month at the Sheriff's office with the president of the armored car company."

"Oh, wow!" Millie looked at her brother and then back to the deputy. "Are you kidding?"

"There is also a reward."

"And this morning I thought life couldn't get any better," Jeremiah looked at Millie. "I guess we really struck gold!"

While they laughed together, Deputy Black put his arm around the boy. "Now, my second reason for dropping by. This is Caleb."

Jeremiah greeted him.

"Hey, Caleb," Millie joined in. "What's that you've got there?"

Caleb showed her a crumpled photo. It was a quad rider racing through the desert.

"Hey," Millie took the photo from him to get a better look. "Number 37. He looks fast."

Caleb smiled and pointed to the deputy.

"Is that him riding?" Millie looked over at Deputy Black.

"Uh-huh," Caleb whispered. "He's nice."

"His mom is going through a hard time," Deputy Black looked at her parents. "She'll be going away for a few months."

Millie wondered if that meant jail.

"Jeremiah," Dad held out his keys. "Why don't you take Caleb down to the shop and let him sit on your motorcycle?"

The deputy waited for them to leave. "I hate to get child protective services involved. His mom asked if I would find someone to take care of him."

"Do you have anyone in mind?" Mom asked.

"No, but I know you're praying folks, so I wanted to ask you to pray about finding a family."

"Are you a believer?" Dad asked.

"I'm trying to be, Max, but it's hard. When I see kids who've been mistreated and abused." He stared up in the sky, then looked back at Dad. "Where is God in all of this?"

Millie could hardly breathe. It was a question she had struggled with most of her life. She really needed to hear Dad's answer.

He looked in her direction. She hoped he wouldn't send her to the shop too.

"Millie, run inside and get my Bible."

When she returned, he touched her shoulder. "Stay right here."

"I don't have all the answers. But I can tell you a few things." He held his Bible out. "First, this book tells me that Jesus loves me and it is filled with promises for those of us who have given our lives to Him."

He stepped behind Millie, placing a hand on her shoulder. "The second thing I will tell you, is about this special young lady. When I think..." he paused. It sounded like he was sniffing. She heard him inhale deeply then slowly breathe out. "When I think of all that she has gone through and the evil she has seen, it breaks my heart and I wonder, just like you, where was God?"

Millie turned. "Oh, Dad! I didn't know you felt that way," she said through tears while hugging him. Then Millie stepped back and wiped her eyes, wanting to hear more. She needed an answer for the question that had haunted her.

Her dad continued. "When I was ten, my grandpa died. He had been in a coma for a few days but one afternoon, I saw tears on his cheeks. Then he mumbled something and became animated."

Dad took another deep breath. "I believe Grandpa saw the angels coming to take him to heaven. Just like the Bible promises us."

"Is that when he died?"

"Yes, Millie, and it was an amazing experience to be there."

Dad looked back at the deputy. "I don't understand why God doesn't stop the evil from hurting the children and it breaks my heart. But I will not let that evil also destroy my faith in Jesus."

"Trust in the Lord with all your heart," Millie said. "just like you taught me the Bible says."

"What did your Grandpa say there at the end?" Deputy Black asked.

"He said, 'Don't forget the dream, Max.'"

"What was he talking about?"

"I know!" Millie said. "He was talking about the dream to buy the land and take care of kids."

"That's right, Millie," Dad put his arm around her shoulders and pulled her close.

"So it was your grandpa's dream to help kids like Caleb? Do you suppose God led me here to talk to you about Caleb?"

Dad looked up in the sky and mouthed the words, "Thank you, God!"

"I bet your grandpa would be dancing up a storm if he knew about Caleb!" Millie said.

"Absolutely!" Mom agreed and looked at Deputy Black, then over at Dad.

"Let's all go tell Caleb the news."

Acknowledgements

I am especially grateful for those who helped bring this story to life:

Deputy Sheriff Larry Hammers for answering questions about law enforcement. Realtor John Elliott helped me to understand real estate deals. Science and math teacher David Woltz for providing logistical information.

Justinna Kukla and Jana Foley read the completed manuscript and gave valuable feedback. An extra measure of thanks to my Aunt Jana for letting me bounce hundreds of ideas off of her as the project drew to a close.

My sister, Regina Jensen, for prayer support throughout the project. My son Byron Kukla for discussing plot ideas with me.

My husband, Steve, for 45 awesome years of adventures to draw on for story ideas and for surprising me by reading the entire manuscript and marking it all up to make it better.

Finally all the praise to God for inspiration and creativity and for His wondrous gift of salvation and abundant life.

In Memory of Black

May 2, 2013 - March 23, 2019

K9 Partner of
San Diego County
Deputy Sheriff Larry Hammers

Ghost Lights of Dry Brook

BOOK 2

SHERRI KUKLA

In Memory of Emilie Elizabeth Puricelli
Her story inspired me

Chapter 1

Millie

"M o-o-o-o-m-m-m-i-e-e-e-e-e!" Caleb's scream for his mother pierced the darkness causing Paisley's little brother Donovan to join in. Millie dropped the spotlight she held and rushed to clamp her hand over Caleb's mouth.

Her brother Jeremiah ran out of the bushes where he had been hiding and making animal noises.

"It's a joke, Caleb." Jeremiah whispered. But the tears streaming down his cheeks didn't stop.

"I feel like crying, too." Millie looked at her brother. "We're dead meat if Mom and Dad come out."

Paisley got Donovan to calm down, but they couldn't get Caleb to stop crying.

"I want my mommy!" His voice rose.

In the three months since Caleb moved in with the Andersons, Jeremiah and Millie had never seen him like this. Millie wrapped her arms around him.

Caleb clung to her, resting his head on her shoulder. Millie kept one eye on the house hoping her parents or Paisley's hadn't heard the commotion. They'd be in so much trouble for playing a trick on the little kids by pretending wild animals were close by.

"I want my mommy." Caleb kept crying. "I want my sissy."

Sissy? Millie looked at Jeremiah and then over at Paisley who knelt down, with her arm around her brother. None of them knew anything about Caleb having a sister.

He moved in with the Andersons when his mother went to jail. The Deputy Sheriff they'd become friends with introduced her parents to Caleb and told them about his need for a home. They had moved to this big property in the desert where their parents planned to give a home to kids who needed help. Caleb moved in a week after they arrived in the desert.

"Where is your sissy?" Millie rubbed his back, hoping to stop his tears. She glanced at the door again to make sure they were safe. So far it seemed their parents hadn't heard the commotion.

Paisley knelt on the ground close to her. Her little brother, now calm, leaned against her, ready to fall asleep.

Caleb grew quiet, but whispered again, "I want my sissy."

"Do you mean your mommy?" Jeremiah said, then leaned over to Millie. "Does he have a sister?"

"Not that I know of."

"Not my mommy!" His voice raised. He pointed across the desert. "My sissy, she's where the lights are."

Millie and the others looked where he pointed. Bright lights shone in their direction from off in the distance.

Chapter 2

Jeremiah

"Why do you think Caleb would suddenly start talking about a sister?" Millie and I sat at the kitchen table eating brownies after Paisley and her family left. Mom and Dad were putting Caleb to bed. What a relief we made it this long without them finding out about the problem outside.

"Beats me. But that is weird." Millie talked with her mouth full. Good thing Mom didn't see her. She could never get that girl to quit talking with food in her mouth.

"You know that's gross, don't you?"

She shoved another brownie in her mouth. "What's gross?" Her words were garbled and when she burst into laughter, she almost lost the mouthful of brownies.

"That's just wrong!" I looked away, but couldn't stop laughing.

Millie wiped her mouth. "I know, I know. I need to work on my manners."

"So back to this mysterious sister." I poured milk in both our glasses, waiting for her take on this. But instead of answers she fired another question at me.

"And why would he say she's by the lights?"

"Right." I took a big swig of milk, but rather than wiping the milk mustache off with my sleeve, I used a napkin to set a good example. "That was just some truck driving off Sunset Hill. What made him think it had to do with his sister?"

"Yeah, a sister we don't even know is real. And why did you call it Sunset Hill?" Millie shocked me when she wiped her own milk mustache off with a napkin instead of using her shirt like she did when Mom couldn't see her. Maybe there was hope for that girl.

"Haven't you noticed all the off road vehicles parked up there on a busy weekend, right about sundown?"

"I guess I haven't."

"Must be a good view of the sunset."

"Yeah," Millie nodded her head. "Let's ask Dad to drive us up there one of these days."

"Uh-huh, after he gets something to drive us in."

"Well," Millie said, "he promised we'd get a dune buggy after we moved in. It's time now."

"Time for what?" The deep voice startled us and we both jumped.

"Did I interrupt top secret conversation?" Dad smiled and reached for the last brownie.

"Time to get a dune buggy, Dad." Millie looked right at him. I was glad she answered his question. If there was something to talk about or ask for, it was easier to let her. She had a habit of just speaking up without thinking. All the time. And I was happy to let her do it. I'd get the answers, and she'd get the consequences if she was being too pushy or greedy or nosy or just about too much of anything. Which she often was.

"Well, before we talk about that dune buggy," Dad pulled out a chair and sat near us. "Let's talk about what happened outside tonight."

I wanted to glance at my sister but resisted the urge. And wouldn't you know it? This was one of those times the mouthy one stayed quiet. Dad looked from Millie to me. Waiting for an answer.

I was trying to decide if I should try the play-dumb-scenario like I don't know what he's talking about or just admit we made a bad choice in scaring the little boys and get the consequences over with. Before I made my decision, Millie opted for the play dumb routine.

"What do you mean, Dad?"

I knew by my dad's face that was the wrong thing to say. He didn't look happy with her less than honest answer. Man, was I glad I hadn't given that answer.

"Millie, you of all people should know what I'm talking about."

Chapter 3

Millie

"Why would I know more than Jeremiah would know?" Millie was ready to throw her brother under the bus. She wasn't going to take all the punishment when it was Jeremiah's idea to hide in the bushes and pretend to be a wild animal.

Dad sighed. "Why do I feel like there is more going on than I know about?"

Millie looked at her brother. "You tell," she said. Luckily she wasn't close enough to him so that he could kick her under the table.

"Do you two know something about Caleb having a sister that you're hiding from us?" Dad sounded stern. He was definitely tired of their vague answers. Millie wanted to laugh out loud with relief. This wasn't about them scaring the boys at all.

"No, Dad." Millie jumped at the chance to carry the conversation in another direction far removed from them playing a mean trick.

"That's what we were just talking about," Jeremiah said. "We've never heard anything about Caleb having a sister."

"Did Deputy Black say anything about other kids in the family when he helped Caleb move in?" Millie asked.

"No, nothing." Dad looked puzzled.

"So what did he say to you and Mom tonight?"

"We were getting ready to pray with him and Mom asked, like she always does, if he wanted to pray about anything." Dad took a glass out of the cabinet and poured some milk.

"And?"

"Ever the impatient one." Jeremiah looked over at Millie. "Let Dad get a drink."

She gave her brother a dirty look.

"And he usually says no," Dad continued. "But tonight he asked Mom to pray for his sissy. He said he saw her over by the lights tonight and he wants her to come live here."

"What did Mom say to him?" Millie asked.

"She said she'd pray about that and he was satisfied." Dad took another drink of his milk. "He drifted right off to sleep."

"Dad," Millie said. "Why did you say that I should have known what you were talking about?"

"Caleb said you were helping him to feel better," Dad looked over at her. "I guess he was sad because he was thinking about his sister."

Millie glanced at her brother with a quick eye movement, rather than turning her head, then looked back at her dad. But she didn't say a thing.

"Hey Dad," Jeremiah spoke up. "Can we have a campfire?"

She was glad for the change in topic. Even though she hadn't actually lied about what happened outside, she felt guilty.

Dad glanced at the clock on the wall. "I'll give you two about 30 minutes outside. Your mom and I have some things to discuss, so that will work out fine."

223

Millie looked over at Jeremiah. She was torn between being more interested in what her parents were going to discuss than going outside to have a campfire. But she knew it would look suspicious to stay inside now. She reluctantly followed her brother.

As they gathered kindling and firewood, the bright lights they saw earlier were back again. This time it seemed like they were coming right for them.

Chapter 4

Jeremiah

I dropped the wood and motioned for my sister. "Let's get closer to the fence line and see if that truck really is heading this way."

Millie set her wood down more quietly than I did and glanced behind her. I looked too, relieved to see that our parents were nowhere near the window looking out over the firepit.

We half ran, half walked through the brush and rocks, as we headed to the fence, but the truck that appeared to be coming our way, turned, heading a different direction.

"I think we're just spooked because of the weird way Caleb acted tonight," Millie whispered as we stopped to catch our breath.

"I think you're right." I pointed to the house. "Let's get back before they find out we're not building a fire."

"I'm sure Deputy Black would have told Mom and Dad if there were other kids," Millie said.

"Right, and even Dad said he didn't know about any."

"That kid hardly ever talks," Millie said, "and now to be so bold with all of us, insisting he has a sister, it's just weird."

"We need to talk with Deputy Black." I dropped the wood into the fire ring and lit the kindling.

"Maybe Paisley's family knows something about Caleb's mom." Millie poked the fire with a long stick she kept hidden from me. Someday I'd pay attention to where she puts it when she's not poking the fire. The fact she kept it hidden made me want to find it and poke the fire myself. With her watching.

"Why are you laughing?" She looked over at me.

"Because you're so protective about that stupid stick." I couldn't stop the laughter.

She poked the fire even more. "I love living out here." She settled back in one of the chairs and looked into the sky. "I love the stars, and the dirt and the trees . . . "

"I love riding my motorcycle every day before school," I interrupted.

". . . I love the moon and the sunrise and the hills . . ." she continued as if I hadn't even said anything.

"Millie, for Pete's sake! I get the point, you love the desert."

"Don't you?"

"I love riding my motorcycle every day, did you know that?"

We both burst out laughing. It felt so good to be done with all the troubles of trying to get this house and property and being chased by the bad guys, of worrying about Millie's adoption. It was a good feeling to just have all that over with and everything going good.

"Did you hear that?" Millie said.

"Hear what?"

Millie stood and was looking toward the edge of the property. "I can hear something, like a rumble." She stopped talking and stared intently.

I stood next to her but didn't see or hear anything.

"It sounds like a truck. A big truck. It's getting louder."

She was right. "Come on," I motioned and I started down the path toward our gate. "Let's go look."

She followed behind me a little ways until we saw the silhouette of one of the big gypsum mine trucks creeping along slowly in the moonlight, way out on the dirt road. I stopped walking and Millie bumped up against my side. She seemed scared.

"Why aren't his lights on?" she whispered.

"I don't know, and look how slow he's going."

"He shouldn't even be on that dirt road," Millie said. "They're usually on the highway."

We both watched as the truck rolled to a stop.

"He probably broke down." I turned and motioned for Millie to follow. "We better get back up to the firepit before our time is up."

"What do you think Mom and Dad wanted to talk about?" Millie asked as we walked back to the house.

Before I could answer, we heard Dad's voice.

"Millie? Jeremiah? Where are you two?"

We jogged the last little bit until we were in sight of the house. "Right here, Dad," I called out.

"It's time to come in. We need to talk to both of you."

Chapter 5

Millie

"Best part of homeschooling." Millie leaned back against the rough wood of the abandoned store and watched the sun come up.

Jeremiah took a drink of his orange juice before agreeing. "Yeah, setting our own schedule, and going riding every morning before schoolwork starts."

"You know, when I was in school," Millie looked at the brother she had come to love so deeply. "You know, before . . ." she choked up a little.

Jeremiah turned his head in her direction. "Before?"

"Yeah, you know, before this family."

That was one thing he never teased her about. He understood the challenges they'd each been through in foster care, hoping, praying for a family. It was something they probably would never joke about.

"I would hear kids talk about things they were doing with their families, and it was so hard not to be jealous." She scoffed. "Well, who am I kidding? I didn't even try not to be jealous. I didn't know then what the Bible says about it. I just flat out was jealous." She crushed her orange juice container and wadded the trash from her breakfast burrito. "And I was angry that I didn't have my own family."

Jeremiah took her trash and stuffed it into his fanny pack, ready to ride some more. Millie could tell he was listening intently. "But you have a family now, Mil. No reason to be angry. Just grateful."

"Even though I dreamed and hoped that one day I would," she looked over at Jeremiah. "I don't think I ever really believed it would happen."

He waited for her to continue. As if he could tell there was more to this conversation than just reminiscing.

Millie picked up her own fanny pack, breathed deeply and stared at the motorcycle in front of her. She had more to say, but it was hard to get it out. But she felt she had to tell someone. And Jeremiah was the only one she could tell.

"What is it, Millie?"

She appreciated his gentle voice.

"Well." She looked over at him. "This is going to sound mean, especially since I know what it's like to need a family. But I really like being the only daughter. I feel special. So important to Mom and Dad."

"You are important to them."

"What I'm getting at is, what if Caleb really does have a sister out there somewhere?"

Jeremiah waited. She appreciated that about him. He didn't rush her when it was really serious, he seemed to know she needed time to get the words together.

"What I mean is, I know how Mom and Dad are. I know they're following Great Grandpa's dream to give a home to kids who need one. And what scares me is, I don't want them to find Caleb's sister and give her a home too. You heard what they said last night. I know that's what they're going to try to do." She barely got the words out before tears fell.

Jeremiah handed her some crumpled napkins he found in his fanny pack, but stayed quiet while she cried.

"I'm ashamed to say it, but I don't want to share Mom and Dad with another girl. I want to be the only daughter. The important one."

Jeremiah smiled. "Oh, so it's okay for me to share them with another boy in the house?" He nodded his head. "I see how it is."

Millie smiled through her tears. "Yeah, I guess I didn't think about it that way."

Jeremiah stood and cinched his fanny pack around his waist. "Here's the thing, Millie," he looked right at her as he grabbed his helmet from where it hung on the handlebars. "God understands. He'll help you through it if that time comes." He pulled the helmet down over his head. "But we don't even know if there is a sister out there."

Millie wiped the last of her tears and joined her brother by the motorcycles. "Thank you for listening." She looked into Jeremiah's eyes. "And for understanding."

As she pulled her helmet on, something caught her eye behind the dingy windows of the abandoned store. She gasped.

"Jeremiah! Look!"

Chapter 6

Jeremiah

Millie took off running in her clunky riding boots and helmet before I could even get turned around to see where she pointed.

I saw nothing out of the ordinary, anywhere, except my sister disappearing onto private property clearly marked with a "No Trespassing" sign. She rounded the back side of the abandoned store and vanished.

I looked over at our motorcycles, then back in her direction and sighed. Loudly. Sometimes it was all you could do with that crazy sister of mine. I'm afraid she's on her own for this one. I wasn't about to leave our bikes sitting here unguarded for all the world to see. Well, not that all the world was driving down this road the old store was on. But I did see one car earlier. Oh and a big gypsum mine truck lumbered by us while we were eating the breakfast we brought along.

I straddled my motorcycle which was pointing in the direction Millie went. This way at least I could see if she ever decided to come back.

The sun rose higher and I knew we'd need to get back soon. Mom said no more than two hours and we were at least halfway through that much of our riding time, if not a little more.

"Millie!" I hoped she could hear me yelling. She probably expected me to follow her. But no way was I leaving my bike here. Just as I was about to yell again, I saw movement through the dirty window of the old store. I took a second look, but there was nothing. That was strange. I kept my eyes glued on that window in case it happened again. Maybe that was what Millie saw. Knowing her, she went around back looking for a way into the store. I sure hope she didn't find one. That would be breaking and entering. At least that's what they called it on the cop shows.

Speaking of cops. Suddenly there was one standing by my side. I looked at the man in uniform, wondering where he came from. I sure didn't see a cop car.

"Can I help you?" His words seemed nice. But the way he spit them out sounded anything but nice.

I looked around for the car I didn't hear and realized why. There wasn't one.

"Uh." I had no clue what to say and really wondered who this guy was. He had a uniform and a gun, but he sure didn't look like a Sheriff's Deputy. "Do you work with Deputy Black?"

"I'm asking the questions around here, sonny boy!"

"Excuse me, what did you want to know?" Something didn't feel right, but I played it safe hoping we could get out of here without trouble. Out of the corner of my eye, I saw Millie heading our way.

Mr. Uniform Guy must have seen her too. "Well, well, what have we here?" He turned in her direction, hands on his hips. "A trespasser!" He spoke the words like Millie had committed a major crime.

"You know I could impound this motorcycle for trespassing on clearly marked private property!"

Millie looked at me and I knew she didn't understand. "He means he can take your bike." I whispered, hoping the guy didn't hear.

"Who are you?" Millie challenged. "You're not in charge of this town. Let me see your badge."

Whoa, sister. Wrong thing to say. Big time wrong thing.

"You wanna see a badge, do you, little lady?" The man leaned his face close to her helmet, yelling. "Well, how about I just show you something else instead?"

He pulled out a set of handcuffs.

"Turn around, hands behind your back!"

Millie stood frozen in place. I couldn't move either. Was this really happening?

"Now!"

Chapter 7

Millie

"Jeremiah!" Millie whispered. "Do something!" The look on his face reminded her that she got them into this mess. "Please!" she tacked on to her hasty demand.

Jeremiah looked in her direction, then turned to the uniformed man.

"Excuse me, sir, uh, Officer."

"Yeah, what is it?" The man looked away from Millie and straight at Jeremiah.

"Well, would you please reconsider? My sister didn't think. She rushed off when she thought she saw a critter."

The man looked over to Millie. When he turned his attention back to Jeremiah, Millie's hopes lifted.

"She's always on the lookout for stray dogs who need help. If you let her go, I'll see to it that she never goes on that property again." Jeremiah seemed to grow more confident as the man listened. Millie had her doubts she could keep the promise

Jeremiah just made without consulting with her first. She knew she saw something move behind that dusty window.

A few scary moments passed while the man, who Millie really doubted was a cop, seemed to be deciding what to do, still dangling the handcuffs. "All right," he finally said. "You kids get on outta here. But don't let me catch you on that property again."

"Thank you, God," Millie whispered when her bike started on the first kick. She took off after Jeremiah so fast she nearly ran into his rear tire. She wanted to get away from this place. At least for now anyway. There definitely seemed to be something going on there worth exploring.

Jeremiah pulled over a few miles from the old store.

"Well, you just about got us in a world of trouble back there," he said as he pulled his helmet off.

Millie pulled a water bottle out of her fanny pack and sucked half of it down on the first gulp. Her mouth had gone completely dry when she saw the guy in the uniform waiting near Jeremiah.

"Who was that guy anyway? He sure didn't look like any cop we've ever seen around here."

"Oh, you mean in the three long months we've lived here?" Jeremiah grabbed her water bottle and finished it off. "It's not like we know every character in this town yet."

"Yeah, character, that sure describes him," Millie said. "I'm going to ask Deputy Black about him next time we see him."

"Oh no you don't!" Jeremiah stared at her.

"Why not?"

"What are you going to say? 'Who was that man who wanted to arrest me and impound my bike when I was trespassing?'"

"Oh, good point."

"Not to mention mouthing off to him." Jeremiah shook his head. "You need to learn to control that mouth of yours."
"I'll work on that."

"We better get back, our time must be about up." Jeremiah pulled his helmet on.

"Someone was inside that store." Millie said and then put her helmet on too.

"You heard what I told that officer." Jeremiah pointed his index finger at her.

"Yeah, yeah, I heard you," Millie said as she kicked her bike over.

"But that doesn't mean I'm going to do what you said," she whispered as she twisted the throttle and followed Jeremiah in the direction of home.

Chapter 8

Jeremiah

"Did you see something move through that window?" My sister whispered when we were sitting at the kitchen table doing schoolwork.

Mom and Caleb were in the living room working on his reading lesson. Even though he was seven years old he had never learned to read. We each took turns reading to him and encouraging him as he learned letters and sounds. He seemed excited about discovering he would be able to read books soon just like everyone else.

"Did you hear me?" My impatient sister poked my arm with the eraser on her pencil, bringing me back to the present, where instead of contemplating why a seven-year-old had never learned the alphabet, I had to put up with an impatient sister cooking up schemes that would get us in trouble. Like today, when she nearly got arrested. Which reminded me of something I wanted to talk to her about.

"I don't think that guy was really a cop." I looked over at her. "What do you think?"

"Well, you're most likely avoiding my question on purpose," she said, "but now that you mention it, there seemed to be something weird about him."

"Right." I tapped my pencil on the table as I thought back to what happened this morning. "Like he just suddenly showed up next to me and I never even saw a car. I don't even know where he came from."

"But he had that uniform on, and a badge and a gun," Millie said. "And for sure he had handcuffs." She grimaced, most likely at the thought of how close she came to feeling them clamp shut around her wrists.

"Can you imagine how much trouble we would have been in if he had impounded your bike?" I shuddered at the thought. "That would have been the end of our freedom for awhile."

"Why would he care if I was poking around that old ghost town of a store?" Millie squinted her eyes. She always did that when she was deep in thought, trying to unlock mysteries. I don't know how it helped her think. It was just plain funny looking if you asked me.

"I wonder how long that old store has been vacant," I said, not caring if I was interrupting her mental analysis of the facts. "Dad said he used to go there when he was a kid and get ice cream and candy when they were camping in the desert."

"Maybe he knows when it closed down, I'm going to ask him."

"Are you two deep in a discussion about social studies or science?" Mom opened the refrigerator and took out a pitcher of iced tea, then looked our way. We both gave her those deer-in-the-headlight looks wondering how much she heard.

"We were talking about our ride this morning." Millie recovered faster than I did. I was worried Mom heard us talking about the fake cop. "We ate our breakfast outside that old abandoned store. We just wondered how long it's been closed."

"As long as I've been coming to the desert with your dad," Mom said, pouring herself a glass of tea. She grabbed a cold water bottle out of the fridge when she put the tea pitcher back.

"Here you go, Caleb," she called out and then turned back to us. "I know your dad used to go there as a kid, but I don't ever remember it being open."

"Why does it just sit there empty?" I said. "Seems like someone would buy the place and open it again."

Caleb shuffled into the kitchen in his sock feet and took the water bottle. He was carrying a Dr. Seuss book under his arm and had a big smile on his face. "I'm going to learn to read this," he said softly, holding it up to show us. His voice was always so quiet you could hardly hear him. Except for last night, when he was so adamant about seeing his sissy. That was strange.

Mom patted Caleb on the head as he shuffled back out of the kitchen carrying his book and his water bottle. "I'll be right there, Caleb," she said.

"I heard once there was some strange goings-on where that store was concerned." Mom got back to my question.

Millie looked over at me. I could see her out of the corner of my eye, but I kept my eyes on my mom.

"You'd have to ask your dad more about it when he gets back from his trip." She picked up her tea glass and took a sip before she added, "But if I remember the story right, someone died there many years ago."

Chapter 9

Millie

"A murder?! There was a murder at that store?"

"Millie, shush," their mom said. "You'll frighten Caleb and I didn't say it was a murder."

"Well you said someone died there. What else could have happened?"

"How about they got sick and died?" Jeremiah said. "How about they were old? How about they had a heart attack?"

"Okay, okay," Millie said, "I get the point."

"You two get back on your schoolwork," Mom said as she left the room. "Your dad can answer questions for you when he gets home."

Millie waited until she was out of sight. "I'll bet it was a murder," she whispered.

Jeremiah was making notes in his science workbook. He looked up at her. "Millie, you heard Mom. She said it wasn't a murder."

"No, she did not say that."

"We both heard her," Jeremiah sighed. "You can be so exasperating."

"Well, that's a nice big word for today. Is that on your spelling test?" But before he could answer she continued. "She never actually said the words 'there was no murder.' She said 'I didn't say there was a murder.'"

Jeremiah looked at her and shook his head.

"Big difference," Millie insisted. "Big. And the fact that she didn't tell us any other way the person died, tells me it very likely was a murder and she didn't want to talk about it."

"Whatever." Jeremiah looked back down at his science workbook. He seemed to be done with the conversation.

Millie was far from finished with this topic.

She opened up her binder and began scribbling notes on a blank sheet of notebook paper.

Jeremiah glanced over at her. "Finally, you're doing what Mom told us."

"Uh-huh," she said without looking up.

She kept writing. Her list was growing.

Ask Dad when the store closed
Ask dad about the murder
Find out when the murder happened
Find out who the fake cop was
See if Paisley knows any of these answers

"What subject are you working on?"

Jeremiah's question interrupted her focus and she tried to ignore him as she continued writing.

Ride bicycle over to store and try to see inside (maybe Paisley will go)

"Millie!" Jeremiah whispered.

She looked up to see him staring at her. "What?"

"I asked you what subject you're working on."

"Why? What's it to you?"

"I've just never seen you so eager to make notes when you're studying."

"Oh," she chewed on the pencil's eraser as she studied the list. Then she noticed he was still staring at her. "English," she said.

"Oh, that's interesting." His monotone answer didn't match his words.

"Why, what's the big deal?" Millie said.

"Just that you have your Social Studies workbook open, but you say you're working on English."

Jeremiah reached toward her binder, but Millie shoved it farther away.

"I'm working on my spelling words," she said.

"Uh-huh, sure." He stared at her. "But remember, you just about got arrested today."

"By a fake cop," she said.

"Curiosity killed the cat you know," Jeremiah whispered.

"I'm not a cat," Millie said.

Chapter 10

Jeremiah

What a relief to stand outside and watch my mom drive off with my sister and Caleb in the car. I was ready for a break from her yakking about that old store.

Caleb waved from the back seat, a big smile on his face, as he headed off to play with Paisley's little brother, Donovan, his new best friend. It took about 15 minutes to get to the Ridge Riders Lodge from our place, where they lived. Paisley also homeschooled. Some days she worked in the store of her parents' lodge after school, but today they had invited both Millie and Caleb over to visit.

Well, they invited me, too. But spending the afternoon listening to two girls obsessed with conjuring up a new mystery was not my idea of fun. Not when I had a motorcycle I could work on. Unless they were going to take the family dune buggy out. I hadn't thought of that when I declined the offer.

"Too late now," I said as I headed toward Dad's shop. Thankfully, he left the keys for me when he took off for the city yesterday.

"Well, now, lookie here who I jist ran into!" The booming voice echoed through the shop just as I got all the lights on and opened my tool box.

"Minnesota Mike!"

"Who else did you expect to come sneakin' up on you like that?" The Santa Claus look alike came into the shop and gave me a bear hug.

"It's good to see you. Where have you been?" Even though we had only known him for a few months, it seemed like he'd been a family friend for years.

"Where else, but out looking for more adventure!" He reached in his pocket, bringing out a folded paper. "Lookie here at this beauty!" He shook the paper open.

I stepped toward him, looking at the tattered paper with pinholes in it. Must have been on a bulletin board somewhere. It was a handwritten ad with a photo of a red four-seater dune buggy.

"Hey, are you going to get that?" I took it out of his hand to get a better look. Minnesota's face reflected the excitement I felt. I knew he'd be taking us for rides if he got it. "Look at that light set-up," I said before he could answer.

"Boy, we could see halfway across the desert driving around at night in that beauty, couldn't we now?" Minnesota Mike agreed. "Where's your pops? I figgered on taking him with me to check this here thing out. Ya know, get his opinion. He's one right smart guy."

"Dad's not home, he went to the city to visit Mr. Smith."

"That the older feller that sold you the property?"

"Yes, but Dad and Mom say he gave us the property."

"Right generous thing to do," Minnesota Mike said. "I think he was eager to see yer folks use the land to help kids."

"Mom and Dad want him to come for a visit. They said he misses the desert."

"It'll do him a world of good to spend some time with you folks." Minnesota Mike folded the paper and slipped it back in his pocket.

"Well now, I guess I'll jist have to go look at this beauty by myself. It's only about a half hour drive from here." He turned to leave, then stopped and looked back at me.

"Unless you know anybody else what might want to tag along." He let out one of his belly laughs and turned back toward the door.

Chapter 11

Millie

"Did your parents find out about the wild animal trick we played on the boys?" Millie asked her new best friend as they headed up to her bedroom. She had become instant friends with Paisley several months ago when her family stayed at the lodge that Paisley's parents owned. Once they moved to the desert, the girls became inseparable.

Paisley breathed a sigh of relief. "Thankfully, no."

"I don't know why we did that. It was mean," Millie said. "Guess I'm not used to having a little brother. But that's no excuse."

"Caleb's a sweet kid."

"That reminds me, I wanted to ask if you know anything about his family. What do you think about him talking about a sister?"

"I asked my mom." Paisley shook her head. "She knows nothing about Caleb's family, but maybe you could talk to the deputy. I bet he would know."

Millie reached into her backpack and pulled out her list. "Yeah, that's what Jeremiah and I were talking about. But I have other questions for you, too." She looked up and smiled at her friend. "You're my information source, you know, since you've lived here your whole life."

"Okay, what's up?"

"First, what do you know about that abandoned store a little way off the highway? I can't remember the name of the road it's on."

"Oh, you must be talking about the old trading post. It's on Monument Road."

"Yeah, that's the one. How long has it been closed down?"

"Since before I was born."

"My mom said someone died there." It tempted Millie to say it was murder, but she wanted to get Paisley's take on it without influencing her. She didn't know why, but she hoped it was a murder. That seemed more mysterious and exciting.

"I never heard that." Paisley went to her bookcase. "But I never asked." She pulled out a book and returned to the bed where they both were sitting.

"What's that?" Millie asked.

"It's about southwest desert history." She shuffled through pages, then stopped on the table of contents. "Maybe something is in here about our town."

Millie scooted next to her so she could see the contents page. "Look right there," she pointed. "Is that it?"

"Ye Olde Dry Brook Trading Post," Paisley read out loud. "That's what they called it." She flipped to the page. She must have been reading faster than Millie or skipping parts of it because suddenly she looked up, her eyes big and mouth open.

"Wow, Millie, listen to this!"

Chapter 12

Jeremiah

"Woo-hoo are we going to have a blast in this thing!" Minnesota Mike bounced in his truck seat as we drove down the highway towing a trailer carrying a flashy looking red four-seater dune buggy. Room for me, Dad, Mike and Millie. I couldn't wait for Dad to get home from his trip to give us permission for a ride.

Our windows were down and Mike's beard and hair were blowing in the wind as he bounced around in his seat while he drove. This guy was more excited than me.

But then I thought of a problem.

"Hey, Mike." He glanced over at me, then back at the highway, still wearing the biggest smile I ever saw on this old guy. "Where will you keep the buggy? You don't even live around here."

"Well, sonny boy," he glanced over and smiled even bigger, if that's possible. "There's another thing I been meaning to tell you and your folks."

This sounded exciting.

"I bought me a right cozy trailer in that nice place over where your friend lives."

"At the Ridge Riders Lodge?" I asked.

"That be the place, sonny boy. I am now a permanent resident of this little town. And wouldn't you know it? There is room to park my truck and new buggy right next to my trailer."

"That's the best news ever!"

"I agree," Minnesota said. "I guess my traveling days are over. I'm having too much fun hanging out with you and your family. You kids seem to have a knack for finding adventure. So what's the point of me driving all over the country looking fer what I can find right here with the likes of you?"

I turned to stare at the trailer and buggy. "Yeah, and I see lots of future adventure following right behind us. I can't wait to go for a ride in that buggy."

"You and me both, sonny boy. We'll wait for yer pops to get home and we'll plan an outing real soon like."

The truck jerked hard to the right. I turned to see what happened, as a car almost sideswiped us. Minnesota Mike held on tight to the steering wheel as we hit rough dirt on the side of the road while avoiding the oncoming car.

"What's that guy thinking?" Minnesota's voice sounded strained.

"That scared me! I was looking at the trailer and didn't see it coming."

"You didn't get a look at the feller driving?" Minnesota glanced over at me, then back at the road. "Almost looked like he were a cop the way he dressed, but that shore weren't no cop car."

"I caught sight of a uniform," I said. "It almost reminded me of the guy who tried to handcuff . . ." I stopped before I gave away the trouble Millie got us into this morning.

I stared straight ahead, but out of the corner of my eye, I saw Minnesota Mike look over at me. No way was I going to make eye contact. First off, I was a bad liar, and second, this was Millie's secret too.

"What's that sonny boy? You stopped talking awful fast."

The car was quiet except for the sound of the wind whistling past us through our open windows as we sailed down the highway. I wasn't sure where to take the conversation next. I didn't want to lie to Mike, but I didn't want to tell him what happened either.

"Were ya gettin' ready to say it's the guy what was going to handcuff Millie?"

My head jerked in his direction, and I'm sure my eyes were bulging out. "How did you find out?"

Minnesota chuckled. "Well, I didn't know for sure."

He looked over at me and smiled. "But I sure know now."

Chapter 13

Millie

"The proprietor of Ye Olde Dry Brook Trading Post closed the business and left the area within days of his partner's untimely death. He was never known to return. As of the writing of this book, Ye Olde Dry Brook Trading Post stands deserted and abandoned. Who knows what secrets are hidden in the walls and halls of the beloved store that served travelers and locals for decades?" Paisley read the passage aloud and looked at her friend.

Millie stared, eyes and mouth wide open. "Wow!"

"You're not kidding, 'wow!'" Paisley said. "So your mom was right, someone died there."

"Untimely death, it said." Millie grabbed the book from Paisley and re-read that portion. "Untimely! That could mean murder!"

"Murder?" Paisley looked startled. "Why would you assume that?"

"Well, he couldn't have been sick. That wouldn't be unexpected."

"He could have had a sudden heart attack, or maybe a car accident," Paisley said.

"And it could also have been murder."

"Why are you so sure it's murder?"

Millie shrugged. "I don't know, I guess because it's more exciting." She looked over at her friend. "It's the stuff legends are made of."

"You're right about that," Paisley said. "So how do we find out?"

That's what Millie loved about Paisley. Instead of acting like her ideas were stupid or weird like other so-called friends from her past, she went along with Millie's adventures and even more important, Paisley was also excited about them. "It's not only the past we need to find out more about," Millie whispered.

"What do you mean and why are you whispering?" Paisley whispered.

Millie smiled. "Why are you whispering too?"

The girls were both laughing when Paisley whispered again. "I guess because you are."

"Well, I'm whispering because I don't want anyone but you to hear me." Millie stood and walked across the room to the closed bedroom door. She opened it and peered out to see if anyone was in the hallway. Satisfied they were alone she sat back down on the bed.

"Well?" Paisley said.

"Something is happening at the store right now."

"Why do we have to whisper about it?" Paisley said.

"Because," Millie leaned closer. "I almost got arrested today."

"You what?" Paisley blurted out.

Millie put her hand over her friend's mouth. "Shush, you'll get me in trouble. Big trouble. And the worst part would be I couldn't go back to investigate."

"You better start at the beginning."

After Millie filled her in on the happenings of the morning, she finished with a question. "Will you go with me to get a look in the windows, since I can't count on Jeremiah to help?"

"When and how are we going?"

"I've got it all figured out. Spend the night on Friday. Saturday morning we'll go for a bicycle ride. That will give us the perfect opportunity." Millie said.

"That's a great plan. Then we can also watch for the lights together on Friday night."

"What lights?" Millie asked.

Paisley looked surprised. "You mean you haven't heard about them?"

"No, what lights?"

Paisley looked at Millie for a minute before she spoke. "I'm not sure I should tell you what kind of lights."

Chapter 14

Jeremiah

I held my breath, waiting for Minnesota Mike to speak. Wondering how I would answer. How could he have known about Millie almost getting arrested?

The desert rushed by my open window. I stared straight ahead. The brisk wind blowing in the window helped cool my burning face. I kept waiting for him to say something else. My heart beat hard, wondering how much he knew.

"It shore got quiet in here, did you notice that, sonny boy?" Minnesota Mike chuckled.

Nothing seemed funny to me.

"Tell you what, sonny boy, I can take a hint. I know when someone doesn't want to talk about something. How's about we move on to another topic?"

My entire body relaxed. What a relief. For now, at least. I know how sly that old man could be. I knew he would catch me off guard and spring it on me. "Okay," I said after much thought. "I like that idea."

"You and that sister of yours been checking out the ghost lights?"

I turned to see if this was some kind of joke. He wasn't laughing. Just staring at the road as he drove.

"What are you talking about?"

"Well, they been around these parts for decades, I been told. I jist now heard about them the other night."

"Why did you call them ghost lights?"

"Don't rightly know why folks call them that, maybe cause they're spooky looking." Mike clicked his blinker on and slowed the truck.

I still wanted to talk about the so-called ghost lights, but now another question popped into my mind. Like, why did he turn here on Monument Road? This wasn't the way to our house.

"Where are we headed?"

He chuckled and looked over at me. "This road a little familiar to you?"

My body tensed. I thought at least he'd wait a couple days before he tried to get me to talk about Millie's near arrest again. Now we were heading right to the scene of the crime, as they say.

I tried to think of some nonchalant comeback, but I'm bad at lying and anyway, even if I had something to say, I couldn't have gotten the words out. I wasn't used to feeling awkward around Minnesota Mike. He was one of those guys that just puts you at ease. Except for now, while approaching the abandoned store.

I closed my eyes, waiting for the truck to come to a stop, so he could pry the truth out of me, right here where it all happened. Once Dad and Mom found out, we'd never get to ride off the property by ourselves again.

"Let's go check out where those spooky lights might be comin' from." Minnesota's words interrupted my fretting.

Relief flowed through me as the truck passed by the old store. I couldn't resist turning around to look.

What a mistake that was.

Chapter 15

Millie

"What do you mean you shouldn't tell me what kind of lights?" Millie's voice raised. "Why even bring it up then?" She stood to leave.

"Millie!" Her mother's muffled voice through the closed bedroom door provided an escape from Paisley.

"I gotta go." She hurried to open the door. "Be right down, Mom."

She no sooner got the words out than the door banged shut. Stunned at the force Paisley used to slam the door, Millie stared at her friend. "Why are you so upset with me?" Paisley said.

"Because you're reminding me of girls where I used to live. All the time keeping secrets. Like I'm not smart enough, or cool enough, to be told."

"It's not like that." Paisley held her palm against the door, keeping it closed. "I would never treat you like that, Millie."

Millie shoved her hand aside and tried to open the door. "Well, you sure coulda fooled me." The words shot out of her mouth as she squeezed through the barely open door and approached the stairwell.

She felt she stepped back in time. Back to where the kids were mean. Always mean. The girls in particular. Maybe it was all a glorious dream, that she'd discovered a genuine best friend. Unwanted tears formed. As she lowered her foot to the first step, Paisley's loud whisper caught her off guard and she almost lost her balance.

"Ghost lights!" The whispered words blasted out of her mouth like cannon fire.

Millie looked back at her. "Ghost lights?" she repeated. "What are you talking about?"

"That's what they call the lights." Paisley said.

Millie stepped back up onto the landing outside Paisley's bedroom. "Why couldn't you tell me before?"

"I wasn't sure how you'd feel about it."

"How could you not know?" Millie gave her friend thumbs up accompanied by an enormous smile. "I'm always up for adventure, especially a spooky one."

"They say the lights have been around a hundred years," Paisley said. "Come see." She went back into her room. "I'm sure it's in the book."

"Bring it when you come over. My mom's waiting for me," Millie said. "But why haven't we seen them before if they've been around that long?"

"I don't know. I've never seen them as long as we've lived here, which is practically my entire life. But now people are talking about them."

"What are they saying?"

"Millie, we're waiting!" Her mom's voice drifted up the stairwell.

"Come on, quick, tell me," Millie started down the stairs.

"Ghost lights," Paisley whispered as she followed her downstairs. "I don't know any more."

"Then how do you know how long people have been talking about them?"

"Oh," Paisley whispered when they saw the little boys and their moms waiting at the bottom of the stairs. "I guess I know a little more."

Chapter 16

Jeremiah

Millie would never forgive me for not telling her what I saw as we sailed by. But if I told her, she'd return to the store for sure. Why did we have to take this road?

"What are you so fidgety about, sonny boy?" Minnesota Mike reached out to the dash and turned the radio on.

The static gave me time to answer while he searched for a station. I hated feeling nervous and scared. This day should have ended on a high note going with Minnesota Mike to pick up the cool old dune buggy. But it sure didn't seem so fun right now. This was almost worse than seeing the guy threaten to handcuff Millie.

"See somethin' that shook you up back at the store, did you now?" Minnesota said.

"Why do you ask?" I tried to sound casual, but figured he heard the shake in my voice.

"Because I saw something too."

My head jerked in his direction without me meaning to. "You did?"

"Sure did, sonny boy, and I'll tell you, something ain't right."

I turned and look back over my shoulder, but we were too far past the store. "Who were those people?"

"Not sure, but I know one thing. They don't belong there."

"Maybe they're buying the place."

"Well they got a mighty suspicious way of acting if they're looking to buy the place." Mike continued trying to tune in a station as he drove.

"Were they yelling at those kids?" The scene etched itself in my mind. One man stared at the truck as we drove by. Another tried to herd children into the old store.

"I couldn't tell for shore," Mike said. "I just knowed they's ain't supposed to be anybody prowling around."

"How do you know?" I felt calmer discussing the strange happenings. The strange thing was, I hadn't seen anything definitely wrong going on. But something didn't seem right.

Mike got a radio station tuned in, sort of. We heard music now mixed in with the static. "There now, that's what I'm talking about!" He seemed pleased with his accomplishment. And he also used that minor accomplishment to ignore the question I asked.

"Mike," I said. "How do you know no one should be there?" He looked at me, then back at the road. "Well now, sonny boy, some things you just can't talk about."

Chapter 17

Millie

"I thought Friday would never get here," Millie said as the girls settled back in their sleeping bags.

"I can't believe your dad is letting us sleep out here by ourselves." Paisley fluffed her pillow then laid back, gazing at the stars.

"That's what he built this tower for. So we could have outdoor sleepovers and be safe from nocturnal desert critters roaming around."

Paisley tore open a bag of chips and offered some to Millie.

"Now tell me about these ghost lights." Millie's words were muffled with her mouthful of chips.

"Your brother is right. You have the worst manners!"

"Hey, you offered me the chips when you knew I had a million questions for you." Millie reached into the bag and stuffed her mouth again.

"Okay, I'll talk," Paisley said, laughing. "You just chew quietly and listen."

Little puffs of crunched up chips slipped out of Millie's mouth as she tried to chew while laughing.

"So the story goes back to the 1800s," Paisley said. "My dad and I looked it up on the office computer the other day after one of our guests mentioned something about seeing ghost lights."

"What do you mean, one of your guests? How many people were visiting you that day?" Millie interrupted.

"No, silly," Paisley hit her on the shoulder. "That's what we call the people who stay at the lodge."

"Why don't you just call them customers?" Millie asked.

"It's hotel etiquette, my dad says."

"Oh, okay, I guess that makes sense. So what did you and your dad discover?"

"A stagecoach driver first told the story of the ghost lights back in the 1800s. He called them 'fire balls.'"

"Sounds like fireworks," Millie said.

"Same thing I thought."

"I wonder if they had fireworks back then?"

"Yes." Now it was Paisley's turn to munch on chips while she talked. "Fireworks were first used by the Chinese back in the second century and the first we could find mention of their use in the United States was in the early 1600s."

"You sound like an encyclopedia."

"Well, it's just that my dad and I had the same question about the possibility of the ghost lights being fireworks, so we checked that out too."

"If that's all they were, that takes all the excitement away." Millie was ready to move on to another topic, like the history of the abandoned store. She was sure there was a murder mystery waiting to be solved.

Paisley continued. "It said the lights rose in an arch and then returned to the ground. That doesn't sound like fireworks."

"No, I guess it doesn't." Millie was growing weary of the lights story but she didn't want to be rude since Paisley seemed so interested in thc lights. "Why do you think we're going to see these lights from a hundred years ago?"

"There have been some sightings lately and people are saying the ghost lights are back." Paisley shivered and burrowed down in her sleeping bag. "It's so cold. Do you think we'll last all night?"

Millie zipped her bag up the rest of the way. "We better if we want a chance to see the spooky lights."

The girls grew quiet as they laid back and studied the night sky. There wasn't a cloud to be seen and thousands of stars twinkled, but nothing that could be called ghost lights.

Millie felt herself nodding off when she heard a loud rumble in the distance. She kept her head down on her pillow but turned toward Paisley to see if she had fallen asleep. Her eyes were open wide.

"Did you hear that?" Paisley said.

Chapter 18

Jeremiah

Earlier it seemed tonight would be the perfect opportunity to be miserable. I still hadn't told Millie about the people at the abandoned store the other day. If I did, she would hound me endlessly, wanting to know every single detail, right down to what color shoes they wore. Not to mention the more serious problem it would create. She'd been itching to get back and explore. Knowing what I saw would have sent her running to investigate.

I hated keeping secrets. Especially because I'm so bad at it with my sister and I feel so guilty around my parents. My big plan for the evening, once I heard about the sleepover with Paisley, was to hide in my room with a good book. That way the girls wouldn't talk to me about abandoned stores or ghost lights. Whatever that silly wives' tale was, I didn't even know.

Honestly, I think Minnesota Mike was pulling my leg when he drove down Monument Road, supposedly to check out the lights. We got nowhere with that escapade. More likely he wanted to get a reaction out of me when we drove past the store.

And boy, did he get a reaction. But I don't think it was what he was expecting. Even he seemed surprised seeing people there.

Even if he did try to trick me, I didn't care anymore. He was about to rescue me before Paisley arrived. And since Millie would have a friend here, I got the privilege of being the only one to go out on a night ride in Mike's new red dune buggy.

Now we sat atop one of our favorite desert hills and surveyed all of our property and the surrounding desert. We could see campfires across the highway. Off road vehicles drove all around, lights bouncing up and down as they hit the whoops. Some folks sailed up the big sand hill, challenging each other to get to the top the fastest.

"You know, Mike," I pulled off my helmet and looked over at him. He did the same. "I never imagined we'd really live out here in this off road paradise."

"Well, now, doncha know," he smiled over at me and then took a long swig out of his water bottle. "This is the living, that's fer sure." He patted the aluminum dash panel of his buggy as he switched the engine off, then let out one of his trademark belly laughs. "And this little darlin' makes the off road living even better."

"It sure does. Hey, when are you going to let me have a try at driving?"

"Well now, sonny boy, you'll have to take that up with yer dad, doncha know."

Minnesota Mike was one fun guy, but sometimes not fun enough. I thought I could get him to let me try driving without getting permission. But then again, if he was the type to let me do stuff without my parents knowing, they wouldn't trust him. I guess it's all for the best.

"Hey," he whispered and pointed to some movement off in the distance.

"What do you see?" I whispered back. I didn't know why we were whispering.

"That big mine truck, jist sittin' on the dirt road."

I almost didn't notice the truck in the darkness. All the lights were off. Usually lights glowed all around those trucks.

"That ain't right." Minnesota pulled his helmet back on. "No." He shook his head as he fired up the engine. "Jist ain't right."

Chapter 19

Millie

"It sounds like a big truck," Millie whispered.

Paisley laughed. "Why are you whispering?"

Millie sat up and shrugged. "I don't know." She joined in the laughter. "I guess I always whisper when I think there's something mysterious going on."

"Shh," Paisley said as the rumbling grew louder.

"Yeah, I think it's a big truck out on the road. It must have shut the engine off and now started it up again."

"It sounds like a gypsum mine truck." She looked at Millie. "Why would it be around here?"

Millie rummaged in her backpack. "I don't know, but this isn't the first time. Aha!" She pulled out a pair of binoculars, then stood and peered intently through the lens.

"What do you see?" Paisley whispered. "Let me look."

"Hold on! I haven't even found it yet."

"Maybe you're not looking in the right direction."

"I'm looking in the direction Jeremiah and I saw the truck."

"You've seen one out here before and didn't tell me?" Paisley said.

"Well, it didn't seem that important." Millie swept the area with the binoculars. All the while, the rumbling continued.

"When was it?"

"That night we scared the boys. Ah! I found it!" She pulled the binoculars from around her neck and handed them to Paisley. "Look in that direction." She pointed. "You can barely see it because of the trees along the road."

"Maybe God was trying to scare you guys that night." Paisley laughed as she pulled the binocular strap over her head. "You know, payback for scaring the boys."

"Yeah, never thought about that," Millie said. "The Bible says you reap what you sow."

"Oh, yeah!" Paisley said. "I see it. He's just sitting there with no lights on."

"Jeremiah and I thought maybe he was broke down when we saw him the other night."

"If he was broke down, why would his engine still be running?"

"I don't know, we didn't think that far, because our dad called us. We had to hurry back to the house."

As the girls talked, the truck slowly started rolling. "Look." Paisley handed the binoculars back to Millie. "He's starting to move, but still no lights on."

The engine rumbling grew faint.

"Does your dad know anyone who works at the gypsum mine?" Millie asked as the girls settled back into their sleeping bags.

"Yeah, Hank does. He comes in the store a couple times a month."

Millie rustled around in her backpack again, pulling out her notebook and pen.

"You carry everything in there!" Paisley said.

"Don't have the kitchen sink." The girls laughed as Millie jotted down: Ask Hank about truck on her list of things to do.

"Well, this sure was a big disappointment for seeing the ghost lights tonight." Paisley snuggled into her sleeping bag, eyes closed.

Millie couldn't respond right away, stunned at what she saw heading their way.

"Uh, maybe not. Paisley, look over there!"

Chapter 20

Jeremiah

My teeth chattered as Mike floored the gas pedal and we flew down the hillside toward the big truck. Whether from cold, excitement or fear, I didn't know. I wanted to ask what he had in mind, but knew he wouldn't hear. And even if he could, he probably wouldn't answer. Fully focused, he drove the bouncing car over rocks and through ruts, heading in the truck's direction.

Once down on flat ground we didn't have the bird's-eye view the hilltop gave us, so it was hard to pinpoint where to go. But the bigger problem, at least in my mind, was what if we caught the truck? It could be dangerous.

I hung on as Mike kept the pedal floored. We slid around corners as he maneuvered through bushes and along trails that he must have hoped would lead us to the mysterious truck.

Finally, with no luck, he slowed and headed to Sunset Hill. It was long past sunset, so we were the only ones there. This hill wasn't as tall as the other one, but since it was closer to the highway, we could still see across the road where off road vehicles were cruising around in the desert. On busy weekends, adventurous ones were out all night long. It was fun lying in bed at night listening to the roar of the vehicles exploring the desert.

"Lookie there," Mike shouted over the sound of the buggy engine.

I turned my head in time to see a big mine truck rolling down the highway. "Is it the same one?" I shouted back.

"Don't rightly know fer sure." He rubbed his chin under his helmet. I noticed he did that when he was thinking hard about something.

"The lights on that truck look different from the mine trucks I've seen."

He nodded his head. "You're right about that, sonny boy. Unfamiliar pattern. Some of the lights on top are different colors, too."

"The rest of the truck looks normal though, don't you think?"

"Hard to tell, from up here, in the dark." He looked at me. "But I'm gonna be keeping my eyes peeled watching all those trucks now, doncha know."

If there was something different, Minnesota Mike was sure to figure it out. I saw him looking at his watch.

"Hey now," he said, "I told yer folks I wouldn't keep you out too late and it's pert near midnight."

"Wow! Well, this sure beats having the girls pester me all evening. But I guess we better get on home."

"What're those gals up to anyways?" Mike checked over his seat belts, then pushed the clutch in and shifted the car into gear. I knew I better hang on. We were in for another fast take-off.

"They're sleeping outside in the tower to watch for the ghost lights!" I couldn't help it, but I burst out laughing.

Minnesota Mike joined me, only he seemed to think it was even funnier than I did. "Boy you're gonna love the great idear I jist got me." And we roared off toward home.

Chapter 21

Millie

Paisley stared in the direction Millie pointed. She turned, eyes wide, back to her friend as the two huddled together, the colorful lights dancing and bobbing above their heads.

"The ghost lights!" Paisley yelled and Millie clamped a hand over her mouth.

"Shush! You might make them go away."

"Oh, can the lights hear me?" Paisley burst out laughing.

"No, you dope, but you'll wake my parents."

"What's so bad about that? You don't want them to see the lights?"

Millie watched the lights continue to bob around. "I don't know," she whispered. "I want to figure this out for myself."

"Oh, that's right. We're supposed to be solving the hundred-year-old mystery about the ghost lights in the desert."

"Look!" Millie stared at her friend. "Are you with me in this mystery solving business or not? Maybe you think it's all a joke."

Paisley stood and motioned Millie to do the same. "I'm sorry, sometimes I make jokes that aren't that funny." She hugged her friend. "Yes, I'm with you."

Millie joined Paisley in the corner of the tower holding on to the rail and kept her eyes focused on the colored lights.

"They don't seem to be very far above us," Paisley said.

"You're right," Millie said. "So how would anyone else see them?"

"It's like they're shining just for us." Paisley took hold of Millie's arm, squeezing hard with both hands. "This is creepy."

"How creepy is it?" A deep voice sounded from below the tower.

Millie stifled a scream and wished now they had awakened her parents. "Someone is down there," she whispered.

Paisley's only response was whimpering.

Ready to scream for her parents, she waited to see what would happen next. They heard the voice again, closer this time, from on the ladder. The tone different, a high-pitched sound. "Oh, Millie, it's so creepy."

The lights stopped and a familiar belly laugh echoed from the back side of the house, joined by Jeremiah's loud laughter as his head popped up over the railing of the tower. He balanced on the ladder, laughing at the girls.

"I oughta push you off that ladder, Jeremiah Anderson!" Millie shouted. Now she was the one yelling and didn't care if her parents woke up.

"That was a mean trick," Paisley said.

"Oh, come on, little gals," Minnesota Mike's voice called from down below. "Doncha know, we was jist having some fun." He turned the colored spotlights back on and shined them up in the sky again. "I couldn't resist buying these at the discount store the other day after all the talk about the ghost lights."

"You've been hearing the stories, too?" Millie called down to him.

"Shore enough have, little missy."

"What have you heard?"

Minnesota Mike tipped his head down and rubbed the back of his neck. He looked back up at her. "Well now, this ain't the best way to carry on a conversation. Let's talk in the morning."

Jeremiah backed down the ladder and joined Mike on the ground. Minnesota put his arm around Jeremiah's shoulders. "I was a little late gittin' this here feller home, so I got to be going."

"Okay," Millie said. "Well I want to hear everything you know about the lights first thing tomorrow."

"Well, now, let's make a deal." Minnesota chuckled as he looked up at her. "I'll trade you my light story for you telling me about almost gittin' handcuffed."

Chapter 22

Jeremiah

I saw the first signs of daylight out my window, but I wasn't in any hurry to get out of bed. Millie was probably camped out in the hallway by my bedroom door waiting to pounce on me for spilling the beans to Minnesota Mike about her troubles the other day. Honestly, I hadn't meant to tell him. That old codger tricked me into admitting it. I wonder if he really knew the whole story already? And if he did, how would he have known? There was a lot more to that guy than just a fun-loving old drifter.

I stared up at the ceiling, pondering what Saturday had in store for me. Hopefully Paisley and Millie were still sound asleep in the tower and not stalking me. A chuckle slipped out though as I pondered Millie's predicament. She always wants new information about the latest happenings, but she wouldn't want to give up any information to get it. Hmm, how would she find out what Minnesota had heard about the ghost lights? For that matter, I'd kind of like to know too since he never told me anything about the lights.

The safest thing for me to do was get up and disappear before the girls woke up.

My dad must have had the same idea this morning. He was already at work in his shop when I got down there. Which was good, since I didn't have keys to get in. My plan was just to get away from the house before I had to face Millie.

"What's up, Jeremiah?" Dad shut off his band saw and pushed his safety glasses up on his head. "You're up mighty early."

"So are you." I laughed and rubbed my hands together. "It's cold in here."

"Flip on that heater, will you?" Dad said. "I was so eager to get back on this project I forgot to do that."

"Well, I thought it was best to get away from the house before the noisy girls took over the kitchen."

"Aha." Dad nodded. Not sure if that "aha" was for what I said or for the piece of steel he was studying.

"Girls talk a lot, Dad." I held my hands close to the warm air flowing from the electric heater. "I mean a lot!"

"Don't I know it." Dad laughed. "Why do you think I love the shop?"

"Are you kidding me?" I never thought about a dad wanting to get away from so much talking.

"Yeah, just don't tell your mother."

"I'm sure she already knows."

He really laughed at that. "I'm pretty sure you're right."

Our conversation was interrupted by a knock on the door. That was unusual for this early. I looked over at Dad, but before he said anything the door opened.

"Well, how are you doing, Griffin?" Dad crossed the room quickly, his hand out to shake with Deputy Black. We hadn't seen him in several weeks. He'd been away on a special assignment.

"Max!" Deputy Black said, "It's great to see you, and you too, Jeremiah. I thought this might be too early, but looks like you're a couple of early birds."

I shook his hand, but looked at the other man who had followed him into Dad's shop. I'd never seen him before. He was in some kind of cop uniform, not riding gear like Deputy Black. It didn't look like the uniform Deputy Black wore on duty. A little different.

"I didn't hear you pull up, with the door closed and the heater running." Dad said. "Must be a little chilly riding this early."

"Boy, you can say that again," the other man said. "Max, Jeremiah, this is my friend, Leon."

We all shook hands. "Are you a deputy, too?" I asked, thinking about the fake cop we had encountered earlier this week. I still had much to learn about this area we moved to.

"Border Patrol." Leon smiled at me. Friendly guy.

"That's why you look familiar," Dad said. "Were you working the checkpoint a few days ago?"

"Sure was."

"I think I chatted with you there."

"You may have at that," Leon said.

"Hey, can I ask you a question I've been wondering about?" This was my chance to find out why every time we went grocery shopping we had to sit and wait in a border check line on the way home.

"Sure, what's on your mind?"

"How come there's a border check when we're probably 20 miles from the border?"

"Actually, it's 54.4 miles from the border." Leon and Deputy Black chuckled. "But it's a good question."

Leon was the one to answer. "Things slip through the border and we're a secondary checkpoint they have to get through. You'd be surprised how much criminal activity gets discovered there."

"So you fellows got the day off?" Dad asked.

"Well, yes and no," Deputy Black said. "I've got the day off, so I told Leon I'd ride along with him on his patrol since he's doing it by quad today. I never pass up a chance to go riding."

"Do you think there are illegals crossing the border around here?" I felt like Millie, but I couldn't resist a few questions.

"Jeremiah." One look from Dad and I knew I overstepped the bounds.

"It's okay, Max," Deputy Black said. "We know your kids have a history of crime fighting, so it's not surprising the curiosity."

"We haven't spotted anything in this area recently," Leon said. "But we're always checking. Do you ride much off the property?"

"Sure, my sister and I go out just about every morning for a couple hours before we start our schoolwork."

He turned to head out the door. "Well, if you ever see any activity that seems suspicious, be sure to let us know."

I nodded my head but didn't speak. Why did I feel so guilty?

Chapter 23

Millie

Millie pulled the sleeping bag over her head to block out the creeping daylight. She made it a habit never to get up too early on Saturday, and especially sleeping outside, she didn't want to leave the warmth of the bag too soon.

"Millie, you awake?"

Paisley's whisper sounded muffled through the sleeping bag. What was she doing awake so early? Millie wondered.

"No."

Paisley pushed her shoulder. "I thought you wanted to get up early to track down Jeremiah."

Millie threw off her sleeping bag and sat straight up. "That's right! That rat! He told Minnesota Mike about me almost getting arrested." She looked over at Paisley, already dressed and rolling up her sleeping bag. "I wouldn't be surprised if my parents don't already know."

"Well, let's get going," Paisley said. "He's probably still asleep and you can sit outside his bedroom door so he can't hide from you."

"Good idea." Millie grabbed her sleeping bag and backpack and followed her friend down the ladder.

The smell of cinnamon rolls drew the girls to the kitchen before they could hunt down Jeremiah.

Millie's mom appeared to be the only person awake. "Oh good, we get first pick of the cinnamon rolls," Millie said as she took two from the center. She licked her fingers and poured a cup of milk before carrying her plate over to the table. "Glad we're the first ones up this morning, Mom. I love cinnamon rolls!" Paisley followed her to the table, also with two rolls.

"Well, you're the first ones to get the cinnamon rolls, but you're not the first ones up." Her mom joined them at the table with a glass of tea and piece of toast.

Millie dropped the roll back on her plate. "What do you mean?"

"Your dad and Jeremiah have been out of the house for at least an hour."

"Where did they go?" Millie did her best to sound nonchalant. She didn't want to alert her mom to how upset she was with Jeremiah.

"Well, they're most likely at the shop." Mom took a sip of her tea. "Your dad was up early to get back to the project he was working on. I saw Jeremiah head down that way shortly after your dad left the house."

Paisley and Millie exchanged a knowing glance. Her mom didn't miss that. "Why, what's up?" she asked. "Did you need to talk to one of them?"

Millie was already standing, gulping down her milk. She motioned to Paisley. "Come on, we can finish our cinnamon rolls while we walk."

"Millie?" Mom asked.

"Oh, nothing's up, I just want to let Jeremiah know I got first pick of the fresh cinnamon rolls," she said as the girls rushed out the back door.

"A likely story!" Paisley whispered once the door shut. The girls snickered as they rushed away from the house.

"Shush," Millie said. "My mom's already like a super sleuth. I'm sure she knows it's something more than the cinnamon rolls on my mind."

"Gee, maybe it runs in the family, ya think?" Paisley said.

But Millie wasn't listening. Her attention was fixed on the action down the road at the shop.

Who were those people? And what were they doing here so early? Didn't anyone sleep in on Saturdays?

Chapter 24

Jeremiah

I've heard the phrase "between a rock and a hard spot" before, but never understood what it meant. Until now.

Standing outside with my dad, we watched as Deputy Black and his friend Leon started their quads and waved goodbye. At the sound of their throttles accelerating, movement on the trail leading to the shop caught my eye. Oh no. It was Millie and Paisley headed right for me.

I had nowhere to go. Back into the shop to have my dad question why I looked sick when Leon said to watch out for suspicious activity or stay outside and get hammered by my sister for spilling the beans about the handcuffs?

This keeping secrets stuff was for the birds.

Now Millie was running and waving her arms like a wild woman. "Deputy Black!" I could hear her shouting his name over and over.

This might be my perfect opportunity to escape. Maybe it was my lucky day after all. Deputy Black must have glanced up toward the house before he headed to the gate, because now he and Leon were riding their quads in Millie's direction.

"Hey Dad, I'm going to head up and get some of those cinnamon rolls I saw Mom baking." Was my dad staring at me or was it my imagination? I wasn't waiting around to find out. "I'm starving!" I called over my shoulder as I took off in a slow jog toward the house.

As I got close to them, Millie was suffocating the deputy in a bear hug. Good thing for him he had a chest protector on. I thought I could jog right on past them undetected.

No such luck! "Where are you going, Jeremiah? I need to talk to you." She let go of the deputy and turned toward me.

"Hey, I'm starved." I kept heading toward the house. "Besides you need to visit with Deputy Black and meet his friend."

I'm sure I could hear the deputy laughing under his helmet. Maybe he had a sister once, too.

"Jeremiah, you're not getting off that easy!" I tried to ignore the sound of her annoying voice. Paisley hadn't caught up with Millie. She stood in the trail, looking a little tired, but I couldn't risk getting stuck talking to either of the girls. This might have been a trick. I waved and jogged right past her. Right now the cinnamon rolls were calling my name.

Chapter 25

Millie

Millie shoved the last of her breakfast in her mouth and took off in a run once she recognized the #37 quad down by the shop. She hadn't seen their friend in several weeks.

"Deputy Black!" she yelled and waved her arms as she ran. "Deputy Black!"

"Millie, you're going to wake up the entire neighborhood," Paisley said breathlessly as she ran along next to her.

Millie gave her a strange look. "What neighborhood? All three people who live on this dirt road? Deputy Black!"

"He sees you," Paisley said. She slowed to a walk. "You can stop screaming."

"I'm not screaming. I'm talking in a loud voice."

"Oh, brother." Paisley took a deep breath. "Wow, I'm out of shape, if that bit of running left me panting." Millie watched as her friend stopped, and leaned over with her hands propped on her knees.

"Are you okay?"

"Yeah, you go on ahead," Paisley said. "I'll catch up."

Millie resumed running even though she saw the deputy and his friend heading towards them on their quads.

She nearly attacked him with her enthusiasm as she threw her arms around his neck while he still sat on his quad. She heard the other man laughing.

"Millie, it's good to see you," he said.

"Deputy Black, we've missed you!"

He reached over and patted her shoulder. "You and your brother should start calling me Griffin. Deputy Black sounds so formal."

"Griffin?" Millie looked surprised. "Why would we call you something like that?"

He looked over at his friend and they both laughed. "Well, because it's my name. Is that a good enough reason?"

Millie felt herself blushing. "Oh, I'm sorry." An escaping giggle made her apology seem less than sincere. "I never heard a name like that before."

"Well, I'm happy to be the only Griffin you know."

Paisley caught up with them while they talked. "You remember Paisley, don't you?"

"Of course, she's the one who gives me free popsicles in the summer." Griffin smiled at Paisley. "Does your dad know you're cheating the store out of $2 every time I come in?"

Paisley's laugh sounded weak. "It was his idea," she said, her voice just above a whisper.

"Boy you are out of shape," Millie turned to her friend. "We didn't even run that far."

Paisley nodded, then collapsed in the dirt.

Chapter 26

Jeremiah

I couldn't believe we were in the waiting area of the emergency room again. It was only a few months ago we had been here for Minnesota Mike.

Millie sat next to me sniffing while our parents stood across the room talking in low voices to Deputy Black. Millie definitely wasn't her usual self, or she would have been pacing the floor trying to get close enough to hear what they said.

We both stood when the door from the emergency room opened. Paisley's mom approached our parents.

"Oh, thank God!" I heard my mom say. Mrs. Morgan smiled in our direction and motioned for us.

"Paisley would like to see you, Millie." She hugged my sister, who continued to cry.

"It will be okay." Mom patted Millie on the shoulder. She handed her some tissues before Millie followed Mrs. Morgan through the door.

"Oh, Max," Mom said, tears falling down her cheeks. Who could figure adults? Why would she tell Millie everything was okay, but cry as soon as Millie left? Dad was comforting her when Deputy Black put his arm around me and headed toward the door, dragging me along. "I'm thirsty." He smiled at me. "How about you?"

Deputy Black, okay, Griffin. I felt weird calling him by his first name, but he insisted. I have to admit it was easier than using his formal title. Anyway, Griffin prayed for the table full of food and I bit into the cheeseburger in front of me. I guess we were more than thirsty because a big plate of food sat in front of him, too.

As delicious as the cheeseburger tasted, it was hard to enjoy wondering what was going on downstairs in the emergency room. I kept waiting for Deputy, I mean, Griffin, to tell me what was happening with Paisley, but he just munched on his food. Maybe he was waiting for me to ask. I wished Millie was here. She would have asked a dozen questions by now.

He finished the last bite of his sandwich, wadded his napkin and dropped it on the plate, then looked at me. "Are you wondering what's going on with Paisley?"

I nodded. I'm not one to cry about everything, but I wasn't sure I could talk over the lump in my throat. I'd never had a friend get sick enough to go to the hospital before. And the worst part was seeing my mom cry.

"The good news is," Griffin smiled. "She is getting good care right now."

"But what is wrong with her?"

"Well, they will run tests to find out what it is."

"Maybe she got dehydrated," I said, "like when Minnesota Mike passed out and hit his head."

Griffin nodded. "I'm sure they're checking on that." His smile faded.

I could tell he had more to say, but I wasn't sure I wanted to hear whatever it was.

He reached across the table and patted my hand. "Remember what your parents have taught you."

He confused me. What did my parents teachings have to do with Paisley lying in an emergency room bed? "What's that?" I asked.

"Trust God in all things."

I took a deep breath. He definitely knew something.

Chapter 27

Millie

Millie followed Paisley's mom past the rows of curtained off beds. It reminded her of the time Minnesota Mike went to the emergency room. But this was worse. Paisley was just a kid. She shouldn't be having serious health problems. Millie wiped her eyes as a nurse pulled back the curtain near the end of the room.

There was Paisley. Even though she was hooked up to tubes and machines, she still had her usual big smile. Millie struggled to return the smile. "Did you bring your backpack?" Paisley asked.

"My backpack? Why in the world would you ask me that?"

Paisley smiled. "You always have everything in there we need."

"Oh." Millie looked around the little cubicle, listening to the beeps of the machines, watching the numbers bounce and change. Then she turned her attention back to Paisley. "Well, what do you need? I can check when I get home."

"A new heart."

Millie felt her own heart skip a beat. Was Paisley kidding? How could she sit there so calmly, even smiling, and say she needs a new heart? Millie's eyes went wide, and she looked from Paisley to her mother to the nurse. She wasn't often speechless. But right now, she had no idea what to say.

The nurse put her palm on Paisley's forehead, then smoothed her hair back. "Now Paisley, no one said anything about your heart." Millie heard Paisley's mother inhale deeply, but she kept her eyes on her friend.

She finally found her voice.

"What does she mean, Mrs. Morgan?" she whispered.

Paisley's mother didn't respond.

"It's common for patients to be hooked up to a heart monitor in the emergency room." The nurse reached over and took Millie's hand. "But that certainly doesn't mean she needs a new heart."

Paisley looked around the cubicle at the three of them, still smiling. "Well, I thought it was good for a little joke."

Millie grabbed Paisley's foot through the bedsheet. "Don't do that! You scared me!"

When her friend giggled, Millie felt herself relaxing.

"In fact, I think I get to go home soon. Isn't that right, Julia?"

The nurse's smile seemed forced. "Well, that's a possibility."

"I thought the doctor on duty said if she continues to be stable, it would be okay for her to leave later today." Mrs. Morgan looked over at Nurse Julia. "Or did I misunderstand him?"

Julia stared at the laptop on the bedside table, intently studying the information on the screen. Her breathing seemed heavy and Millie wondered if she was having health problems of her own. She finally looked over at Mrs. Morgan. "You didn't misunderstand him, but I'm hoping we can run a few more tests."

"Did the doctor order more tests?" Paisley said. It surprised Millie. Paisley rarely spoke up. Maybe she had been spending too much time with Millie. She stifled a chuckle at the thought.

"No, Paisley," Julia looked at the girl in the bed. "No, he didn't."

Chapter 28

Jeremiah

"On the surface, it appears Paisley is okay. Tests aren't showing any reason for her shortness of breath and fainting," Griffin said.

"I thought you told me her heart was racing after she fell."

"When I checked her pulse after she collapsed it was faster than the normal rate."

"Does that mean there is something wrong with her heart?" I asked.

"The doctor doesn't believe so. He feels it could be exertion from running in cold weather." Griffin looked away. He stopped talking, but it looked like a million thoughts were running through his head.

"Well, what are they doing for her, then? How are they going to figure out why this happened?"

"That's just the thing." Griffin looked back at me. "Sometimes there are no definite answers right away with health issues."

"Well, the tests should tell them something, right?"

"That would be nice if they did, but the tests they've run so far are showing nothing abnormal."

"Is that why my mom was so happy when Mrs. Morgan came out with the news?"

"I imagine so."

"Why did she cry then after Millie went back there?" This was so confusing. It's like he was saying she was all right, but maybe she wasn't all right.

"My guess would be she was holding back the tears while she was with Millie, and then, even though she was relieved, she was still scared."

"Huh?" If you're relieved, how can you be scared? I wished I could just go back to this morning when my biggest worry was my sister griping at me.

Griffin piled all the trash on our tray. "Emotions are complicated," he said. "Let's get back to the waiting room and see what's happening."

I followed him to the trash container and dropped everything in but my drink. That I wanted a refill on. As I watched the bubbling soda fill the cup, I remembered something Griffin said earlier.

"Hey," I said as we headed for the elevator. "Why did you say it would be important to remember to trust God?"

He smiled. "That's always important."

"Yeah, but it was like you knew something. Something bad."

Griffin pushed the call button next to the elevator and didn't look over at me. "Oh, is that what it sounded like?"

Chapter 29

Millie

"Why are you saying it like that?" Millie looked at the nurse. She was thankful her mom wasn't nearby to tell her it wasn't her place to ask questions. She held her breath, waiting to see if Mrs. Morgan would correct her. But the room was silent. Both Paisley and Mrs. Morgan also looked at the nurse. Maybe they wanted to hear the answer too.

"Well," Julia said. "Professionally, I'm not the one to order tests or make recommendations." Her voice trailed off.

"But?" Millie asked, probably more forcefully than she should have. She had to know. She knew something was going on. This nurse knew more than she was saying. And for whatever reason, neither Paisley nor her mom were asking any more questions.

"Millie," Mrs. Morgan said. "Let's wait for the doctor."

"Is Jeremiah here, too?" Paisley asked. She was like that, wanting to keep everyone calm. She probably figured changing the subject would help.

"Yes, he's with my parents and Deputy Black," Millie said, not happy about the new direction the conversation took. She wanted information, and she wanted it now.

Nurse Julia looked up and smiled. "Are you talking about Griffin Black?"

Shocked, Millie said, "Yes, do you know him?"

"I sure do, he's been friends with my husband and I for many years, but I haven't seen him in a long time. He used to work in this area, but once they transferred him we haven't crossed paths much."

"That's how we know him," Millie said. "He's the deputy where we live."

"I'm sure he loves it out there, especially being able to ride his quad whenever he's not on duty." She looked over at Paisley. "How are you feeling right now?"

"I feel good. Do you want to go out and say hi to him?"

"We're fine," Mrs. Morgan said. "We'll be okay waiting here until the doctor gets back to discuss discharge."

Millie saw a flicker of something in Julia's eyes. But the nurse smiled. "I'll check back with you in just a few minutes."

Determined to find out what the nurse really thought about Paisley's situation, Millie said, "I'll go along with her and let Jeremiah know how you're doing, Paisley."

Millie wasted no time digging for information as she walked beside the nurse. "So how did you meet Deputy Black?"

"Oh," Julia said as they headed toward the door to the waiting room. "We had an emergency at our home many years ago and Griffin was the first officer to respond."

"An emergency?" Millie probed.

"Yes, and we've been friends ever since." Julia pushed security buttons to unlock the waiting room door and Millie knew her window of opportunity to get more info was over.

Chapter 30

Jeremiah

"**J**ulia!" Griffin crossed the waiting room floor in three giant steps.

My parents looked as surprised as I did to see Deputy Black and a nurse hugging and laughing together.

"It's been so long since I've seen you," the nurse said.

I looked at Millie for answers. She stepped over near me. "This is Paisley's nurse, and she knows Deputy Black."

"He said to call him Griffin," I reminded her.

"It's hard to get used to that."

"But it's a lot quicker to say."

Griffin released Julia and turned toward our parents. "Max, Norah, this is my good friend Julia."

While the four of them exchanged greetings, Millie grabbed hold of my sleeve and led me across the waiting room. "Something is going on," she whispered.

She probably expected me to scold her for finding a mystery everywhere we went, but this time I agreed. "I'm thinking the same thing."

Her eyes grew big. "Why do you say that? You weren't even in the room."

"I can't figure it out for sure, but Griffin is acting strange about what's wrong with Paisley. What is the diagnosis?"

"I feel the same way about the nurse. She says the tests don't show anything, and Mrs. Morgan is even saying the doctor's talking about Paisley going home soon."

"So why do you think something is wrong?"

"It's the way the nurse acts. She kept staring at Paisley's info on the laptop, and she acted funny when Mrs. Morgan said something about Paisley going home. She wants them to run more tests."

"So are they going to?"

"That's just it, she said the doctor didn't order more tests."

"Well, how is Paisley?"

"She seems okay, smiling as usual. She wants to go home."

"Maybe the nurse is extra cautious." I looked up as Griffin motioned for us to join them.

He moved in between Millie and I and put his arms around our shoulders. "Julia, meet my good friends, Millie and Jeremiah."

"Well, Millie, I've met. In a manner of speaking," Julia said. "She's got a good head on her shoulders."

"Oh dear," our mom said. "Was she being too outspoken?"

I couldn't hold back a chuckle as Millie tensed up. Julia smiled. "No, she's inquisitive. I like that."

The nurse shook my hand. "I'm very glad to meet both of you."

She turned toward the door leading to the emergency room, then looked back. "I need to get back now, but I hope we can all get together sometime. I'm sure my husband would love to see Griffin again."

Griffin looked serious. "Let's do that and include Paisley's family. Then you can talk to them when you're off duty."

Julia dipped her head, looking at the floor, then reached into her pocket. When she made eye contact with him again, she wiped her eyes with a tissue. "No, Griffin. I can't. Will you talk to them, please?"

Chapter 31

Millie

Millie made it through the door before it shut by nearly walking on the heels of Julia. When the nurse turned, she was still wiping her eyes. "I'm sorry," Millie said. "I know I didn't ask, but I wanted to see Paisley once more before we leave."

Julia sniffed and tucked her tissue back in her pocket. "It's fine, Millie. I'm sure Paisley would like that."

"Millie!" Paisley said. "I'm glad you came back. Mom said you were leaving so my dad can come and get us."

"Oh, no! That must mean we will be taking care of the little boys."

The girls laughed together.

"Millie," Mrs. Morgan said, "you'll only have Caleb. Donovan is coming with Paisley's dad to pick us up. But you know the boys aren't that difficult."

"I know. But sometimes it's just fun to complain. How was their sleepover last night?"

"Well, I'm afraid there wasn't much sleeping until late in the night, which is why they weren't awake when we got the call this morning."

"That was nice of Mr. Morgan to keep Caleb so we could come to the hospital."

"He knew how much it would help Paisley having you and Jeremiah here." Mrs. Morgan smiled. "I'm so glad you two long lost best friends finally met each other."

Millie and Paisley laughed at her description. It was definitely the perfect way to explain their fast friendship.

"So, Millie, can you do something for me?" Paisley said.

"Sure, anything."

"Okay, go home and figure out what the source of the ghost lights are that people have been talking about." Paisley smiled at her friend.

"Are you kidding me? How can I even think about some silly ghost light legend when my best friend is lying in a hospital bed?"

"That's why I asked you to do it. I don't want you worrying about me. You might as well be finding things out to tell me until I can look for clues with you."

"I don't know how soon that will be, Paisley," Mrs. Morgan said.

"Mom, you said yourself the doctor found nothing wrong. You're not going to turn me into an invalid, are you?"

"Your mom is wise to want to keep a close eye on you for a few days," Julia joined in their conversation when she stepped back into the cubicle.

What does she know? Millie wondered. She was dying to tell Paisley what she heard Julia say to Griffin in the waiting room, but she didn't want to talk in front of Mrs. Morgan.

Paisley's mom lost her smile at Julia's words. Maybe she too sensed that Julia knew more than she was saying.

"So it will be important to keep her close by me for a few days?"

Julia blinked several times as if to hold back tears. "Yes," she said. "I think so."

Chapter 32

Jeremiah

The roar of Minnesota Mike's buggy broke the silence before I could see him. A trail of dust gave away his location out on the dirt road leading up to our property. I knew Caleb was loving his first ride. He'd been begging for one ever since Mike brought the buggy over to show the family. What a weekend this was for him. Last night his first sleepover with Paisley's little brother, Donovan, and now his first ride in a dune buggy.

I'll bet Mike would slide sideways into the gate, since he liked to see how long he could wait to hit the brakes before making the turn. I thought about walking down to watch, but knew I'd never get there in time.

I could hear the giggles over the sound of the engine as the buggy cruised up and skidded to a stop in front of the porch.

"Jeremiah!" Caleb shouted through his helmet. "That was so much fun!"

I'd never seen the boy so excited. What a welcome relief to see so much happiness. It was a big change from our day so far. Hopefully Paisley would be coming home soon, but for now, I just wanted to put that out of my mind and soak up the excitement of this little boy.

"You weren't scared at all?" I helped him out and unfastened his helmet.

"No sirree." Minnesota answered before Caleb could. Mike was already out of the driver's seat and coming around to the porch. "I'm telling you, he wanted me to go faster and faster." He reached over and tousled Caleb's already messed up hair. "I don't think there's a fearful bone in this feller's body."

Caleb reached up and grabbed hold of Minnesota Mike's hand, pulling it down and holding on to him. "I trust you," he looked up into Mike's eyes. "I know you wouldn't hurt me."

Minnesota knelt and hugged him. He looked about as happy as a man could be.

"Caleb! You're home." Mom stepped out the door and hurried down the porch steps to where Mike and Caleb were embracing. "Look at you, you're glowing!"

She looked over at Mike once he stood back up. "Thank you so much for bringing him home. This is the happiest I've ever seen him."

"Well, it was a little selfish of me," Mike said. Then lowered his voice as Mom hugged the boy. "I was hoping to get some word on Paisley."

"I'm starving, Miss Norah! Are there any cookies?"

Mom took hold of Caleb's hand. "I believe there are three cookies left with your name on them. Let's go find them." As they stepped up to the front door, Mom turned to me. "Jeremiah, can you tell Mike what we know?"

"Sure, Mom."

The excitement had gone from Minnesota's face, replaced by what was probably worry about Paisley. He must have been hiding it from Caleb.

"Well, there are two different versions about Paisley's condition," I said. "Which one do you want, the official hospital position, or mine and Millie's?"

"I want them both," Minnesota said. He motioned me toward the driver's side of his buggy, then stood with his back to the house. I followed.

"Before you fill me in," he said. "There's something I need to tell you."

Chapter 33

Millie

"Mike!" Millie burst out the front door and down the porch steps into Mike's waiting arms. His long beard tickled her cheek as she hugged him. He squeezed her tight, then held her at arm's length. She swiped at tears. "We don't know what's wrong with Paisley."

"Jeremiah and I was jist talking about that special little lady." Millie saw a look pass between Mike and Jeremiah.

She turned to her brother. "What are you talking about that I don't know?"

"Millie, you know good and well I don't know any more than you know."

She looked back to Minnesota Mike. "I saw the look you gave each other. You were talking about something else."

Jeremiah took a deep breath. "Honestly, we barely got started when you burst on the scene like a whirlwind."

"Well, now, little lady, you are just enough of a little detective that you pick up on ever last little thing," Minnesota said.

"You lost me there, Mike," Jeremiah said. Millie saw Jeremiah stare at the older man and realized he must have been telling her the truth.

"Well, we was gittin' ready to talk about Paisley, but then I said first there was something I needed to talk about."

"Oh, that's right," Jeremiah said.

"And you don't want to talk about it in front of me, so that's why you were staring at each other like that," Millie accused.

"I'm still lost, Mil, because I wasn't staring at anyone. Haven't you heard about innocent until proven guilty?"

"Well, little lady, yer right, I did take a quick like glance over to your brother, because I wasn't sure I was ready to tell the both of you."

"So, I was right," Millie turned to her brother. "I told you. It's something you're hiding from me."

Jeremiah threw up his arms. "Okay, Millie, you're right. I'm hiding something from you. In fact, I'm hiding it so well, I'm hiding it from myself too, because I've said ten times I don't know what's going on."

"Hey, hey, what's all this yelling out here?"

Millie jumped at the sound of her dad's voice.

"I was trying to talk on the phone and couldn't hear over all the yelling."

Before either of them could respond to the reprimand, Mike intervened. "I'm sorry, Max, I think I've got them all worked up."

Their dad stepped down off the porch and shook Mike's hand. "Well, it's easy to do right now," he said.   "We're all a little on edge with Paisley in the hospital."

"I feel real bad about that," Mike said.

"You were a big help to bring Caleb home, he sure was excited about getting to ride in your buggy."

Mike's smile vanished. "Well, that's what I was getting ready to talk to the kids about."

"What about Caleb?" Millie interrupted. "Is he all right?"

"Now, now, there's nothing wrong with that little tyke."

"Well, what is it then?" Millie pushed and heard her brother growl under his breath.

"Millie, give the man a chance to talk."

Someday, she would do that, she vowed. She would wait for people to get around to whatever it is they were trying to say, instead of butting in with so many questions. But today wasn't that day. "What's wrong with Caleb?" She pushed again when he still hadn't responded.

Mike stared off into the distant hills to the south of them. Then he looked over at their dad.

"It's what he said just as we were turning into your gate, that's got me concerned."

Chapter 34

Jeremiah

I stepped closer to my sister. I wanted to clamp my hand over her mouth but I just whispered, "Wait for him to finish!"

Millie glared at me, but I could tell she knew I was right. She surprised me when she did what I said. She didn't take kindly to orders. Especially from me.

"Go on," Dad said. "What did Caleb say?"

"Well, he pointed over to them hills in the distance." Mike motioned toward the hills. "There was a glare coming from there. Kinda like the sun hitting some shiny object. He got real excited, in fact I slowed down to a full stop 'cause I never seen the little feller so excited about something."

"So did he say something while he was pointing?" Millie asked. I thought about jabbing her in the side, but figured that would slow the story down. She would never change.

"Yep, he shore did. He said 'it's the light, let's go find Sissy.'" Mike looked at Dad, then over at me and my sister and shook his head. "I ain't never heard him talk like that and I didn't even know he had a sissy."

"Did you ask him what he meant?" Dad said.

"Well, I tried," Minnesota said. "I said something like, 'Where is Sissy?' and he jist kept saying 'at the light, Sissy's at the light.'"

"Then what happened?" It was my turn to throw out a question.

"I didn't rightly know what to say to the little feller so's I jist said, I gotta git you back to Max and Norah, they miss you something awful. We'll check on Sissy some other time."

"Was he okay with your response?" Dad asked.

"He was more than okay." Minnesota Mike smiled. "His eyes lit up, and I knowed he was smiling under his helmet. He said, 'Let's go! Miss Norah's probably got cookies!' And no more talk about his sissy."

"Dad," I said, "did you ever ask Deputy Black if Caleb has a sister?"

Dad nodded his head. "Yes, as a matter of fact, we discussed Caleb's mom today."

Chapter 35

Millie

"What did he say, Dad?" Millie knew her question would annoy her brother, but her dad was taking too long to answer.

"He said he didn't know of a sister."

"Well, is he going to look into it? I mean, can't he get in touch with the mom and ask her?" She avoided looking at her brother as she fired off the questions.

"Yes. He said he'd try to visit her at the jail in the next few days."

"Good, then we can figure out what that kid's talking about," Millie said.

"Well, now, little missy, I wouldn't count on that too much." They all looked over at Mike's unexpected words.

"Why do you say that?" Jeremiah said.

"Well, could jist be my suspicious mind." He looked at their dad, smoothing his beard down as he turned his head in the other direction. Millie noticed he always fiddled with his beard like that when he had something on his mind.

"Well, you must have a reason," Millie prodded.

"Sometimes I jist git a feeling about people. And she don't seem too trustworthy to me."

The front door banged open and Caleb barreled down the steps, "Mike! You're still here!" Caleb threw his arms around the older man. "Can you take me out for another ride? Can you?"

Even Dad looked like he'd have a hard time saying no to the little guy. Mike was looking in Dad's direction, probably trying to figure out how to answer.

"Tell you what, Caleb. If Mike has time, he can take all three of you out for a short buggy ride."

"Now doncha know, that's jist what I was thinkin' on doin'." Mike nodded.

Any other time Millie would have been excited, especially since she was the only one who hadn't been in Mike's buggy yet. But now she just wanted to wait for Paisley to come home from the hospital.

"You kids go git your helmets on," Mike said, "and I got the best idea yet. We'll head back over to the lodge and see if'n Paisley has come home yet."

With that destination, Millie was fully on board with this change of plans. She and Jeremiah turned toward the house as their mom stepped through the open door.

"Max." She motioned for their dad. "A phone call for you."

Her dad continued to fasten Caleb's helmet. "I'll be right there," he called over his shoulder.

"It's urgent," Mom said. "Griffin says he needs to talk with you right away."

Chapter 36

Jeremiah

"So, Caleb, how's about we go hunt for yer sissy before we check on Paisley?" Minnesota Mike's voice was low, but I caught wind of what he was saying. I looked up to see Millie heading into the house.

"Hey, Millie, grab my helmet too." She'd kill me if she knew I was making her get my helmet so I could stay and hear this conversation. But I'd make it to up to her later. Or maybe I already made it up to her when I kept her from getting handcuffed the other day. I stepped over near the buggy. Mike was fastening the belts on Caleb's seat.

"Is the light still shining over there?" Caleb said. "Cause if the light ain't shining, she won't be there no more."

Minnesota looked up at me, and I shrugged. Who knows what this kid is talking about? But it was the same way the other night. When he saw bright lights shining in our direction, he started talking about a sister.

"No, sonny boy, there ain't no more light shining."

"Then we missed her again." Caleb grabbed hold of the straps on his safety harness with both hands. "I'm all ready to go!"

"Who did we miss?" Millie appeared next to me and shoved my helmet into my hands. I wasn't sure what to say. I didn't know if I should talk about it in front of Caleb.

"Jeremiah!" She jabbed my arm with her pointy index finger, then pulled her helmet down over her head. "What did I miss when I was waiting on you hand and foot?"

"What do you mean, waiting on me? You had to get your own helmet, anyway."

"Yeah, but you didn't tell me there was something interesting going on out here."

"You two stop yer jawing and git those helmets on so we can take off, afore your pops forgits he told us we could all go out." Minnesota Mike climbed into the driver's seat.

"Look, I'll tell you about it later." I could tell my sister was not happy about having to wait. "I promise," I said, fastening my helmet.

The buggy roared to life as Millie climbed in the seat behind Mike. I stepped up on the outside rail to get in behind Caleb, just as I heard Dad call out my name.

Millie must have heard him too. She tapped Mike on the shoulder, and he shut the engine off. Dad stepped around to the driver's side.

"That was Griffin." Dad looked serious. Maybe he learned something about this mysterious sister Caleb keeps talking about.

"He wants to talk to all of us later today."

"All of us?" Minnesota said. "That include me?"

"Yes," Dad said. "Yes, it does. And it includes Paisley's family too."

Well, it must have nothing to do with Caleb, I figured. "What's this about, Dad?"

Millie looked at me, probably startled that I asked a question before she did.

"He didn't say, just said it was important he talks with all of us as soon as possible. He already lined it up with Mr. Morgan. We'll meet at their house"

"Does that mean we don't get to go for our ride?" Caleb tugged Mike's arm. "Ask Mr. Max if we can still go for a ride."

Dad smiled at Caleb. "Tell you what, why don't you all go for your ride anyway and Mom and I will meet you over at Paisley's house in about an hour."

"Yippee!" Caleb howled, then squirmed in his seat trying to turn around. "Did you hear that, Millie?"

"I sure did." Millie reached up and patted Caleb's shoulder. "He said we get to go."

"No, not that," Caleb said. "He called Miss Norah my mom!"

Chapter 37

Millie

Caleb's words startled Millie. She thought he missed his own mother. Before she could dwell on the reasons for him being so excited about her mom, a shriek flew out of her mouth as Minnesota Mike floored the buggy. They took off so fast her head bounced back against the high back seat.

Millie hung on to the safety harnesses cinched over her chest and looked over at her brother as they flew along the bumpy road heading to the back of their property. Jeremiah held both thumbs up as he whooped and hollered.

She peered ahead to see if Mike would skirt around the drop-off she knew was ahead, but he kept the pedal to the floor and the steering wheel straight. She opened her eyes wider and looked over at her brother to see if it worried him, but she saw no such thing. His head jostled around and muffled laughter escaped from his helmet. Before she could worry much more, she felt the car sailing as they launched off the embankment.

Caleb's happy screeching from the seat in front reassured her this ride wasn't scaring him, not one bit. She tensed, waiting for the landing, but to her surprise it was softer than she expected. Must be that suspension she heard her dad raving about with Mike when he was checking out the buggy. She remembered all she cared about was the color.

Once off their property Mike headed the buggy in the direction of the old abandoned store. Millie was glad for the chance to pass by. She hoped she'd get another glimpse of the phony cop. But instead of following the road all the way to the store, Mike cut off in a sandy wash, speeding up and sliding the buggy right and left all to the thrill of Caleb who howled with excitement at every slide and bump.

Too soon their adventure ended, and they were cruising into the driveway of the Ridge Riders Lodge. Millie wanted to undo her helmet when she saw Paisley climbing out of the family car parked in front of the store entrance, but her dad had drilled safety into her. She waited until the buggy came to a full stop a few parking spaces away from her friend.

In record time she got her safety harnesses undone and leaped out, running over to embrace Paisley, helmet and all.

"Millie, it's so good to be home." Paisley's voice sounded muffled as she hugged Millie.

"Here, let me take this off, so I don't knock you out and send you back to the hospital." Both girls laughed as Millie stepped away. She slipped off her helmet, then smoothed her hair, eyes glued on her friend. It was so good to see her out of the hospital bed and back home.

"Hey, isn't that your parents pulling in over there?"

"Yeah," Millie said. "Didn't you know?"

Paisley's head jerked back toward Millie. "Know what?" Then she clapped her hands. "Is it a welcome home party for me?"

Millie's stomach flip-flopped when she realized her friend didn't know they were coming over to hear something Deputy Black wanted to tell them. She wasn't sure why, but she felt scared. And since Paisley hadn't been told anything, she felt especially scared for Paisley.

"Look!" Paisley's excitement grew. "It's Deputy Black! I bet this is a party! My mom couldn't wait for them to let me out of the hospital."

Millie forced a smile. The girls watched as Paisley's mom met Millie's parents at their car. "Maybe we should go see if they decorated." Millie said when she saw that Deputy Black wasn't alone.

It seemed best to distract Paisley. Even though Millie didn't know any details, she was sure it wasn't a party.

Especially when she saw Julia, the nurse, in the passenger seat of Deputy Black's car.

Chapter 38

Jeremiah

I didn't envy my sister right now. I watched as she tried to figure out how to respond to Paisley who had the mistaken idea we were all here for a welcome home party. The look on my sister's face when she saw Deputy Black drive into the parking lot with the nurse in the passenger seat matched how I felt.

Something wasn't right. I knew Griffin was acting strange in the hospital cafeteria.

"Dad!" I did one of those whisper-yells trying to catch his attention and crossed the parking lot in a couple big steps to catch him before he went in. "What's going on? Why are we all here?"

Dad's arm felt good around my shoulders as he led me away from the others. "I'm not sure, Jeremiah. But we'll find out soon."

"Why is the nurse here?"

"That's a surprise to me too. Griffin didn't say anything about bringing her. He just said he had some information about Paisley's health and her parents wanted our family to be here with them to hear it."

"Okay, that's weird." I shook my head. "We were all just at the hospital, why would a cop know more about Paisley's health than the doctor in the emergency room?" I inhaled deeply and watched as Griffin and Julia got out of his car.

Dad nodded. "You got me. I'm as confused as you are." He pointed back toward the car. "Let's go help Mom."

She had the back doors to the SUV open and looked like she was pulling out something bulky. Just as I was about to ask what she was doing, giant colorful balloons popped out of the back, bouncing around on ribbons my mom held.

"Those are beautiful, Norah!" Dad said. "I can't believe you came up with something like that on the spur of the moment."

"I told you that helium tank would come in handy one day," Mom said. "Jeremiah, will you get those presents? Max, can you carry the cake?"

"Mom, you're amazing." I reached in and grabbed a gift bag and two wrapped parcels. "Did you know Paisley thinks we're all over here for a welcome home party?"

Mom wiped tears from her eyes with her free hand. "I didn't, but God did." She reached out and hugged me. "I've been accumulating party things and gifts recently and I didn't even know why. But today God showed me what they were for."

Dad shoved the back doors shut with his elbow as he balanced the double layer chocolate cake with both hands.

"I didn't have time to write anything on the cake," Mom said.

"I don't think Paisley will mind," I said. "I sure don't. I can't wait to get a piece."

"Well, let's go get this party started," Dad said.

"And whatever happens at this party, God's got it all under control." Mom sounded confident, but was still wiping tears as she turned to follow Dad, the helium balloons bouncing all around her head.

Chapter 39

Millie

As much fun as the impromptu party was, Millie figured everyone, even Paisley, was relieved that the time had arrived to find out what this get-together was all about.

The room grew quiet. Even Caleb and Donovan stopped talking where they sat near the stairwell playing with cars. Or at least they had cars in their hands. Mostly they were watching the adults. Probably wondering, just like everyone else, what was happening.

Griffin scooted to the edge of his chair, his elbows propped on his knees as he leaned forward and surveyed the room. Julia sat in a folding chair a few feet from him, close to Paisley. She smiled in her direction and reached over and patted Paisley's shoulder. Millie was across the room next to her mother.

After Griffin looked around at each one of them, he took a deep breath. "I know this seems strange to all of you." Millie noticed that Julia dipped her head down and fidgeted with a tissue in her lap.

"Julia has some information that might be helpful. It may or may not apply to what happened with Paisley today. If it doesn't, that's wonderful, but if it does, it's important that we share this."

"Thank you," Paisley's dad said. "We appreciate it and we'd like to hear what you have to say."

"Julia is the one with the knowledge about the subject, but it's difficult for her." Griffin paused to look at Julia, but her head was still down. "We decided I would share the information and then if you have questions, she'll answer them."

"How come she didn't talk to us about this at the hospital?" Millie said.

"Millicent!" Both parents scolded her at once. She didn't look, but no doubt her brother was giving her a dirty look too. Someday maybe she'd learn to stop blurting out whatever she wanted.

"We will explain all of that, Millie." Julia's voice was kind. At least she didn't seem to mind Millie's curiosity getting the better of her all the time.

"I met Julia and her husband on a 9-1-1 call many years ago." Griffin took another deep breath and looked at Julia again. Her head was up. She nodded for him to continue.

"They found their infant son unresponsive in his crib. We could not resuscitate him."

Gasps were heard around the room.

"Why did that happen?" Paisley's soft voice asked what they all wondered.

"At the time it was referred to as Crib Death." Millie could see her parents nodding their heads like they were familiar with the term. "It was accepted as an unexplained death that sometimes occurs with infants."

"Do you know something now about what caused the baby's death?" Paisley's mom said.

"Yes." Griffin looked at Julia again before he continued. "About ten years ago, there was another sudden death in their family." His words hung heavy in the air.

Even Millie couldn't bring herself to ask who it was.

Chapter 40

Jeremiah

"Hey now, what do you all say, if I take these young'uns out for a little walk right about now?" Minnesota Mike's voice was a welcome interruption. I mean, where was Griffin heading with this story? Was he saying that Paisley might die? How did we go from worrying about ghost lights, fake cops and handcuffs to learning that one of our friends might die? This didn't seem real. I couldn't even bring myself to look at my sister.

Mike was already moving across the room toward Caleb and Donovan. The little boys gathered up their cars. They seemed more than willing to go with him. Hopefully, they didn't understand what Griffin was talking about.

"Thank you, Mike," Mrs. Morgan said. "I think that's a good idea."

Caleb stopped by my mom on his way out and gave her a hug. "I love you, Miss Norah," he whispered. I think the little squirt could tell she needed some comfort.

Mr. Morgan left the room then, too. He returned carrying a tray with a pitcher of ice water and empty glasses. The welcome break gave us all a chance to stand and stretch. We hadn't been sitting very long, but this conversation made it seem like we'd been talking for hours.

Once everyone sat back down, Julia surprised us by picking up where Griffin left off.

"It was my daughter." She smiled at Paisley. "She was your age."

Mrs. Morgan moved over to Julia and embraced her. "I'm so sorry." Paisley's mom looked like she was struggling not to break down.

"To make a long story short, we discovered that my husband and I carry a gene that causes problems with electrical impulses in the heart. We passed it on to our daughter, and we suspect to our son. It doesn't happen in every family that carries it, but there is the risk of sudden cardiac arrest if it isn't treated."

Mrs. Morgan covered her face with her hands and breathed a loud whisper, "Thank you, Jesus." Then she looked at Julia. "So this is treatable?"

"Yes," Julia nodded. "And if that is what caused our son to die and it had been discovered, we could have had our daughter tested and treated."

"Were there any symptoms?" my mom asked.

"Not that we recognized," Julia said. "She fainted a few times, and we took her in for testing, but no one connected it."

"Which explains why you want us to know about this?" Mr. Morgan said.

"Yes," Julia said. "I'm not allowed to make medical recommendations, which is why I couldn't discuss this at the hospital, but as one mother to another, I urge you to get her checked out by a pediatric cardiologist."

The door banged open suddenly. "My sissy! Can I go see my sissy, Miss Norah?" Caleb flew into the room like a whirlwind. "She's shining the light for me."

I don't know if it was right to feel like this, but it relieved me in a big way to have Caleb interrupt us. I was ready to get out of this room. Sorry Paisley.

"Come on, Caleb!" I grabbed the young boy by the hand and led him back out the door. "Let's go see where your sissy is."

Chapter 41

Millie

Millie watched longingly as her brother escaped the depressing conversation. She looked over at Paisley and saw that same desire in her eyes.

"So, can I say something?" Millie said to no one in particular.

"Well, that's a refreshing change, Millie." Her dad laughed.

"What do you mean?"

"You rarely ask, you just jump right in with both feet."

"Oh." Even though her dad was laughing, she wasn't sure it was okay to laugh yet.

"Yes, Millie, what did you want to ask?" Julia said.

"Well, it isn't really a question. And it's kind of off topic."

"That's okay," Mr. Morgan said. "I think we can all use a breather here."

"I didn't know nurses wore cowboy boots." The suede boots with the little bit of fringe had fascinated Millie the entire time she'd been listening to Griffin and Julia talk. Maybe it was her mind distracting her from the scary conversation.

Julia reached down and touched her boots while relieved laughter spread around the room. "Well, sure, when I'm not on duty, it's what I live in."

"Wow."

"Nurses are people too, Millie." Paisley smiled at her friend, then looked over at Julia. "I wouldn't mind having a pair just like that."

"Say, while we're moving on to new topics," Griffin said. "I'm sure Julia wouldn't mind if someone offered her a dune buggy ride while we're here visiting."

Millie saw Julia's face light up. "I would love that! I haven't been out cruising around in the desert since I was a kid."

"Really, Julia?" Millie said. "Did your parents have a buggy?"

"Millie!" Paisley laughed.

"I know, I know, Paisley," Millie said. "Nurses are people too."

"They sure did, Millie. I have so many wonderful memories. We used to stay at an RV park out here somewhere. I don't think I could even find it now."

"What was it called?" Griffin seemed surprised to learn about this side of Julia.

"The campground, I'm not sure, but it was right near a store called Ye Olde Dry Brook Trading Post. I loved that store!"

"That's the store!" Millie jumped up. "Jeremiah and I were there recently." Her eyes grew large as she looked over at Paisley. She had almost given away the trouble she'd gotten into there. She needed to get back there to figure out what was going on. How was Paisley going to help her with that now?

"So, it's still there?" Julia clapped her hands together and turned toward Griffin. "Can you take me by there on our way home? I wonder what time it closes."

"Well, the building is there," Millie said, "but the store is closed down."

Julia looked disappointed. "They had so many fun things to look at in that store. I'd save my money in between desert trips just to buy trinkets from the trading post whenever we came to the desert."

No one had noticed Minnesota Mike step back into the room, but he must have been there long enough to hear part of the conversation.

"Well, now that store's for sale, doncha know?"

"Oh, so maybe it will re-open soon?" Julia looked hopeful.

"It's been for sale for quite a few years," Mr. Morgan said.

Minnesota Mike pointed in Julia's direction. "But doncha know, if'n the right person were to come along and buy it, then it could open back up again."

Chapter 42

Jeremiah

I stirred the fire with my roasting stick, watching the charred remains of the marshmallow turn to black crust. After the last of the marshmallow dropped into the fire, I dropped the stick onto the edge of the firepit and leaned back in my chair. It felt so good to sit out here, staring up into the stars. What a day this had been.

"Hey, maybe we'll see the ghost lights while we're out here tonight."

I looked over at my sister when she spoke. She was doing the same thing I was, gazing up into the dark sky.

"You don't give up on this mystery solving business, do you?" I said.

"Why should I?"

"Well, look what's going on with Paisley."

"Even Paisley told me to watch for them."

"Are you kidding me? Isn't she scared?" I hadn't talked with Paisley after we heard Julia's story today, but when Minnesota Mike and Griffin took Julia out in the buggy, I saw Millie and Paisley sitting on one of the outdoor benches talking.

"I'm not kidding you and no she isn't scared."

"Would you be if you heard you might have something you could die from?" I sat up in my chair and stared at my sister. I'm not sure I understood girls.

"Well, I don't think we can really know if something would scare us until we're experiencing it for ourselves," Millie said.

That made a lot more sense than I would have expected my sister to make. It's easy to say how we think we would handle something, but she's right, we don't really know.

Millie continued. "Paisley said they don't even know if she has the same thing Julia's kids had and even if she does, Julia said there is treatment. She said maybe it's a good thing she fainted today."

"Wow." I nodded my head. "I'd like to think I could have that much faith not to worry about health problems."

"Why focus on health problems when there are more fun things to focus on?" Millie said.

"Like ghost lights, no doubt?"

"Yes, and speaking of lights, look over in that direction." Millie stood and stared toward the dirt road.

"I don't see any light," I said.

"No, but listen. It's like the other night. We hear the loud rumble of a truck, but don't see any truck lights."

"Well, what's that have to do with ghost lights?"

"Maybe nothing, but it sure is strange. We've heard that three times now."

"That reminds me," I said. "I never told you what Minnesota Mike and I saw the other day when we drove by the trading post."

Millie jerked her head in my direction. "What?" she demanded. "And why didn't you tell me?"

"Because you would have ridden right back to the store and got arrested for real this time."

"You can't get arrested by a fake cop."

"Really? Well, he was doing a good job of starting to arrest you the other day."

My sister shivered. "Don't remind me."

The front door opened, and Dad wandered over to the firepit. "It's been quite a day, hasn't it?" he settled in a chair. I saw Millie slump down in her chair. I knew what she was thinking. She wouldn't get to hear about the trading post now that Dad was out here.

"Yeah, sure has," I said. "That's the last thing I ever expected to hear Griffin telling us."

"Paisley's parents are handling it well," Dad said. "They see it as a blessing to have the chance to get her tested. They're grateful the incident today wasn't more serious."

"Paisley doesn't want to dwell on it," Millie said. "At least, that's what she told me."

"Yeah, she just wants to get back to solving mysteries with Millie." I said.

Dad smiled. "Well, that's probably a good way to deal with it. Wait for the tests and in the meantime focus on other things."

"That reminds me of something I've been wanting to ask you." Millie turned toward Dad. "Paisley and I read in a book that the old store closed down because one of the partners died. Was he murdered?"

I couldn't hold my laughter back. "You and your mysterious stories." Millie gave me a dirty look and turned back to Dad.

"Sorry to burst your bubble, Millie." Dad smiled. "It wasn't murder, but it was tragic. He fell from the roof while doing some repairs. His partner was grief-stricken at losing his best friend and just locked up the store one day and left."

"Oh, that's pretty sad. Well, at least I can tell Paisley I solved one mystery."

Dad reached into the marshmallow bag and poked one onto the end of the stick I left on the fire ring. "Speaking of mysteries," he said, as he held it over the flames. "What did you find out from Caleb about his sissy shining a light?"

Chapter 43

Millie

Millie sat straight up in her chair at this new topic. She didn't mind waiting to hear what happened at the trading post if she could finally learn something about Caleb's mysterious sister.

Jeremiah leaned forward in his chair. "Well, when I got outside, Caleb was staring toward the mountains south of us. You can see them better from Paisley's house."

"Did you see a light shining?" Millie said, and then cringed, expecting Jeremiah to get annoyed.

"No, so I asked him where the light was. He shrugged his shoulders and said it went away again."

"What about Mike?" their dad asked. "Did he say if he saw the light?"

"I didn't ask him." Jeremiah said. "But I asked Caleb why he thinks that is his sister."

"And?" Millie said. He didn't have to drag this out and keep them in suspense. She wished she had been out there with Caleb, but she knew she did the right thing by staying inside with Paisley.

"He said he hasn't seen her in a long time. That she went away when he was a little boy. Before she left, she told him she would shine a light for him."

"Well, how does he know it's that light? Did he say where she went?"

"Millie, I didn't ask him a thousand questions like you would have."

"That's probably best," their dad said. "It may be his imagination. We don't even know if he has a sister."

"Has he mentioned it since we've been home?"

"I haven't heard him say anything, Millie." Their dad popped his roasted marshmallow into his mouth, stood and stretched his arms over his head. "This has been a long day, we should all get some sleep, so we're refreshed and ready for church in the morning."

Millie looked at her brother, but neither of them moved as their dad turned toward the house. "Can we have 30 more minutes, Dad?"

"Make it 15, Millie," Dad said, "I'll have Mom let you know when it's time."

Millie waited until the front door latched shut. "Okay, now tell me what you saw at the store and it better be more useful than the lame info you had about Caleb's sister."

"Well, it's kind of hard to have news about someone who probably doesn't even exist," her brother said. "And don't be so bossy about it."

Millie watched as he stood and stared into the darkness. She was tempted to push him for info, but their dad was right. This had been a long day, and her brother was edgy. She'd get no information from him if she made him mad. Being patient seemed wiser than risking him turning and heading into the house.

"It's nothing big," he said. "The other day when Mike and I were picking up his buggy, he drove me down Monument Road."

"Why?"

"Millie!"

"Okay, okay, no more questions. I'll be satisfied with whatever you tell me."

"He wanted to check out the area where he's heard people talking about the ghost lights. But when we went past the old store, I saw that guy, you know, the fake cop. He stared right at me, even pointed his finger at me threateningly."

"He recognized you?"

"Yeah, but that's not all," Jeremiah said. "There were other people there, probably two or three others and several kids. They were heading into the store. Even Mike seemed to think it was strange."

"Do you think they want to buy it? Maybe a realtor was showing it to them?"

"That's what I said to Mike, but he said no one should be there. He seemed to know something about the place."

"Mike seems to know stuff about a lot of things."

"Yeah, like how did he know about the man trying to handcuff you?"

"I thought you told him. I've been mad at you ever since."

"Then why have you been talking to me?" Jeremiah snickered.

"Well, in all the confusion with Paisley I forgot I was mad," Millie said. "But now I remember."

"No, I didn't tell him. Well, part of it slipped out, and I tried to stop it, but then he seemed to know anyway, maybe not the whole story, but some of it."

"I guess if I want to find out what he knows about the ghost lights, I'll have to give in and tell him the story."

"Tell who what story?" their mom said.

"Mom!" Millie jumped, almost tipping her chair over. "You scared me, I didn't hear you come out."

"I've been calling you two, but you're so engrossed in your conversation, you didn't hear me."

Millie looked at her brother and he shrugged. "I never heard anything."

"So what story are you two wanting to hear?" Their mom looked back and forth between them.

Chapter 44

Jeremiah

"We really shouldn't be doing this." I don't even know why I bothered to say anything. Millie's mind was made up, so what I said made no difference. I backed out of the overgrown mesquite trees where we stashed our motorcycles and helmets and squinted at the sun's rays peeking over the hillside.

"You didn't have to come with me," Millie whispered. I don't know why. There was no one anywhere around.

"Well, I sure wasn't going to let you go alone."

"Why didn't you just tell me not to go?" She couldn't even get that sentence out without laughing.

"No kidding?" I said. "Look, let's just get this over with. You and I both know telling you not to go would have done no good."

"Come on, Jeremiah." She pulled the breakfast sandwiches out of her backpack. "You could at least enjoy the adventure. Let's eat first."

Millie peeled open the sandwich Mom wrapped for her and was just about ready to take a bite. "Wait!" I yelled. The look on her face made the whole risky trip worth it.

"You scared me to death!"

Well, get used to it," I choked out the words around my laughter. "Since you're leading us into the path of disaster, get used to being scared to death. Anyway, we might as well pray first, for our breakfast and for safety."

"Oh, you're right." She closed the wrapper on her sandwich and her eyes.

"Oh God, save me from this sister you gave me," I said, thankful we could joke around even with God. I was tempted to sneak a look at Millie's face, but kept my eyes shut tight. "And thank you for the food You provided and please watch over us on our adventure this morning and give us wisdom to make right choices. Especially my sister. Amen. Ouch!" I barely finished the prayer before Millie slugged me in the arm.

"Give me my sandwich," I rubbed my arm and pulled bottles of orange juice from my fanny pack. "Mom said be back by 8:30, for chores and school."

"Don't remind me." Millie's words were muffled as she chewed a way too large bite of her egg and cheese sandwich. "Don't spoil my morning."

"Well, we've got a little over two hours. I figure it will take us 20 minutes to walk to the store from here, especially in these heavy boots."

"Twenty there, twenty back, and twenty minutes to ride home. That gives us an hour to investigate," Millie said.

"Less than an hour since we're using time enjoying a leisurely breakfast." I downed the rest of my orange juice. "At your suggestion I might add."

She didn't even take the bait and argue back. Instead, she jumped up and wiggled her backpack into place. "Come on," she motioned. "Let's hit the road."

I took one last look at our bikes, as we stepped away from the trees, to make sure they couldn't be seen from the road. Confident they were hidden I turned toward my sister and pointed boldly toward our destination.

"Onward!"

Despite the soft sand we trudged through, we made better time than expected as we approached the back side of the abandoned store property.

"Let's watch where we're stepping," Millie said, "so we don't cover up tracks that might tell us something."

"Look, I already see tracks."

Millie stared in the direction I pointed, then looked back at me, eyes wide. "Those are semi-truck tracks."

"Exactly," I said. "And I'm wondering if it's the truck we've been hearing at night, the one without lights."

"Look!" Millie whispered. "There's two people. I wonder if it's the same ones you saw the other day."

I edged a little closer, hugging the brush-covered fence line of the property, so the shrubs would hide us. Millie followed at a distance.

Once I got close enough to see the couple peering into the windows of the store, I knew I had seen the woman before. But it sure wasn't here. My heart beat hard as I turned back to my sister.

"It's Julia," I whispered. "The nurse."

Chapter 45

Millie

"No way!" Millie looked up from her science textbook and stared across the dining room table at her brother.

He didn't budge. His nose was glued in the sci-fi novel he was devouring. That boy could lose himself, forgetting the rest of the world with whatever novel he was immersed in. Millie nudged his foot under the table, once, twice, then a third time, hard enough he couldn't ignore.

"What?" He looked up as if suddenly realizing someone else was in the room with him.

"There is no way that was Julia."

"That's a delayed reaction, don't you think?" He shoved a bookmark in between the pages and set the book aside, picking up his pencil and jotting some words in his notebook.

"What are you writing?" Millie said.

Jeremiah grinned. "I'm writing in my journal that my sister doesn't believe I know what I'm talking about."

"No, really," she said. "Are you writing something about what's going on?"

"Yes," he said, scribbling a few more sentences. "I'm writing about what's going on in my book so when I work on my book report I'll remember what to say." He reached over and grabbed for Millie's notebook, but she shoved it out of his reach. "You should try it sometime, you know. Take notes on your schoolwork instead of your detective work. It comes in handy if you actually want to learn something."

Jeremiah let his pencil flop to the table where it rolled to the edge. He opened his book again, but Millie slammed it shut.

"Tell me, it isn't so, Jeremiah. Why would Julia get mixed up in whatever is going on at that old store? I mean, she's a nurse. She's supposed to be respectable. Besides, she acted like she knew nothing about the store being closed down the other day."

"Hey," Jeremiah whispered. "I'm as surprised as you are. That's why I wanted to get out of there so fast. I didn't want to take a chance on her seeing us."

"Did you get a good look at the man? Was it the phony cop?"

"No, I didn't recognize him."

"Maybe it was her husband. He might be in on this too."

"Well, she sure had me fooled," Jeremiah said. "At the hospital and at Paisley's house the other day, she seemed like someone you could trust. Not like someone that would sneak around a closed down store."

"And what about those kids you saw the other day, do you think she has something to do with them being there?"

"I'm clueless." Jeremiah opened his book.

"Well, that I've always known." Millie threw her pencil at his book. "Come on, do you have to be such a bookworm? We've got problems to figure out."

"My biggest problem," Jeremiah pointed at her. "Is trying to figure out how to get my schoolwork done with your constant distractions."

"Millie, how is your schoolwork coming?" She could tell she was giving her mom that deer-in-the-headlights look when she turned to her. She was so surprised at the sudden appearance of her mom, it left her without a response.

"Uh-huh, I thought so," their mom said as she reached into a cabinet, pulling out a big crock pot.

Millie sighed and turned a page in her science book. There went any chance to talk more to her brother if Mom was getting ready to put dinner in the slow cooker. She surprised herself by discovering something interesting in the passage she was reading and was just getting engrossed in science when her mom's words startled her.

"What did you kids think of the nurse, Julia?" Millie's stomach flip-flopped and she wondered if her mom had heard them talking. Mom smiled at both of them. "I like her a lot," she said.

Chapter 46

Jeremiah

"Mom is a good judge of character." I'm not sure if I was trying to convince Millie or myself. I pulled the plates out of the kitchen cabinet and handed them to Millie. She took them without responding, so I continued. "She's always had some sort of special sense for figuring people out."

"Discernment," Millie said as she set the plates around the table.

"What?" I followed behind her with silverware and napkins.

"That's what it's called. Mom says she has the gift of discernment." Millie brought glasses over to the table and plopped them all down in one spot. "I think her discernment is off on this one, though." She picked up a glass and held it in mid-air, staring out the window.

"Well, maybe if she knew that Julia was snooping around the store today, she'd have a different opinion."

"That's not how discernment works," Millie said. "It doesn't have to be based on facts, it's a feeling."

"Okay," I picked up the glasses and set them on all the placemats while Millie still stood frozen. "Then her feelings are off on this one."

"What if we're wrong?" Millie set the glass down and stared at me. "What if that wasn't Julia at the store, maybe just someone who looked like her? We weren't that close."

"Trust me. It was her."

Millie stared, unbelieving.

"Look, believe what you want. I know what I saw."

"It's not that I don't . . ."

"Boy, does it smell good in here! Caleb, let's go tell Mom we're starving!" Dad and Caleb passed through the kitchen like two hungry animals on the prowl.

"It's not that I . . ." Millie tried to finish, but soon Dad and Caleb were back with Mom in tow.

We joined everyone at the table, forced to stop our conversation for now.

"So, did Mom tell you two about the adventure she discovered for you?" Dad didn't look our way after the prayer, as he focused on piling his plate high with beef.

I looked over at Millie, who didn't seem to know any more than I did. Mom buttered a dinner roll for Caleb. "No, I didn't get a chance to tell them yet, Max."

"Well, I could have figured that out for myself by their lack of response." He chuckled as he scooped carrots onto the side of his plate. "They probably wouldn't even be here at the table with us if they knew what treasure awaited them."

"What are you talking about?"

"The meteorite, Jeremiah." He motioned toward the dining room window. "It's out there somewhere in the desert waiting for you two."

Chapter 47

Millie

"Wait a minute." Millie looked from her dad to her mom. "You mean what Mom was telling us out by the fire the other night is true?"

"Well, young lady." Mom pretended to be hurt. "Are you saying you didn't believe me?"

"Oh, Mom. I didn't mean it like that."

"Explain it for us then, Millie," Jeremiah said. "What does it mean when you sound so surprised that something Mom said was true?"

The family enjoyed a laugh at Millie's expense as she looked around the table, speechless.

"I have to admit," Jeremiah said. "I found Mom's explanation of the ghost lights being a meteor a little too simple. Who knew it was just an atmospheric phenomenon?"

"Oh, my gosh!" Millie blurted out. "What have we here? A walking, talking dictionary?"

"I told you, sister dear." Jeremiah took a bite of his dinner roll. "You should try paying attention to your schoolwork once in a while."

Millie threw a dinner roll across the table at her brother. "Get real, you expect me to believe that was in your school assignment today?"

"Millicent!" Mom said. "When are you going to learn some manners?"

"I'm sorry, Mom."

"Yeah, Millie," Caleb said. "You will set a bad example for me."

Millie laughed and reached over to hug Caleb.

"And no," Jeremiah said. "It wasn't in my assignment today." He smiled as he scooped a second helping of the casserole. "It was on my vocabulary list last week."

"So, if you two are finished arguing over schoolwork and the trustworthiness of your mother, maybe you'd like to know what she discovered today," Dad said.

"Okay, well, hold on," Jeremiah said. "Because I admit I was only half listening the other night when you said something about a meteor. Are you saying that there aren't really ghost lights? It was a meteor shooting through the sky that people saw?"

"That's what I'm saying." Mom picked up a piece of paper next to her plate. Millie watched her unfold the paper she hadn't even noticed laying on the table.

"I found this online today and printed it out to share with you." Mom held the paper up and read, "Scientists Search For Fallen Meteorite."

Millie reached over to grab the paper, but her Mom pulled it away. "Millie, it's polite to ask, not just grab it out of my hand."

"Yeah, Millie," Caleb said. "Don't set bad examples."

Okay, the first time Millie thought it was funny, but this time she was not laughing with the rest of the family.

"I'm sorry, Mom." It took so much effort to admit fault, but she was dying to know what the rest of that paper said.

"I'll summarize it for both of you."

"And, you, young man," Dad looked at Caleb, "please leave the disciplining to the parents."

Caleb smiled up at their Dad. "Does that mean you're my parents, too?"

Dad reached over and tousled his hair. "Well, Caleb, I'd be honored for you to call us your parents while your mom is away."

Caleb grabbed hold of their dad's hand and looked toward their mom. "Well, Mom, tell us what the scientists said fell."

Millie loved the warm feeling that spread through the room. She watched Caleb glowing as he listened to the good-natured laughter around the table. But enough of the warm fuzzy feelings. It was time to move forward with the information gathering. "So what does the rest of the article say, Mom?"

"At 8:02 p.m. Saturday evening, a bright meteoritic bolide was . . ."

"A meteoritic bolide, what in the world are they talking about?" Millie interrupted.

"Let her finish, Millie," Jeremiah said.

But before Mom could resume reading, the sound of car tires crunching on the gravel outside interrupted them.

Chapter 48

Jeremiah

"It's Deputy Black!" Caleb shouted from where he stood by the window.

I jumped out of my chair, nearly knocking it over, and ran to the door. Maybe he had been to see Caleb's mom and had news for us.

Caleb beat me to the door and was outside hugging Griffin before the rest of us made it out to the porch.

"Do you have news for us?" Millie said. I could tell by the look on his face he did, but he just nodded his head as Caleb clung to him.

Griffin knelt down to talk to the boy face to face. "And how are you doing? You look like you've grown since you've been here."

Caleb stood straight and puffed out his chest. "I have! I'm having so much fun here. Thank you for bringing me here!"

Griffin stood back up. "You're sure welcome, Caleb," he said as he reached out to shake hands with Dad. "Well, what's everybody up to today?"

Millie groaned, and I gave her a dirty look. I knew she just wanted to get right down to the business of finding out whether or not Caleb had a sister, but she must know Griffin couldn't talk in front of Caleb.

"Well, Norah was just telling the kids the news about the scientists searching for a meteorite in this area."

"No kidding?" Griffin said. "Nearby?"

"Somewhere in or around Dry Brook, according to the news report I found online today," Mom said.

"That must be what sparked all the recent talk about ghost lights," Griffin said. "How about that? It wasn't ghostly at all. Just a few people who had the fantastic opportunity to view a meteor falling from the sky."

"Kinda disappointing if you ask me," Millie said.

"Not exciting enough for my sister. Ghost lights sounded so much more adventurous when there wasn't a scientific explanation."

"It would be a big adventure if you were the one to find the meteorite," Mom said. "Don't you think, Millie?"

"It's not likely that would happen." She moaned.

"Well, why not? The news report said they believe it's in a two-mile area between the Superstition Hills, Dry Brook Badlands and Dos Palmas Wash."

"That's close to here," Griffin said.

"Your mom says they're encouraging people to search for it, Millie." Dad patted her on the shoulder.

For as annoying as she could be, none of us liked seeing her discouraged.

"I'll bet we could find it, Millie. In fact, it sounds so educational, Mom might even give us extra riding time tomorrow." I looked over at Mom. "Wouldn't that count toward schoolwork?"

"Well, let me give that some thought. Maybe you can start in the morning by reading the complete news report, then mapping out a plan for where to search."

Millie groaned. "Oh Mom, do you have to wring all the fun out of it?"

Dad and Griffin laughed, but I kept my chuckle to myself so I didn't get a dirty look.

I saw Griffin looking at his watch, and Mom must have seen it too.

"Caleb," she bent over to look him in the eye. "How would you like to come in with me and test the dessert before we serve it to everyone?" Mention sweets and Caleb would do whatever you asked.

Griffin winked at Mom as she took Caleb's hand and headed inside.

Millie practically rushed Griffin, and Dad and I weren't far behind in gathering around him.

"So I take it you have news for us?" Dad said.

"I sure do," Griffin looked around, making eye contact with each one of us. "I had an interesting visit with Caleb's mom today."

Chapter 49

Millie

Finally. Millie couldn't believe after all this waiting they were going to get some answers about the mystery sister Caleb kept talking about. At least she thought they were.

"Before I get into that, what is happening with Paisley?" Griffin said. "I've had no contact since Julia and I left the other evening."

Millie cringed at the mention of Julia. She looked over at Jeremiah and knew by the look on his face he felt the same way.

"What?" Griffin said. "Is there bad news about Paisley?" Millie tensed. She should have known with Griffin being a cop he was probably aware of even slight changes in demeanor.

"No," their Dad said, oblivious to the silent communication between them. "In fact, they've gone to the city to see the specialist Julia recommended. Their appointment is tomorrow, but they're staying in town for a few days."

Relieved her dad hadn't caught on to their attitude, Millie avoided looking at him. She didn't want to answer questions about their reaction to the mention of Julia. That would open up a whole can of worms about what was going on at the abandoned store. Not to mention the trouble it might get them into.

"We better get to the news about Caleb's mom before he comes back out," Millie said.

"Good idea." Griffin motioned for them to follow him away from the house. "To make a long story short, she says there is no sister."

"Why would that be a long story?" Millie asked.

"You tell me. My thoughts are there is more to the story than she is telling. She talked all around this sister thing. She rambled about Caleb having quite an imagination, how he always wanted a sister, how he would pretend he had a sister. But she was adamant there is no sister."

"Did you tell her what he said about the light being a signal?" Jeremiah asked.

"I sure did. She laughed. Said she couldn't understand why he would make up a story like that. Insisted Caleb is her only child."

"Boy, she did turn that into a long story," their Dad said.

"You got that right. In fact the only reason the story finally ended is because I told her I had to leave."

"Wow," Millie said. "What do you think? Do you believe her?"

"Good question. And the answer is, I'm not sure."

"But why would she lie about it, if he had a sister?" Jeremiah asked.

"To protect herself," their Dad said. "If what Caleb is saying is true, then something is very odd about the situation."

"But wouldn't you have heard about a sister long before this?" Millie said. "You've known the family for a while, haven't you?"

"About a year, and yes, it seems like I would have heard about another child. But there was never any mention of it until you folks told me about it."

"Hey, what about the deputy that was with you the other day?" Millie said. "The day Paisley got sick."

"Leon?"

"I don't know his name. Would he know anything about Caleb's family?"

"He wasn't a deputy, Millie," Jeremiah said. "He's Border Patrol."

"Border Patrol?" Millie looked from Jeremiah back to Griffin. "What was he doing here? How come you were out riding together?"

"I brought him here to meet your dad," Griffin said. "I had the day off and rode along with him while he was on patrol. And you sure ask a lot of questions."

"No kidding!" Jeremiah said. Millie ignored both of their comments.

"Why was he patrolling this area? I've never seen Border Patrol around here."

"They're around," Griffin said. "You better crank up your spy senses, you're slipping there, young lady."

Millie ignored the laughter from all of them and pushed for information. "What are they looking for?"

"What do you think, Millie?" Jeremiah said. "Smuggling. Drugs. People. Why do you think we go through the border checkpoint every time we come home from the grocery store?"

Chapter 50

Jeremiah

I could tell Millie didn't like me implying she should have known all that. As annoying as she could be, I felt bad when my teasing upset her. I turned to Griffin. "Millie has a good idea, though. Do you think Leon might know anything about Caleb's family?"

"He just might," Griffin said. "He's worked this area for quite a few years. Even before Caleb was born."

"Deputy Black!" Caleb threw open the front door and leaped off the porch, running toward Griffin. "Mom said to invite you in for dessert."

"Mom?" Griffin looked in Dad's direction.

"Yeah!" Caleb tugged on Griffin's hand. "Max and Norah said I could call them my parents while I'm here."

"That is a great idea." Griffin smiled at Caleb and took hold of his hand. "So lead me to the dessert that Mom has waiting for us."

We sat around the table enjoying cinnamon crumb cake and vanilla ice cream. Caleb had cinnamon all over his chin and cheeks. He was looking happier every day. Quite a change from the quiet, sad little boy who moved in a few months ago.

"Hey, Mom," Millie said. "Can you finish reading the news report now? Griffin might like to hear it."

"I sure would, I've always been interested in astronomy, but never been lucky enough to see a meteor." Griffin sliced himself a second piece of crumb cake and looked at Mom. "This sure is delicious. I might have to get me a wife one of these days."

Mom laughed as she picked up the paper and continued reading. "Anyone who saw the meteoritic fireball Saturday evening, and especially anyone who was in the area of Dry Brook or Dos Palmas Wash at the time of sighting, should contact either Professor James R. Goles or Professor Gordon G. Arnold at the Space Museum and Science Center. Also, anyone who intends to visit the area, should keep their eyes open for an object coated with a shiny black fusion crust which looks as if it might have fallen from the sky. The meteorite is of great scientific value."

"Wow," I said. "I can't believe we live right in the area where such an important scientific event happened."

"I guess it's too late to go searching tonight?" Millie turned her puppy dog eyes on Dad.

"You guessed right, Millie." Dad reached over and patted her hand on the table.

"It's safer not to go out after dark anyway," Griffin looked from Dad to Mom. "Best to keep the kids near the house after sundown for the time being."

Chapter 51

Millie

"Why do you think Griffin said what he did about not going out after dark?"

Jeremiah took a long swig of his water, then twisted the lid back on and leaned against his motorcycle. "I'm guessing it has something to do with illegal border crossing, either drugs or people."

"Did you talk with the Border Patrol guy the other day?"

"I got to meet him when Griffin brought him in the shop. He seemed to be looking for something specific in this area, but he didn't give details. He said one thing that kind of worried me."

"What was that?" Millie scrounged in her backpack, then brought out a couple packs of trail mix.

Jeremiah took the trail mix she offered and struggled to rip it open. "Leon told me if I see anything suspicious I should let him know."

Millie took the little package back and ripped the top off.

"How do you do that?" Jeremiah dumped trail mix into his palm, then tossed it into his mouth.

"Talent," Millie talked around the nuts and raisins she chomped on. "What did you say when he asked if you'd seen anything suspicious?"

"Well, I felt guilty, that's for sure. But thankfully he didn't ask if I'd seen anything, he just said if I ever do, I should let him know."

"Were you thinking about the old store?" Millie crumpled her trail mix packet, stood and wiped the dirt and twigs from her riding pants.

Jeremiah did the same, then straddled his motorcycle and grabbed his helmet from where it was hanging on the handlebar. "That's exactly what I was thinking." He balanced the helmet on the gas tank and leaned his elbow on it. "If he had asked me directly if I'd seen anything suspicious, I would have had to tell him."

"Yeah, I see what you mean. I guess this way you weren't actually lying."

"No, but I sure wasn't being honest either." He picked the helmet up and tugged it down over his head.

"Do you think we should tell Griffin what we saw?" Millie copied his actions, then fastened the strap under her chin. "I want to search around the store more. And if we tell, we won't be able to do that."

"And what if we don't tell, and we get in big trouble, or worse, get hurt or something while we're searching?" Jeremiah pulled out the kick starter. "Isn't it good enough to search for a meteorite?" He kicked the starter, and his bike roared to life.

"That's why I wanted Paisley to search with me," Millie thought. "She wouldn't bail out on me. At least she wouldn't have if she hadn't gotten sick."

Out loud she said, "I'll think about it while we ride." Millie kicked her bike over and yelled over the sound of the engine. "We sure haven't had any luck yet this morning."

Jeremiah wasn't looking at her, his eyes focused on something behind her.

"Millie, look over there."

Chapter 52

Jeremiah

I cut the engine and just about fell when I jumped off my bike and ran toward the object glistening in the sun. Millie followed right behind.

We were both huffing and puffing by the time we got midway up the hill.

"Check this out, Millie." I knelt down, shielding my eyes from the glare. Millie moved around until she stood in just the right spot to block the sun from shining on the metal.

"Millie, it's a bumper from an old car."

"It looks like it's polished."

"How could that be?" I picked it up. "This thing is heavy. How could it be so shiny laying out here in the wilderness? It doesn't even look weathered."

"Look," Millie pointed to both ends of the bumper. "They're weathered."

"So someone keeps the middle section polished." I set the bumper back in the brush. It looked like someone moved it often, not like something that was laying in one place for a long time. There were several areas where the brush look flattened and the dirt gouged as the metal dug into it.

"Jeremiah, this is the area Caleb keeps pointing to. We're right on the hillside. Look, if we turn and look to the north, our property should be over there somewhere. We'd be able to see the reflection from a few miles away."

"Millie," I whispered, wondering if someone might be nearby. "Someone keeps the bumper polished and moves it around. Maybe there is a sister."

Her eyes were large as she stared around the area, then back at me. "And she could be the one polishing the bumper. And maybe she picks it up to reflect the sun."

"Yeah, because right now, the early morning sun reflected from where it was. But Caleb has been seeing it at different times of the day. So someone is picking it up and causing it to reflect."

"I hope our bikes are safe back there," Millie looked down the hill where we left them. "I feel like someone might be watching us."

"I wondered the same thing, like is someone nearby?"

"Let's look for footprints." Millie picked our helmets up from the ground. I took mine as we walked.

The ground was hard, and we couldn't even see our own prints. I looked toward home.

"Millie, if Dad would let us use those expensive high-powered binoculars he had for his job, I bet we could see all the way to this hill from our house."

"If we could look when the light was reflecting we might see someone holding this bumper up." Millie clapped her hands, while jumping up and down. "That would be awesome. If there is a sister, we might spot her."

"Yeah, but that's a big 'if' for Dad to let us use those. I think I will ask Caleb why he thinks his sister is up here and see what he says."

"If we have a really good reason I'm sure Dad would let us use them. And this is a really good reason."

"Well, Millie, you're the one to ask him. Or should I say beg him?" As we headed toward our motorcycles, a drone caught my eye. It was circling the area south of us. "Millie, look at that drone."

"Jeremiah!" She pointed. "Something just fell from it."

I watched a box falling to the ground as the drone circled, then increased elevation and headed south.

Chapter 53

Millie

"Jeremiah, let's ride over and find that box," Millie called over her shoulder as she jogged toward the motorcycles.

Her brother caught up with her. "I don't know, Millie. We're supposed to be looking for the meteorite."

"Yeah, well, we haven't found it yet and at least if we find the box we will have found something."

"It's not safe. They were probably dropping the box for someone expecting it."

"Look around," Millie said. "Do you see anyone? Besides, I think it just fell from the drone. You know, by accident."

"How would you even know?"

Millie had her helmet on and motorcycle running. "Humor me." She yelled over the sound of the engine. "Let's ride in that direction a little way." She took off before her brother could argue.

Millie struggled to keep her bike upright as she maneuvered around the growing number of sagebrush and creosote bushes the higher they rode up the mountain. She wasn't used to leading when she and Jeremiah went riding. Venturing into the desert mountains with so much tangled shrubbery and no trails to speak of tested her skill, or lack of it. She looked back for Jeremiah, but lost control. The handlebars twisted hard to the right, tossing her off the bike and into a thorny bush.

"Jeremiah!" What a relief to see him so close.

Her brother grabbed hold of her arms and tugged. "Cat's Claw!" she yelled as she picked at the thorns clinging to her riding jersey.

"What are you talking about?" Jeremiah said once she was out of the bush and standing.

"That stupid bush." Millie brushed at the leaves and twigs on her shirt and pants. "That's what it's called."

"Since when do you know something?" Jeremiah laughed as he picked her motorcycle up.

"Botany Adventure." Millie took her helmet off and set it on the seat of her bike. She shrugged out of her backpack. "I need some water."

"I must have missed out on that adventure." Jeremiah grabbed a water bottle out of her backpack.

"Mom was trying to make science more fun for me last year." She guzzled down the water. "And it worked. That's how I know the name of this stupid plant that grabbed hold of me."

"Are you okay?"

"Yeah, I'm fine. And you will not believe this," Millie wiped her mouth on her sleeve and tucked the empty water bottle into her backpack. "I'm ready to go home."

Millie zipped the backpack and slung it into place on her back, then turned to see why Jeremiah hadn't responded to her startling decision about going home.

"Jeremiah? Where are you?"

Chapter 54

Jeremiah

Millie would not believe this. I took off running while she was jabbering about something. I wanted to get back with the box in time to surprise her when she finished fiddling with her backpack and turned around.

Running in riding boots was hard, especially dodging bushes and boulders. I sure didn't want any Cat's Claw plants grabbing hold of me. I couldn't believe my sister actually learned something in science.

The box was bigger than I expected, but when I picked it up it hardly weighed anything. There were no labels or marks of any kind. Just a plain brown box that fell from the sky.

"Millie!" I yelled out as I turned to head back. This took a little longer than I thought, and she might be worried. "Millie!" I rounded the bush she had crashed into and could see her looking all around.

I knew the second she spotted me.

"Jeremiah!" she screamed and ran toward me. "You found it! You found it!"

Well, if anyone else was in the area, they would know, too, that I found the box.

Millie took it from me as soon as I got to her. "It's so light," she said.

"Yeah, I wonder what we should do with it? It doesn't even have a name on it."

"Let's take it home." Millie pulled on her helmet.

"It's not ours," Jeremiah said.

"It is now." Millie straddled her motorcycle and balanced the box on her gas tank.

"I don't think so," I grabbed the box and set it on my bike, then pulled my helmet on. "If we're taking it home, I'll ride with it. At least it will get there in one piece."

"Oh, you're real funny," Millie said and then kicked her bike over. She revved the engine and sprayed dirt and pebbles on me as she steered the bike around to head downhill.

That girl. She could be impossible sometimes. Why couldn't I have gotten a nice, calm, quiet girl like Paisley for a sister? I felt a lump in my throat at the thought of Paisley. She was probably going through the testing right now. "Oh God," I prayed out loud in my helmet as I followed Millie down the hillside. "Please take care of Paisley. Please tell the doctors what to do."

"Mom! Dad!" Millie raced through the house yelling for our parents as I followed carrying the box. "We found something!"

Dad and Mom came hurrying out of the office, meeting up with us in the kitchen. "Did you find the meteorite?" Mom asked. She looked so excited, I hated to tell her no. So I let Millie do that.

"We found something better," Millie said. "And it fell from the sky too!"

Chapter 55

Millie

"What in the world?" Mom said when Jeremiah set the box on the table.

"You say this fell from the sky, Millie?" Dad looked unbelieving. "Jeremiah, is that right?"

"Oh, so you believe Jeremiah, but not me?"

"Well, face it, sis, you get some wild ideas, sometimes." Jeremiah gave her one of those patronizing looks she hated. But right now she was so eager to see what was in the box, she ignored the pest.

"Well, we were riding south looking for..." Jeremiah started.

"The meteorite!" Millie interrupted. She didn't want them to know they were looking for the shiny object that Caleb talked about. She wanted to make sure Mom trusted them to keep going out in search of the meteorite. There were so many interesting things waiting for them to discover out there in the desert.

Jeremiah took a deep breath. "I love being interrupted. Said no one ever." He gave her a dirty look.

"Well, that's quite a story," Dad said after they related the strange events of the morning. Not including finding the bumper.

"So can we open the box now?" Millie looked from one parent to the other.

"No."

"No?" Millie said a bit too loudly. "Why not?"

"It isn't ours," Dad said. "And it could very well be connected to a crime."

"I have the business card from Griffin's friend Leon," Mom said. "I saw it with your keys and wallet, so I filed it."

"Thanks, Norah. I think we should call him."

"Why not just call Griffin?" Millie asked.

"This seems like something the Border Patrol should check out," Dad said. "I've read about smugglers dropping items from planes and drones for their associates on the ground."

"Oh, Max!" Mom's hands went up to her face, her eyes opening wide in fright. "They could have been in danger." She looked at both kids. "Did either of you see anyone in the area?"

"No one," Millie said.

"We looked all around us too, and there was no sign of anyone," Jeremiah said. "I thought maybe it dropped from the drone by mistake."

It didn't take long for Leon to show up.

"Thanks for the call," he said after he greeted them. "I was on my way to check out a potential drop. They caught the drone on radar when it crossed the border. Sounds like your kids made my job a little easier."

He looked at the box sitting on the table, then over at Jeremiah. "Boy, you really paid attention when I said to call if you saw anything suspicious."

Jeremiah smiled, but Millie wasn't going to let him get all the praise. "Well, it didn't take a rocket scientist to know that a box falling from the sky was suspicious."

They all laughed, while Leon pulled out a knife and sliced through the tape on the box top. He looked inside and whistled, then spoke, almost to himself.

"Well, I've heard about this, but I've never seen it for myself."

Chapter 56

Jeremiah

I watched as Leon pulled a slender potato chip can out of the box. He laid it on its side on the table and we watched, stunned, as the can moved back and forth.

Millie gasped. "What is inside that thing?"

Leon pulled a pair of gloves from a pouch on his belt and slipped his hands into them before lifting the potato chip can from the table. He pulled the plastic lid off and tipped the can with one hand. A large lizard wrapped in masking tape slipped out of the can into his other hand. He dropped the can, then used both hands to hold the reptile.

"Oh my goodness," Mom said. "That poor creature."

"What is going on?" Millie asked.

"Smugglers." Leon peeled the masking tape off the bound legs. "Lizards are just one of many animals sold on the black market." He looked up at their parents, shaking his head. "It's a billion dollar business around the globe, smuggling wildlife."

They watched as the lizard stretched and moved his legs. "Do you have some cardboard boxes I can put them in?"

"Them?" I looked inside the box. My mouth dropped open when I saw 15 or 20 more potato chip cans. "Millie, look at this."

She had tears rolling down her cheeks, which explained why she had been so quiet. I never knew she had a soft spot for critters. She reached out and touched the head of the one Leon held. "I used to own a big lizard, kind of like this one."

Mom put her arm around Millie's shoulders. "Oh, honey, I'm so sorry. This must be extra hard for you."

Dad returned with Caleb in tow. They both carried boxes. "Come on, Caleb, let's get more." He steered him away before Caleb could see what the boxes were for.

"How about if Millie and I get some branches and shrubbery to put in the box?"

"You go get that stuff," Millie said. "I'm going to cut up some banana and see what veggies we have that lizards can eat. I remember what they like from when I owned one."

"Whatever happened to your lizard?"

I knew by the look on her face, I shouldn't have asked.

"We'll talk about it another time, Jeremiah." She was already peeling the banana.

"I'm going out to my car to radio this in," Leon said. "Then I'll get the rest of them out of the cans." He looked over at me. "If you don't mind, get enough for all these boxes."

Caleb helped me carry in the branches, rocks and bits of shrubbery. I found enough to house an army of lizards.

Leon followed us inside. He watched as Millie, Caleb, and I made nice little habitats in each of the boxes. The kitchen had turned into a reptile preserve.

"This is nice, kids," Leon said. He looked at each one of us. Mom and Dad looked proud.

Then Leon looked over at my parents. "Now, I've got a huge favor to ask."

Chapter 57

Millie

Millie hoped against hope Leon would ask her parents the same thing she wanted to ask. In a rare show of self-discipline, she kept her mouth shut, waiting to hear what he had to say. It was well worth it.

"It really impressed my supervisor how Jeremiah and Millie," he reached out and patted Caleb's head, "and Caleb too, have all pitched in to help."

"I would have to agree," Dad smiled at all three of the kids.

Leon cleared his voice and nodded. "In fact, he's so impressed he wanted me to ask if you all would be willing to keep the lizards here until our Customs Field Officer can get out to assess the situation and make arrangements to transport and care for the lizards."

"Yes!" Millie shouted.

"I'm surprised you kept quiet this long, Mil," Jeremiah said.

"Please, Mom! Please, Dad!" Millie turned pleading eyes to her parents. "This would mean so much to me."

"Do you have any idea how long that will be, Leon?" Dad asked.

He hesitated, rubbed his chin, then took a deep breath. "Honestly? It could be a few weeks to a month or more. He covers a big territory that encompasses all the rural communities out this way."

"Even better!" Millie knelt down next to the box that contained the freed lizard. "Can we let the others loose now?"

Leon touched her shoulder. "Not just yet," he said. He looked at her mom and dad.

"Sorry to push, but your answer has a bearing on whether I free the others now."

"You mean you'll leave them in the canisters if we can't keep them here?" Millie moaned. "That's so not fair."

"It's a practical matter, Millie. I appreciate all of you gathering up the boxes, but I wouldn't be able to fit them in my car."

Millie could see Dad and Mom whispering to each other while Leon talked with her. Surely they wouldn't force these poor reptiles to stay bound in the containers.

"Dad," Jeremiah spoke up. "I know Millie and I could take care of them and she's had a lizard before, so she knows what to do."

Millie wanted to hug her brother, but she stayed put on the floor next to Chippie. She smiled. There was no way she could let this little critter go now that she had already named him. She peered in the box and watched the lizard looking up at her.

"He trusts me," Millie said. "I can tell."

Leon watched Millie interact with the reptile. "You know, I believe he does."

Millie held back tears. This reminded her so much of the pet she said goodbye to several years ago in foster care. She remembered crying for weeks when she didn't get to take the lizard with her when she moved to a new foster home.

Dad and Mom were still whispering, but Millie couldn't wait any longer. "Please, Mom and Dad! Please don't make me say goodbye to Chippie!"

Jeremiah burst out laughing. "Chippie? That's hilarious."

Mom knelt down next to her and smiled. "I know where you got that name."

Caleb picked up the potato chip can. "I know too, Millie. 'Cause he came out of a chip can." He sat down next to Millie, staring into the box. "I love Chippie, too." He reached into the box, then jerked his hand back the lizard hissed. Caleb glared into the box. "Bad Chippie!"

"Oh dear," Mom said.

Millie cringed. It seemed like her mom had been close to agreeing, and now she'd probably say no because it was too dangerous.

"Caleb, you were smart to pull your hand back from the box." Dad joined them on the floor. "We must be careful with these creatures. They're scared and probably angry too. And they have good reason to be angry. Someone has mistreated them."

Millie felt hope rising in her. Dad talked like they would keep them. She was afraid to look up in his face, afraid to ask. She wanted to hold on to the hope that Dad would say yes they could take care of them. As long as she didn't know yet, she could still hope.

Chapter 58

Jeremiah

I was torn between not wanting to spend my days taking care of needy reptiles that were just waiting to bite my finger off in retaliation for being captured and stuffed into canisters, but not wanting to see my sister fall apart if we couldn't keep them.

Millie looked ready to cry, and it was crazy how that lizard seemed to bond with her already. It was clear though he hadn't bonded and probably wouldn't bond with Caleb. Wow, that hiss sounded crazy mean.

Dad patted Millie on the shoulder, then turned to face Leon.

"We'll be happy to help." I expected Millie to go bonkers with excitement, but instead she cried. Whew, she wore me out trying to keep up with her emotions. I felt sorry for the guy she might marry someday. I hoped all girls weren't like this.

Mom stayed next to Millie with one arm draped around her shoulders. Leon pulled his gloves back on and took another canister out of the box. Caleb lost interest after getting hissed at and disappeared into another room. I sure wasn't going to ask if I could help pull those angry critters out of the canisters, so I was content to watch as one by one they were freed and placed in their new homes.

Millie went from box to box, checking on the welfare of each one, placing food and water. I don't know where she came up with all those water bowls. It was as if she had been expecting a tsunami of reptiles to descend on us and she had the supplies to care for them.

Before long, all the canisters were empty. There were 16 live lizards and two we would bury. I'm sure if Millie gets her way, it will be with a full-on funeral with music and a speech before burial.

"Jeremiah, will you go tell Caleb lunch is ready?" I hadn't noticed Mom making sandwiches and setting the table while we were busy with lizard rescue.

"He's sound asleep on the floor in his room surrounded by his cars," I said when I returned to the kitchen. Everyone, including Leon, was seated when I joined them at the table.

Dad said grace, and Millie and I dug in before anyone else. My appetite raged after our adventurous morning. Millie hardly talked since we found out we were keeping the lizards. I think she was so overcome with joy she couldn't talk. Wow, I wish she could be this overcome all the time. I snickered at my joke.

"What's so funny over there, Jeremiah?" Dad said. "And pass me that bowl of chips while you share your joke."

Hmm, I needed to get out of this without hurting Millie's feelings. Sometimes I didn't care, but today wasn't one of those days. I passed the chip bowl down his way. "I was just thinking how funny Caleb looked sound asleep with cars in both his hands." Mom enjoyed that, and I sure hoped God would forgive a lie like that.

"I can't tell you all how much I appreciate you helping with the lizards," Leon said. "And to feed me a delicious lunch too, well, it's turned out to be a great day." He wiped his mouth and dropped his napkin on his plate. "I can tell you not all our days are great. In fact, some are very much not so great."

Mom nodded. "I can imagine you see some tough things in your line of work."

"Say, Leon," Dad said. "On a different topic, we wanted to ask you about Caleb's family. Griffin said you might be familiar with them."

"Sure, what do you want to know? I didn't get to know the boy as well as Griffin did, but I've known of the family for quite a few years."

Millie surprised me by coming alive. "Does Caleb have a sister?"

Chapter 59

Millie

"He does, but she didn't live with the family," Leon said.

"Where did she live?" Millie asked before anyone else could get a word out.

"Well, I take that back." Leon paused, as if remembering. "When the family first moved to this area, oh, say, five or six years ago, the sister lived with them. It was the girl and Caleb, who was quite a bit younger, and an on-again, off-again boyfriend of the mom's."

"So when did the sister move out?" Jeremiah glanced at Millie triumphantly. She smiled, knowing he was glad he beat her to a question for once.

"About a year or two ago. She went to live with her dad in some other state," Leon said. "I don't remember where."

"How do you know that's where she went?" Millie's question came out more like a challenge than a polite inquiry.

Leon looked startled, but it seemed to cause him to think. "Well, I guess I just took the mom's word for it. But now you got me thinking."

"Thinking?" Millie challenged again.

"Millicent." Mom was firm. "Stop interrogating, Leon."

Remembering the lizards he had just entrusted to her care, Millie felt ashamed. "I'm sorry."

He smiled. "It's okay, Millie. I'm impressed by your thoroughness. You might make an excellent detective someday."

"Okay," Jeremiah said, "now you both got me curious. What did Millie's question cause you to think about?"

Mom brought a plate of cookies to the table and set them in front of Leon and Dad. "She would have to do that," Millie thought. "Now he's distracted with oatmeal raisin cookies, and it will take forever to get an answer." He surprised Millie by reaching for a cookie and then just holding it while staring in space, like he'd gone back in time.

"I remember now that I had been by the house several times and not seen the girl. Don't remember her name." He stopped and looked at the cookie in his hand like he wasn't sure how it got there.

"Leon, would you like some coffee to go with that?"

He looked sheepish. "Actually, ma'am, I'd prefer a glass of milk." He looked over at Millie. "I never acquired a taste for coffee, but milk with cookies, now that's living."

Millie laughed politely, although she just wanted to get back to the story.

"So I asked the mom about the girl, said I hadn't seen her lately, when she used to be outside most of the time. She was always stacking rocks in piles or hunting for bugs. I remember I'd get such a kick out of seeing her puttering around outside when I would be in the area." He stopped talking and took a couple bites of the cookie when Mom set the glass of milk in front of him.

Millie decided she might as well join in and grabbed a few cookies. She would have preferred chocolate chips rather than raisins.

"So I never thought anything about the mom's answer until today." He looked over at Millie. "Something tells me you're suspicious about that answer, and now I am, too."

Millie was dying to ask another question, but she was close enough to Jeremiah for him to kick her under the table.

"When I asked the mom where the girl was . . . why can't I remember her name?" He stopped and stared into space. "Well, anyway, when I asked, I remember now the mom hesitated just a split second. Enough to make me think now that she was making up an answer. Then she blurted out something like 'oh she's gone with her dad, yeah, she's gone with her dad.'" He took a drink of milk and finished his cookie, then looked around the table at all of them. "She repeated herself after having to think about it. See what I mean about it seeming strange?"

"I sure do," Dad said.

"Well, I was suspicious," Millie said, "because she told Griffin she didn't have any other kids besides Caleb."

"What other kids besides me?" Caleb stood in the kitchen doorway, rubbing his eyes, his hair frazzled from sleep.

Chapter 60

Jeremiah

We were so engrossed in talk about Caleb's sister that we didn't notice him at the kitchen door. I felt bad that he heard us talking about his family and wondered how much he heard.

"Hey there, little buddy." I jumped up from my chair and went to greet him. "You slept right through lunch."

"I did?" he said, still rubbing his eyes.

Taking his other hand, I led him to the table. "You sure did, but I bet Mom will make a sandwich for you real quick."

Caleb spotted the cookies. His face lit up. "I can just eat cookies." He reached for the plate. "You don't have to go to all that trouble for me, Miss Norah." He looked over at Mom, then corrected himself with a huge smile. "I mean Mom!" Before she could answer, Caleb bit into a cookie. He looked over at Leon. "Miss Norah said I could call her Mom."

"Well, how about that?" Leon said.

"My mom's gone somewheres." He finished the cookie and grabbed another one before Mom could stop him. "Did you know that my mom was gone somewheres?" He directed his question to Leon.

Leon smiled. "I did and I'm sure glad you found such a great family to live with while she's gone."

"It's okay if she don't come back for a long, long time," Caleb talked around the bite of cookie he was chewing. He was as bad as Millie. Mom didn't even correct him, she was probably too concerned he might have heard us talking about his family. "I can just stay here the rest of my life if she can't come back." Caleb looked around the table and smiled, then back at Leon. "I'm happy here. Did you know that?"

We all laughed. "Well if I didn't know," Leon said, "I sure know it now."

Leon scooted his chair over and leaned close to him. "Caleb, I haven't seen your sister in a long time. Do you know where she moved to?"

Caleb reached for another cookie, but this time Mom was faster. She pulled the cookie plate away and placed a sandwich in front of him. "Peanut butter and strawberry jelly, Caleb. Your favorite."

Caleb took a big bite, then turned back to Leon, jelly on both sides of his mouth. "She knows I love strawberry jelly."

Leon wiped the edges of Caleb's mouth with a napkin.

"See why I like living here so much?" Caleb said, "They're nice to me." He took a few more bites, then looked back at Leon. "Sometimes my mom wasn't nice to me. You remember that, don't you?"

This was news to all of us. Leon looked upset. He took a deep breath before answering. "Well, your mom had some problems, Caleb. But she's taking care of those now and look what a special place she found for you to live."

"She didn't find this place," Caleb said. "Deputy Black said it was God who brought me here."

"Well, how about that?" Leon said. "God's pretty special now, isn't He?"

"Yeah, He is." Caleb finished the first half of his sandwich and eyed the cookie plate across the table. "I hope God will bring my sister here next." He bit into the other half of his sandwich and while chewing said, "I miss her."

"Do you know where she lives now?" Leon asked.

This was perfect with Leon here to get all this information. It helped because he knew Caleb's family. I felt funny asking questions of Caleb because it seemed like prying.

"Yeah," Caleb pointed. "She lives over on the mountain. Where the shiny thing is."

Chapter 61

Millie

"I can't believe we're getting to go with him to find Caleb's sister," Millie said as she fastened her seat belt in the back seat of the Border Patrol SUV.

"Millie, he's told you a hundred times, we're not going to search for her sister. We're just going to show him where we found the polished bumper."

Millie sighed. "A hundred times, Jeremiah? Isn't that a bit of an exaggeration?"

"Well, not by much," their Dad said and laughter filled the car. Only Millie wasn't laughing. She left that to Leon, her dad and her brother.

"Well, why can't we look for her while we're up there?"

"Quit whining," Jeremiah said.

"I'm not whining." Millie tried to defend herself, but even she recognized the whine this time. "Well, not too much, am I?"

"I know you're disappointed, Millie," Leon glanced at her in the mirror as he drove the car out the gate and down the dirt road. "I'd feel the same way if I were you, but it's too dangerous to search while I have all of you with me. The only reason you're here now is to show me where the bumper is and where you found the box. After that I'll bring the three of you back home and probably have Griffin accompany me when I go back to search the area."

"What will happen if you find her?" Millie said.

She saw Leon look over at her dad and then back to the paved road he had just turned onto. "What do you mean?" he said. Millie couldn't believe that adults could be just like kids. She figured it was clear what she meant, and he probably didn't want to answer the question. So just like a kid, he pretends he doesn't know what she means.

She thought about explaining what she meant, but decided she wasn't ready to hear the answer. The way Leon looked at her dad, she knew her parents already offered to let the sister move in. Out of the corner of her eye, she could see Jeremiah looking at her. She hoped the tears wouldn't fall. She didn't want him to know the thought of sharing her parents with another girl still upset her.

"Hey Dad," Jeremiah said. "I wonder if Griffin will confront Caleb's mom about lying."

Millie looked at him. Her brother was awesome. He winked at her and she knew he was changing the subject to get her out of an uncomfortable conversation.

"I imagine he will."

"Depending on what we find," Leon said, "there may be more criminal charges filed against the mom, too."

"Really?" Jeremiah said.

"I wouldn't doubt it," Leon pulled off the pavement and slowed to put the SUV into four-wheel-drive mode. "Sure, if she's lying to Griffin about the daughter, that means wherever the girl is probably isn't safe or it may involve her in illegal activities."

Millie felt her heart beat harder. She never thought about this girl being in danger. "Will she be in trouble if she is doing something illegal? Could she go to jail?"

"I don't know the circumstances, but my guess is if she is doing something illegal, it's probably against her will. She would be a victim, not a criminal."

Millie's hand went to her mouth and her breath came faster. All this time she only thought about herself. How selfish could she be? She looked over at Jeremiah. "This changes everything," she whispered.

"What did you say, Millie?" Her dad turned to look at her.

"Oh, nothing, Dad."

Chapter 62

Jeremiah

I knew once Millie realized Caleb's sister might be in trouble, most likely scared and mistreated, that she would want her to live with us. She didn't even have to say anything to me, I could read it in her eyes. I hoped that we would see the sister when we got up there. Even though Leon said we couldn't be there when he searched for her, what would he do if she was near the bumper when we got there?

"This is the way, right?" Leon said as he maneuvered around the rocks and bushes on the rutted road.

"Yes," Millie answered before I could. "About halfway up the hill. Look! You can see the sun shining on it right now."

"Isn't that something?" Dad said. "All this time Caleb knew what he was talking about, and we just thought it was a little kid rambling and confused."

"It's amazing what you learn from listening to children," Leon said.

"Have you had to listen to kids tell you stuff?" I asked.

"Twenty years in law enforcement, you better believe I've heard my share of stories from kids." Leon shook his head. "And most of them are not stories you'd want to hear."

"I'll bet your job is tough," Dad said.

Leon looked over at Dad, then glanced in his rearview mirror at both me and my sister. He was smiling. "It is, but there are good days, too. Like today. You've got some special kids there and because of them we might rescue another special kid."

CHAPTER 63

Millie

Millie tried not to sulk when Leon turned the car around and headed back down the hill. She had hoped they'd see the sister hanging around and could be there for the rescue.

"Millie," Jeremiah whispered.

Her dad and Leon talked about four-wheel-drive vehicles on the drive down the hill, a conversation that held no interest for her. They pulled back onto the pavement at the foot of the mountain when she looked over at Jeremiah. He pointed to the north.

A good distance ahead of them on the paved road was a big 18-wheeled mine truck. But this wasn't the road that led to the gypsum mine. What was it doing way out here? She and Jeremiah kept their eyes on the truck. As they got closer, Jeremiah whispered to her again. "It's the truck."

"What truck?" she mouthed. Her dad and Leon's conversation had tapered off, and she didn't want them to hear what they were saying. She pulled a notepad and pen from her backpack and handed it to her brother.

It's the one Mike and I saw the other night, he wrote.

Millie nodded and kept her eyes glued to the truck. It slowed and turned onto a dirt road.

She pointed to Jeremiah, but he was already watching it. He nodded. She wished her dad and Leon would start talking again so she and Jeremiah could talk. She picked up the pen and scribbled: *That road leads to the old store.*

Jeremiah nodded his head, then took the pad and pen from her. *And we're not going there!!!!*

Millie wished so hard that Paisley hadn't gotten sick. Paisley would have been willing to go with her. She had to know what was happening at the store and why that truck was heading there.

Then I'll go by myself!!!! she wrote and glared at Jeremiah when she showed it to him.

Millie watched him shake his head and stare out the side window. She could tell he was finished with this discussion. But she sure wasn't.

"Millie!" Mom was on the porch waiting for them when the car pulled up to the house.

Millie jumped out to greet her mother, wondering why she was so excited.

"Paisley is coming home!"

"Oh, Mom, I'm so glad!" Millie hugged her mom. "I thought they would be gone longer."

"They're eager to get back. Mrs. Morgan said they headed home as soon as they got out of the doctor's office. They should be here in about an hour and a half."

"I can't wait to see her. What did the doctor say? Is she okay?"

"Mrs. Morgan didn't say, and I didn't ask," Mom said.

"Why ever not?" Millie was too bold, as usual.

"Said the girl who won't ever stop asking questions." Jeremiah glared at her.

Millie snarled in return.

"They've been through a lot, Millie," Mom said. "They'll tell us when they're ready."

"Well, the fact that she didn't say everything is okay, tells me a lot." Millie's head dropped as she stepped through the front door.

A few minutes later she heard a knock on her bedroom door. "What?"

No answer. Just more knocking. Knocking that wouldn't quit. She stomped over to the door and jerked it open. "What?!" she said before it was all the way open. Then her mouth dropped. Jeremiah stood there in his riding gear, holding his helmet.

"What are you doing?"

"Come on, Mom said we can go back out and look for the meteorite for another hour."

"Really?"

"Yeah, really," Jeremiah stared at her. "And if we happen to look for something else while we're out there, maybe you'll cheer up."

Chapter 64

Jeremiah

"Why is Minnesota Mike parked over there in those trees?" Millie whispered as we sat on a hill overlooking the old store. For an abandoned store, there sure was a lot of activity at this one.

"Maybe for the same reason we're here watching. He seems to know there is stuff going on there. But he hasn't told me anything."

"He tried to chase down the truck that night," Millie said.

"That's true. So that's probably why he's watching it now, just like we are."

The mine truck we saw earlier was sitting with the engine idling in front of the store.

"I wonder if Mike sees us up here?"

"Maybe we should park somewhere else." Millie pulled out her kick starter. "I don't want him seeing us. He'll tell Mom and Dad."

I kicked over my bike and waited til Millie got hers started. She surprised me by taking the lead, so I followed, figuring this spy business was her idea. I was just along for the support or protection. Or maybe just so she wasn't the only one to get in trouble. Sheesh, sometimes it was hard to be a nice brother.

We pulled over near some trees close to the store.

"Let's leave the bikes here and get closer so we can see if that truck driver went into the store." Millie leaned her bike against the tree.

I wasn't thrilled with the idea of getting closer to that building, especially going in the back way, but I knew there was no stopping Millie now.

"Hopefully we don't run into Julia."

"I've been thinking about that, Millie. I don't see how she could do something illegal."

"I know. She seemed nice. And I can't figure a nurse who cares enough to go to someone's home to talk about their health, sneaking into an abandoned building."

"I wouldn't believe it if someone had told me."

Millie nodded her head. "Yeah, even seeing it, it's still hard to believe."

"Well, if she's here again today, then we definitely know she's not the person we thought."

"I would hate for Paisley's family to find out." Millie motioned me to follow. "Come on, let's get to the store before the truck drives off."

We followed along the same overgrown fence line, protected by the trees and shrubs, until we were close enough to see the truck. Millie stopped so suddenly I almost ran into her.

"Jeremiah," she whispered. "Look, there's a ladder leaned up against the truck."

"Maybe that's how the driver checks on stuff in those metal tanks." Even as I offered that lame suggestion, I knew it didn't sound right. I wondered if Minnesota Mike could see the truck and ladder from where he sat in his buggy. He'd probably have an idea what it was all about.

"Jeremiah, look!" Millie's whispers were getting louder, and that seemed dangerous.

I watched as a group of people streamed out the front door of the store and headed to the ladder. Millie gasped as we watched them one by one climb the ladder and disappear down into the metal tank of the truck.

"Smugglers, Millie." I couldn't believe what we were seeing. She never looked back at me or responded. She focused on a little girl crying at the foot of the ladder.

Chapter 65

Millie

"Ven rápida!" A woman's voice from the top of the ladder yelled at the young girl. Millie knew she was telling her to come quick. "Ven rápida!" This time the woman sounded angry. Millie watched as the little girl cried harder. "She's afraid to climb the ladder," she whispered. Without thinking, Millie darted from her hiding spot out to the girl and knelt on the ground, comforting her.

"Está bien," Millie whispered, "it's okay." She smoothed the girl's hair and held her close. "I'm here. Estoy aquí." She didn't look back at Jeremiah. She knew he'd be angry with her for doing this. But she couldn't let that child cry. She remembered too many days and nights when she was a young girl, crying and scared. She would have loved for someone to show up out of nowhere and comfort her. Like an angel. A guardian angel.

The girl clung to her and cried harder. Millie looked up and saw the angry woman at the top of the ladder disappear into the tank with the others.

"Oh, God," she prayed. "What have I done? What do I do now?" She had always been impulsive, but this was probably the most dangerous situation she had ever gotten herself into. Before she could make a choice, it was made for her.

A deep, angry voice from behind startled her. "Entre ahora!" She turned to face a large man pointing at the ladder. "Get in, now!"

Millie's heart beat hard as she stood and held onto the girl's hand. He must have thought she was with the rest of the group. She hesitated long enough for him to take a good look at her. He motioned to her boots, then stared at her riding apparel. She trembled as she recognized the man who threatened to handcuff her.

"Who are you?" his voice boomed, speaking only English now. She had no idea what to say, but a Bible verse popped into her mind. Do not worry about what you are to say, for it will be given you in that hour what you are to say. Oh, how she hoped that was true, even when she got herself in this dangerous situation.

The sudden roar of an engine took them by surprise and a red buggy charged in their direction. Millie grabbed the little girl and jumped out of the way as the buggy slammed into the ladder, knocking it to the ground. The loud crash intensified as the car drove over the fallen ladder, then circled the truck, coming back around again.

"Millie, run!" She heard Jeremiah's voice and without looking to see where the man was, still holding onto the young girl's hand, she ran faster than she ever had before, dragging the child along with her.

Chapter 66

Jeremiah

"¿Cuál es su nombre?" Millie knelt by the little girl and looked right in her eyes as she spoke to her.

Was this really happening? Did my sister really just rescue a little girl from smugglers? And surely this was the hand of God who rescued Millie.

Thankfully, Minnesota Mike was nearby for God to use. And how did Millie learn to speak Spanish? There was still a lot I had to learn about this sister of mine. Like where did she get this incredible courage to set her own safety aside to help a young child?

"My name is Mía," the girl said. "I know English."

"You do?" Millie sounded stunned.

Mía smiled, as if happy she surprised Millie. "I saw you before." She pointed at Millie.

"Me?" Millie stared at me, then looked back to Mía. "Where did you see me"

She pointed to the front of the store. "There. I saw you out the window."

Millie gasped. "I knew I saw movement in that window."

Wow, my sister was on to something even then and I thought she was just running off in a tangent.

"Where did you learn English?" I asked Mía.

She smiled at me and seemed to sense she was safe now. "The orfanato. A lady there teached it to me."

I looked at Millie. "What's an orfanato?"

"I think it means orphanage," Millie said. "She probably doesn't know that word in English."

"I didn't know you spoke Spanish, Millie."

She laughed. It didn't sound like one of her relaxed, carefree laughs though. I think the adrenaline was dwindling, and fear was setting in. "A little. They spoke Spanish at one of the foster homes where I lived."

"Did they teach it to you?"

"Ha!" Millie scoffed. "More like the other kids talked about me in Spanish, so I couldn't understand. That's why I learned some words, to figure out what they were saying."

She pulled a granola bar from her backpack and offered it to Mía. I watched as the bar disappeared. Mía chomped noisily, crumbs covering her mouth and cheeks. I wondered how long it had been since she ate.

We could hear the big truck driving away. I breathed a sigh of relief the man didn't follow Millie. I half expected to hear Minnesota Mike driving around looking for us, but it sounded like his buggy took off in the truck's direction.

"What do we do now, Jeremiah?" Millie looked like she could cry. It's funny how she could go from being so brave one minute, to being a scared little girl herself the next. That left me no choice.

"Let's take Mía home so Mom can feed her. She looks starved."

"What is Mom going to say? And Dad?" Now tears fell. "Oh, Jeremiah, what have I done?"

I couldn't help but laugh. "Well, you've topped yourself this time, Millie. I will say that." Mía listened to our conversation.

"Wrong or right, I think you've made a big difference in this little girl's life right now."

Millie took a deep breath. "You think so?"

I was almost tempted to hug my sister. Almost, but not quite. "I think so." I smiled and patted her on the shoulder.

Chapter 67

Millie

The ride home was slow with Mía on the back of Jeremiah's motorcycle. It was risky because they had no helmet for her. Millie chuckled at the thought of this being risky after what she had just gone through that brought Mía into their lives. She knew she would pay a big price for that risk later.

Their parents were out front watching for them when they pulled up. They both stepped off the porch, right over to Jeremiah's motorcycle, and greeted Mía as if they were expecting her.

"How did you know?" Millie said when she took her helmet off.

Dad lifted Mía off the bike.

"Minnesota Mike called and told us," Mom said.

"And then we called Leon." Dad set Mía on the ground and Mom knelt to greet her.

"Oh, no, Dad," Millie said. "Did you have to call him so soon?" She knew that meant they would come and take the little girl away. Somewhere that would be scary to her. Millie hoped she could spend a few days with them first.

"I told him about the mine truck and gave him Mike's number. Mike is following the truck. He's driving in the dirt alongside the highway, hanging back but keeping it in sight, until the Border Patrol gets there."

Millie's hopes rose. "So you didn't tell him about her?" Mía was already heading into the house with their Mom.

Dad smiled. "Not yet, Millie. I told him to stop by later so we could talk about something."

Millie threw her arms around him. "Thank you, Dad."

Jeremiah stepped up onto the porch and opened the door. Before he could get inside, Caleb rushed through the open door, running into Jeremiah. "Hey, who is that girl in there eating all our cookies? And where is my sissy? I thought you went to look for my sissy." His lip quivered, but he held back the tears.

"It's okay, big fella." Jeremiah sat on the porch step, pulling Caleb to his side. "Her name is Mía, and she's visiting us."

"But where is Jenny?"

"Jenny?" Millie took a seat on the porch step next to Caleb. "Is that your sister's name? You never told us before."

"I know." Caleb rubbed his eyes and hung his head down. "My mom told me I'm not supposed to talk about Jenny to anyone."

Millie locked eyes with her dad. She didn't know what to say.

Her dad knelt down. "It's okay, Caleb. Leon and Griffin are looking for Jenny, and you can talk about her now."

Caleb looked into their dad's eyes. "You won't tell my mom, will you? You know, my other mom, the one that went away."

Dad hugged him. "You don't have to worry about that anymore."

Mom and Mía joined them on the front porch. "Caleb, come and meet Mía. She's close to your age."

"I don't have to share my room with her, do I, Miss Norah?" He smiled up at her. "I mean Mom."

"Is she your mom?" Mía surprised Millie when she spoke to Caleb.

"Sure, she's my mom," Caleb stood and took Mom's hand. "If you want, she can be your mom, too. She's a good mom."

"Well, it isn't that easy, Caleb." Mom smiled at the boy. "Leon will help Mía find her mommy."

Mía smiled up at her. "I never had a mommy, Miss Norah."

Chapter 68

Jeremiah

Both Mom and Dad looked startled at Mía's comment, but before they could answer, Minnesota Mike's buggy roared in through our gate. We could hear him approaching the house, and I jumped up to greet him.

Paisley's family followed in their car. Millie flew off the porch steps. I watched as Paisley jumped out of the car just as fast. The girls hugged and cried. Sheesh. Girls.

I felt a small hand patting my leg and saw Mía looking at me. "Who are those people? Are they going to take me away?"

As much I would have liked for my parents to comfort her, they were both following Millie out to the car so I sat back down on the porch to look into Mía's eyes. "No, they won't take you. They'll be happy to meet you."

Mía smiled and followed me. Caleb and Donovan ran around chasing each other and laughing like they hadn't been together in weeks instead of just a couple days.

"Well, now if this ain't the purty little girl what Millie rescued." Minnesota Mike pulled his helmet off and joined them.

"Is he Santa Claus?" Mía whispered.

Mom rushed over and embraced Mike. "Thank you, thank you, thank you!" She wiped tears from her eyes. "I don't know what would have happened to Millie if you hadn't been there to intervene."

"Well, I'll tell ya." It looked like Mike was also wiping tears away. "I don't think I ever been so scared myself and," he pointed to Dad who had joined Mom. "It's your God, that One you been telling me about. That's the only reason I was in that spot this morning."

Paisley's parents joined us by Mike's buggy. "It sounds like we all have stories to share," her mom said. She was smiling, so it must be good news. At least I hoped so.

But then I saw Millie and Paisley talking, heads close together. When Millie threw her arms around Paisley and started crying again, I knew Paisley had already given her the news. And it sure didn't seem good.

Chapter 69

Millie

"Millie." Jeremiah startled her when he was so close. She wiped her eyes before looking his way. "Are you going to show Paisley our new pets?"

"Pets?" Paisley squealed. "You got pets? Plural, as in more than one?"

"Sixteen!" Caleb said. He looked at Donovan, eyes wide with excitement. "Lizards!"

"Lizards?" Mía screamed. "I hate lizards!"

"Where did she come from?" Paisley whispered. Millie, glad for the change in topic, put her arm around Mía and introduced her.

Minnesota Mike joined the girls. "You wouldn't believe what yer good friend did for this little gal."

Mom called out from the porch. "Let's all get some refreshments and share our stories."

"Well, how about this?" Mr. Morgan said. "We go away for a couple days and everything changes."

Mrs. Morgan sat with her arm around Millie while they all related the events of the morning. "God was surely watching over you today." She looked across the room, "And thank you Mike for being His instrument to care for her."

"I like the lizards best!" Donovan said. "I can't wait to hold one."

"It will be quite some time before those critters are ready to be held," Millie's Dad said. "They're angry now because of being mistreated."

"What about me?" Mía stood with her hands on her hips staring at the boys. "Aren't you excited about me?"

Millie hugged the girl and held back laughter at the look of horror on Caleb and Donovan's faces.

"The only girl I will get excited about," Caleb said, "is my sister Jenny. She'll be here soon."

"Leon is out looking for her, honey." Millie's mom smiled at Caleb. "We're not sure if he'll be able to find her."

"He'll find her, she lives by the light. She told me so."

This was news to all of them. "When did she tell you that, Caleb?" Jeremiah asked.

"I'll be right back, I gotta get something."

Millie followed Jeremiah to the hallway, curious to see what he was up to. He went into his room and came back out carrying his box of toy cars. Disappointed, Millie followed him back to the living room. She thought he had something to show them about his sister.

Caleb sat on the floor and spread the cars out near Donovan, then looked over at Jeremiah. "She came back to visit once and when my mom went outside, Jenny whispered and told me when I see the light shining on the hill, that she was there." He looked around the room at everyone staring at him. "And that's how I know."

Mía scooted over by the boys. "Can I play with the cars, too?"

"Oooh!" Caleb said. "Girls don't play with cars."

Mía reached for a bright blue car with orange decals. "I never had cars to play with." She ignored the boys complaints and joined in.

"I had to get stucked with a needle today," Donovan said to Caleb as they drove their cars around the chair on the far side of the living room.

"I hate needles." Caleb chased Donovan's car, overtaking him as they rounded the chair.

Millie looked over at Paisley. "I thought it was you they were checking out?" She turned to her mom and dad and saw a look of concern on their faces.

Paisley's dad stood and motioned for them to follow. "How about if we go in the kitchen for some coffee?"

Millie knew there was a lot more than coffee drinking they were going in the kitchen for.

Chapter 70

Jeremiah

"Why did Donovan get stuck with a needle today?" Millie demanded in her typical rush-right-in-style as soon as we were all in the kitchen. Minnesota Mike offered to stay with the little ones in the living room. Who knows, maybe he'd rather play cars with them than face the news about Paisley. And now maybe even Donovan?

Mom set out cups, while Dad brought over the coffeepot as we gathered around the table. It's probably hard for a mom to hear another child might be in danger, and maybe that's why she busied herself getting cream and sugar and cookies and napkins. It was as if as long as she didn't sit down and look into the faces of Paisley and her parents, she didn't have to admit that her daughter's best friend might be in some danger.

I'm sure it wasn't far from her mind, the sad story Julia told about her children. Julia. I shuddered as I thought of her again. How was she involved in Mía being at the store?

Finally, Mom joined us at the table, and Mrs. Morgan broke the silence. It was amazing how long Millie waited for the answer to her question without demanding again to be told. But maybe, she, too, was afraid to hear.

"The doctor believes Paisley has the condition Julia told us about."

Mr. Morgan reached over and squeezed his wife's hand where it was resting on the table. I watched Millie's face go white. She avoided making eye contact with any of us, especially Paisley, sitting beside her. Millie, my tough-as-nails sister who just rescued a little girl from a smuggler, looked like she was ready to fall apart at this news about her best friend.

Paisley reached over and clasped Millie's hand, much the same way her dad did with her mother. Millie still refused to look at her. "There are treatments to keep me safe," Paisley said. "Julia most likely saved my life."

"Praise God for bringing Julia into our lives," Mom said.

"Amen," both Paisley's parents spoke at once.

"But why were they testing Donovan?" I repeated the question I knew Millie wondered about, but could no longer ask.

"Because it's very likely genetic, they tested all of us. We'll have the results in a few weeks," Mr. Morgan said.

"What led them to think that Julia may have been right?" Dad said.

"Paisley's electrocardiogram showed some irregularities, the kind typical with this condition. It's called Long QT Syndrome, and it's a problem with the electrical impulses the heart sends between heartbeats," Mrs. Morgan said.

The kitchen was quiet as we all took in the scary fact that Paisley could have died the day she passed out.

"Tell them about the treatment, Mom." Paisley, always the upbeat one, let go of Millie's hand and put her arm around her shoulders, squeezing her close. "It's okay, Millie, now that we know, the doctors can treat it. I will be fine. I can lead a normal life and still be as active as I want to be."

"Is that right?" Mom asked.

"Yes and no, Norah," Paisley's mom said. "A doctor will monitor her and they will treat it with medication. It's an excellent chance that she will be fine, but we have to be careful. I'm so very thankful for Julia."

"But you don't know the truth about Julia!" Millie blurted, startling everyone, especially me. We weren't supposed to talk about that until we found out why she had been at the store that day. Millie continued. "She's involved in the smuggling."

"Millicent!" Mom said.

"Now, hold on there, missy," Minnesota Mike's voice took us all by surprise. I sure hadn't seen him come into the kitchen. "You don't know what you're talking about."

Chapter 71

Millie

"Excuse me. I'll be right back." Millie stood and ignored the stares of everyone in the room, including Mike, as she passed him on her way out of the kitchen. Glad that the young ones were now in the playroom, she slipped out the front door with no one seeing her.

She felt so mature as she climbed the ladder to the tower. Just a few months ago she would have run off screaming or crying. This time she said "excuse me" before she left. It was almost funny. But she had no energy to laugh.

She winced at the memory of the time she ran crying far into their back acreage at night, climbed a hill, then fell and sprained her ankle and couldn't get back home. That was scary, listening to the coyotes howl. At least now she was more polite and stayed closer to home where it was safe.

Millie slumped down on the floor of the tower, hidden by the wooden walls her dad had built, and let the tears fall. This day was too much. First the poor lizards taped and stuffed in small containers, then finding Mía and that angry man scared her to death. Worst of all, finding out her best friend has something wrong with her heart. Something people, kids even, have died from. It was just all too much.

She laid down on the floor, her face buried in her hands, and let the tears flow.

"Millie?" The voice sounded far away. She didn't recognize it. "Millie?" It was a soft, comforting voice. Had she heard that voice before? She felt a hand touch her shoulder, then rub her back. "Millie? Can we talk?"

She struggled to open her eyes. Darkness surrounded her. How long had she been asleep?

Chapter 72

Jeremiah

"Jeremiah, why would your sister say such an outrageous thing about Julia?" Mom looked stunned.

That Millie. Well, she started it, so I'm just going to spill the beans on everything. That's what she gets for bringing up seeing Julia at the store and then taking off, leaving me here to answer the questions with a roomful of people staring at me.

"Jeremiah, do you know?" Dad said.

I guess all my thinking was taking too long. Well, here goes.

"Yes, I know." I took a deep breath and looked around the table. Minnesota Mike came the rest of the way into the kitchen and took a seat.

It's a weird feeling when you're getting ready to spill your guts and you know it will get you in lots of trouble. But I had no choice. Thank you, Sister Millie.

"We knew something strange has been going on at the old store for a couple weeks. So whenever we would go out riding, we would go by the store to see if we could see people there or what was happening."

"What do you mean something strange and what does this have to do with Julia?" Mom was just as bad as Millie with asking too many questions.

"Norah, give him a chance to explain."

Thank you, Dad.

With no more hesitating, I told them everything from the day Millie got handcuffed right up to seeing Julia and going back there today. Mom looked horrified, and Dad sat there shaking his head. I could just imagine the punishments they were lining up in their minds. We'd probably get grounded the rest of our lives.

"Well, I got to say that I'm a bit to blame here, too." Minnesota Mike's unexpected words interrupted the awkward silence.

It helped me out because everyone quit looking at me. It was like a ping-pong tournament, all the faces at the table turned away from me and toward Mike.

"I'm ashamed to say, I knowed about the trouble at the store when Millie got herself handcuffed and I shoulda told you."

Mom did not look happy hearing that confession. Maybe Mike would get grounded, too. I almost laughed out loud at that thought, but caught myself. Probably not a smart thing to do at a time like this. That's more like something Millie would do, except she was hiding somewhere and missing out on all this fun.

"Well, at first I didn't know fer sure, but I was up at the ice cream store about a week ago and I heard some fellers talking about some kids poking around the store. Heard 'em say something about handcuffing the girl to scare them away."

So that's how Mike knew. I wondered how he found out.

"Well, a few days later I sorta tricked Jeremiah into telling me it was them two at the store." He looked over at Dad and Mom with the sorriest look on his face I'd ever seen. "I never once thought them fool kids would go back there after a scare like that. I shoulda told you."

"Is that why you were there today?" Mom said.

"Well, now, ma'am," Minnesota said, "you know, I was sitting in my recliner watching an old black and white movie and then I just got the strangest urge to go fer a drive in my buggy. And once I got out there I saw that truck I suspected, so I started following it. And," he turned toward Mom, a pleading look in his eyes, "ya gotta believe me, I never in my wildest dreams expected to see your young'uns there at that store, too."

"Well, it was the hand of God that led you there, that's for sure," Dad said.

The sound of tires crunching on the gravel outside interrupted the conversation.

"Sounds like you've got more company," Mr. Morgan stood and motioned for his family to join him. "We'll go ahead and leave now. We've had a long day."

"Tell Millie I said goodbye," Paisley hugged Mom as she stepped away from the table.

Before any of us could get out the kitchen doorway, Caleb came barreling into the kitchen yelling for all the world to hear. "It's my sissy! Deputy Black has my sissy with him! Come on, everybody!"

Chapter 73

Millie

Millie opened her eyes, stunned to see the nurse sitting next to her on the tower floor. Julia smiled. "How could I ever have thought she was a bad person?" Millie wondered and felt shame looking into the gentle eyes.

"Julia?" She sat up and rubbed her eyes. Julia reached out and smoothed her hair, then leaned over and hugged her.

"Can we talk, Millie?"

"I'm so sorry." Millie felt tears welling up in her eyes again. She wondered if she would ever stop crying so much. "They must have told you what I said."

"Shh," Julia whispered. "It's okay."

"How can it be okay? I accused you of something so bad."

"It's okay because you did it out of love for the little ones like Mía. You weren't being mean just for the sake of being mean. You care so much for others and you want to heal their hurts." Julia smiled. "You're very special, Millie. You risked your own life to save hers."

"I'm not sure it was the smartest thing I've ever done, but it worked out."

"Yes, it was dangerous and I'm sure Leon will talk about that with you, but for now, look how wonderful it turned out for little Mía." Julia clapped her hands together. "Now, let me tell you why I was at the store that morning."

"So it was you?" Millie asked.

"Yes, and my husband Tucker." Julia beamed. "When I went home the other evening and told him that the store I have such fond memories of was for sale, he wanted to go see it."

Millie couldn't believe what she was hearing.

"Tucker has been wanting me to change careers."

"He doesn't like you being a nurse?"

"Well, not that so much, as the environment I've worked in for some time has been hostile. To me, at least."

"Is that why you couldn't talk about the heart condition with Paisley's mom at the hospital."

"Yes, it is."

"Does that mean you are buying the store?"

Julia's broad smile answered that question. "We just came from visiting Paisley's family and telling them the news."

Millie got on her knees to peer over the wall of the tower, looking for Paisley's car. "Did they go home?"

Julia laughed. "Quite some time ago. I'm told you've been out here sleeping for several hours. Did you know it's almost ten o'clock?"

"Oh no, I've missed everything. Did Leon ever come back? What about Caleb's sister?"

Chapter 74

Jeremiah

I knew as soon as I saw this girl she was nothing, and I mean nothing like Millie. Caleb clung to her like he hadn't seen her in years. And who knows, maybe he hadn't? She hugged him back just as hard and I wondered where has she been living and what's been going on in her life? Her hair looked like she didn't own a brush and not sure the last time they washed her clothes. But the biggest contrast between her and Millie was how timid she was.

Mom embraced the two kids. Caleb wiggled out of Mom's arms, then grabbed hold of her hand and his sister's hand. "Jenny, this is our new mom. Her name is Norah." I saw Mom turn and look at Dad and then Deputy Black.

Jenny didn't even look at Mom. "Where is our mom?" she whispered to Caleb. Millie would be glad to know I stood close enough to hear what they were saying so I could pass the info along to her.

"She's gone away somewheres," Caleb said.

"I hope she went to jail." Jenny still whispered, looking only at her brother.

He seemed surprised. "Jenny? Why would you say that?"

Jenny didn't answer. Just stood there and cried. Uh-oh. She had at least one of Millie's characteristics. But crying wasn't as bad as being pushy.

Mom put her arm around Jenny. "Honey, let's go in the house and get you something to eat."

I never saw Paisley's family leave. They must have slipped out the back door which probably was best. I think it would have been even harder on Jenny for so many people to be here. Caleb looked torn between following Mom and Jenny inside or staying outside. He looked up at me. "Why did she say our mom should go to jail?"

"Hey buddy," Deputy Black rescued me. "Jenny's upset. She's tired and hungry and scared." He knelt down and looked into Caleb's eyes. "We all say things when we're feeling overwhelmed." He hugged Caleb. "Do you know what I mean?"

"I guess so. But I told her we got a new mom now." He looked into Deputy Black's eyes, then over at Dad. "She can live here too, can't she?"

Chapter 75

Millie

"We should go in the house quietly," Julia followed Millie down the ladder.

Millie looked up at her, puzzled.

"Jenny and Caleb are asleep on the couch."

"She's here? They found her? Why didn't anyone tell me?"

"So many questions, girl." Julia tucked her arm around Millie shoulders when she reached the ground. "Your parents just wanted to let you sleep, you were exhausted and upset. And honestly, so was Jenny they tell me."

"You didn't talk to her?"

Julia took Millie by the hand and headed to the garden. "Let's chat for a bit and I'll tell you what I learned."

Millie grabbed her stomach at the loud growl. "I think I slept through dinner."

"It sure sounds like it." Julia laughed as they both took a seat on the garden bench.

"My husband and I went to visit Paisley's family after we left the realtor's office late this afternoon. I wanted to hear about Paisley's test results and tell them our news about the store."

"So Paisley already knows? Was she happy about it?"

"Oh yes, very and especially her parents. I'll be close by and able to help them learn about living with Paisley's condition."

"And if there's an emergency?"

"Well, I'm not a doctor, but I can be there until they get medical attention." Julia nodded. "But with proper treatment and monitoring any symptoms, I'm not expecting any emergencies."

"I'm so glad," Millie said. "I was worried about her. Did you know I never had a best friend in my life until I met Paisley?"

"You two are perfect for each other." Julia patted Millie's knee. "And I think you'll be a perfect friend for Jenny, too."

"What were you going to tell me about her?"

"Leon and Griffin found her living in a shack close to where you two found the box this morning."

"Oh, no, that's awful." Millie felt ashamed of her earlier selfish thoughts about not wanting the sister to live with them.

"Her mother was getting paid for Jenny to live there and help with the smuggling of the reptiles. Before they started using drones, it was Jenny's job to signal the pilots of the planes. That's what the bumper was for, to reflect the sun so the pilots knew where to make the drop. Then she would get the boxes."

"Did she know what was in them?" Millie felt sick at the news.

"Griffin doesn't think she knew what was in the boxes or that it was smuggling. She just knows her mom was making her live there and work for the couple. She got paid a little, but Griffin and Leon think her mom was getting most of the money."

Another long growl from Millie's stomach distracted them. "We better get you inside to eat." Julia stood and pulled Millie up with her.

Millie stretched and rubbed her rumbling stomach, then headed toward the house. She looked over at Julia as they walked. "So how did you come to be over here so late, anyway?"

She regretted asking that question when she heard the answer.

"Paisley's family told me you thought I was involved with the smugglers."

Millie felt her ears burning. "I'm so sorry." She kept her head down, unable to face Julia.

"It's okay." Julia put her arm around Millie's shoulders as they walked. "I just wanted to clear that up right away and your parents said it was okay for us to stop by after we left Paisley's."

"Millie! There you are!" Mom's enthusiasm warmed Millie's heart as she stood waiting on the porch with open arms.

Chapter 76

Jeremiah

"This house is filling up with kids faster than I thought it could happen." The smile on Griffin's face as he came through the door followed by Leon gave me some sense of relief. When Mom and Dad told us they were coming over this morning to talk to me and Millie, I had an uncomfortable feeling. I doubted this time it would be to tell us about a big reward like before.

Mía and Caleb bickered over the toy cars. Poor Caleb. Mía was like a miniature Millie. Give up now, kid, I felt like telling him. You don't even have a chance. Jenny sat on the floor next to her brother, whispering to him. Caleb didn't look happy about whatever she said, but I saw him let go of the car Mía wanted.

Minnesota Mike sat on the couch chuckling about it all.

"Jeremiah, Millie." Dad motioned for us to follow him. "Let's go in the kitchen and chat with the officers while Mike watches the kids."

Uh-oh, he called them officers. That sounds so much more formal than calling them by their names. I thought they were our friends. Officers? I wondered if we were in trouble. By the look on Millie's face, she must have been thinking the same thing.

"How are those lizards doing?" Leon looked over at Millie as he took a seat at the table. Mom sat cups of coffee on the table but gave Leon iced tea. I noticed she didn't put out any cookies or muffins. So definitely not a social call. Come on, Millie, I thought, tell him about the stupid lizards so we can get on with the bad news. If I had said that, Millie would have had a fit because I called them stupid.

"They're doing good."

A three word answer? Not like her at all. Definitely nervous.

"Well, kids," Leon looked from Millie to me. "Some good things have come out of the risks you've taken. Mía and Jenny were rescued." He smiled, but not too big, I noticed. Mom and Dad stayed quiet. I'm sure they'd have plenty to say later.

"The reptile smuggling ring has been discovered."

"Julia said Jenny didn't know about the lizards." Millie's curiosity must have overcome her fear.

"That's true," Leon said. "She thought the dropped boxes were supplies. It was her job to retrieve the boxes." He paused and took a long drink of his iced tea.

"But you took risks." Now he wasn't smiling. "Serious ones. You could have been hurt or worse."

It was hard to make eye contact with Leon while he spoke, and no way could I look at our parents. Silence filled the room. I couldn't even hear the other kids. Mike must have taken them outside.

"Do you remember when I told you to report any suspicious activity to me?" Leon was stern.

"I do."

"Did you do that?" Leon looked over at Millie. "Either of you?"

We were both speechless, at least I assumed Millie was, I sure heard nothing from her and I couldn't take my eyes off Leon. I shook my head.

"It's your decision," Leon looked at my parents, "but I'd recommend that they not leave the property for a few weeks, maybe longer."

"Absolutely," Dad and Mom both said at the same time.

"And when you go riding again off your parent's property," Leon looked back at both of us. "Only ride between here and Ridge Riders Lodge, or over in the off road park. There are park rangers over there. No going back to those hills south of here."

"Okay." We both spoke at the same time.

"You two are awesome kids." Griffin smiled. Wow, what a relief. Leon nodded his head at Griffin's words. "You're curious, you're adventurous, you're brave. Maybe a little too brave." It seemed funny, but I didn't know if it was okay to laugh. "Leon is right, when you see something suspicious, never investigate yourself. Tell your parents and contact us."

"Besides the risks you took," Dad said, "there was a fair amount of dishonesty going on too."

"Dishonesty?" Millie asked what I wondered about.

"Didn't you tell us each time you went riding this last week that you were searching for a meteorite?" Mom did not sound happy. "Whatever happened to that plan?"

Chapter 77

Millie

"Why do you think Jenny didn't want to roast marshmallows with us?" Millie dangled her stick in the fire, letting the marshmallow flare, before pulling it back out.

"She's probably scared. She doesn't know us."

"Do you think Mom will make her do schoolwork? And Mía?" She pulled the way too hot marshmallow off the stick, wincing when it burnt her fingertips.

"You're not going to put that in your mouth right away, are you?" Millie was bouncing it around with her tongue before Jeremiah even got the words out. She gasped for cool air and waved her hand in front of her mouth. Jeremiah shook his head like he thought she wasn't too smart.

"Well, are they?" Her words were garbled, coming from her marshmallow filled mouth.

"Are they what?" He lifted his roasting stick out of the fire, waving his marshmallow around in the cool air.

"Are they going to be doing schoolwork?"

"Millie, you heard Mom and Dad. They don't even know how long the girls will be here. You don't just find kids and bring them home and keep them."

"Yeah, but you know Mom and Dad," Millie shoved another marshmallow on the end of the stick. "They'll make this work somehow. You can tell, both those girls need a home."

"Not my problem whether or not they do schoolwork." Jeremiah popped his barely browned marshmallow into his mouth.

Why he couldn't roast them to a decent brown, she just couldn't understand. "Well, it isn't fair."

"What isn't?" He stared at her like he had no clue what she was talking about.

"It isn't fair if they're doing nothing, while we're doing school. I mean, if it wasn't for us, they wouldn't even be here."

"Sounding a little boastful there, aren't you?"

She had to admit it didn't sound like the right thing to say. "I guess what's bothering me the most." She stopped to focus on shoving three marshmallows on the end. "Why is Mom making us do that stupid 15 page report on meteors on top of all our regular schoolwork?"

"Millie, I think we got off pretty easy with what we did. I mean, for one thing, we're still alive in spite of all those dangerous risks. For another, they could have taken our motorcycles away for good."

"But why a report on meteors? I don't even care about them."

"Well, maybe because that's what we were supposed to be searching for, the meteorite that fell to the ground last week."

She saw Jeremiah watching as she waved the flaming stick around. She thought about shoving all three hot marshmallows in her mouth at once just to annoy him. But she figured that might hurt. Instead, she put the stick back in the fire and let them burn.

"Look at it this way," he said. "Maybe we'll learn something about hunting for meteorites and we can find it when we're allowed to go out riding again."

"Yeah, I guess that sounds like a good idea. I wonder if we can sell it when we find it, and get rich? Or famous? Yeah, we can get famous. Those professor dudes will be so excited when we contact them." She shoved four marshmallows on the stick.

"Don't fill that whole stick." Jeremiah grabbed the bag from her. "In the meantime, maybe we can get off the property by offering to help Julia and Tucker clean up the new Dry Brook Trading Post."

"Wait a minute, what happened to calling it Ye Olde Dry Brook Trading Post."

"That's the old name." Jeremiah popped the lightly roasted marshmallow into his mouth. "This is the new Dry Brook Trading Post. That's what Julia told us when you were hiding out in the tower."

"So how did Minnesota Mike know about Julia and her husband buying that store, anyway?"

"You missed out on that when you ran off."

"I didn't run." Millie shook her finger at her brother. "I politely excused myself."

"I guess you're right," Jeremiah said. "Well, turns out it was Minnesota Mike's idea all along. He met Julia when he was in the hospital and knew she wasn't happy in her job. Once he found out the store was for sale, he started checking to make sure no one had put an offer on it. The realtor told him the place had been deserted for years with no interest from anyone."

Jeremiah stood and stretched, then sat back down. "That explained why when he and I drove by the store, he knew no one should have been there."

"So, how did he know Julia and her husband bought the store? You haven't even answered that question in that long history lesson."

"Remember at Paisley's house when he hinted to Julia about the right person buying the store?"

"Yeah."

"When they went out in the buggy he drove her to the store and talked to her about his idea. He said he was even more sure it was the right thing to do when he learned she had gone there as a kid. So Minnesota Mike was the first one she told after they worked out the deal."

"Wow," Millie said, staring into the fire. "The things you miss when you get upset and walk out on everybody."

"Hey."

Millie and Jeremiah both jumped at the sound of a voice near the garden. They stood and looked around.

A boy about Jeremiah's age stood near Millie's rock formation, barely discernible in the dim firelight.

"Where did you come from?" she said.

He took a few steps toward the fire. "Is this the place that takes in kids?"

Millie looked at Jeremiah. His eyes were as wide as hers felt. "What should we do?" she said.

"What do you think?" Jeremiah looked at her like she was brainless. "We need to go tell Mom and Dad about this right away."

"Be right back, kid," Millie said, and they took off running for the house.

Acknowledgements

It takes the help of many people to bring a story to life. I am grateful to my family members who patiently listen to never-ending talk and questions about my book adventures. They offer suggestions and are the first readers, providing valuable feedback:

Summer, age 14, Granddaughter – First Reader
Jana Foley, Aunt – Second Reader
Steve Kukla, Husband – Third and Most Critical Reader

For helping with accuracy and authenticity in this book, thank you Jolene Crouse, RN with Palomar Health in San Diego County (who also races her quad in the desert) and Terri Peterla, middle school teacher at New Hanover Township School in Wrightstown NJ. These ladies gave their time to read the manuscript while it was still a work in progress, then provided feedback and answered questions, to help with the final editing.

Thank you to my sister and brother-in-law for prayer support and encouragement: Regina and Alan Jensen; to my grandson, Wyatt Kukla, age 7, who loves previewing and helping choose book covers.

I am especially grateful to the members of the LQTS Kids & Families Facebook page who gave valuable input: Shelby Nicole Balk, Thomson IL; Stephanie Lentell, Port Orchard WA; Melissa Marie, Ohio; Eileen Pike, Westchester NY; Jan Schiller, SADS Foundation, www.sads.org; Dianna Walters, St. Louis MO; Jasmine Wylie, San Francisco CA; and Amy Whittle, teacher, Idalou Middle School, Idalou TX.

Thank you Christine Puricelli, mother of Emilie, to whom the book is dedicated, for providing these resources to learn about children and adults who may be at risk for heart related sudden death: Parent Heart Watch, www.parentheartwatch.org; Mayo Clinic (search Long QT Syndrome), www.mayoclinic.org; SADS Foundation, www.sads.org and Sudden Cardiac Arrest Association, www.suddencardiacarrest.org

Read Emilie's story at
www.sads.org/healing-wall-entries/Emilie-Puricelli

Lastly, I give all praise to God, the Creator, for blessing us with creative abilities and for His wondrous gift of salvation and abundant life.

Phantom Ship in the Desert

MotoMysteries

Book 3

For two of my greatest encouragers
Jana Foley
My very special aunt
and
Susan Stephens
My friend and neighbor

Chapter 1

Millie

Millie hung on tight to the handlebars as her dirt bike bumped and bounced down the rocky hillside. She twisted the throttle hard when she reached the bottom of the hill, taking a quick glance over her shoulder to see if her pursuers were in sight.

"Jeremiah!" she yelled as she gassed it up the next hill. She grimaced at the jostling of the backpack slapping against her. "I'm sorry lizards, I'm sorry," she said into her helmet, thinking about the poor creatures inside getting bounced around.

Her heart pounded as she realized she was nearing the top of the hill quicker than she expected and was about to be launched into outer space.

"Jeremiah!" she screamed as she crested the top with only blue sky visible. Where was her brother when she needed him? He told her not to go rescue the lizards by herself. Why hadn't she listened?

She thought about the reptiles with limbs taped, stuffed inside the potato chip cans. She couldn't leave them, she couldn't wait for the authorities to come.

But now, knowing she was about to be launched into thin air with the smugglers chasing her, she'd been no help to them at all. They would probably pick over her dead body and steal the lizards back.

She wondered if lizards could scream. Because if they could, this would be a good time!

"Jeremiah!!!!" It was a deep guttural grunt as fear robbed her of the ability to speak.

Millie, the motorcycle and the lizards in the backpack left the safety of the dirt and launched into the atmosphere. She didn't know if she should hold on to the handlebars or let go. Her last thought as she sailed through the air was, "I'm going to die."

Chapter 2

Jeremiah

"Jeremiah!"

I sat up in bed like an electric shock went through me, the early morning sky still dark outside my window. There was no sound other than the wind howling outside. "Did someone call me?" I wondered, then heard the muffled sound of my name again, coming from the direction of my sister's room.

Millie sounded terrified. Leaping from my bed I bolted toward her room, hoping my dad would be there for back-up. With Millie you never knew if it was a masked intruder or if she lost her favorite rock. She was a girl of extremes.

"Jeremiah." This time the low pitched sound was barely discernible. I crossed the carpeted floor in a hurry as she thrashed and moaned in her bed.

Flipping the bedside light on, I could see her wince at the light through her closed eyes. I had hoped that would wake her. "Millie," I whispered. She continued to moan. "Millie." Shaking her shoulder, I jumped when her eyes popped open and she jerked her head in my direction.

She sat up panting and looked around in a daze.

"Millie, you were having a bad dream."

Her eyes grew large as she stared at me, then looked frantically around her room. "I'm safe!" she said, breathing hard. "Where are the lizards? Are they okay?" She slipped off her bed onto the floor and rummaged through her backpack.

"Millie." I knelt next to her, not sure if she was awake yet. I didn't know people could dream when they look awake.

"Millie, it's okay. Agent Leon took the lizards. They're safe."

I didn't want to be the one to remind her that yesterday we said good-bye to the lizards we helped rescue from the smugglers. She had stayed in her room most of the day after Agent Leon left. It didn't help that her best friend Paisley was also gone. She had left for the city last week and wouldn't return for a long time.

"Millie, you were dreaming."

She stopped searching through the backpack and looked up. "I was?"

"You kept calling out my name. What was going on?"

She breathed deeply, "I was running from the smugglers . . ."

"Jeremiah!" Dad appeared at the doorway. "Come with me! There's trouble at the Ridge Riders Lodge."

Chapter 3

Millie

"I hate the wind!" Millie stood at the large front window watching the wall of dust blowing by. Through the brown haze of sand she could make out the faint view of trees and bushes flapping wildly. She watched as leaves, bits of paper and even a trash can lid blew by. "It never stops howling!"

"Millicent, hush!" Mom's stern whisper caught her off guard. "You'll wake the younger ones."

"Mom, I mean it," she continued to stare at the object of her anger. Not that she could see the wind. But the results had been visible for days. "The wind just never stops."

"Springtime in the desert." Mom spoke from across the room.

"I can't even go riding or work in my garden," Millie grumbled. "I'm just stuck in the house." She groaned. "With ten million kids. Why do you have to let all these kids live here, anyway?"

She braced herself for a lecture from her mother. About

kids needing a home, just like she once did. How God called them to open their home to kids in need. How she should set an example for the younger ones. She continued to stare out the window, shoulders tense, waiting to hear the words that would make her feel guilty for resenting their growing family.

But no reprimand came. That was strange. Mom always had something to say. Especially when Millie was doing or saying something wrong. She waited, still glaring out the window. But the silence puzzled her. Millie listened to the wind and wondered if her mother had simply walked away.

"If only I could get that lucky," she thought. Finally, curiosity got the better of her. She turned to face the music, as they say.

Only the "music" in this case was much worse than she expected. Millie stood frozen in place, speechless. A feeling she rarely experienced

Chapter 4

Jeremiah

The tow truck arrived at the Ridge Riders Lodge just as Dad drove our truck in. Minnesota Mike wore his goggles with a bandana covering the rest of his face. He directed the tow truck driver down the first row of trailers to the damage. The toppled trailers had been no match for the powerful wind. Dad parked across the road from the overturned trailers and we both put our goggles on for eye protection against the wall of sand we would step into.

The wind grabbed hold of my door the second I opened it. "Hang on to that door, Jeremiah!" Dad yelled. I meant to, but it happened so fast. I sure hope the door hinges didn't break again. I never realized until we moved to the desert how destructive wind could be. Before that, it seemed the worst thing the wind did was ruin our camping trips.

"Should we try to upright these while the wind's still blowing?" Dad shouted over the howling wind.

Minnesota Mike nodded his head. "That old coot that owns these trailers might have gas or propane on and, doncha know, I don't want no explosions while I'm in charge."

Figures a major windstorm would happen right after Paisley's family left the lodge in Minnesota Mike's care. This is the last thing they need to worry about. Especially with their daughter's life in danger. We weren't even sure when they would return.

I remembered the first time we stayed at the lodge before we moved to the desert. We never realized then what close friends we would become with the owners. The fact they had a daughter our age who homeschooled like us gave my sister a ready-made best friend in the desert. We were all stunned when the doctor diagnosed her with a serious heart problem a few months ago. I hoped we would hear soon the results of their appointment with the heart specialist. Without even asking her, I could tell my sister thought about Paisley constantly, even though she only left a few days ago.

M&M, that's my sister's nickname for Minnesota Mike, watched the driver secure his truck to prevent rolling, grab hold of the winch and head to the trailer. I knew Mike wanted to help, but they have their rules and you can't just jump in and help the guy do his job.

"Jeremiah." I turned to see Dad motioning for me. "Why don't you walk around the RV park and check for other damage while they raise the trailers?"

"Maybe I'll even spot Samuel," I grumbled, which wasn't like me. I usually left the grumbling to my sister, except once in a while. Like now. That kid should help us, instead he just takes off like he's free as a bird and can come and go as he pleases. I don't get why Dad lets him do that.

Minnesota perked up at Samuel's name. "Hey, where is that boy of mine?" He chuckled and winked at me. And that was another thing. At the risk of sounding like I've acquired even more of my pesty sister's bad habits, it irked me that Minnesota had grown so fond of the new kid Samuel. I mean, I thought I was Minnesota's best buddy. Well, in the way a kid can be a buddy to an old man. His sidekick when he needed someone to hunt down skeletons or ghost lights. Me and my sister were the ones who got to hang out with him. Now this new kid comes along and life changes for all of us.

"Jeremiah." Dad's reprimand interrupted my pity party.

"Oh yeah, I'm going right now." I waved as I took off down the row of RVs and trailers. "But if I find that kid," I said under my breath, "I'm going to give him a piece of my mind."

Oh man. I'm turning into my sister.

Chapter 5

Millie

Millie's eyes grew large when she saw Samuel standing next to her mother. He held a dusty looking old knapsack. The kind she imagined soldiers might have once carried as they trekked across the desert during some ancient war.

She glanced at her mother, long enough to know she had really blown it this time, then back to Samuel. "I'm sorry, I didn't know you were there."

He tossed the knapsack on the floor near her feet. "Yeah, no kidding." Then turned to leave the room. "At least I know what you're saying about me when you think I'm not around."

"Samuel, wait!" Millie called out as he disappeared. She started to go after him, but stopped when the back door slammed. Millie wanted to complain to her mom. It wasn't fair that Samuel could slam doors without getting in trouble. She figured this probably wasn't the right time.

"So much for my quiet time this morning," Mom said. It startled Millie. She expected her mom to scold her for being rude.

Millie turned and looked at her. "I'm sorry."

Mom smiled. "I'll get another chance tomorrow morning. I need to get up even earlier to beat all of you early risers."

Mom put her arm around Millie's shoulders and led her to the kitchen. Millie, glad for the opportunity to speak without having to look in her eyes, said, "I mean I'm sorry I made Samuel think he isn't welcome here."

"But you meant what you said, didn't you?" Mom turned to Millie. "It feels to you like our family is growing too fast."

Millie sighed, then plopped down in a kitchen chair and stared out the window. She watched Samuel kicking rocks out by her garden. That jerk, she thought, he's going to ruin my rock garden. "Well, is that bad? I mean, I know these kids need homes, but I'm losing my little family I loved."

"And what if you were the last one to join our family, Millie?" Mom pulled out the baking pan and placed muffin papers into each slot.

"I know," Millie said, "I've thought about that. And if I just came along and Samuel had been here first, I'd think he was a big jerk for not making me feel welcome." She meant that to be funny, but tears started falling. She realized that none of this was funny and she didn't have any answers.

Mom stopped what she was doing and put her arms around Millie, hugging her tight. "We might need to take a breather. Put a brief hold on growing our family and take time for everyone to adjust."

Millie pushed away from her mom and looked into her eyes. "Do you mean it?" Tears flowed faster now. "I feel like I'm the awful one who is complaining about great-grandpa's dream of helping kids. Like I wonder if he would say I'm selfish."

Mom smiled and reached into the cabinet for the mixing bowls and measuring cups. "He would say no such thing. He would know you were every bit as special as we know you are." She motioned to the sink. "How about washing your hands and helping me with the muffin batter?"

"Maybe I should apologize to Samuel first." Millie saw him out the window replacing all the rocks he kicked out of her garden. "He must think I'm such a jerk."

"Sounds like a good idea."

"Hey, kid!" she yelled as she got closer to the garden. She hoped he heard her over the howling wind. Why would a kid want to be out in this weather if he didn't have to?

Just when she decided he hadn't heard, he turned. "Why do you call me that?"

"That's the first time!" She almost forgot she came to apologize, but stopped before saying more.

"My first night here." He pointed to the fire ring. "Be right back, kid!" he mimicked her voice in a high pitch.

"I do not sound like that!" she said.

"But you can't deny those were your words."

"You're right," she admitted. "I said that."

"I'm older than you, you know." Samuel glared. "So don't call me kid."

"You know what your problem is?" Millie stared right back at him. "You should have gotten here sooner. Then you could boss me around."

She saw a flicker of a smile, then he said, "Well, you know what your problem is? You don't even know when a gift has landed at your feet."

"What do you mean?"

"Did you even look in that knapsack?"

Chapter 6

Jeremiah

I thought getting out and walking around would work off my anger at Samuel, but it increased as I saw the mess in the RV park. Fences down, trash cans blown over, debris strewn all over the place. I headed to the swimming pool where plastic chairs were scattered, some even in the pool. And was Samuel here to help me? Was I supposed to pick all this up myself while he was out doing who knows what?

I took a deep breath and remembered all the fun we'd had here before and after moving to the desert. Now everything had changed. Too many new kids at home, and even worse, one older than me. I'm supposed to be the oldest. Samuel seemed to displace my role in the family. And besides all that, Paisley was sick. She could even die. Who knew there was a disease called Long QT Syndrome? What kind of name is that? We don't even know how long her family will be in the city taking care of her. And why did we all have to live so far away from civilization, anyway?

I kicked a rock and watched it bounce across the parking area. Picking up an overturned bench, I sat down and stared at the mess. This must be how Millie feels when she gets all grumpy. I guess I should be more patient with her. It's a crummy way to feel. I wanted everything to go back to the way it was when we first moved to the desert. Nothing but fun. Well, except for a few bad guys, a skeleton, car chases and a car wreck.

I stood and looked around, then realized something. I did not want to become a Millie clone. One of her was enough. Maybe Samuel had a good reason for taking off like he did today. Maybe I should get to know him before deciding I don't like him. Especially if he's going to be my brother. My big brother. That was the hardest part to accept.

As I headed back toward Dad and Minnesota Mike, the sound of the tow truck accelerating, prompted me to pick up the pace. I watched it pull onto the main road in the RV park, heading toward the highway. I jogged back to the trailers, both upright now.

Dad worked on a door banging in the wind. "Looks like the latch is busted clean off," Minnesota Mike yelled to Dad as I walked up. "Hey, there's my man," Mike winked at me. "I got a job fer you, doncha know and you're gonna love it."

I wondered what kind of job would be fun, but it was nice to know he remembered we're still buddies. "What job?" I asked.

"Well I figgered you'd be a good one for this 'cause I know how much you and that sister of yers enjoy exploring and discovering things."

This sounded a lot more interesting than picking up trash.

"How about you go inside this trailer and check things out, make sure nothing's leaking like liquid or gas? Kind of pick things up." He winked at me. "And this old coot that owns this trailer hasn't been around in a long time. So it's okay to do a little snooping too." He let out his trademark belly laugh that was louder than the wind howling.

"Jeremiah," Dad said, "I'm not sure that's a good idea about the snooping."

Leave it to Dad to take away the fun.

"Just make sure everything is okay. And clean up things that fell."

"Okay, Dad." I looked over at Mike.

He winked again. "You be sure and listen to yer dad now, I get a little carried away fergittin' what's right sometimes."

I looked around at the mess inside and wondered if it looked any better before the wind blew the trailer over. You wouldn't even have to be trying to snoop because things were scattered all over the place. I started with cups and plates and silverware I was tripping over. After getting those piled into the sink, I shuffled through papers, boxes, couch cushions and pillows to get to the back of the trailer, looking for anything dangerous like Dad said. Among the debris lay a half crushed cardboard box covered in tape and stickers. The box looked like it had traveled around the world and back.

Bending down to pick it up, I saw words written in large letters on one side of the box. I knew what Dad said. But there was no way I could resist looking inside.

Chapter 7

Millie

"Why?" Millie moved closer to Samuel so she didn't miss hearing his answer in the howling wind. "What's in the knapsack?"

He smirked. "You'll have to see for yourself. If it's still where I left it." He turned to walk away.

"Wait, a minute!" Millie yelled, following him. "Why wouldn't it still be there?"

"I don't know," Samuel called over his shoulder. "Lots of people live in this house. Maybe someone else was more curious than you."

"Ha!" She yelled. "That's impossible. I am the queen of curious."

He turned to look at her. "So you say." He headed toward the back hills of their property.

Millie couldn't be bothered any longer wondering why someone would be crazy enough to hike in a windstorm. She had to get to that knapsack and see what was so important that he would call it a gift.

All was quiet when she opened the back door and passed through the kitchen. Mom's back was to her as she stood in front of the oven, placing the muffin tin on a rack inside. She didn't seem to hear Millie enter the room. Thankfully, all the kids must still be asleep, since there was no noise.

Millie rushed into the living room where Samuel had tossed the knapsack and stopped cold in her tracks. It wasn't there. Maybe that rat doubled back and came in the front door and took it while she was going in the back door. She stepped over to the window to look for him but couldn't see anything through the wall of sand still blowing.

"Hey, give me that!" Caleb's voice rang out down the hallway and Millie cringed, realizing the kids were awake. Maybe they had it.

"It's my turn to play with it." Mía's voice meant business.

"Those kids probably have my gift," Millie muttered. "There are too many kids living here." She knew it was selfish, but today she didn't care. It was too much to deal with being cooped up in the house. This wind had been going on for days.

"Mía, give that back to Caleb." Jenny's soft voice coaxed the little girl to return whatever it was she had taken.

"Of course she'd defend Caleb, he's her brother. Her real brother," Millie thought. "She'll side with him over any of the other kids in the house. And it's probably my knapsack."

Millie rushed down the hallway to see what the bickering was about, ready to take the knapsack away from all three of them.

"I'll take that!" She burst into the playroom. Jenny sat on the couch reading a book while Caleb and Mía argued over a bright orange Hot Wheels car. The knapsack was nowhere to be seen.

"You want my Hot Wheels car, Millie?" Caleb asked.

Chapter 8

Jeremiah

Just as I sat on the couch with the box in my lap, the door banged open. My heart beat hard wondering how my dad could have known I was getting ready to snoop. When he didn't step inside, I figured it was just the wind.

Peeling up the old dusty packing tape from one side of the box, my heart pounded with excitement, wondering what I would find inside. So engrossed in removing the layers of tape, I didn't realize I had an audience until a young boy shuffled closer to me. I jumped as if my dad was standing there watching me do what he told me not to do.

"Who are you?"

The boy ignored my question. "Did Emmett say you could come in his trailer?"

"Who is Emmett and who are you?"

"I'm Tyler and Emmett is my friend." He stared at the dusty, crumpled box I held. I couldn't believe some little kid could make me feel so guilty. I gave up and put the box down where I found it. The kid stared at the writing in big letters on the side, then looked at me. "What's that say?"

"You can't read it?" He looked about 8 or 9 years old.

"No one ever told me how."

"Where do you live?"

"Next door to Emmett. Only I ain't seen Emmett in a long time."

"Next door? You mean in the other trailer that the wind blew over?"

"That wasn't the wind." Tyler picked the box up and stared at the words. Thankfully he didn't ask me again what it said. I didn't want to tell him.

"What do you mean it wasn't the wind?"

"It was the bad guys. They tipped the trailers over because they was mad at my mama for somethin'. But I don't know what."

"Where is your mom?"

"Well, me and her were staying with my mama's friend last night 'cause we knowed those bad men were gonna try to hurt my mom and Emmett. But they didn't know Emmett ain't even been around for a long time."

"Does your mom know you're in here?"

"Nah, she don't get up too early. She's tired a lot."

"Jeremiah?" Dad poked his head in the trailer door and looked surprised to see Tyler.

"Well, who's your friend here?"

"I'm Emmett's friend."

The little fellow sure wasn't shy.

"And who is Emmett?" Dad looked from Tyler to me and back again.

Before Tyler could turn this into a long conversation, I jumped in. "Dad, there is something you and Mike need to know."

Chapter 9

Millie

"I'm going to kill that kid!" Millie didn't mean to say that out loud.

"Millie!" Caleb yelled. "You can't kill someone."

"I'm going to tell Mom." Mía dropped the toy she was trying to take from Caleb and ran out of the room.

"She's not even your mom," Millie wanted to yell after the little girl, but this time she kept the words in her head. Good thing because she was in enough trouble already.

Millie headed toward her bedroom, but Samuel stood in the hallway, blocking her path.

"Give me that knapsack!"

"I already gave it to you," Samuel said. "What are you yelling at me for?"

"You know why!" She struggled to resist the urge to shove him out of her way.

"I don't have the slightest idea what you're talking about."

How could he lie with such a straight face? That's the thing about liars, especially ones who are so good. They don't even look guilty when they lie.

"You know you snuck back in the house and took it."

"Why would I do that, when I gave it to you?"

"To get back at me for being mean."

"You were pretty mean."

"Well, you're just as mean, taunting me outside, saying you gave it to me, but you don't know if it would still be there."

"You mean it wasn't there?" He looked surprised, but Millie knew it was part of the act.

"You know it wasn't there! You snuck back in and got it when I went around to the back door." Millie's voice was so loud she figured by now her dad could hear her wherever he was. Who cared? She was in trouble already, and she was sick of all these kids in her house. Telling on her. Playing tricks on her. Doing all the talking at the dinner table so she couldn't even get a word in to her parents. This business about letting a bunch of kids move in with them sure wasn't as fun as she thought it was going to be.

"Millicent!" Mom's voice sounded from the end of the hallway. Mía was close behind.

"It's probably Samuel she wants to kill," Mía's whisper was so loud she may as well have been shouting.

"I'm not going to kill anyone!" Millie shouted. "It's a figure of speech, and I didn't even mean to say it!"

"Are you sure about that MILLICENT?" Samuel glared at her.

"That's enough, Samuel," Mom said, then turned to Mía. "And you go back to the playroom and stay out of this."

"Millie, what's this about?"

"The knapsack." Millie glared back at Samuel. "He gave it to me, then he snuck back in the house and hid it from me."

"No, I . . ." Samuel started, but Mom interrupted him with her hand up.

"No, he didn't Millie."

"How do you know? You don't even know what he said to me outside. I know it was him."

"Well, I know it wasn't," Mom said.

"How can you?" Millie could feel tears threatening to fall. Even her mom was siding with the new kids.

"Because I know where it is."

Chapter 10

Jeremiah

Minnesota Mike joined us in the trailer. He didn't seem surprised to see Tyler. "Hey there old buddy, I was worried you got tipped over in your trailer when the wind knocked it over."

"That's the thing . . ." I started.

"The wind didn't blow it over," Tyler blurted. "Those bad men did it."

Dad looked at me. "That's what I wanted to tell you, Dad."

"Tyler, buddy, you sure you ain't funnin' me?"

"That don't sound very fun to me, Mr. Mike." Tyler shook his head from side to side staring into Minnesota's eyes.

"Where's yer mom now, little fella?"

"She's over at her friend's. We slept there last night."

"Does she know you're here, Tyler?" Dad asked, looking at Minnesota Mike, then back to the boy.

"She's still asleep. But she lets me walk around when she's asleep."

"Pretty windy for you to be outside, don't you think?" I said.

Tyler looked at me like he had forgotten I was there. "Well you're out in it."

I held back a chuckle, but before I could think of a comeback, Minnesota jumped in.

"Well, now sonny boy, that's 'cause we needed to get these trailers set back up that the wind done blew over."

"I told you . . ." Tyler started.

"Hold it there now, I heard what you told me, but I got to think on that some."

Tyler stepped over to the crumpled box on the floor, picked it up and showed it to Mike. "Well, while you're thinking, can you tell me what this says?"

I saw a look pass between my dad and Minnesota when they read the words. Dad glanced at me, then Minnesota said, "Now why do you care about some old box that looks a hundred years old?"

"Because," Tyler said, "Maybe it's a message from Emmett. I ain't seen him in a long time. He might have left a message for me."

Wow, what was going on here? I could tell by the way Minnesota looked at my dad, this kid just may know what he's talking about.

Chapter 11

Millie

The only thing worse than being wrong, in Millie's mind, was to be wrong in front of all the kids. Especially Samuel, whose gloating stare taunted her.

"What are you all doing in the hall?" She looked past Samuel as she scolded the younger ones. "Mía, you heard Mom tell you to leave."

Caleb, Mía and Jenny scampered off down the hall, disappearing into the playroom. Thankfully they were gone before Mom spoke.

"Millicent!" It was a stern whisper. She might as well have been shouting. "What has gotten into you today?"

Millie struggled to hold back tears. She would not give Samuel the satisfaction of seeing her cry, but as she rushed past him on the way to her room, she caught a glimpse of what looked like sympathy in his eyes. Gone was the gloating and in its place, something she wasn't expecting.

Millie stormed through her bedroom doorway, slamming the door behind her, as tears fell. The worst part of it all, she didn't even know what was wrong. She really did like kids and she wanted to follow Great-Grandpa's dream to help others. But lately it seemed too much had changed. Her best friend had heart problems and had to go to the city for months maybe.

And right after Paisley left, the lizards she had nursed back to health got taken away. After she and Jeremiah had rescued them from the smugglers they became her pets. She really thought she was going to get to keep them.

She picked up the framed photo from her dresser and plopped down on the floor next to her bed. At least she had a picture of them. Not like the lizard she lost when she was in foster care. She loved that creature. Littlefoot was the only pet she'd ever owned. She wished she had a picture, but even without one she would never forget him. She remembered the day she had to move to a new foster home and the social worker told her she couldn't take Littlefoot. She cried her heart out inside, but never once let a tear fall. It was her secret pain and there had been no one she could trust to share it with.

"Millie." Mom's voice accompanied a soft knock on her door. "You have a phone call."

Millie wiped her tears. "Who is it?" she said without moving from her spot on the floor.

Mom stepped into the room, carrying the phone. When she saw the framed photo Millie held she said, "Perfect timing. It's Agent Leon. He has news for you about the lizards."

Chapter 12

Jeremiah

"Hey little feller, you just done reminded me of something," Minnesota Mike clapped his hands, then patted Tyler on the shoulder. "I almost fergot to tell you."

"He did leave a message for me?" Tyler asked.

"Someone did, that's for dang sure." Minnesota grinned. "You better come along with me and I'll show you. You got a letter and I been hanging onto it in the office for you."

"Who's it from?" Tyler jumped up and down, shaking the trailer. "I ain't never got a letter before."

Dad and I glanced at each other, then back at Minnesota. Wow, if he was making this up to distract Tyler, how was he going to produce a letter for the boy when they got to the office?

Tyler leaped out the door, missing both steps and landing on the ground. Mike turned to my dad as he stepped closer to the door. "How 'bout you folks button this place up good and tight fer me." He glanced at the box with the message on it, then back to us. "And do somethin' about that, if ya know I mean, doncha know?" He winked and stepped out the door, banging it shut behind him.

"Boy, do you think he made up that story?" Before my dad could answer, I fired off another question. "And what's he going to tell him when there is no letter?"

"I sure don't know, Son. But this is one time I'm glad a kid his age couldn't read."

I picked the box back up, studying the crude thick letters. "Yeah, I know what you mean."

Dad took it from me. "It's so light." He looked startled.

"That's what I thought, almost seems like there's nothing in it."

Dad shook it, holding his ear close to the box.

"Do you hear anything?"

"Well there is something in it, maybe papers." He set it on the counter. "Let's pick up the rest of these things on the floor and clean the place a bit." Dad moved toward the back of the trailer gathering papers and boxes as he went.

I know he told me to help clean, but I couldn't get my mind off the box, wondering what was in it and if Tyler's story about a couple bad men was true.

I held the crumpled dusty box and stared at the words. "Open this box if I disappear." It was signed "Emmett."

CHAPTER 13

Millie

"Leon! Are you bringing my lizards back?" Millie saw her mom give her one of those looks, like she shouldn't have said that. Before Leon could answer, she added, "I'm kidding. Sort of."

"I wanted to let you know," his voice was strong and loud coming through the phone. "We found a reptile sanctuary for the lizards and the owner was very impressed with the condition they were in."

"Really?" Finally something good was happening today.

"She said they usually get the smuggled ones still in the small containers. She also said she wouldn't have known these were smuggled because you did such a great job caring for them."

"Oh wow! Hold on a minute," Millie jumped up and hugged her mom.

"What's going on?" Mom returned her hug, planting a kiss on her cheek. She shoved the phone in her mom's hand and plopped back down on the floor clutching the framed picture of the lizards she and Jeremiah had rescued. Overcome with emotion, she knew she couldn't finish the conversation.

"Leon?" she heard Mom say. "Millie is overjoyed, can you let me in on what's happening?"

Mom nodded and smiled, staring at Millie as she listened. Then, "Thank you so much for letting us know. Talk to you later."

"Well, it looks like you might have a future in reptile rescue," Mom said as she hit the off button.

"Do you mean it?" Millie wiped her tears and jumped up off the floor. "Did he say that? For real?"

"He said the lady who operates the sanctuary would like to meet you someday."

"When can we go? Today?"

"We're not going anywhere in this windstorm," Mom said, "besides the sanctuary is a thousand miles away."

"So I'll never get to go, in other words." The smile disappeared from Millie's face.

"Oh Millie, must you be so dramatic?" Mom knelt down by her where she had dropped back to the floor. "Someday can be any time in the future, it doesn't have to be today or tomorrow."

"I guess." Millie agreed without wanting to.

"Besides I think you have some unfinished business here today."

"Oh yeah, like I'm probably grounded the rest of this year for being mean to the other kids?"

"Well, that is a thought," Mom smiled. "But I was thinking more along the lines of you checking out that knapsack Samuel gave you."

Chapter 14

Jeremiah

"Dad, I think Mike wants us to look in this box." Jeremiah headed to the back of the trailer clutching the lightweight box.

"To tell you the truth, I'm not sure what he meant," Dad said. "I just don't know if it's our place to look into this man's private papers."

"Well, Paisley's dad can't do it while they're out of town, and you told him we would help Minnesota take care of the Lodge while they were gone."

Dad sighed. I could read his mind. He was wondering why all this happened right after Paisley's family left town for a few months. But I was glad for the way it turned out. This was an unexpected adventure I was looking forward to being a part of.

"So can I open it?"

Dad folded some towels that looked like they had fallen from an open cabinet, shoved them back into place and latched the door. I waited impatiently.

"Tell you what, Jeremiah." He continued tidying things as he talked. "Let's get this trailer back in shape and then . . ."

"Then we'll open it?"

"Hold your horses, I feel like I'm dealing with Millie here." Dad's smile took some of the sting out of his insult.

"You didn't just call me Millie, did you?" I set the box down on the counter. I really needed to work on my attitude if even my dad could see my sister's impatient qualities coming out in me.

"Well, if the shoe fits," he said as he picked up a pair of mismatched slippers and tossed them in my direction.

I caught one in each hand and headed for the back bedroom area. "Let's get this done," I said and started hustling. Nothing like a mystery box to get me motivated

The wind still howled outside and the trailer shook as we finished the job. "This place probably looks better now than before it got blown over." I wiped the counters with wet paper towels. The thick dust turned to mud as I reeled off more paper towels to tackle this last task.

Dad lifted the box off the counter as I cleaned under it, then dropped the dirty paper towels into a makeshift trash can.

"Here you go, Son." He handed me the box. "You've earned the right to investigate."

I think Dad was as curious as I was to find out what was inside. Lucky for me I always have a knife in my pocket. I slit the tape down the middle and sides. Dad reached over and pulled the flaps back to reveal the contents.

"Wow, Dad!" I looked inside, then up at him. "Wait til Millie hears about this!"

Chapter 15

Millie

"So you really know where that knapsack is, Mom?"

"Follow me."

Mom headed down the hallway toward her bedroom and Millie could feel the stares of four curious pairs of eyes peeking out of the other rooms along the hallway. Yet none of the other kids dared to step out in her way or say anything as she passed the rooms they were in.

Mom closed the door behind her and sat on her bed, motioning to the dusty heap on the floor.

Millie knelt down, studying the dirty canvas material. Picking it up, she rubbed her hand over the dust, revealing a greenish color underneath the brown dirt.

Studying the straps and buckles she wanted to open it to see if there was anything inside. Samuel said it was a gift. But maybe he just meant the bag was the gift. And besides, now, after making such a big fuss over it and causing problems with all the kids in the house, she felt too guilty to look inside.

"Well?" Mom urged.

"Well, what?" Millie placed the bag back on the floor.

"For Pete's sake, Millie." Mom laughed. "After all the fuss, you're not even going to look inside?"

"Do you know what's in it?"

"No, I just brought it into my room so the kids wouldn't get into it."

"Oh."

Mom dropped down to the floor next to Millie. "Honey, what is wrong? I can't believe you're not going through the bag inspecting every inch of it. This isn't like you."

"It's like you said, Mom. I made such a big fuss." Her voice trembled. "I just feel ashamed of all the trouble I've caused this morning and I don't feel right looking in the bag."

She picked it up again, studying the buckles, examining the worn straps, then dropped it back to the floor. "I can't. I just don't feel right."

"Samuel will be disappointed."

Millie looked over at her mother. "Why? He probably is sorry he even gave it to me."

Mom smiled. "I don't think he's sorry. He just can't figure you out."

"Why does he need to figure me out?" Millie jumped up from the floor and walked to the window. Why did she love to stare at the wind she hated so much? "Did he tell you that?" she said without looking at her mom.

Mom joined her at the window. "No, not with words."

"Well, how else does someone tell you something? And look at that wind, it's been blowing like this for months."

Mom's laugh annoyed her even more. "Millie it's only been a couple weeks."

She sighed and turned back to the knapsack. One buckle was broken and undone. The other two opened easily. Millie peeled open the flap and peered inside to see yellowed papers covered in dust. Reaching her hand in felt like reaching into the desert sand. To keep from spilling it on the floor, she knelt back down, balancing the knapsack on the floor in an upright position. She pulled a few pieces of paper out.

Mom sat on the bed watching. "Can you make out any writing on the papers?" Millie knew her mom was also curious, but she let Millie do all the discovery work and waited for a response.

"It looks like a map," Millie studied the worn and dusty paper, following the hand drawn lines and arrows with her finger. The printed words were smudged and hard to make out. In the upper right corner was a rough drawing that looked almost like a ship with tall masts.

"Is that a ship?" Mom peered closely after she dropped to the floor next to her.

"That's what I thought," Millie said.

"Millie?" Mom sounded excited. "Do you know what that reminds me of?"

Chapter 16

Jeremiah

"She does love an adventure, doesn't she?" Dad reached in and pulled out the black and white photo.

I watched as he studied it closely. I really wanted to get a good look at it, but Dad seemed so interested I waited. Not very patiently. But I waited.

"Look at this, Jeremiah." Dad pointed to a grainy portion in the middle of the photo. "It looks like a ship's mast sticking up out of the ground." He handed the photo to me to get a better look.

I could make out a tall post that leaned to one side. Three cross boards, each one a little shorter than the other, looked like a ship's mast from long ago days. The picture was too grainy to make out any other details.

"You know what I think, Dad?" I handed him back the photo. I think this was a section of a wider angle shot and when they printed this picture they enlarged this portion so much that it lost the detail."

"I think you're right, Son."

"Why would this old picture be in a box with such a strange message written on the outside of it?" I held it up to the window trying to shed more light on the image.

"Look on the back there, Jeremiah." Dad joined me at the window.

I turned the photo over and read the words: "I'm gone looking for the ship – Emmett."

"Wow, Dad! Do you suppose he knew something might happen to him when he went looking for the ship? And why didn't he tell anyone where he was going? And . . ."

"Hold on there, now." Dad put his hand up to slow me down.

"Hey, there's one of them bad men!" Tyler's voice was muffled coming through the closed trailer door and windows.

I bent down to look out the window, just in time to see his small body streak past the front of the trailer. Minnesota Mike was ambling along after him trying to catch up.

Dad popped the door open and stuck his head out while I hurried to look out the back window.

A sound outside caught my attention when I stepped into the bedroom area. I raised the bent and broken blinds to get a glimpse outside.

"See anything Jeremiah?" Dad called from his post at the door. "I've lost him."

"Not yet," I rubbed the dust and grime off the scratched glass.

Just as I put my face to the window, I gasped so hard I nearly lost my breath. The last thing I expected to see was a face staring back at me.

Chapter 17

Millie

"**M**ommyyyyyyyy!"
Millie and her mom jumped at the sound of the loud scream coming from the hallway.

Her mom dashed out the bedroom door ahead of her with Millie right on her heels. This better be serious, she thought. Those kids just interrupted something important Mom was getting ready to say. Maybe she saw the lost ship when she was a kid.

Millie was ready to scold the kids again if this was something as stupid as fighting over a little car, but stopped dead in her tracks when she saw Caleb rolling around on the play room floor, holding his knee and crying out in pain. Mía looked terrified and once again hollered with mouth wide open, "Mommyyyyyyy!" So scared, she didn't even realize Mom was already in the room.

Millie put her arm around Mía and quieted her while Mom knelt to see what happened to Caleb. He brushed tears from his cheeks and rolled over on his back, looking up at Mom. He held on tight to his knee, bent nearly to his chest.

"Caleb, honey." Mom's voice was soft as she brushed his hair back off his forehead. "What happened?"

Whimpering sounds that Millie thought were from Caleb, continued as Mom comforted him. Millie turned and saw Jenny sitting on the floor holding her own legs closely to her chest, head buried in her knees. "What is going on here?" she wondered as she moved from Mía to the other side of the room.

"Jenny," she whispered, "it's okay. What's wrong?"

Jenny cried harder at Millie's words and Caleb distracted her when he suddenly jumped up and said "I'm okay, Jenny, see I'm okay."

Jenny lifted her head a tiny bit and stared in the direction of her brother. She seemed unsure whether to believe him or not. Caleb limped over to his sister and hugged her. Mía watched speechless, but only for a few minutes.

Before Millie or her Mom could ask what was going on, Mía blurted out, "Jenny had a paper with a picture on it and Caleb wanted to see it and she wouldn't give it to him and he tried to take it from her and I pushed Caleb – but only a little itty bitty push . . ."

"That wasn't itty bitty," Caleb turned from his sister, and glared at Mía. "She pushed me so hard she tried to break my leg."

"You were being mean to Jenny," Mía hollered.

"Was not!" Caleb, forgetting to limp, rushed toward Mía as if to push her back but Mom stepped in between the two.

Jenny's whimper turned into silent sobbing, her body shook, her head again buried in her knees she hugged to her chest. She clutched a crumpled piece of paper in one hand.

"Goodness," Mom said. "What's this all about?" Millie, was glad, for once today she wasn't the cause of the commotion. It was about time the other kids got in trouble.

"Caleb?" Mom looked directly at him. He stared at Mom, but didn't speak. It wasn't like Caleb not to respond when adults were talking to him.

"Caleb was being mean to Jenny so I pushed him away from her," Mía said. "It's not my fault. He started it."

Jenny's sobs grew louder.

"I wasn't being mean, I just wanted to see the picture and she wouldn't show me."

"What picture?" Millie asked.

"I'm really sorry, Millie," Jenny lifted her head and held the crumpled paper out.

Millie took the paper and smoothed it out, studying the crude drawing. Then realized what she was looking at it.

"Where did you get this?" she demanded.

"Millicent, don't be so harsh with Jenny."

Millie shoved the paper in her mother's direction. "Look what she has."

Mom examined the drawing then said softly. "Jenny, where did you get this?"

Chapter 18

Jeremiah

"Dad!" I yelled as I flew by him on my way out the door of the trailer, hoping he'd get the hint and follow me.

I wanted to find the guy, but preferably not face him alone.

Rounding the back of the trailer I could feel my dad right behind me, as I glimpsed a man running down the row of trailers. I was in full chase mode when I felt Dad's hand on my shoulder as he ran next to me. "Hold up, Jeremiah."

I slowed my pace to a walk, turning to face Dad who came to a standstill. "But Dad, we need to catch that guy."

"Why?"

"Well . . ." He had me stumped with that question. I felt foolish as I realized I really didn't know why. "He was looking in the trailer window."

Dad nodded. "But that's about all we know."

"I saw Tyler chasing someone. It was probably him."

"Hey Mister!" the young voice called from a few trailers

away. The wind had let up and we were able to hear and see clearly as Tyler ran toward us waving an envelope over his head. "Look what I got!"

So much for convincing his dad they should follow Tyler and hunt that guy down. "What do you have there, Tyler?" I asked when he caught up to where we stood behind Emmett's trailer. Minnesota Mike was not far behind and his smile was about as big as the kid's smile.

"I got me a letter in the mail! I ain't never had a letter before!" His grin was huge as he held up the envelope to show us. "Mr. Mike says that's my name on it."

Wow, it's pretty sad that a kid that old can't even read his own name. Wait till my mom hears about this. She'll want to start teaching this kid.

"Who sent you a letter?"

He handed it to me and I saw Donovan's name in the corner. "So you're friends with Paisley's little brother?" I gave him back the letter, pointing to Donovan's name in the corner.

"Hey, how do you know Paisley and Donovan?"

"The same way you know them," I said. "They're our friends."

"Well now, let's quit all this jawing and get this trailer buttoned up," Minnesota Mike looked right at me. "Did you get those papers I done told you to get?"

My heart pounded when I realized he was going to let me take them. "I'll go grab the box now."

"Now hold yer horses there, leave that box where ya found it, but just grab the contents."

"Hey, I wanna know what's in that box!" Tyler demanded.

"Now don't you think you got enough to worry about with a letter you need help reading?" Minnesota patted his head and motioned to Dad. "How about you all take this young feller home and feed him some breakfast?"

We were almost home when Tyler quit staring at his letter. "Boy, I hope that bad guy don't find Emmett's secret box!" he blurted out as if he suddenly remembered his chase.

"Well, I think you chased him away," I said, hoping to take his mind off what might be trouble at the resort.

"Not the other one, I didn't." Tyler's eyes were big as he stared up at me from where he sat between Dad and me.

"What other one?"

"The one hiding under the trailer when we left."

Chapter 19

Millie

"I can tell you where she got it."

Every person in the playroom turned to stare at Samuel who stood in the doorway. What did he have to do with this? Millie wondered.

"No, don't tell!" Jenny jumped up from where she sat on the floor and rushed out of the room. "She'll really hate me now," she yelled as she ran into the hallway.

Millie followed, reaching the living room in time to see Jenny collide with her dad and brother coming through the front door.

"Hey, you almost ran me over!" a little boy said.

Who is that little pipsqueak? Millie wondered. Right now she was too curious about Jenny to care. But later she'd take this up with her mom who promised, well it seemed like a promise, that they would take a break from adding kids to the family.

"Millie, this is Tyler," Dad said. She took one look at the disheveled, scrawny kid and made a mental note to worry about this later. Right now, she just wanted to find out what was going on with Jenny.

"Tyler!" Caleb ran across the living room and embraced the new kid. "How did you get here?"

"This man brung me," the new kid said. "Mr. Mike told him to feed me."

By now the living room was full as the rest of the family filed in. Mom looked stunned at the new addition and Millie decided to go easy on her. Maybe she didn't know their dad was trying to sneak a new kid into the family.

Millie saw Jenny slip out the door as everyone made a fuss over this Tyler kid. "Uh-uh," Millie thought, "she's not getting away that easy."

"I'll be right back," she said, hurrying out the door before her mom or dad could ask questions.

She spotted Jenny running toward the back of their property and took off after her. "Jenny, wait!"

Jenny glanced over her shoulder and ran even faster.

Millie was out of breath but kept pushing. "Wait!" The word barely came out she was so breathless. Jenny might have been a faster runner, but Millie's determination propelled her through the soft sand and wouldn't let her stop.

She shouldn't have been happy when she saw Jenny trip and fall, but it gave her a chance to catch up. Jenny laid in the dirt.

"Are you hurt?" Millie dropped down next to her, overcome with guilt.

Jenny stayed face down, but shook her head.

"Jenny, please," fear filled Millie's voice. "Where are you hurt? Should I go get Dad?"

"I'm not hurt," the words were muffled, barely discernible.

"Then why can't you get up?"

"You'll hate me." Jenny sat up. Sand covered her body and her hair hung in her face. She held out the crumpled paper. "This is yours."

Millie opened the paper and again studied what looked like a rock carving of a ship. "Where did you get this?"

Jenny finally made eye contact with Millie. "I took it out of the knapsack Samuel gave you."

Millie took a closer look at the drawing. "This is the ship the map leads to!" she shrieked, then reached over and squeezed Jenny in a tight hug.

"You're not mad I took it?"

"Well, I should be, but I'm too excited about this picture to care right now, besides . . ." Millie looked around the vast desert, remembering the time she was so angry and scared she took off running down this very same path to get away from everyone.

She looked at Jenny and realized that maybe they had more in common than she wanted to admit. She almost felt like they could be kindred spirits. Almost.

Chapter 20

Jeremiah

Freedom! I couldn't believe how good this felt as I held the throttle on and followed my sister through the desert on our motorcycles. She didn't usually like to lead, but today she was so excited about searching for the mysterious ship that she didn't even give me a chance to get out in front.

The deep rumble of the four stroke engine was a comforting relief after days of being cooped up inside. It seemed like it had been months with listening to Millie's constant complaints, not to mention getting used to all the new kids. Well, let's just say . . . I let off the throttle as Millie also slowed to make a hard right-hand turn on the rocky path . . . let's just say I needed this dirt bike ride more than I realized. I couldn't believe Mom and Dad let us go out today, with so much going on at home.

Millie was on the gas, her pigtails flying in the wind as she rode harder than I'd ever seen. This girl was on a mission to find the missing ship. "It was a sign from God," she'd said when

Dad and I showed everyone the information about the ship we found in Emmett's trailer. I couldn't believe it when Millie and Mom also had papers about some ghost ship supposedly lost in the desert. I don't know if it was a sign, but once Dad said we could go hunt for it, I sure felt it was a gift from God. We both needed a break like this. Even the wind cooperated by dying down.

      Honestly, I didn't believe for a second that there was a ship in the desert. I mean, really, we're how far from the ocean? I've never seen a ship sail through sand, but if it's going to keep my mouthy sister from complaining so much, I'm all for following her on this adventure, pretending that I believe we're going to find the mysterious ship.

      Hopefully it would take her mind, well, and maybe mine too, off all the kids that were joining our family.

      It's funny, because when we were first planning to move to the desert and get the big house Millie and I were excited about the plan to help out kids who needed a home. We both knew what it was like to need a family, to live in foster homes where you knew you didn't quite belong. Some places were okay, but it seemed like just when you'd get a good foster home, then something would go wrong. A foster parent would get sick or lose their job, and then next thing you know, you're being moved to a new place, with kids who weren't very happy to have you there.

      Wow. I felt like someone just punched me in the gut.

      I twisted the throttle harder, standing up to smooth out the ride over the rocky section we were on. I rode faster to overtake Millie.

      I motioned with a nod of my helmet for her to pull over as I came alongside her.

      She slowed to a stop and yelled through her helmet, over the sound of our engines. "Did you see something?" She sounded excited. Yep, this girl was definitely on a mission to find a ship's mast sticking up out of the desert somewhere.

      I hit the kill switch on the handlebars to shut off the engine. "No."

"What then?" She revved her engine, impatient to return to the search.

"There's something I need to tell you."

Chapter 21

Millie

"If this isn't about the lost ship, I don't even want to hear it!" Millie killed the engine, but refused to take her helmet off. She defiantly sat on her bike even as she watched her brother take his helmet off and dismount.

"They only gave us two hours to search," she said. "You're wasting time."

Jeremiah stared at her without speaking.

"You're wasting time!" she repeated.

When he didn't respond, she got off the bike and jerked her helmet off. "There! Are you happy?" She stopped short of throwing her helmet. She'd been in trouble enough for doing that.

"Jeremiah, what did you want to tell me? And if it isn't about the ship, why do we need to talk about it now when we only have a little bit more time?"

He sucked on the tube connected to the water pack on his back, staring at her.

Giving up on getting any information out of him, she

pulled off her backpack and dug around inside, producing a couple of granola bars. She held one out to her brother

"Wow, I can't believe you're going to let me eat one of your snacks."

"Just take it and shut up."

"Well, first you ask me to talk, then you tell me to shut up." Jeremiah tore open the granola bar and bit off a chunk, laughing as he chewed.

She didn't appreciate the joke.

"What is it with you lately, anyway?" he asked. "You're always grumpy."

"I thought you had something to tell me."

"Did you ever have to live at a foster home where the other kids made you feel unwelcome?"

Millie's heart fluttered and unwanted memories came back to her. But even worse, a heaviness settled over her. She knew it was guilt, but didn't want to face it. Not right now.

"That's a question not a statement." She knelt down and examined some rocks in the shadow of her bike.

"Well?"

"Well what?" Millie stood and dropped the rocks into her backpack then pulled out the map for the ship.

Jeremiah took the paper from her.

"Hey! Give that back."

"Millie, you know what I'm getting at. I can see it in your eyes."

"It's not the same!" She shrugged into her backpack and pulled her helmet on, then grabbed the map out of Jeremiah's hands. "If we're not going to search for the ship, I'm going home!" Millie tucked the map in between her chest protector and riding jersey and kicked the bike over.

Without waiting for Jeremiah she revved the engine and spun the bike around, throwing rocks and dust with her rear tire as she roared off.

Chapter 22

Jeremiah

"Well that didn't go well," I said to no one. Grabbing my helmet, I took my time pulling it on and weaving the strap through the buckle. She won't go far, she knows we're not allowed to ride alone.

I kicked over my bike and headed in the direction Millie went. She'd probably be waiting at the bottom of the next hill.

Accelerating up the hill, I dodged rocks and ruts and followed what could be her tracks. Cresting the top of the hill, she was nowhere in sight. The trail leading down twisted and turned, so she was probably around the bend where I couldn't see her. I aimed the front wheel in the direction of the path and gave it a little throttle, letting gravity propel me down the hill where she'd be waiting.

But she wasn't there waiting.

I rode up to the next hilltop and parked, looking all around trying to spot that crazy girl. What was she thinking?

If she shows up at home without me, we're both going to be in trouble for getting separated.

"Thanks a lot, Millie," I muttered. "There goes our riding privileges."

I sipped water from the pack on my back as I pondered which way to head back. I had no clue how to think like my sister. Would she go back the way we came or would she take a different path hoping she'd spot the ship's mast on the way? She never gives up on an idea once she gets it into her head. Right now she was driven to find that ship. And she was mad. So my guess was she'd take a different route back, not caring if I found her or not.

I opted for staying pretty close to our original route. I scanned the right and left of the trail as I rode, searching for a crazy pig tailed girl on a dark blue dirt bike with an overstuffed backpack bouncing around on her back. Weaving my way along winding trails filled with ruts and rocks, up and down hills and through sand washes, I never caught sight of her.

"I'm telling you, Millie," I mumbled under my breath as I got closer to home, "you better be waiting for me at the gate."

She wasn't. I rolled through the gate and looked for her bike parked in front of our dad's shop. A funny feeling started to grow in the pit of my stomach when I didn't see the bike. But it didn't compare to how I felt when my dad stepped out of the shop and looked over at me.

"Where's your sister?"

Chapter 23

Millie

Millie twisted hard on the throttle throwing dirt and rocks as she rode away from her brother. It wasn't allowed. Riding alone, that is. Why did she do it?

Even knowing she was doing the wrong thing, she kept the throttle on, standing on the pegs to keep from taking a beating over the whoops. She should have remembered this path with the evenly spaced short bumps that never seemed to end. So focused on not losing control of the bike, it didn't occur to her to pull over and wait for Jeremiah. Or better yet, to turn back.

She knew he was right. Her attitude was bad about all the new kids. It wasn't so bad when Caleb moved in, and she was the one who found Mía and rescued her from the smugglers, so how could she be mad about her moving in? When it came down to it, it was the older kids, Jenny and Samuel. They were the straws that broke the camel's back, if that saying was even true. Hard to believe one extra little piece of straw could hurt a big lumbering animal like a camel. Maybe that old saying wasn't even true. But in her case, those two extra kids, too close to her own age, were what did it for her. She wanted her small family back. But it was too late for that.

Lost in thought she didn't notice a vehicle approaching until the quad was right alongside her. "Hey, this trail isn't wide enough to pass on!" she yelled under her helmet as she maneuvered to the right, not wanting to get taken out by the big wheels passing too close.

Nearing the end of the whoop section, Millie veered off at the fork in the road to get on a completely different trail from the unwanted quad rider. But as she did she could hear another engine roaring right behind her.

Glancing over her shoulder she saw a different quad following her. She twisted the throttle harder and jumped the berm on the side of the trail heading off the path to cross the desert through the bushes and ruts. She kept focused, without taking her eyes off the ground in front of her. There was no trail to follow, she was making her own. As much as she wanted to look back over her shoulder to see if she'd lost them, she knew that could lead to disaster if she missed an unexpected rock or ditch ahead of her.

Even without looking behind, she could hear and sense, the sound of engines getting closer. Now it seemed both riders were gaining on her. This couldn't be a coincidence. This was no regular riding path she was on, she was making her own trail and these people seemed to think they could join her on this adventure.

As she increased her speed, the sound of their engines grew louder. They were keeping pace with her.

"Jeremiah, please come find me," she whispered as she rode. Then fear took hold as she remembered. "This is just like my dream!"

Millie hung on tight and twisted the throttle as far as it would go. If only this time she could wake up and find herself safely in her room at home.

Chapter 24

Jeremiah

I've heard that familiar saying "deer in the headlights look" and I'm guessing that's exactly how I looked to Dad right now.

A heavy lump in my stomach worked its way up to my throat and I couldn't get any words out. I don't know what scared me more, facing my Dad after breaking one of the main rules of riding, or worrying about what might have happened to Millie. Most likely a combination of both. "Dad . . ." I squeaked out.

"Jeremiah! Where is your sister?" He crossed the short space between us in a couple of giant steps and surveyed the desert area from where I had ridden in. I turned my head, hoping and praying I'd see Millie riding in behind me. Hoping this was one of her crazy stunts to try and get me in trouble. And that after seeing Dad scold me, she could then saunter in. If you can saunter on a motorcycle. No such luck, there was no sign of her.

"Where's Millie?"

Samuel startled me when he appeared by my side. He must have been in the shop with Dad.

"That's what I'm trying to find out," Dad said.

"She got mad and took off without me after we stopped for a break."

"That figures."

"That's enough, Samuel!" Dad barked.

I felt sorry for Samuel, he looked sheepish. Poor kid just hasn't been around long enough to learn when to talk and when not to.

"I'm sorry, sir, I just meant that she's been mad at me all morning."

He really sounded sorry. It wasn't that kind of sorry that kids say sometimes when they're just trying to get out of trouble. Dad must have felt bad for taking his anger out on him. He put an arm around Samuel's shoulders. "I'm sorry too, Son."

A flicker of surprise flashed in Samuel's eyes as he looked over at Dad. I remembered how good it felt the first time Dad called me his son when I moved in years ago. Maybe everything was going to work out okay having Samuel here. Well, once we find Millie, that is.

"Where is the last place you saw her, Jeremiah?"

"We were probably three miles east of here, where the mud hills start . . ."

"Three miles?" Samuel interrupted.

Dad and I both looked at him, probably wondering the same thing. When is he going to learn to keep his mouth shut? Not any time soon, it seemed.

"Don't go anywhere," he said and turned toward the house. "I'll be right back!" he called out over his shoulder taking off in a sprint.

Chapter 25

Millie

"At least I'm not going to go flying off the top of some hill," Millie thought to herself as she stayed on the gas with the quad riders keeping pace a short distance behind.

She maneuvered around bushes, then crossed a dirt trail, continuing her cross country trek making trails where there were none before. "Why are these people chasing me?" she wondered as she made a sudden hard right to follow a whooped out trail that looked familiar. Standing on the pegs to smooth out the ride, she held the throttle on, hoping the unstable terrain would cause problems for the four-wheeled vehicles pursuing her.

She wondered briefly if she should stop to see what they wanted. Maybe they weren't bad people. They could be friendly and just wanting to check on her since she was riding alone.

She contemplated slowing down, but a gut feeling told her not to. Just ahead she saw a familiar trail. "Yes!" she yelled inside her helmet. This would be the perfect place to lose these guys.

Millie slowed the bike just enough to veer off into the creviced trail. She maneuvered through the tight winding path. The tall dirt walls closed in on her the further she got into the hideaway, slowing her speed as she found herself bumping the walls with the handlebars, as the path grew more narrow.

The sound of the quads was long gone, as there was no way they could fit their wider vehicles through the crevice. Thankfully Dad had taken Jeremiah and her along this trail once before, otherwise she wouldn't have known it was wide enough for a dirt bike to fit through. It looked more like a crack in the earth than an actual riding trail.

She remembered when they all rode this trail together that it eventually led into a ravine that dumped them down a rocky cliff into a sandy dry wash. She also remembered she had been afraid to ride down the cliff. She stood and watched as her Dad rode down, then climbed back up on foot and rode her bike down for her. She followed behind half walking, half sliding down the steep bank.

Today she was on her own. She hoped the quad riders didn't know the desert as well as her Dad did. If so she just might have a welcoming committee waiting for her in the wash. What did they want from her anyway?

The only thing she had of interest was the map to the lost ship, but there was no way they could have known about that. Unless they had been nearby when she and Jeremiah stopped. She tried to remember what she said or did. All she remembered for sure was taking out the map and then hiding it in her chest protector. They couldn't have seen that, could they?

Before she could give it another thought, her engine died and the bike coasted to a stop. The eerie silence of the desert reminded her she was completely alone, a long way from home. And it was her own fault.

Chapter 26

Jeremiah

Dad and I knelt down next to the shop while I drew a map in the dirt of the route Millie and I had taken earlier in the day. He knew the spot where we stopped for our break and we both knew there were a hundred different routes Millie could have taken from there. Well, a hundred might be an exaggeration, but depending on her mindset, it was anybody's guess which way she might have gone if she chose not to head home.

"Dad." I brushed my hands off as we stood. "As crazy as Millie can get, and even with her being mad, I can't believe she would deliberately not head home or at least wait for me a little ways down the trail."

"So what are you saying?"

"I'm not sure." I gazed across the desert trying to imagine what could have happened. A wild thought crossed my mind. What if someone kidnapped her? Too wild to even say out loud. "What if she's hurt?"

"That's a possibility," Dad wheeled his motorcycle out of the shop, then began suiting up in his riding gear. "We'll head back out, you lead." Dad clamped his riding boots tight, then stood and pulled his chest protector on over his head. As he fastened each side he continued, "Take a route different from the one you rode home. If we don't see her, stop when you get to the place where you took your break."

"Then what?" I pulled my helmet on and watched Dad do the same. He didn't answer.

"Dad, what if we get there without finding her, then what?"

Dad looked choked up. I felt like Samuel, not knowing when I should just be quiet. Now I realized he didn't answer, because he couldn't answer. Maybe I wasn't the only one scared.

"I'll ride up to the house and tell your mom what's going on," Dad said and started his bike. Before he took off, we heard Samuel yelling.

"Wait! Wait!" He ran toward us but was slowed by a bulky object he carried.

"What in the world?" Dad shut off his bike as Samuel reached us.

"It's my drone," he said. "It can fly up to five miles away."

This kid was getting on my nerves. Why did he think we cared about his stupid drone when Millie might be in danger? Dad looked like he had the same thoughts.

He started his bike again. "I've got to go tell Mom what's happening so she can pray."

"She already is," Samuel said, "I told her."

"Did you tell her we're going to go search for her?" I asked.

"I told her I can search for her with the drone."

Dad and I exchanged looks, then focused back on Samuel. Once again, I may have misjudged the kid. Maybe he knew something we didn't.

"What do you mean?" Dad said.

"My drone is connected to Ms. Norra's laptop. I can fly it up to five miles away, filming the whole time. I should be able to see Millie anywhere in a five mile radius from here."

I wanted to hug the kid, but held back. I mean I'm worried a lot about my sister, but not enough to hug a kid I'm trying to learn to like. "Are you kidding me?" I yelled out instead. "That is awesome!"

Samuel set the odd looking contraption on the ground. Dad and I watched as he pressed a few buttons and the drone slowly lifted off the ground and hovered above us, then flew toward the gate.

"I'm sure I can find her." Samuel took his eyes off the drone as he attempted to convince Dad. I turned back to watch the drone only to see it list sideways and plunge into a large tree near the fence line.

Chapter 27

Millie

Millie leaned her bike against the wall of the crevice and pulled her helmet off, balancing it on the seat. She slipped out of her backpack and pulled out a water bottle and granola bar. She'd never run out of gas before. And she'd never been out riding alone. Thankfully she was always prepared with her survival pack.

She wondered if Jeremiah had made it home or if he was out looking for her. "I've really messed things up good," she said as she tore open the granola bar, wishing for a repeat of their earlier stop when she handed her brother a snack.

"They'll probably take my bike away for a year this time," she moaned. "Why did I ride off like that?"

Millie thought about scaling the wall to see if she could spot the quad riders, but decided against it. She didn't want to risk them seeing her.

If Dad was out looking for her, hopefully he would spot her tracks heading into the crevice. Only one set of tracks should give him a clue it was a single rider. She was glad she chose a trail they had all been on before. Hopefully Dad would remember.

She stood still, listening for the ominous sound of the quads or the familiar sound of her dad and brother riding to her rescue. Silence. It was probably too soon. She wondered if her dad would run across the quad riders while out looking for her. Of course he wouldn't know they had been following her.

She wondered what the first words she'd hear from him would be or if he'd have any gas with him. Probably not. He wouldn't have any way to carry fuel on his bike. The sun was straight up in the sky and she guessed it to be around noon. She sure was glad she hadn't done something like this on an early morning ride in the summertime. Pulling a stunt like this in the summer could do more than get her into trouble. It could kill her if she was lost and stranded in the 120 degree heat.

Finishing her granola bar, Millie tucked the wrapper into the backpack along with the half empty bottle of water. She decided to conserve the water, even though she had a few more bottles. She didn't know how long she would be out here alone.

She could sit and fret or she could explore while she waited.

"God, please help my dad find me and I sure I am sorry for this mess I caused," Millie prayed out loud as she trudged through the sandy sections of the trail in her heavy riding boots.

She ran her hands along the rough dirt on both sides as she walked. Rounding a tight bend her heart beat hard at the sight of an opening that looked like a cave. She hadn't noticed that the time she and Jeremiah followed her dad through here. The faint sound of quad engines dampened the excitement she felt at the cave discovery.

Chapter 28

Jeremiah

Samuel took off running toward the crashed drone. I followed Dad's lead and started my bike, heading slowly toward the gate.

"Samuel," Dad yelled over the sound of his engine. "There's a ladder on the side of the shop you can use to get the drone."

"I know I can find her with this," he said. "Let me try!"

Dad reached over and patted Samuel's shoulder. "That will be fine. You search for her with that and we'll also be looking."

"What if I find her?"

"Call my cell phone," Dad said. "And tell Mom we're going to look."

Samuel looked discouraged as Dad rode off, I gave him thumbs up hoping to be encouraging and stopped before I passed him. "It's a good idea that we're all looking. She could be anywhere."

Samuel nodded, but the excitement was gone from his eyes. His drone tangled up in the tree didn't help.

I pulled away slowly, then gassed it as I rode out the gate to catch up with Dad. He motioned for me to lead as I caught up with him.

This was a new experience when riding with Dad, usually he was the one leading. I wanted to look all around for my sister as I rode, but kept my eyes on the path I chose, so I didn't crash. Dad sure didn't need to be taking care of me with Millie missing.

No sign of her, not even any fresh tracks to follow. We pulled up to the place Millie and I had taken a break not long ago.

"Let's ride up there where we can get a better look." Dad pointed to nearby hill and led the way.

We both shut off our engines at the top. In the distance we saw a couple of quad riders heading in our direction. But no sign of a lone dirt bike rider.

"Dad, check your phone to see if Samuel has called."

He maneuvered his fanny pack around to the front, retrieving his phone. I scanned the skyline hoping to see the drone. "Do you think we're more than five miles from home?"

"I'd say three or four" Dad examined his phone, then shook his head. "No calls."

"Maybe those guys have seen her." I pointed as the riders got closer.

Dad started up his bike and headed down the hill in their direction.

We met up with them at the base of the hill.

"My daughter is missing," Dad said to the men. "Have you seen a girl riding a motorcycle by herself today?"

The men glanced at each other, then back at Dad. Both of them shook their heads. "No, man. We ain't seen anyone 'cept you two," the bigger fellow said. His partner revved his throttle and appeared anxious to get going.

Dad pulled a business card from his fanny pack. "Can you give me a call if you see her?"

"Sure thing," the anxious guy stuck the card in between his seat and gas tank and roared off. His friend nodded to them, then followed.

"Dad, did you think the taller guy looked familiar?"

"No, can't say that he did."

"I've seen him somewhere, just can't figure out where."

CHAPTER 29

Millie

Millie worked to maneuver her motorcycle into the opening in the dirt wall. She'd always wanted to explore a cave but it would have been more fun if she wasn't being hunted by some crazed quad riders.

She thought the crevice she rode through was narrow, but this make-shift cave was even smaller. If she turned the front wheel just right she could angle the bike in so the handlebars didn't scrape the walls too much. She wondered how far back in it went and hoped she wasn't sharing this safe space with any wild critters. A jack rabbit or bunny would be okay, but snakes, coyotes or a badger would not be fun.

Once the bike was safely inside the cave, Millie stepped out to listen for the quads. "I wonder if I should have stopped to see what they wanted?" she said out loud. "Maybe they could have helped me."

It was too late for that now though and anyway, each time she heard the sound of their engines an uncomfortable feeling came over her. Like now. But she couldn't tell if it was the guys chasing her or someone else riding. How would she get help if she wasn't sure who to trust?

She opted to wait in the cave for her dad to find her. No matter how much trouble she was in, one thing she knew for sure. Her dad would find her.

Back in the cave, Millie pulled out her notepad and pen, and settled down in the dirt next to her bike, to write a letter.

Dear Paisley,

I haven't stopped thinking about you since you left. I'm asking God to fix your heart and bring you back soon!

You won't believe where I am sitting while I write this letter. I'm sure you'll be shaking your head when you read this. I'm hiding in a cave with my motorcycle that ran out of gas and hoping my dad will find me soon. Well, it's a long story why I'm here, but it probably won't surprise you that it's my fault because I got mad at my brother.

Julia has been asking about you. If I ever get rescued I will go and help her with cleaning out the old store since you aren't here to help. I'm glad she and Tucker moved to our town to open the store.

Come home soon and help me find the ghost ship. I just learned about it. I have a map for it and a picture. That is another long story. Samuel really annoys me, but he gave me an old bag with the ship info in it. Maybe you can pray that I will start liking that kid. Especially since it seems like he's going to be living with us for a long time.

I miss you.

Love, Millie

She folded the letter and stood to tuck it into her backpack when a buzzing noise caught her attention. It sounded like a gigantic bumble bee. Peering out of the cave she saw a strange looking object hovering above the crevice.

She jumped back into the cave, wondering if that was a device for spying.

Chapter 30

Jeremiah

"What now, Dad?"
"I'll call home and see if she's there."
I think we both knew that wasn't likely. Mom would have called already.

It seemed like it had been hours since I watched Millie ride off. According to my watch, it was only a little over an hour ago since I last saw her. I could kick myself for not going after her sooner. I thought sure she would have been waiting a little ways down the trail.

Dad shoved his phone in his fanny pack. "Let's go home and get the truck."

"The truck? Why?"

"If she's hurt or broke down we'll need it."

"Did Mom say anything about the drone?"

Dad nodded as he pulled his helmet on and fastened the strap. "It sounds like he got it going. They've been watching the footage on the laptop, but haven't seen her."

My stomach fluttered with excitement. "Dad!" I already had my helmet on and bike started. "We should watch it before we head back out. Maybe we'll see tracks or something Samuel wouldn't notice."

Dad pulled the phone back out and got Mom on speaker. "Norra!" he yelled to be heard through his helmet. "Get the truck out and ready to go with water, snacks and first aid kit."

"I'm on it." Mom's voice crackled through the speaker. Thankfully there was enough service where we were parked to get through.

"And have Samuel get the footage up so we can watch it before we head out."

We flew back to the house with Dad leading, still glancing to the right and left of the trails for signs of Millie.

All the kids were silent as we rushed past them and into Mom's office where Samuel was waiting.

Samuel hit play and stepped away from the desk so we could get closer. We watched the familiar terrain scroll by. He had covered a different area than we were on, which was good so we didn't duplicate each other's efforts.

"Hey Dad, there's those quad riders!"

"That's them bad guys!" I hadn't noticed Tyler near us at the desk until he startled me with his yell. "That's them! They're gettin' away!"

"Samuel," Dad said. "Can you get us back to those quad riders and freeze the image?"

"Those are the guys that talked to us, Dad. See, one's bigger than the other."

Dad nodded, then looked over at Tyler. "You recognize those men?"

"Yeah, they're the bad guys I was telling you about. I seen them riding those quads before."

Dad locked eyes with me, then said "Samuel, can you start it again?"

"What are you going to do about them, Mr. Max?" Tyler insisted.

"Shhh," Dad said, his eyes glued to the desert terrain scrolling by. "First we have to find Millie."

"Dad, there's the crevice trail you took us on once."

"Samuel!" Dad said abruptly. "Can you stop this and enlarge it?"

"Bike tracks!" Dad turned and hugged Samuel. "You're a genius, you and that gadget!"

"And it's just one bike, Dad." I pointed to the entrance.

"I can start the play again in slow motion," Samuel said, "Then we can follow the tracks."

We all held our breaths as we followed the tracks part way up the crevice trail.

"Stop it here Samuel," Dad said. He leaned his head closer to the screen. "Look here, the tracks are different here, there are footprints next to the tire tracks."

"Keep going, I think we're on to something," Dad motioned for Samuel to hit play.

"Lookie! Lookie!" Tyler yelled. "A head just poked out of that wall!"

Chapter 31

Millie

Millie pulled the crude map out of its hiding place between her chest protector and riding jersey and studied it. She wondered how the photo of the cave drawing tied in with this map. And wouldn't it be awesome if the cave drawing was in this very cave she was hiding in?

She squeezed between her motorcycle and the dirt wall, staring back into the darkness. It was hard to tell how far back this opening went. The dirt ceiling above her head was only about a foot away. She wished she had a long stick to poke into the ceiling to check for stability.

Millie knew she had a flashlight in her backpack, but she hesitated to use it. If the light exposed a deeper cave it would increase her desire to go exploring. She already caused enough trouble for herself and everyone else with her impulsive action.

She stared into the dark but felt like the flashlight was calling her name.

Millie turned and leaned over the handlebars to grab the

backpack off the seat of the motorcycle. It couldn't hurt just to shine the light and take a look from where she was.

She was in awe at the narrow cave that led back to a larger area, the ceiling rose as the walls widened. Near the back wall it looked like the cave branched off to the left.

"It couldn't hurt to get a little closer," Millie said aloud, taking a few steps away from the motorcycle, trying to see around the bend where it branched off.

She looked back at the motorcycle and realized she had stepped more than just a few feet away. She could still see the opening where she pushed the bike in.

"What if this was the cave where the drawing was?" Millie studied the walls, looking for carvings. She held the flashlight with one hand and rubbed the wall with her other hand feeling all around for indentations. She didn't know if the drawing she saw had been carved in dirt or etched into the side of a rock wall.

Millie picked up a rock and scraped at the hard dirt. She carved a big M, then stood back to admire her work. Continuing her name she was almost to the end when the flashlight slipped from her hand, hitting the ground, leaving her in total darkness.

"Wait?!" she yelled. "Where is the light from the entrance?" She turned back the way she had come and saw only darkness.

"Did I really come this far into the cave?" Millie stepped a few feet away from the wall she had been carving and turned to look for the motorcycle. She couldn't see anything.

She looked over her shoulder, then turned around wondering if she was looking in the wrong direction.

"No!" she yelled. "How can I get lost just carving on a wall?"

Her voice echoed back at her. "How big is this place anyway?" This could have been fun if she wasn't alone and lost.

Millie stood silently, staring unseeing, trying to decide what to do.

"I need to get back to my bike." She took a couple of steps in the direction she thought would take her there.

Suddenly the ground dropped out from under her.

"Daaaaaaad!" she yelled as she fell through the air.

Chapter 32

Jeremiah

Before Dad even spoke, Samuel stopped the video and reversed it, to replay what looked like a head popping out of a wall of dirt.

"That has to be her, Dad!" Relief washed through me for the first time since I watched my sister ride off alone. Everything was going to be okay.

"How did she get inside the dirt wall?" Tyler poked Dad's arm to get his attention. "Huh? How did she?"

Dad looked deep in thought, most likely already planning what to load in the truck for the rescue. He finally looked down at Tyler, standing next to his side. "It's a cave in the side of the dirt wall . . ."

"A cave?!" Tyler's yell brought the other kids scrambling to get into Mom's office.

"What cave?" Mía said. "I want to see a cave."

"Is Millie hiding in a cave?" Caleb asked.

"Did you find Millie, Mr. Max?" Jenny's quiet voice could

barely be heard over the noisy younger kids.

"Everyone come with me." Mom intervened and Dad looked relieved about the distraction for the kids. "I've got brownies in the kitchen and we need to let Dad think."

Samuel turned to follow Mom.

"No, Son," Dad reached out and touched his shoulder. "Mom meant all the others."

I watched as Samuel's countenance changed. It seemed like for the first time since he moved in, he felt like he really belonged. A pang of guilt rose up in me, knowing how much I had resented his intrusion here. I was part of the reason he hadn't felt welcome. That was going to change.

"Samuel, can you make that gizmo of yours work with my phone?" Dad asked.

"Sure can. I just need to download the app."

"Okay, how about you go put it in the truck while I get some tools?" Dad turned to me. "Jeremiah, get the loading ramp in the truck with the tie-downs so we can get Millie's bike back home. And might as well throw in a pillow and blanket."

Samuel attempted to download the drone app on Dad's phone as we raced over the bumps and ruts. The seatbelts held us in place but Samuel's hands with the phone would fly up in the air as we sailed over the large bumps. The plan was to get to that trail and find Millie with no problem. But Dad wanted Samuel ready for Plan B in case we needed to search more once we got to the crevice trail.

"Should only be about another mile," Dad said as he held tight to the steering wheel to keep it from jerking out of his hands when he hit boulders and ruts.

What a crazy day this had been. I went from intensely disliking Samuel to feeling respect and almost brotherly love for him. Hard to believe we started the day battling the windstorm and all the damage at the Ridge Riders Lodge to heading out on a search and rescue mission.

Thoughts of the Ridge Riders reminded me of that startling face in the window

"Dad!" Iß yelled. "I know where I've seen that big quad rider before!"

Chapter 33

Millie

Millie landed hard on the ground before she had time to realize she was falling. She sat up slowly, still in pitch darkness, then tried to stand.

"Ow!" Her voice echoed. She winced at the pain in her ankle and gave up on the idea of standing. Feeling around with her hands, she was able to scoot back a few inches to lean against the dirt bank. She had no idea how far she had fallen and couldn't stand to see if she could reach the ledge.

This would have been an amazing discovery if she wasn't lost, alone and now hurt. She didn't even have her backpack. "That was stupid!" she said to no one. "I should never have left Jeremiah. I don't even have water now."

She wondered how long it would be before her dad found her. For the first time that day she gave into the fear that had been skirting around in her mind, threatening to consume her.

Leaning against the dirt wall she scooted her knees up to her chest and buried her head in her knees. Tears seeped out of her eyes and she remembered Jenny sitting in this very same position just a few hours ago.

She lifted her head, wiping her eyes and tried to look around, but the darkness still blinded her. "Is this how Jenny felt? Scared and alone?"

Millie sighed. Why was life always changing? She didn't want to feel guilty for resenting Jenny and Samuel, but she did. And now she couldn't even feel sorry for herself in this predicament she'd gotten into because she kept picturing Jenny crying this morning.

"God," she looked up even though it was just as dark above her as it was all around. She just knew that was a good direction to look to talk to God. "I'm not trying to make any deals, I hate it when people pray those kinds of prayers. But I'm just saying if I do get out of here, I'm going to be nicer to Jenny and to Samuel and to all the kids."

She stopped praying to listen. She thought she heard a sound. But now all was silent. "And one more thing God, I know while I'm down here it seems like I'll be able to be nice to everyone . . . but I'm sure when I'm back home safe, I'm going to need Your help being nice."

This time she knew for sure she heard a noise. It sounded like the rattling of a sidewinder.

A scream escaped her throat so loud it could probably have been heard at home. That was the last thing she remembered before she passed out.

Chapter 34

Jeremiah

"That quad rider looked like the same guy at the window of Emmett's trailer this morning." I hung on and tried to talk while bouncing around in the front seat. "I'm sure it's him!"

Dad stared straight ahead, flying along the dirt road. We were almost to the crevice. "How can you be sure of that?" He glanced over at me. "We couldn't see his face."

"Remember, I saw him running past some trailers this morning. They're the same size, and I'm sure he's dressed the same."

"Turning into quite the detective, aren't you?" Dad laughed despite the seriousness of our outing.

"Hey, Millie's not the only one who's observant."

Dad slammed the brakes on as we got to the trailhead. "I should have brought my bike," he said, shutting off the engine. We all jumped out and heard a loud and long scream coming from the crevice trail.

Dad took off in a run, with Samuel and I following close

behind. For an old guy, he could move. The scream stopped and the silence scared me even more. Thankfully, this trail was hard packed dirt. Running in soft sand is a killer, and that would have slowed us down.

Worried about Millie, I felt like we were running in slow motion. Dad was ahead of us, but suddenly he disappeared. The huge dirt wall swallowed him. When he led us on a ride through here, I never noticed a cave. Samuel and I pushed harder.

We got to the cave entrance, barely large enough for a bike to fit. Dad stood alone near Millie's bike. She was nowhere in sight. My heart fell in my stomach imagining those guys dragging Millie away. That's probably why her scream stopped. They clamped something over her mouth to quiet her down. My heart beat so hard I thought Samuel would hear it.

"Millie!" Dad's voice boomed and echoed through the darkness. We couldn't see much past where her bike leaned on the dirt wall, but from the echo it sounded like this cave could be larger than it appeared.

"Why didn't I bring a flashlight?" Dad slammed his fist down on the seat of Millie's bike. "Where is that girl?"

A beam of light startled us as it shone about the cave, revealing a much larger cavern than we expected. I turned to see a smiling Samuel holding a flashlight. "I'm always prepared for a search."

Wow, was he a Millie clone or what?

Dad clapped him on the back. "Samuel we couldn't have done this without you."

"Dad, look there!" Samuel's light focused on Millie's name carved into the wall deeper into the cave. We stepped that way, careful not to cover her footprints.

"Millie's flashlight." I picked up the pieces of the flashlight she never left home without.

"Millie!" Dad yelled again.

"Dad." The faint voice seemed to come out of the ground. "Dad, help! Snake!"

Chapter 35

Millie

The muffled voices sounded like her dad and brother. Millie's eyes fluttered open, and she wondered if she just dreamed she heard them talking.

"Millie!" The unmistakable sound of her dad's voice floated down into the dark pit where she huddled against the wall. Before she could respond, she heard the rattle again. She couldn't tell how close it was in the darkness, and she stifled a scream.

"Dad, help! Snake!" She sat frozen in place, remembering that advice about a sidewinder, if you couldn't retreat.

She heard a commotion above her. A flashlight beam bounced around the walls, but she still couldn't see the ground. The rattling sound increased. "Dad, hurry, I'm in a snake pit!" Millie felt dizzy, like she might pass out again.

The sound of running feet calmed her, knowing she'd soon be safe.

The calm disappeared when a flashlight beam from

above illuminated a coiled sidewinder inches from her boots. She gasped and jerked her feet closer to her, wincing at the pain shooting up her ankle.

"Millie, don't move." Dad's calm voice carried such a sound of authority Millie hoped he could order the snake to retreat.

She heard whispering and wondered who came with Dad, but to twist her body to look up seemed risky. She kept her eyes trained on the snake.

"Millie," Dad whispered from above. "Sit tight."

"Get me out of here, Dad!" She tried to sit still, but the longer the snake stared at her from its coiled position, the more she shivered in fear. Would that movement cause the snake to strike?

Millie could feel drops of sweat forming on her forehead as she stared, her body trembling.

"Millie, hold still." She whimpered at her dad's words, knowing she couldn't force her body to follow his commands.

The snake's head lifted, the tail rattling so fast she couldn't discern the movement. This would have fascinated her, if she wasn't inches away from the poisonous reptile. She didn't know a lot about snakes, but it seemed to her this one was getting ready to strike.

"Dad." The whimpering sound escaped her lips.

A rustling sounded above her and the flashlight beam bounced around, leaving the snake in darkness.

Millie clamped her eyes shut, expecting to feel the fangs sink into her at any moment. She held her breath. A loud thud nearby forced a pitiful scream out of her.

"Samuel!" Dad's yell echoed through the cavern.

Chapter 36

Jeremiah

Dad and I watched in disbelief as Samuel leaped from the ledge, landing near the snake. I recognized the frustration in Dad's voice. Samuel hadn't been in the family long enough to know what things Dad doesn't want us to do, like Millie and I had learned.

I thought about the predicament Millie was in and realized, "Well, maybe not." Look how long she'd been in the family and she did stuff all the time Dad didn't like.

Which was why we were on this wild goose chase in the desert, now watching a poisonous snake staring down my sister.

"Samuel, don't!" Dad caught my attention, but obviously not Samuel's.

We heard him wince as the snake struck his hand. The jerk of his arm sent the snake flying deeper into the cavern.

"Millie," Samuel turned to her. "I'll help you up."

I stood frozen, not believing what I saw. Samuel didn't even act like a poisonous snake had bitten him. Millie still whimpered. Dad jumped down next to them. "Samuel, let me see your hand." He reached out to take hold of him.

Samuel jerked his hand back, "I'm okay, it's probably just a dry bite." He struggled to lift Millie.

"You don't know that." Dad's stern voice failed to deter Samuel, who had Millie up on her feet. She looked back and forth between the two.

"I know." Samuel placed her arm around his neck, then appeared to be trying to pick her up.

"Son," Dad helped him support Millie's weight. "We don't know without an exam. We've got to get you to the hospital."

"It's not my first time to get bit, I'll be okay."

I stood still, shining the flashlight at the three of them, feeling useless and hating the feeling. I felt like a coward, content to let my sister face the venomous snake alone. And I had no clue what a dry bite was.

"Jeremiah," Dad took his eyes off Samuel and Millie briefly. "Check the reserve tank on her bike and see if it will start."

Finally, something I could do that Samuel couldn't. I kicked a rock as I got near the bike, only to have it hit the wall of the cave and bounce back at me. What an idiot I felt like.

I straddled the bike, reached under the tank and flipped the petcock to reserve. The bike fired right up. Couldn't believe Millie didn't think of this herself. Something must have scared her just before the main tank ran dry.

"Jeremiah." The three of them were out of the pit and almost to the bike. "Move forward and we'll put your sister on behind you," Dad said. "Ride her to the truck, then come back for Samuel."

"I can walk," Samuel said.

Once Dad got Millie on the bike, she wrapped her arms around me in a bear hug. I turned to nod at Dad and Samuel as we rode out of the cave. Samuel was nowhere to be seen.

Chapter 37

Millie

Millie clung to her brother as they flew down the hard pack dirt of the creviced trail. She hated being a passenger on her own motorcycle, but had no one to blame but herself.

"My backpack!" she cried out, realizing she didn't have it with her.

Jeremiah brought the bike to a skidding halt. "What happened?" he sounded alarmed as he strained to look back over his shoulder.

"My backpack, I forgot it!" Millie yelled through her helmet.

Jeremiah let out a groan, then gassed the motorcycle, causing Millie to grip his sides even harder as she felt her body thrust backwards.

At the truck, Millie stumbled when she got off the bike on her bad ankle. Her brother caught her and shoved her into the back seat, in a hurry to get back to Dad and Samuel. "Dad made me bring a blanket and pillow for you." He tossed the blanket over her head, then grabbed the helmet from her. She threw the blanket off.

Jeremiah nodded a goodbye to Millie, then kicked the bike over.

"I'm not sick, I just ran out of gas!" she yelled.

He revved the bike extra loud. "Yeah, really out of gas, aren't you!" Dirt and rocks flew as he spun the tires, taking off before she could get another word in.

Millie slammed the truck door and twisted in the seat to watch her brother head back through the narrow trail. Her growling stomach reminded her she still didn't have her backpack that always had snacks and water in it. She flopped down, stretching out on the back seat, pondering the poor decisions she'd made that day. "What a mess I've caused," Millie said to no one, and yanked the blanket up over her shoulders.

Staring at the ceiling, she shivered at the memory of the snake rattling and Samuel jumping off the ledge to stop it from biting her. Pulling the blanket tighter to her chin, she closed her eyes, begging God for forgiveness. The shame of how she treated Samuel overwhelmed her. "Why did he do that?" she yelled, unable to imagine taking a snake bite for someone who had treated her so badly.

Millie sat upright at the unexpected sound of Jeremiah returning already, but she couldn't see him on the trail. The sound grew closer.

She turned to look out the windshield and saw the quad riders barreling for the truck.

Millie threw herself down on the floorboard, flattening out, trying to look invisible and pulling the blanket the length of her body.

She held her breath as the engines shut off and willed herself to stay still.

"Jay!" A deep voice yelled. "Look what's in the truck!"

Millie's heart stopped when she heard the back door open and felt the breeze ruffling the blanket.

"Well, lookie what we have here," a raspy voice said.

Chapter 38

Jeremiah

"I wonder if you can die from a sidewinder bite?" The question echoed in my head as I pinned the throttle and flew along the narrow path. Millie has really done it this time with her shenanigans. Why in the world Samuel would put himself between a poisonous snake and a girl who treated him like dirt was a mystery to me.

Roaring around a blind corner, I grabbed the front brake lever and stomped hard on the back brake, skidding to a halt, barely missing my dad and Samuel in the middle of the trail.

Samuel looked fine, not at death's door, as I was imagining. "Where were you when I left?" I said as I killed the engine. "I thought you passed out and were on the ground."

"Nah." Samuel held up Millie's broken flashlight. "I went back in to get Millie's backpack and this."

Two small bloody spots on his puffy wrist stood out when he held up the flashlight. Dad saw me staring at the fang marks. "We've got to get Samuel to the hospital."

"I told you," Samuel shrugged. "I'm okay, I've been bit before and I was fine."

Backing the motorcycle up, I angled it around to return to the truck. "Hop on, Samuel." Looking over at Dad, I said, "I'll be back for you."

"I should be almost there." Dad took off in a jog.

"Look at that!" Samuel tapped my shoulder when we were almost back to the truck, yelling into the side of the helmet. His arm extended over my shoulder, pointing ahead of us.

Focusing on some rocks in the path, I hadn't seen the commotion at the truck. It looked like a couple of quads parked nearby, and a man standing near the open truck door.

"Hang on!" I yelled and twisted the throttle as far as it would go.

"He's got my drone!" Samuel leaned into me, as if to push the motorcycle faster than we were already going.

The roar of the engine must have startled the man as we got closer. He turned toward us, still holding the drone. His partner fired up a quad and took off into the desert.

Suddenly the truck door burst open from the inside, knocking the man off his feet. I cringed as I imagined Samuel's drone breaking in pieces when it flew out of the man's hands.

At least Millie was safe.

CHAPTER 39

Millie

"That guy was lying!" Millie's voice wobbled from the jarring of the truck as her dad raced along the dirt road heading toward the two-lane highway. "They were chasing me!"

"Dad knows that." Jeremiah shared the back seat with her. "It's okay."

Her dad didn't respond, just focused on his driving. Millie tried to read his expression in the rear-view mirror. She wondered how much trouble she was in. Maybe her dad didn't believe the quad riders were chasing her. In fact, now she even wondered if they were. He told her dad they were trying to check on her to see if she was okay.

"You don't chase someone down like a scared jack rabbit just to see if they're okay," she whispered.

"Millie, I almost forgot," Samuel turned to look at her from where he sat in the front passenger seat. "Your mom gave me something for you."

Millie looked at Jeremiah for a clue, but he shrugged.

Samuel unzipped his drone case and pulled out some papers. "She said she remembered about this when you two were looking through the knapsack." Millie could see the ugly red fang marks on his wrist when he handed the papers over the seat. His hand looked swollen. She wanted to know if it hurt, but her shame wouldn't let her mention the snake bite. She knew she should say something, but she couldn't bring herself to.

"Millie," Jeremiah's voice startled her, interrupting her guilty thoughts. "Aren't you going to take the papers?" He reached up, taking them out of Samuel's hand.

"Lost Ship of the Desert," he read aloud, but Millie couldn't even pretend to be interested. She'd done so many stupid things today and now maybe put Samuel's life in danger. Why didn't he yell at her, at least? Why did he have to save her from getting bit by the snake?

Her guilt overwhelmed her.

Samuel stared at the two of them in the back seat. Even Dad glanced in the mirror in Millie's direction. She ignored them both, and stared straight ahead. She just wanted to disappear.

"Fine!" Samuel jerked the paper out of Jeremiah's hand and jammed it back into his case. "You hate me so much, you won't even take information about your precious ship from me."

"That's not it!" Millie mumbled. She felt the stares of her brother and her dad in the mirror.

"Well, what then, Millie?" Jeremiah seemed to be taking his side. "Have you even thanked Samuel for saving you from the snake?"

Millie turned a stunned look toward her brother. Even he was against her now.

Her guilt vanished, replaced by anger.

"Stop the truck, Dad!" she yelled and grabbed hold of the door handle. "I want out!"

Chapter 40

Jeremiah

"**M**illie! Stop it!" I grabbed my sister and drug her away from the door before she could pull the handle.

Dad kept the gas on, but glanced over his shoulder, then turned back to watch the road. We were just about to the highway. "It's okay, Dad."

Millie struggled to get free, but I held on. I'd never seen my sister like this. Crazy she could be, but right now she was bordering on out of control.

Samuel never looked back. He stared straight ahead, stiff as a stone statue.

Once the truck hit the highway, Dad floored it. From where I sat, I could see the speedometer climbing. Fifty, 60, 70, leveling off at 80. We should be to the hospital in less than an hour at that rate. What an unreal day this was turning out to be. Millie settled down, but I still didn't let go.

"Can I go live with Minnesota Mike?"

Dad's head jerked to the right of him, at the unexpected question from Samuel.

"No, Son," Dad said, concentrating on his driving. "Why would you ask that?"

Samuel didn't respond. An awkward silence settled inside the truck. I think it was pretty obvious to all of us why Samuel asked. If my sister had any sense at all, she'd use this opportunity to apologize to him. Stubborn Millie clinched her jaw shut and stared out the window of the door I wouldn't let her open.

I would not want to be in her shoes when Dad gets a chance to give her a piece of his mind. Not to mention the consequences he'd have lined up for her.

I was glad Dad had me accompany Samuel into the emergency room while he waited with Millie. I'd had enough of her for today. "I'd hate to see you move out," I said.

Samuel looked surprised at my comment. I had to admit I hadn't been super friendly to him either, and unlike my sister, I was feeling bad about that.

Samuel shrugged.

"I don't blame you for wanting to get away from Millie."

"She treats me like trash." Samuel stretched out on the emergency room table and picked at the IV needle the nurse had placed in the back of his hand. "I don't even need this," he said.

It seemed kind of weird they hooked him up to an IV needle that didn't have any fluid flowing through it yet.

"I admit she's not always the nicest girl to be around."

"I don't see her treating you that way." This time Samuel looked right at me.

"Oh believe me, she can treat me that way too."

"Doesn't it bother you?" Samuel looked back at the

needle, continuing to pick at the white adhesive tape. He didn't know it, but in some ways he was a lot like Millie.

"Why would it bother me? She's just a dumb sister."

Samuel's head jerked up and the look in his eyes answered my question more plainly than if he had spoken it aloud.

Chapter 41

Millie

"Gerard's Motorcycles." Millie read the name aloud on the engraved wooden sign. "Gerard. I like that name."

She fiddled with the crutches the hospital gave her while she studied the large wooden sign outside the motorcycle shop. Someone took a long time carving that sign. There was another smaller one over the doorway that her dad, Jeremiah, and Samuel disappeared through.

They didn't get into town often, so it made sense to make the most of this trip, once the hospital confirmed what Samuel had been saying all along. He wasn't in any danger, the snake hadn't released venom when it bit him.

"So, he didn't really save my life," Millie said out loud in the empty truck. She wouldn't have dared mentioned that to anyone, knowing she was already in a lot of trouble. Besides, she had to admit, even without the poison, those fang marks on his hand looked painful. She was grateful to him for helping her. But she just could not tell him.

Millie stared past the carved sign, through the fence, and into the side yard of this little motorcycle shop. It was filled with dozens of old motorcycles in various stages of completion. A giant RV with pop-outs on both sides sat in the middle of the lot. She wondered if Gerard lived right there, surrounded by his hobby.

She'd been wanting to go in this shop ever since they moved to the desert, but there had never been time when they'd come to town. And now, instead of taking advantage of the opportunity, here she sat. In the truck, sulking, licking her wounds. Not that she would admit that to anyone. She was too proud to struggle with the crutches in front of everyone, especially on the heels of causing so much trouble.

Millie leaned forward to grab the paper she had refused to look at earlier. She wondered what that funny contraption was in the front seat? No one mentioned it, and as much as she wanted to know, she couldn't bring herself to ask. And speaking of questions, she wondered how her dad found her so soon when she was nowhere near the trail she and Jeremiah had ridden on.

Before she could settle back and read the paper, she saw the door to the RV open. An older man looked out, then stood on the top step. He struggled to lower his foot to the next step, but missed it and tumbled down onto the asphalt.

Millie, forgetting her discomfort with the crutches, threw the truck door open and shuffled to the fence. She struggled to get the gate open. The man was trying to get up on his own by the time she reached him.

"Well, look at you, little lady," he smiled up at her. "You look like you had a tumble yourself today."

Millie rested one crutch against the RV and leaned on the other, then used her free hand to help the man up. He rose as far as the lower step, where he plopped down to catch his breath.

"Are you hurt?"

He chuckled, "Well, I think I'm better off than you are right now. How did you earn those crutches?"

"I did something stupid."

He threw his head back and laughed. Before he could ask her anything else, she saw her dad and the boys approach the truck.

"I better go now." Millie grabbed her other crutch. "Are you sure you're okay?"

"I'm right as rain." He chuckled again. "Stop by and see me again sometime. I don't get many visitors and you seem like you'd be fun to visit with."

Millie smiled, for the first time that day. "Okay, I'll try." She reached out to shake his hand. "I'm Millie."

"Glad to meet you, Millie. My name's Emmett."

Chapter 42

Jeremiah

"Millie!" I was too excited to wonder what she was doing behind the fence. "Wait till you hear what we discovered in there!"

She hobbled over to the truck with surprising speed. "What did you find?"

"This guy, Gerard, has a big picture hanging on his wall of a Spanish galleon and underneath the picture is a caption that says 'Lost Ship in the Desert'!"

Millie's eyes grew enormous, and she looked from me, to Samuel and Dad and back. "Are you kidding me?"

"He's not kidding," Samuel said.

"That's not the best part." I couldn't believe how relieved I felt seeing a smile on Millie's face.

"What?!"

"Hey, hop in the truck. We'll talk on the way," Dad said. "I'm sure Mom is anxious for us to get home."

"Yeah, she'll want to see for herself Samuel and Millie are okay." I took Millie's crutches and helped her into the truck.

Dad drove a few blocks, then turned into the Dairy Queen. "But first, milkshakes!" he said.

"So, what's the best part?" Millie asked after we all got settled around the picnic bench with our ice cream and shakes. She talked around the straw in her mouth as she slurped her banana shake.

I took a big bite of my ice cream sundae and heard her groan. Probably because I was taking too long to answer.

Samuel surprised me when he jumped in with the explanation. "Gerard and a friend have been searching for the ship and he invited us to go along with them sometime."

"Wow? Are you kidding me?" Millie turned to Dad, "Can we do that, Dad? Can we go with them?"

Dad continued sipping on his chocolate shake, then nodded and set his cup on the table. "That might be a possibility."

"When are they going again?" Millie asked. "I should have gone in the store with you."

"In about a week," I said.

"Let me talk to Minnesota Mike," Dad said. "Maybe he'll take all of you." Dad turned to Samuel. "Do you want to go too, Son?"

"Well, if it's okay with everyone." Samuel went back to looking unsure of himself around Millie. And maybe even me.

"Yeah, of course," I said and noticed that Millie didn't respond to that comment.

Apparently Samuel noticed too.

"And can you also ask Minnesota Mike if I can live with him?" he said to Dad.

Chapter 43

Millie

"The Spanish vessel sailed into the delta area in the 16th century filled with pearls and other treasure," Millie read aloud.

"Listen to this one," Jeremiah said, reading from a different paper. "Some speculated it might be a craft from the navy of King Solomon . . ."

"Wonderful!" Mom said as she passed through the room. "This could be a Biblical adventure searching for the ship."

Millie jumped up and hugged her mom. "Thank you for printing these out for us."

Mom pointed out the window to the sunrise greeting them with no wind in sight. "Looks to be a better day than yesterday."

"When are Julia and Tucker expecting us to work at the store?" Millie said.

"Dad set it up for 7 a.m. so you'll have time for adventure later."

"Adventure?" Millie couldn't believe there was no punishment for yesterday. "What kind of adventure?"

"Is searching for a lost ship adventure enough?" Mom said, walking out of the room.

"Jeremiah! Did you hear that?"

Samuel followed Mom out of the room. "Where's he going?" Millie said to her brother.

Jeremiah shrugged. "I don't know, he probably noticed you didn't include him."

"Oh man," Millie said, "I'm not good at this. Every day it's a challenge trying to make the other kids feel welcome."

"Millie, don't be so annoying about it," Jeremiah said. "It's not that big of a deal to be friendly."

She groaned. This couldn't be a replay of yesterday's bad day. Millie took a deep breath. Determined to make Samuel and all the kids feel welcome, she cringed at the memory of her prayer while trapped in the cave. Today she needed to try harder.

"Listen to this," Jeremiah resumed reading from the papers. "The ship could be from the '10 lost tribes of Israel or a warring people from the Indian Ocean, or a band of pirates.'"

"No matter what, there would be treasure," Millie said.

"I think it would be treasure enough just finding the ship," Jeremiah said.

"How is this for treasure?" Samuel returned and dropped a pile of dusty pearls on the floor in front of Millie.

Millie scooped them up and held them in her palm, studying them. "Where did you get these?"

She looked up when Samuel didn't answer. He stared right at her, still not speaking.

"Samuel! Where did these come from?" she insisted.

"Found them."

Chapter 44

Jeremiah

Tucker left before we got to the Dry Brook Trading Post and Julia only had work for Millie. Not that she could do much on crutches. That opened the door for me to hang out with Samuel and Minnesota Mike, since she didn't need me at the trading post. Somehow picking up debris from the windstorm at Ridge Riders Lodge seemed like it would be more fun today with Samuel helping. Plus, we'd get to talk Minnesota Mike into taking us out in his buggy to search for the ship.

M&M was always up for an adventure. And since Samuel didn't ride, this way we could all go. Besides, Millie won't be riding for a while with her sprained ankle. That's why Dad didn't take her bike away for what she did. She couldn't ride, anyway. Mom said being chased, lost and almost bitten by a snake was punishment enough. Not really lost, but she might as well have been. She couldn't get home by herself.

Tyler ran up to greet us as soon as Dad parked the truck. "Come on, I gotta show you the bad guys," he tugged on my hand when I stepped out of the truck, his voice low. I wondered if they were nearby.

"Why do you call them bad guys?" I asked. Samuel came around to join the conversation.

"Are these the quad riders?" he asked.

"Yeah, they wanted the map to the ship." Tyler looked at Samuel then turned to me.

Wait a minute. How did this kid know about the map to the ship?

"Why do you think that?" Samuel said.

"'Cause the other kids told me about the ship picture. Ms. Norra told us about the map to a lost ship. And I know that's what Emmett was hiding from them guys."

No way this kid could have known what was in that box. But he sure seemed to be full of information.

"How do you know that?" I asked.

"I heard Emmett arguing with them a long time ago. They wanted to hunt for the ship with him. He said no."

"Why did they want to go with him?"

"For the treasure, why do ya think?" Tyler looked at me like I was an idiot.

Samuel burst out laughing. I didn't even know the guy could laugh. He was always so tense. It was worth being the source of his laughter if it loosened him up.

"So where are they?" I asked. "We don't have much time. We're here to work."

"Yeah, I know, Mr. Mike told me you were coming. I like being with you guys. Do you think I could live with you?"

Dad stepped around this side of the truck just then. Thankfully, I wouldn't have to answer that surprising question.

"Well, I don't know about that young fellow," Dad said. "I'm sure your mom would miss you."

"She don't mind," Tyler said. "She's busy or sick, anyway. Besides, she let my sister go live somewhere else once when she was alive."

Wow, this kid dropped some startling statements.

Samuel and I both looked at Dad. How was he going to handle that?

"Tell you what, Tyler. The boys have to work this morning, so we'll talk about this later." He nodded for us to find Minnesota Mike and get started. "Maybe you can come for lunch today. How about that?"

I turned toward the office and spotted the guy from yesterday running from his hiding spot behind the tree.

If he didn't know before we had the map, he sure knows now.

Chapter 45

Millie

Millie leaned her crutches against the wall and balanced on the stool near the counter at the Dry Brook Trading Post. She and Jeremiah worked a couple days a week with Julia and Tucker getting the store cleaned and ready to open. Julia, the nurse who helped Paisley, bought the store with her husband Tucker. It would be fun when the Trading Post opened. As long as Millie had lived in the desert, this store had been deserted.

"So, what do you hear from Paisley?" Julia said as she pulled dusty souvenirs down from the upper shelves and placed them on the counter. Armed with a dust towel, Millie began wiping off the glass figurines of coyotes, rabbits and cactus plants.

"I just got a letter from her," Millie said. "It's in my backpack if you want to get it."

She set the dust cloth down when Julia handed her Paisley's letter.

Dear Millie,

    I miss you so much, but I am having fun, if you can believe that. I'm pretending this is a vacation. The hotel is right near the beach and I don't mind telling you, I won't miss the summer heat in the desert if we have to stay here that long. I wish you could be here.

    Yesterday I saw the doctor, and they told my parents they want to put a pacemaker in my heart. They said that will be the best way to protect my heart. I am so glad Julia told my parents about this disease, since no one at the hospital discovered it. I owe my life to her.

    Millie stopped reading and looked up at Julia. She had tears in her eyes. It reminded Millie of the day Julia told them about her two children dying from the undiagnosed disease Paisley had. She resumed reading.

    The surgery will take place next week. I know you will pray for me.

    I can't wait to see you and until then, stay out of trouble.

    Love, Paisley

    Now Julia was laughing. "Well, you didn't get that advice soon enough, did you?"

    Millie laughed along with her. "I guess Paisley really knows me."

    The two hours of work sailed by. Millie was startled when she heard the loud roar of Minnesota Mike's dune buggy pulling up outside the store. She slipped off the stool and hopped over to where her crutches leaned against the wall.

    The boys bounded through the door with ear to ear grins. "It's adventure time!" Jeremiah said.

    "Are we really going?" Millie asked, struggling to pick up her backpack.

    "We sure are, you got the map and drawings with you?"

"Of course," she said. "I don't go anywhere without all the important stuff."

Millie looked over at Samuel, then dug around in her backpack.

"Look at this, Julia." She set a little pouch on the counter.

Julia untied the ribbon and poured out a handful of pearls. "Oh my!" She looked at Millie. "Where did you get these? They're beautiful!"

Millie pointed to Samuel. "He gave them to me. They were all dusty, but I cleaned them and put them in this pouch I've been saving for something important."

"Samuel, these look quite authentic," Julia said. "Wherever did you get them?"

Samuel looked uncomfortable being in the spotlight.

"Found them," was all he said.

"He showed them to us right after we learned the lost ship may have been filled with pearls." Millie turned from Julia back to Samuel. "But he won't tell us where he found them."

"Well, he likes to go out hiking in windstorms," Jeremiah said. "Maybe he stumbled upon the ship without even knowing it."

Everyone looked at Samuel, waiting for an answer. His response was to turn and walk out the door.

Chapter 46

Jeremiah

Minnesota Mike drove the buggy like he was a teenager, with the pedal smashed to the floor. We all whooped and hollered as we flew over the bumps and rocks on our journey east. He roared up a tall hill about a half hour into our adventure and slammed the brakes on at the top. The view was fantastic. We could see the whole desert from this spot.

M&M shut down the engine and pulled his helmet off. "Lookie here," he said, "I found us a perfect spot to eat that delicious lunch yer mom done packed us."

We piled out of the buggy. Mike reached in for the cooler held down with bungee cords behind the back seat. While he handed out the sandwiches and drinks, Millie dug around in her backpack. "Right on!" I yelled when she pulled out a pair of binoculars. She scanned the desert terrain, making a 360 degree slow spin. Our destination was a salt water sea about 30 miles east of where we lived in the desert.

"See anything yet, little lady?" Minnesota asked as he

munched down his sandwich.

"I can see what looks like shimmering water over in that direction." She held the binoculars with one hand, pointing with the other.

Samuel looked interested, and it surprised me to see Millie hand him the binoculars. "Do you want to look?" she asked.

He seemed shocked, but accepted the binoculars. Samuel looked in a different direction than Millie pointed. I wondered why that was. He studied the area carefully, barely moving the binoculars, as if he was looking for something specific.

"What do you see?" Millie asked. She still hadn't taken her sandwich out. She was like that. Once she got an idea into her head, like being the first one in hundreds of years to find the ship, food was the last thing on her mind.

Samuel continued to stare. He honed in on one specific area. He had me curious now, too. Even Minnesota Mike looked in that direction.

"Samuel, what do you see?" Millie insisted.

He dropped the binoculars down from his eyes, giving them back to Millie. "Just looking."

"Oh, that's great," Millie said. "Now you can't even tell us what you saw. I know you spotted something." She shoved the binoculars into her backpack.

Boy, if he wanted to get on Millie's good side, that was the wrong answer. She hated evasive answers.

"Just like the pearls. 'Where did you get the pearls?' I asked you." She mimicked him. "'Just found them,' you said." Millie grabbed her crutches and hobbled over to the other side of the buggy, most likely to eat as far away from Samuel as she could. I didn't know someone could attack a sandwich with such anger. It was almost comical watching her.

I had to admit, I was wondering myself what was going on with Samuel. Where did he get those dusty pearls? Had he already been out searching for this ship before he came to live with us, when his mom was still alive? What did he see that was so interesting? I was tempted to ask Millie for the binoculars so

I could look in that direction. But with the mood she was in, the last thing I wanted to do was ask her a question.

Finishing my sandwich, I dug into the chocolate chip cookies Mom sent. Samuel joined me.

"Hey, Mike," I said with cookie crumbs spraying out. Bad manners, I know, but I wanted to ask him before I forgot again.

"What can I do fer you, sonny boy?" Mike reached into the container and pulled out a couple cookies.

"What do you think happened to Emmett?"

Millie shocked me when her head jerked around in our direction. She snapped out of her little pouting party and stepped closer to join the conversation. "Who is Emmett?" she asked.

"He lives at the Ridge Riders Lodge, in a trailer that got tipped over in the wind. But he disappeared a couple months ago. We're wondering where he is." I said.

"Well sonny boy, no one knows, 'cepting fer that note you found in the box."

"I know where there is a man named Emmett," Millie said.

CHAPTER 47

Millie

"Dad!" Millie half ran, half wobbled into the house on her crutches. "You won't believe it, Dad!"

Samuel, Jeremiah, and Minnesota Mike followed her into the living room. She was already on her way to the kitchen where she found her dad finishing lunch. "Dad! We've got to go back to Gerard's shop!"

It didn't take long for them to fill their dad in on what they discovered. No one saw Tyler enter the room when he jumped into the conversation. "Did you find Mr. Emmett? Can I go with you? He's my friend!"

An hour later the SUV filled with two adults, three teenagers and young Tyler pulled into Gerard's parking lot. Millie was the first one out of the car. She hobbled over to the gate, disappointed to find it locked. "Emmett!" she called out. By now, the others had joined her.

"Mr. Emmett!" Tyler yelled along with her.

When the man didn't come out of the RV, the group headed inside the store.

"How can I help you folks?" a man, Millie presumed to be Gerard, greeted them.

"Hi there," her dad said. "Is Gerard here?"

So this was an employee, she realized, and noticed Tyler acting strange. He huddled against her dad, clinging to his leg.

"Well, hey there Tyler, is that you?" They all looked at Tyler when the man greeted him. The usually talkative boy stayed silent. "I haven't seen you since you were 3 or 4."

Dad put his arm around Tyler and redirected the conversation. He was good at that. He was also good at figuring out when kids were uncomfortable. "So is it possible to talk with Gerard?"

The man seemed to get the hint. He took his focus off Tyler when Dad repeated his question. "Nah, Gerard and his buddy are out tooling around in the desert today."

Millie desperately wanted to know if the buddy was her newfound friend Emmett. But something about this man seemed untrustworthy. She, like Tyler, remained silent. Even Minnesota Mike left all the talking up to Dad.

Thirty minutes later the group gathered around the picnic table outside Dairy Queen. This seemed to be a new tradition. Millie decided new traditions could be a good thing. Maybe even if they included a family growing more quickly than she expected. She looked around at Samuel and Tyler and a warm feeling rose inside her as she watched them digging into their banana splits with the enthusiasm of kids who haven't had an opportunity like this before. Even though Tyler wasn't a part of the family, it would be okay with her if he moved in.

"Tyler," Dad slurped the last of his chocolate shake. This guy was a creature of habit, always ordering the same thing. He wiped his mouth with a napkin, unlike the boys who used their sleeves or bottom of their shirts. "How did that man know your name?"

The joy went out of Tyler's eyes and he dropped his spoon in his dish. "He's my mom's old boyfriend."

Dad shot a questioning look at Minnesota Mike. M&M shook his head.

"I never met that feller myself," Minnesota said to Tyler.

"It was before we moved to the desert," Tyler said. He stared at the melting ice cream in his dish. Tyler must have some bad memories of that time in his life.

"That was when my sister went to live somewhere else. Back when she was still alive."

Millie's eyes grew huge. Wow, she did not know he had a sister who died. A million questions went through her mind. But this wasn't the time to ask. Millie looked at Jeremiah and Samuel. A slight nod from both of them meant they already knew this. And Jeremiah hadn't even told her. She started to get mad, but realized it was that very tendency to get angry that pushed everyone away. When did he have a chance to tell her? She'd been too angry to talk to.

"What was your sister's name?" Millie asked, breaking the awkward silence.

"Madison." Tyler smiled, then shoved a big scoop of ice cream in his mouth. The other boys joined in and Millie was about to polish off her chocolate chip shake until she noticed her dad.

The color disappeared from his face and he looked like he was a million miles away.

CHAPTER 48

Jeremiah

The following week at day break, I waved bye to Dad and Minnesota Mike and slowly drove the dune buggy off the property of the Ridge Riders Lodge. I didn't even need to look at my sister in the passenger seat next to me to know she had the biggest smile I'd seen on her in weeks.

I couldn't believe Dad and Minnesota let us take his buggy out. All those driving lessons from Minnesota Mike were paying off. They offered for Samuel to drive since he's older, and I shocked myself when I didn't get upset about it. Maybe my reward for a good attitude was Samuel saying he didn't want to drive. I haven't quite figured that kid out yet, except for one thing. His attitude toward Millie. I need to talk to Dad about that.

Once off the property, and out of sight of the adults, I gave it more gas. Millie whooped and hollered and wow, did it feel good to hear her return to normal.

Samuel was quiet in the back seat, but if I had to guess, I hoped he at least was smiling.

Millie insisted we head east, in her ever present quest to find the lost ship, but the rising sun was blinding me. Having never driven this buggy out in the open desert before, I risked my sister's wrath rather than our lives and turned north to get out of the direct sun. Surprisingly, she didn't raise a fuss. I didn't look her way, but expected to feel her poking my arm and pointing back toward the east.

I found a sand wash and powered through the gentle turns, sliding this way and that. I could grow to love driving a buggy almost as much as riding my motorcycle. A long straightaway gave me the courage to floor the gas pedal. There was no speedometer to check, but it felt like we were doing a hundred. Most likely, it was only about 40 or 50. I saw an opportunity ahead to jump a low bank, getting out of the wash onto hard pack dirt. Millie pointed to a covered picnic table and we soon rolled to a stop.

"Wow, that was awesome!" Millie set her helmet on the table, then grabbed her backpack from the floorboard.

Even Samuel was smiling when he took his helmet off.

"What did you think, Samuel?" I tried to draw him out, wishing he would join in the conversation on his own.

"That was a lot of fun," he nodded and accepted a granola bar from Millie. Thankfully, she gave one to him before either of us got one. "I'm glad I came."

"You know why I couldn't keep heading east?"

"Yeah," Millie said. "I wondered how you could see anything at all. Maybe when the sun gets higher, we can go that way."

"We can't go all the way to that desert sea you located."

"I know," Millie said, "but at least we can cover some areas of the desert we don't usually ride on. That map really isn't very clear. I just want to look for a ship's mast sticking out of the ground."

"Millie," I held back the urge to laugh out loud, "Don't you think if it's that obvious, it would have already been discovered?"

She shrugged, and I saw Samuel hide a smirk.

"Did you notice how odd Dad acted yesterday after Tyler told us his sister's name?" Millie asked.

Samuel surprised me when he answered first. "I did." We both looked his way.

"I was too busy getting back to my banana split to notice anything," I said.

"It seemed like that name meant something to him." Samuel confirmed my earlier thought that he and Millie were a lot alike. He noticed things I missed, the things Millie never let get by her.

"I thought the same thing." Millie seemed excited that he shared her suspicions.

"What do you think it means?" Samuel asked. I stared at the two of them, shocked they were having a cordial conversation. Detective minds, kindred spirits. This could be a good thing.

"I don't know," Millie said, gathering up all our trash and stuffing it in her backpack. "But I'm going to find out."

Chapter 49

Millie

"I'm ready to go home," Millie said, pulling on her helmet.

"Home?" Jeremiah lifted his helmet off the table, but didn't put it on yet. "I thought you wanted to search for the ship?"

"You're right, we won't see a ship's mast sticking out of the ground around here. Let's wait til Minnesota can take us to the sea."

Jeremiah looked at her, puzzled. "Uh, I don't think so." He pulled his helmet on and buckled the strap. "You're up to something."

Samuel laughed. "She probably wants to get home and start investigating your dad's reaction to the Madison name."

"Bingo!" Millie gave a thumbs up and headed for the buggy.

She didn't even have to wait til they got all the way home. Once the buggy slowed to a stop at the Ridge Riders, Millie leaped out and went in search of Minnesota Mike. She found him in the office, looking lost as he sat at the desk staring at a computer screen.

Her laughter startled M&M out of his daze. "I can't make heads nor tails outa this thing to save my life," Minnesota said, "and I got people comin' to check into the hotel this afternoon."

"Didn't Paisley show you how to do that before they left?" Millie asked.

"She shore 'nuff did, and it looked right easy when I was watching her do it."

Millie had spent many days beside her friend working in the office and knew how the computer check-in system worked.

"How about if I do it?" Millie couldn't keep the smile off her face.

"Uh-oh," M&M said, "what's it gonna cost me? What do you want from me? I can tell you got something up yer sleeve, little lady."

Millie laughed as she slid in behind the desk and manipulated the mouse to the check-in screen. "Just a little info."

"I don't know where that ship is, if that's the question."

"No, this is something else."

She entered the name and contact info Minnesota gave her into the reservation app, so all he had to do was click the submit button when the hotel guests showed up that afternoon.

"Did you know Tyler's sister Madison?"

"That's a question out of left field." He rubbed his beard and appeared to be thinking. "No, there weren't no sister living with them when they moved into the RV park. Just the mom and the kid and sometimes a boyfriend. Weren't never the same boyfriend though. That's a shame fer that poor kid."

"Do you know anything about the sister?"

"Just what little I hear Tyler talking about."

"What have you heard him say?"

"Boy, you jist don't quit with the questions now, do you?"

"No, she doesn't!" Jeremiah said as he and Samuel came into the office.

"How else will she learn anything?" Samuel said.

"Yeah, Jeremiah!" Millie gloated, realizing that she now had an ally defending her endless questions.

"Hey, Minnesota, can you unlock the store, so we can get a drink and some snacks?"

"Shore 'nuff, can." He stood and reached for a big set of keys dangling from his belt loop. He looked ready to leave the office.

"Wait a minute," Millie said. "You didn't answer my question."

"What question was that, little lady?"

"What have you heard about Madison?"

"Oh, yeah. That." Minnesota went quiet. He stared at the floor, jangled his keys with one hand and ran his other hand along the length of his beard.

"Mike?" Millie persisted.

"Well, it ain't a happy thought." Minnesota looked up, making eye contact with each of the boys, then settling on Millie.

"He's mentioned her a time or two. Always something about things they did before she moved away. Back when she was alive."

Millie nodded. "He said something like that to us too."

"You don't know how she died?" Samuel asked. He seemed to have a soft spot for Tyler. Maybe because they were both new to the family. Not that Tyler had joined the family, but it seemed like that was his goal.

"No, not fer sure," Minnesota Mike said. Then stared out the window, off in the distance, nodding his head. "But I got my own ideas."

Chapter 50

Jeremiah

I felt like we had crossed a line in the sand, and maybe Millie would stop antagonizing Samuel. This could be good for me. I'm up for adventure, but I'm not as curious as these two are. They can do their snooping, leave me out of it, and I'll just wait to hear the outcome. Besides, I've got something to discuss with dad, that neither of them need to know about. I was as eager to get home as they were.

Dad should be here any minute to pick us up from Ridge Riders. I stood outside the store watching for him while Samuel and Millie helped Minnesota restock the store.

"Jeremiah!" Tyler screamed my name from across the RV park and ran toward me. He threw his arms around my waist when he reached me. "Jeremiah! Can I go home with you today?"

"Hey buddy, don't you have some chores or something to do?"

"Chores? I ain't done nothing called chores."

"Wow, what a lucky kid," Millie said, stepping outside in time to hear Tyler's response. "I wish I never had to do chores."

"What are they, Millie?" Tyler turned his attention to her. "I'll help you, then I can come home with you today."

"Where is your mom?" I wondered why this kid was always out running around by himself.

"She went to a friend's."

"Which RV does her friend live in?" I looked in the direction where Tyler lived, wondering if I'd get a glimpse of his mom.

"He don't live around here."

"Wait!" Millie said, "What do you mean? Your mom left here and didn't take you?"

"Nah, she knows I'll be okay, I stay by myself all the time."

I doubted Minnesota Mike knew that. No way would he let a kid sleep in a trailer alone for who knows how long. "You know what, Tyler?"

He turned to me, a hopeful look on his face. "What?"

"I think Millie needs help with her chores today. I'll ask Dad if you can come home with us."

"Better yet," Millie said. "Caleb and Mía are still learning how to do chores, I think you should help them."

"Okay!" Tyler yelled. "I'll help anyone who wants help."

I know my sister. She's got snooping to do, and can't do that with a kid by her side.

"Better stay off Mom's laptop," I said, remembering when that got her into trouble before we moved to the desert.

"I don't need your advice," Millie snapped. Samuel cringed, and she wasn't even talking to him. Millie must have noticed. "But you're right." She changed her tone of voice. "I won't touch that."

Later at home, unlike my sister, I got on my chores right away, faster than I'd ever done them, so I could get down to the shop with my dad. Jenny hummed while she mopped the kitchen floor, a chore I'm sure Millie was glad to share. Samuel ran the vacuum in the playroom. I had no idea what Millie was doing, but I'm sure it had more to do with snooping than chores. Caleb,

Mía and Tyler were raking in the garden as I passed by, although they seemed to be playing more than raking.

"Dad!" So eager to talk to him, I was too loud, and he jumped at the sudden sound of my voice.

"Jeremiah, you startled me." He stopped his work on the motorcycle engine on his workbench, and turned toward me, tools still in hand.

"I need to talk to you."

Dad put the tools down and rolled a shop stool over for me to sit on next to him at the workbench. I was too anxious to sit.

"It's about Samuel."

Dad looked concerned. "Is he okay?"

"Yeah," I said. "Well, no."

"What is it?"

"I don't think he should live here anymore."

Chapter 51

Millie

"Mom, I'm finished with my chores, do you want me to dust and vacuum in your office?" Millie's heart fluttered like a butterfly in her chest while she waited for her mom's response. She had to know what was behind her dad's odd response when he heard the name Madison.

Mom looked up from her recipe cards at the dining room table. "Millie, are you feeling okay?"

The guilt prevented her from catching the joke. "I feel fine."

Mom laughed, "Well, it's just unlike you to want more chores." She took a long swallow of her iced tea, then looked back at Millie. "If you're willing to do that, I'd love it. Then I can keep working on my menu planning."

Millie laughed, hoping it didn't sound as forced as it felt. "The others are still working and I don't mind doing a little more."

"Maybe you can start with the dusting, since Samuel is using the vacuum." Her mom returned to the recipe cards.

Millie hurried to the office, breathing a sigh of relief that her mom suggested leaving the vacuuming for later. She shut the office door behind her, then realized she forgot to get the dust cloth and spray. Good thing she remembered before she started checking the files.

"Millie," Mom said as she passed by the dining room with the supplies. "Instead of vacuuming, I've got a stack of papers that need filing. Would you like to do that instead?"

"Yes!"

"Okay, then." Mom laughed. "If I'd known you were that excited about filing, I would have had you doing that all along."

"I'm an idiot," Millie thought as she hurried away. "Thankfully, Mom wasn't suspicious." Now she'd be able to open the filing cabinet without looking like she was sneaking.

Millie remembered to grab the stack of papers on Mom's desk before opening the top file drawer.

Where to begin? Too bad there wasn't a file folder marked "Things Millie is Curious About." Millie chuckled at her own joke as she skimmed the file categories. Nothing in the first drawer caught her attention.

Four drawers later—wow, her mom had a lot of files—she found the category she was looking for. Foster/Adoption.

"Millie."

She jumped at the sound of her mom's voice and slammed the drawer shut.

"Oh my. Did I scare you that much?"

Another forced laugh. "Yeah, I guess I was concentrating so hard." She was glad she had papers to file in her hand, as a cover for her snooping. "You have so many files, I wasn't sure where to start."

Her mom flipped open the laptop, taking a seat at her desk. "Those papers go in the bottom drawer. The main category is Household Expenses, you'll be able to figure out all the sub categories by reading what's on the papers." Mom immersed herself in her email inbox.

Millie opened the bottom drawer, thankful she now had a legitimate excuse for looking in this drawer, but dismayed that her mom stayed in the office.

She studied the first paper in the stack and then flipped to the file folder marked "electricity." As she dropped that paper in the file, her eyes wandered to the Foster/Adoption category. Behind the main heading were several file folders containing the names of all the kids in the household, plus a few she didn't recognize.

"How's that going?"

Her mom's question startled her.

"Millie, why are you so jumpy this morning?"

"I'm just concentrating so I don't file your papers in the wrong folder," Millie lied. "I guess I forgot you were in the room."

"Okay, so you're figuring it all out?"

"Yeah, piece of cake." Millie studied the second paper in the stack.

As she looked for the maintenance file folder, she again let her eyes wander to the adoption files. Her heart nearly stopped when she spotted a folder midway back labeled "Madison."

Chapter 52

Jeremiah

"Why would you say such a thing, Son?" Dad dropped his tools on the bench and focused his attention on me.

"You heard Samuel ask if he could go live with Minnesota Mike."

"That was when he and Millie weren't getting along. I thought you were all getting along better."

"Oh yeah, that's for sure." My eyes grew wide, and I nodded my head.

"What do you mean then?"

I walked to the door and looked out to make sure no one was nearby to surprise us, then turned back to dad. "Because Samuel likes Millie."

"I know," Dad said. "That's why I'm surprised you think he should move out, now that they're getting along."

"No, Dad, I mean he likes her. You know, really likes her."

Dad's eyes opened wide. "Did he tell you that?"

"He didn't have to."

"How do you know this for sure?"

"Dad, I can just tell. Why else does he care so much what Millie thinks about him?"

"Does he?"

"Oh yes, believe me. And to me, Millie is just a dumb sister. I couldn't care less what she thinks of me."

"Yeah, I noticed that," Dad laughed. He picked up his screwdriver and returned to removing the side case on the engine sitting on his work bench. His mind wasn't on what he was doing, though. Unlike Samuel, I knew when to keep quiet around Dad. I sat on the stool next to him while he thought about what I said.

He got the side case off and placed it on the workbench, then studied the clutch inside the engine. Without looking at me, said, "I'll go talk with Mike this afternoon."

We no sooner finished our conversation than the door burst open and Millie barged in, mouth first. "Dad! I need to go to the Ridge Riders Lodge right now!"

CHAPTER 53

Millie

"Millie, can't you ever enter a room quietly?"

"Dad, I mean it," she said, ignoring his comment. "I left my backpack in the floor of the dune buggy. I need to get it before something happens to it."

"Here's your chance, Dad," Jeremiah said.

"What are you talking about, Jeremiah?" Millie demanded.

"Nothing really. Dad was saying he wanted to talk to Minnesota Mike, so this is good timing."

"What about?" Millie knew something was up when she saw the guilty look on her brother's face. "This is about me, isn't it? What is it?"

"Millie, why do you always think everything is about you?" Jeremiah avoided making eye contact.

"Jeremiah was telling me what you kids discovered about Tyler being left alone."

She saw Jeremiah's head jerk in Dad's direction and wasn't sure she believed that. Something else was up. But right now her backpack was more important than anything her brother had to say.

"Can we go then?"

"Sure." Dad set his screwdriver down and wiped his hands. "Jeremiah, lock up the shop and tell Mom where we went."

Minnesota Mike was in his truck heading out of the parking lot as Millie and her dad pulled in. He slowed and rolled his window down to greet them.

"Where you headed?" her dad asked.

"Got to go to town for some plumbing parts," Minnesota pointed with his thumb back over his shoulder. "A broken water pipe needs fixing."

Dad nodded his head and Millie yelled, "I need to get my backpack out of the buggy."

"Tell you folks what. Let me turn this truck around and I'll unlock the storage garage so you can get it."

"Thanks, Mike," Dad said. "I'll bring the boys over later to help with the repair."

Millie leaped out of the truck when they got parked by the garage. She fidgeted with her crutches impatiently, while Mike flipped through the keys searching for the right one.

"If you've got a minute, I'd like to talk to you about Tyler," Dad said.

"Shore thing, I ain't in no hurry to get to town. I got the water turned off where the break is."

Millie rushed into the large storage garage as soon as Minnesota opened the door.

Minutes later she ran out the door yelling. "It's gone! Dad, it's gone! Someone stole my backpack!"

CHAPTER 54

Jeremiah

I locked the shop for Dad and headed to the house to give Mom the message. Halfway there Samuel met me, out of breath from running.

"Jeremiah, did you talk to Millie?"

"No. She came to the shop, demanding Dad take her back to the Ridge Riders right away."

"So you don't know what she found out?" Samuel changed course to walk with me back toward the house.

"You mean about her backpack?"

"No, about Madison."

This news caused me to stop in my tracks. I had forgotten all about their secret mission. "No, what is it?"

"Your mom has a file folder with Madison's name on it."

"Are you kidding me?" Wow, Millie and Samuel were right when they thought they noticed a change in Dad's demeanor.

"What was in the folder?"

"She doesn't know. Your mom came in the office just as she discovered it. She wasn't able to take the folder out of the drawer to look through it."

"Oh man." I wasn't expecting anything like this. Millie shouldn't be snooping through Mom's private files, but there was something about Tyler's sister that our parents had never told us.

"She said there were folders for each of us kids who live here now plus other names she didn't know."

This was the most Samuel had ever talked to me. The info he was supplying was almost unbelievable. But there's no reason for him to lie.

"Who are those other kids?" I asked.

"Well, I'm guessing kids who lived with them."

This stunned me. I always thought I was the first kid Mom and Dad adopted. Why didn't they ever tell me there were others?

"After she saw that, she went to get her backpack. She wanted to write a letter to that friend of her's."

"That's when she discovered she didn't have it?" I asked.

I looked up to the house and saw Mom headed our way. She's about as curious as my sister, so no doubt she's wondering why Samuel and I are standing in the dirt path halfway between the shop and the house having the longest conversation of our lives.

I motioned to Samuel, and we headed in her direction.

"Hi, Boys," Mom said when we reached her. "You sure looked engrossed in conversation."

Without stopping to think about whether this was a good decision, I said, "Mom, did you know Tyler had a sister named Madison?"

Chapter 55

Millie

"No one coulda got into the garage, Millie," Minnesota Mike said. "I had it locked up good and tight."

"I left it right in the floorboard," Millie's voice escalated. She had too many items valuable to her in that backpack to lose it. "Someone had to take it before you parked it in the garage."

"Did you look good? Make sure it didn't slide around?" Dad said.

"I looked over every inch of the buggy, it's not there." She turned to scour the surrounding area. "It's somewhere in this RV park!"

Before her dad could stop her, Millie took off in a hobbling run with her crutches, heading in the direction she knew Tyler lived. Maybe those bad guys he talked about lived near him. Most likely they took it, probably trying to find the map to the ship. And that's what they would find. The map and a lot more.

Blinded by tears as she stumbled along, Millie's head flitted back and forth searching in vain for the quads. Minnesota Mike and her dad were not far behind her. She turned back to them in despair. "Where do they live?" she called out. "Those bad guys Tyler talks about."

"Millie, keep your voice down," Dad said as he drew near. "If they are nearby, you're going to alert them."

"I want them to know!" she yelled.

"No you don't, little missy," Minnesota said. "They'll just vanish. You never want the bad guys to know you're onto them."

She fell onto her dad's chest, crying. That backpack meant everything to her.

"Listen here, we'll find it fer you." Minnesota Mike patted her back. "If it's here in this park, and I'm sure it is, we'll find it."

"How are you going to do that?" Millie's spoke into her dad's chest.

"You just trust me, we'll git'r done." Minnesota said.

Millie suddenly remembered the GPS tracker she'd put in the backpack. Her parents had given it to her right after she got lost on the bike. She knew they meant for her to clip it on her motorcycle, but knowing she always had her backpack with her, well, almost always, she just shoved it in there.

Her tears stopped, and she pushed herself away from her dad's chest.

"Take me home, there's something I need to do!"

Chapter 56

Jeremiah

Mom scared me. She went white, and I thought she was going to pass out. I shouldn't have blurted that out about Madison. That was a stunt Millie would pull.

About the time I thought she would fall, she recovered, hiding whatever thoughts were going through her mind. "Where did you hear that, Jeremiah?"

I didn't trust myself to speak. I felt shaky inside after seeing her reaction.

"Tyler mentioned it to us the other day at the Ridge Riders," Samuel said.

"I see." Mom turned toward the garden, where the young kids pretended to be raking. She watched them for a while, most likely focusing on Tyler. I wished I could read her mind.

"How did you come to be talking about a sister?"

I waited for Samuel to answer, but he left that question to me. "He asked Dad if he could come and live with us."

"He what?" Mom's attention reverted back to me.

"Yeah, he asked if he could live with us, and Dad said that his mom probably wouldn't like that." I didn't want to finish the rest of the story.

"And that somehow led to mention of a sister?"

"Yes, ma'am." Samuel took over. "He said his mom wouldn't care because she let his sister go live somewhere else once." I waited for Samuel to finish, but he stopped. Without meaning to, I glanced to see if that's all he was going to say.

Mom, of course, noticed that unspoken communication. "And is there more to the story?"

"That's most of it." I said, wishing I had never mentioned Madison. I should know to leave stuff like this to Millie. She's got a lot of experience talking about things she shouldn't.

"And what's the rest of it?"

I took a deep breath. "His entire response was, 'she let my sister go live somewhere else once, when she was alive.'"

Mom bit her lower lip and brought her fist up to her mouth, then turned away from us. We stood, as if frozen in time, with Mom's back to us.

I had a bad feeling that Tyler's sister and the Madison on Mom's file folder were the same person.

Chapter 57

Millie

"Wonder what's going on there?" Dad said as we pulled onto the property.

Mom, Samuel, and Jeremiah stood on the dirt path leading up to the house. Mom's back was to the boys, which seemed strange. But all Millie cared about was getting to her laptop.

Dad, of course, had other ideas. He pulled alongside the trio, rolling his window down. "This looks like an interesting little pow-wow."

Millie saw Mom swipe at her eyes before turning toward the truck. Jeremiah gave her a look that told her something bad was happening. But all she cared about was getting to the house.

Millie hopped out of the truck instead of waiting for Dad to park near the house. "Mom, can I get on my laptop real quick? I need to look something up."

"Sure, Millie," Mom said without looking at her. Unusual. Mom didn't even ask her why. Millie ignored Jeremiah's stare and hobbled toward the house. She was getting pretty good with these crutches. Amazing what a little motivation will do.

Minutes later she sat in her mom's office waiting for the laptop to come on. Thankfully, she had downloaded the app to the GPS tracker after watching her mom load it on her phone and laptop. She wasn't sure if her mom knew, and right now she didn't care. All she cared about was finding her backpack.

Millie stared transfixed at the computer screen as the map popped up. Within seconds, the flashing icon showed her where the backpack was. Millie switched to satellite view and enlarged the screen. Just as she thought. The backpack appeared to be inside or near a car parked at the Ridge Riders Lodge. She had to get back there right away. Millie zoomed out to get perspective on where the trailer was in connection to the office. Flipping her laptop shut, she went in search of her dad.

"What in the world is going on?" she wondered. The only person in the house was Jenny eating a sandwich at the kitchen table.

"Where are Dad and Mom?"

Jenny pointed out the kitchen window.

Millie stepped out the back door and saw her parents in the same spot where she left them. Her dad stood outside the truck, engrossed in a conversation with Mom. The boys stood a few feet away.

"Dad!" Millie yelled and did her hobble run with the crutches. He didn't even look her way. "Dad," she called again when she got closer. "I need to go back to the Ridge Riders. I know where my backpack is!" The urgency in her voice failed to get his attention.

Jeremiah gave her a stern look and shook his head. Samuel looked worried. Neither Dad nor Mom looked her way, almost as if they didn't even hear.

"What's going on?" she whispered after shuffling over to where the boys stood.

"Mom knows about Tyler's sister," Jeremiah whispered.

"How did she find out?"

The boys looked at each other.

"You told her!" Millie accused her brother.

"We both did," Samuel said. That surprised her.

"Does she know I found the file folder?"

"No," Jeremiah said. "Is that all you care about, whether you're in trouble?"

Millie didn't answer.

"Can't you see how upset Mom is?"

"Yes, but what can I do? I'm just as upset, I need to find my backpack."

"Millie, you're unbelievable," Jeremiah's whisper bordered on yelling. "You think a missing backpack can compare to a kid who died?"

She should have been ashamed, and later she would be. But she had only one thing on her mind.

"Are those Dad's shop keys?"

Jeremiah looked at the keys, as if he didn't remember holding them. "Yeah, I had to lock the shop when you left."

"Can I have them?"

"What for?"

"I didn't find my backpack, I want to see if it's in the shop."

"You said yourself you left it in the buggy," Jeremiah shoved the keys in his pocket.

"Well, I was wrong, okay?" Millie tried to stay calm. She needed those keys. "It wasn't there. Maybe I had it in the shop."

"Not likely."

She hated to beg, especially her brother and especially with Samuel listening. But she was desperate. "Humor me, please. At least let me check."

"I probably shouldn't be doing this." Jeremiah dropped the keys in her open hand.

Her heart beat hard as she maneuvered her crutches down the dirt road to carry out Plan B.

Chapter 58

Jeremiah

Torn between watching my parents or looking the other direction to monitor my sister, I watched Millie. As annoying as she was, I didn't want her to fall in her rush to get down to the shop.

"Did you hear Millie ask your dad to take her back to the Ridge Riders?"

I looked at Samuel. "Yes, now that you mention it, I heard her say that."

He nodded his head, but said nothing else.

"She's up to something."

"She usually is, isn't she?" Samuel smiled.

Despite the tense situation, I couldn't help but laugh. "You catch on quick."

Dad and Mom were still talking by the truck. It seemed like a good time for Samuel and I to disappear.

"Want to do some snooping?" I motioned for him to follow me.

"Not if it's going to cause the commotion like mentioning Madison."

"Nah, this will be much more fun. We're going to spy on Millie."

Samuel surprised me when he laughed out loud. That was a first, a very welcome first.

We turned and headed for the shop.

"Look at her struggling with the crutches while she tries to get both locks open." We shared a laugh at Millie's expense when I pointed that out. A more stubborn girl I never met.

I veered off to hide behind some bushes in case she turned and saw us. Samuel followed my lead.

Once Millie was inside the shop, Samuel and I ran down the path, then hid on the side of the shop building where she wouldn't see us when she came back out.

"What do you think she's doing in there?" Samuel whispered.

"I don't know. I'm pretty positive she knows her backpack wouldn't be there. Last place she had it was in the buggy."

"Yeah, I don't think she's been in the shop since we got back from our drive, until now."

I nodded my head. "No way it's in there."

We heard a loud noise like something fell and hit the floor. Samuel and I exchanged glances. "Wonder what that was?"

He shrugged. The next sound stunned both of us.

"That's her motorcycle!" Samuel's eyes were large.

"How did she get that started with a sprained ankle?"

"Well, it's her left ankle that's sprained, and she kicks with her right foot, doesn't she?"

"Yeah, you're right," I said. "I don't know how she would have stood on the bad ankle."

"Where there's a will, there's a way," Samuel said. "That was my mom's favorite phrase."

"Where there's a Millie, there's definitely a will!" We burst out laughing and I hoped she couldn't hear us over the sound of her motorcycle.

Seconds later Millie rolled out of the shop, then roared off the property. My guess would be heading for the Ridge Riders

Lodge. I looked toward the house to see if Dad heard her leave. He and Mom were no longer on the dirt path.

"Now what do we do?"

"We could follow her with my drone."

My eyes lit up. "Now there's an idea," I agreed. "But you know if we don't tell, then we're going to be in trouble too."

"I didn't think about that. I've never had siblings, so I didn't know that's how it works."

"Yeah, just like in the crime shows, we're an accessory to the crime if we know about it and don't report it." I explained the ways of living in a family with a sibling who breaks the rules.

"Okay," Samuel said. "So we should go tell?"

"You pick."

"I'm not picking!" Samuel insisted. "I've never been in trouble here, and I don't want to start now. Plus, I'm on Millie's bad side enough."

"Yeah, speaking of that," I said, "Why do you care so much what Millie thinks about you?"

Samuel looked in the direction Millie had just ridden, then back at me. "Who says I do?"

CHAPTER 59

Millie

Millie struggled to turn her motorcycle around to face the door while balancing on the crutches. She climbed on and straddled the bike, resting to catch her breath. Dropping one crutch to the floor, she used her good leg and the crutch on the other side to walk the bike over to the workbench near the door.

"I hope this works," she whispered as she leaned the bike against the workbench for balance, then kicked the lever with her good foot to start the engine. "Yes!" she yelled inside her helmet. She rarely got her bike started on the first kick and if ever she needed to do that, this was the time.

Leaning the crutch against the workbench, Millie rolled out the door, then pinned the throttle as she flew off the property. The plan: get to the Ridge Riders, get the backpack out of that car, and get back before anyone noticed she left.

She wanted to find out what upset her mom and why there was a file folder with Madison's name in the file cabinet. But this was more important. Jeremiah just didn't understand that some things, like everything in her backpack, were just as important to her as whatever was bothering her mom. He didn't understand how important it was to her to find that ship. She lived for adventure. People had searched for that ship for a few hundred years. If she found it, well she and her brother and Samuel would go down in history. It wasn't even the thought of treasure, it was just the thrill of making history.

"And we'll take lots of water with us," she talked to herself in her helmet as she rode. In the papers her mom printed out for her about the lost ship, she read about a man named Charley Clusker who found the ship in the 1800s then almost died of dehydration. He left the ship to get supplies and when he came back he could never find it again.

"I will not let that happen!" she vowed at the top of her lungs, as she slowed to watch for traffic before she crossed an asphalt road. Thinking about Charley Clusker reminded her of the pearls Samuel had given her. They were also in the backpack.

"Where did he find those pearls?" He brought them out when they were reading about the ship being full of pearls.

Millie stared straight ahead, lost in thought, trying to imagine where those pearls came from. What if Samuel had already located the ship and wasn't telling them? What was he looking at so intently through the binoculars when they were out with Minnesota Mike?

She'd never forgive him if he knew where it was and wasn't telling her. Her anger spurred her on and she twisted the throttle as far as it would go. An unexpected washed out rut in the trail sent her flying when the bike nosedived at full speed and tossed her over the handlebars.

Chapter 60

Jeremiah

"So, here's the plan," I said as we got close to the house. "If Mom and Dad are nowhere around, let's get your drone and start searching."

"What about using your mom's laptop to view the camera feed?"

"Well, if I was Millie, I would just go in and use it and hope she doesn't find out."

"But you're not Millie." Samuel pointed out the obvious.

"Yeah, but it's for a good cause. We're keeping an eye on her, so that would be a good arguing point if we get caught."

"Maybe we won't get caught. Your mom was pretty upset. She might just stay in her bedroom all day," Samuel said. "That's how my mom was when she was sick."

"I hope you're right, but I've never seen my mom stay in her room long."

"Okay, well, we can go with that plan. I'll go get the drone and meet you in your mom's office if we don't see them around."

That plan went right out the window when Dad greeted us at the front door.

"Where's your sister?"

Right then, I wanted to give that girl a piece of my mind. We were going to be in trouble already for not stopping her.

"We just saw her ride her motorcycle out of shop and off the property."

I wanted to hug Samuel for jumping in and breaking the news to him. But I'm not a hugger.

Dad looked right at me and didn't look happy. "How did she get in the shop? I told you to lock it."

Millie owes me big time for dragging me into this. She's going to have to do my chores for a year. That's all I could think of as Dad stared at me.

"She saw I had the keys and said she wanted to search the shop for her backpack."

"She knew it wasn't in there."

"I didn't think of that, Dad, she was begging me for them."

"How can she even ride with a sprained ankle?"

"I don't know, Dad, that's what we were wondering."

"We think she went to the Ridge Riders Lodge, sir."

Nice one Samuel, he was really coming through on helping me. I would be sorry to see him move out. But he definitely needed to go live with Minnesota Mike. There was no doubt in my mind about that.

"I'll get your mom. We put those GPS trackers on both your bikes. She'll be able to tell us where Millie is."

"Oh, that's right! Dad, you're a genius!"

"I'd like to take the credit, but it was Mom's idea," he said on his way through the living room.

"So much for using the drone," I whispered as we followed Dad into the house.

"It's better this way," Samuel said. "We all would have been in trouble if we kept this to ourselves."

In no time, Mom, who had reverted to her usual happy self, opened the app for the trackers.

"This can't be right," she said, studying the map.

"It's not showing where she is?" Dad asked.

"It's showing both bikes are out there, one over in the vicinity of the Ridge Riders and the other one about halfway between here and there."

Dad and Mom both looked at me. Why did I feel guilty?

"It's not me, I'm right here!" I defended myself, probably out of the guilt of knowing I wasn't planning on telling them what Millie did.

"I think I know what it is," Samuel said.

"What's that, Son?" Dad asked. "You've been a lifesaver helping with Millie. Let's hear your idea."

"I think she put a GPS tracker in her backpack, and that's the one at the Ridge Riders Lodge. That's probably why she was asking you to take her there?"

"She asked me that?" Dad seemed puzzled.

"When we were all standing out in the road earlier, she came out and asked," I said.

Dad and Mom looked at each other, then back to Samuel and me.

"Oh my," Mom said. "I didn't even pay attention to what Millie was saying."

"I didn't hear it either." Dad turned to Samuel. "What about the other one? Do you think she was riding Jeremiah's bike?"

"No, it was her bike, but I think she took the tracker off his bike and put it on her's."

"Wow, so at least she's not as stupid as it seems."

"Jeremiah, that's uncalled for," Dad said.

But I couldn't help wondering if he was thinking the same thing too.

"We should be able to watch the one on her bike moving then, as she rides over there," Samuel said.

"I thought so too." I pointed to the blip on the map. "But it hasn't moved since Mom opened the app."

Dad sighed. "That can only mean one thing."

Chapter 61

Millie

"This wasn't supposed to happen," Millie moaned into her helmet where she lay sprawled in the dirt. "I'm going to be grounded for life."

She struggled to sit up, wincing at the immense pain in her ankle. "How will I get the bike picked up now?"

She tried to stand, but fell from the pain in her ankle radiating up her leg. She'd never had a broken bone before and had a bad feeling this might be her first.

Determined to get back on the bike, she crawled, dragging her bad leg, back to the bike. There had to be a way to lift it. She wondered if she could kick it over with her hand. Probably a dumb idea, and not her first dumb idea today.

Leaning on the toppled motorcycle, she could stand up on one leg, but trying to lift the motorcycle proved too difficult. As it lay in the ditch, the front wheel looked bent and the tire flat. She wondered about the forks, she wasn't sure they should be twisted like that, and the front brake lever was dangling. Even if she could have lifted the bike and started it, both impossible tasks, she wasn't sure she could have ridden the bike in this condition.

Millie dropped back to the dirt and leaned on the bike, looking toward the sky. "It's me, God. I've really messed up. Again."

"If I had my backpack, I could write another letter to Paisley," she thought. "I'd have to confess that I didn't follow her directions to stay out of trouble."

Soon she heard the welcome sound of a vehicle she hoped was driving on this trail. Since it was just one of many off-road trails in this area, sound traveled and she couldn't be sure the driver would come her way.

"If they are on this trail, I sure hope they don't run me over!" Millie said aloud as she struggled to stand again. "Just what I need is two accidents in the same day."

She hopped on her one good foot, looking both ways on the trail, not sure which direction the sound was coming from.

The noise grew louder and when she recognized her dad's truck approaching, she didn't know whether to rejoice or cry. They must have found her with the GPS tracker she took off Jeremiah's bike. That was the only smart thing she'd done that day.

"I'm in so much trouble," Millie whimpered.

"Millie, is this a new pastime for you?" Dad said when he stepped out of the truck.

She burst into tears as her dad came over and hugged her. Jeremiah picked the bike up and drug it out of the rut. Together, the three of them surveyed the damage.

"That's going to cost you a pretty penny," Dad said.

Millie didn't know if he was serious. She'd never had to pay for repairs to the motorcycle before. It probably wasn't a good time to ask if he really meant it.

"Ow, Dad, my leg hurts so bad!" she said as he lifted her into the front seat.

After they loaded the bike, the truck pulled out onto the highway, but not in the hospital's direction. "Where are we going, Dad?" Millie said through tears. The jarring of her leg as they drove out over rocks and ruts increased the pain. She knew this wasn't the way to the hospital.

"I need to check on your mom and Samuel before we leave the area."

"Where are they?" Millie's voice wobbled as she struggled to hold back sobs.

"Where do you think?" Jeremiah said from the backseat. "Out rescuing your precious backpack."

Chapter 62

Jeremiah

"Jeremiah." Dad gave me a look in his rearview mirror. "That wasn't necessary."

"Well, I told her she was being selfish, worrying so much about her backpack when Mom was upset. Now look at the trouble she's caused."

"I thought you were on my side," Millie yelled. "You're just a traitor."

"Millie, that's enough," Dad said. "And Jeremiah, let's just let this ride for now. It's not the time."

The truck was quiet for the next few miles except for my sister's whimpering. And then, as only my sister can do, Millie opened up another can of worms.

"What was wrong with Mom, anyway?" She kept her eyes on my dad, but he never looked her way.

"She was sad for a bit," Dad finally answered.

"Because of Madison?" Millie actually went there.

"My gosh, Millie, can't you leave anything alone?" I blurted from the back seat.

We were almost to the Ridge Riders Lodge. "I'm only going to say this one more time." Dad's voice sounded far more serious than usual. "This subject is closed for now, and I want no more talk about it."

I noticed he said "for now." That tells me eventually it is going to get talked about. I wasn't sure I wanted to hear any more. I regretted ever meeting Tyler. Why did it seem like almost every day some new challenge came our way? Is this what life is always like?

I dreaded pulling into the parking lot to look for Mom. I wondered why Dad let her come here to face the people who stole Millie's backpack, but I sure wasn't going to ask.

Looking down the row of trailers where the man was running the other day, I saw no sign of Mom or Samuel.

"There they are!" Millie yelled, pointing to the lodge's store.

I couldn't believe it. "Thank you, God!" I whispered as I saw Mom and Samuel standing with Minnesota Mike.

"My backpack!" Millie hollered out.

Samuel held it up for all to see, like it was the greatest treasure ever found. Maybe that treasure would be good enough for her and we could give up on this crazy hunt for a ship that didn't exist. I couldn't believe how much trouble it had caused us in the last few days. I never should have brought those papers home to Millie.

CHAPTER 63

Millie

The ride to the emergency room with her mom was too quiet for comfort. Millie wished one of the boys would have come along instead of going home with Dad.

She cradled her backpack in her lap. Even with all the trouble she caused, it felt good to have this back.

"Did you look to see if anything is missing?" Mom glanced over at her.

"I didn't even think about that." Millie unzipped the bag and removed items, placing them on the seat next to her. Binoculars, snacks, water, Paisley's letters, notepad, pens, her journal. The bag was growing lighter. She found the pearls in the secret compartment. She thought for sure those would have been gone.

"Mom, did you see these pearls Samuel gave me?" She poured the pearls out of the little satchel into her hand.

Her mom glanced over, then back to the road. "Those are beautiful."

"I don't know where he got them. He won't tell me."

"Well, it isn't polite to ask where a gift came from."

"But he got them from his room right after we read about the lost ship being a Spanish vessel filled with pearls. Doesn't that seem suspicious?"

"Not necessarily."

"How could you think it's not suspicious?"

"Maybe that reminded him he had something to give you."

"But they were all dirty."

Mom didn't respond. We were almost to the hospital. "That makes me think he found them in the dirt somewhere. I think he knows where the ship is. I think that's where these pearls came from and he won't tell us."

"Oh, Millie, you have a wild imagination." This topic was going nowhere with her mom, so she took her chances with something she really wanted to know.

"Mom, what do you know about Madison?"

Mom glanced over, then put her blinker on to pull into the hospital parking lot. "Didn't your father say that topic wasn't open for discussion?"

Millie swallowed hard. She'd blown it again.

"Oh, he told you about that?" she said.

CHAPTER 64

Jeremiah

"Wow, look at these forks." Samuel watched as I surveyed the damage on Millie's motorcycle. We'd been back a few hours. Dad stayed at the house to hang out with the younger kids, but said we could come down to the shop if we wanted. And we both wanted to.

Jenny had a new experience today, getting to be in charge of Caleb and Mía while the rest of us went to rescue Millie, her motorcycle and her backpack. I'm sure she appreciated Dad taking over.

"That looks expensive," Samuel said, "and I don't even know anything about repairing motorcycles."

"Well, if we can repair them, it won't cost as much as replacing them, but either way, Millie won't be riding for a long time unless she's got a lot of money saved."

"What do you mean?"

"Dad told her she has to pay for all the repairs herself. Look at that rim, it's bent. The handlebars look bent. The brake lever is broken."

"I can hear the cash register . . . cha-ching, cha-ching," Samuel said. That comment sent us both into fits of laughter.

"Wow, you think Millie would be mad if she could hear us now?" I squeaked out, and we burst into laughter all over again.

"What's all the laughter about?" Dad startled us when he and the kids came through the door.

"Yeah," Caleb said, "what's so funny, we wanna laugh!"

Samuel and I looked at each other and laughed harder.

Blowing off steam at my sister's expense. It was great. She owed it to us.

"Guess what Jeremiah!" Mía yelled. "Guess what?!"

I wiped my tears from laughing. "What, Mía, what?!" It felt good to have some fun after all the Millie stress and drama of the day.

"Mom's bringing home pizza! Pizza!" Mía clapped her hands, while jumping up and down. Caleb and Jenny looked happy too. Pizza was a rare treat living this far from town.

"Are they on their way home already? What's the outcome?"

"The ER wasn't crowded, and they took them in right away. Broken ankle," Dad said. "I offered to cook dinner . . ."

More laughter. I could not imagine my dad cooking. "But Mom suggested pizza instead?"

"Yes, and what a relief that was. I'm not sure what I would have done if she accepted my offer."

"What happened to Millie's motorcycle?" Caleb climbed on the seat where the motorcycle was cinched down on the rack. "These handlebars don't look right."

"No, they sure don't," Dad said.

"Did you mean it when you said she has to pay for all this herself?" I asked.

"I sure did," Dad said. "Her bike should have been locked up after we rescued her the first time."

"How could she ride with a hurt ankle?" Jenny asked.

"Apparently, she couldn't." Samuel looked at me, and fits of laughter overtook both of us.

"What's so funny?" The voice was stern and familiar.

We looked over to see Millie with a blue cast and crutches standing in the doorway.

Chapter 65

Millie

Millie watched through the window as her dad lit a fire in the outside pit. Her mom went to put the younger kids to bed. Jenny read a book in her room. Not surprising. She was a bookworm. Millie could hear drone videos coming from her mom's office. Jeremiah was fascinated by all the footage Samuel had filmed over the past few months. One day she might watch the video that led them to her. Right now it was too soon, especially after today's fiasco.

"Millie," her dad called from the front door. "Get Jeremiah and Samuel and come join me at the fire."

"What's the occasion, Dad?" Jeremiah said as they took seats around the firepit.

"It's been awhile since we've enjoyed an evening fire, don't you think?"

"Now that you mention it," Millie said, "we haven't built a fire in a long time."

"You and Jeremiah used to sit out here quite often." Dad pointed in Mom's direction. "Here come the marshmallows."

"S'mores!" Jeremiah picked up a roasting stick from a nearby table. "We haven't had those in a long time."

"And I've never had them," Samuel said.

"Well, you're in for a treat," Millie reconsidered the first rude comment she had in mind. Maybe there was hope for her, she thought.

Soon, everyone sat back in the chairs, bellies full of the sweet marshmallow, chocolate treats. The night was perfect. Clear sky, millions of stars, sweet spring temperatures that were neither too hot or too cold. "Nothing could ruin a night like this," Mille thought as she leaned her head back, enjoying the view. She couldn't have been more wrong.

Chapter 66

Jeremiah

I watched as Mom gathered the left over marshmallows, chocolate and graham crackers. Jumping up from my chair, I reached to take the items from her. "I'll help you carry those, Mom."

"It's okay," she headed into the house. "Sit tight, I'll be right back."

She returned minutes later carrying a file folder. I looked at my sister and saw fear in her eyes. We were both thinking the same thing. The Madison folder.

Mom also carried some tissues.

I knew something was up when Dad lit this fire and invited us out.

Mom perched on the edge of her chair and opened the file folder, removing a photo.

"This is Madison," Mom said, without smiling, holding the photo so we could all see it. Everyone stayed quiet, even Millie.

Madison looked to be about 13 or 14. It looked like a school photo. Her hair was brown, shoulder length. She wore a T-shirt in the photo which seemed strange, since kids, girls especially, often wore something special on picture day. She barely smiled.

"I met Madison six years ago when I was volunteering in a runaway shelter. She lived there." Mom studied the picture for a moment, then slipped it back into the folder. Dad remained quiet. I couldn't tell anything by the look on his face. Poker face, I've heard it called.

"I grew to love Madison. We knew nothing about her family, but she had obvious needs." Mom looked over at Dad and he smiled and winked at her. "We inquired about having her come and live with us, even adopting her, if she needed a permanent home."

Mom took a deep breath. "My supervisor at the shelter agreed that would be a good thing for Madison."

Mom stared into the firepit, then looked around the fire ring at each one of us.

I held my breath. This was not one of those "happily ever after" stories I could tell. Millie looked frozen in place.

"Before we could move forward on that, Madison died."

"Died?" Millie cried out. "How? What happened?"

Dad answered for Mom. "She took her own life."

Mom's lips quivered, but she held back tears.

"Oh, Mom," Millie said. "I'm so sorry. I'm so sad for you and for Madison. Why would she do that?"

"Sometimes people, or kids, are hurting so badly they don't want to live. They can't imagine life ever getting better for them." Dad said as he reached over, placing his hand on Mom's shoulder. "But there is always hope, no matter how difficult their circumstances."

"Always," Mom said. "Taking your own life is never the answer to problems."

"What could she have done?" Samuel asked. "I mean, since she thought there was no hope, what could she, or anyone who felt that way, do?"

"Talk to someone, an adult, a police officer, a counselor, a friend," Mom said. "I think that's the best place to start. If she had told someone what she was planning, I believe she would still be alive."

"There are suicide hotlines and organizations to help young people," Dad added.

"Sometimes," Mom said, "people hurt so much they won't talk to anyone. Or maybe they tried, and that person wasn't helpful."

"In one of my foster homes, I heard kids laughing about a girl at school who talked about killing herself," Millie said.

Mom shook her head. "It's so sad. If I could say anything to a young person who didn't want to live, I would beg them to find someone to talk to, someone they can trust."

Dad nodded. "And if there is no one they trust, they can call the suicide hotline."

"Did you know Tyler was her brother when he came over here?" I asked.

Dad shook his head. "We had no idea until Tyler mentioned her name the other day when we were eating ice cream."

"Tyler wants to live here. Did you know that, Mom?" Millie said.

Mom nodded. "Your dad told me he's asked a few times. But, Millie, I gave you my word, we would slow down on growing our family, so we can all adjust."

"Mom, we can't let Tyler stay somewhere he isn't being taken care of," Millie insisted.

Samuel leaned forward in his chair. "I have an idea." He looked at Mom, then over at Dad. "You can trade him for me."

Chapter 67

Millie

Everyone stared, stunned, at Samuel.

"Why would you say that, Samuel?" Millie said. "It's because of me, isn't it? I've been mean to you."

Samuel chuckled. "Well, I won't argue that."

"Samuel had a talk with Mike today," Mom said, "while we were at the Ridge Riders."

"About what?" Millie demanded. Then apologized. "I'm sorry, that came out kind of abruptly."

"Kind of?" Her brother said.

"Well, that's our Millie." Dad's smile reassured her.

"He told me he's struggling to keep up with maintenance at the lodge and RV park while Paisley's family is out of town." Samuel said. "And he doesn't understand the computer in the office at all."

"So what does that have to do with trading you for Tyler?" Millie asked.

"I told him if he'd let me move in with him, I could be

there to help all the time." Samuel looked at Mom. "And I could still get my school work from you and turn it into you."

Millie looked over at her dad. "Can he do that? He can't just pick where he lives without telling anyone."

She saw her brother chuckling. "What are you laughing at?"

"Well, one minute you hate the guy and the next minute you're whining because he's leaving." Jeremiah said. There were muffled giggles around the firepit.

"Millie, he isn't doing this without telling anyone," her dad said. "Samuel and I have discussed it. I knew he was going to talk to Minnesota Mike."

"No one told me," Millie said.

"When could they have told you?" Jeremiah looked at her with a big smile. "You're always out riding somewhere by yourself these days."

Now the chuckles erupted into outright laughter.

"Millie," Samuel changed the subject. "Are the map and all the ship papers still in your backpack?"

"Mom! I totally forgot about those. I need to check." She struggled to get out of her chair with her crutches.

Samuel jumped up, "Where is it? I'll go get it."

"It's still in the car." She looked around at everyone. "I hope."

Samuel returned from the car and dropped the backpack in Millie's lap. He stood nearby, shining a flashlight as she searched through it.

Not finding them, she turned the backpack upside down, dumping the entire contents in the dirt in front of her.

The papers were gone.

Chapter 68

Jeremiah

We all watched as Millie sat speechless, staring at the contents of her backpack laying in the dirt. She was quiet. I would have predicted a screaming rage at this discovery.

Still without speaking, she leaned over, attempting to put things back in her bag. Samuel bent down and took over. "I'll do that, Millie."

"Thank you." This wasn't the Millie I knew. Subdued and defeated.

"Dad, can you help me up? I think I'll go to bed."

Mom went with them, and I helped Samuel with the last of the items. She stuffed an unbelievable amount of things into this backpack she carried everywhere.

"What now?" Samuel stood by the fire, holding Millie's backpack.

I grabbed a couple of pieces from the woodpile and dropped them in the firepit. "Might as well enjoy the night." I took a seat.

"Wow, what a crazy day." Samuel took the chair across from me. "Is it always like this around your house?"

"Do you mean around my sister?"

Samuel nodded, and we both chuckled. One thing I'll say about this day, we've sure shared quite a few laughs over it.

"So tell me the truth," I said. "Where did you get those pearls? Millie thinks you know where the ship is."

Samuel looked surprised. "She really thinks that?"

"Well, you gotta admit, it was kind of strange how you produced a bunch of dirty pearls right after we read the passage about the Spanish ship filled with pearls that went missing."

Samuel nodded. "Yes, I will admit that seems kind of strange."

"Well?"

"Well what?" Samuel asked.

"You're not going to tell me where you got them?"

Samuel stared into the fire, then looked back at me. "You're right. I guess I'm not."

CHAPTER 69

Millie

The light tap on her door wakened Millie from a deep sleep. The sky outside her window had a hint of sunlight interrupting the night sky. Another tap and her mom peeked in the bedroom door. "Are you up for company, Millie?"

She rubbed her groggy eyes, squinting at her mom. "Company? Now?" Her voice had morning gruffness to it.

"Yes, trust me," Mom said as she flipped the bedroom light on. "It will be worth it for this company."

Millie was tempted to grumble, but after all the trouble she'd caused in the past few days, she resisted the urge. She rolled out of bed.

"Meet us in the kitchen in 10 minutes," Mom said. "I'll have muffins and juice waiting."

"Meet us?" Millie repeated to herself after Mom left the room. "Who is she talking about?"

Millie dressed as fast as she could with a clunky cast on the lower half of her left leg. Ten minutes later she lumbered into the kitchen, trying to be as quiet as she could with the crutches and the cast.

Minnesota Mike nibbled on a muffin at the kitchen table. Next to him sat Emmett, the man from the motorcycle shop. "Well, now lookie who I brung over to visit you, little missy." He toned down his signature loud belly laugh, probably so he didn't wake the rest of the household.

"What have you done to yourself now?" Emmett said with a big grin, pointing to the bulky blue cast on her leg. "Do you remember me?"

Mille sank down in a chair across from the two men. She welcomed the muffins and juice her Mom placed in front of her. She smiled. "Yes, I remember you. And as far as what I did, believe me, it was something else stupid."

The three chuckled together. Minnesota Mike finished his breakfast treat, wiped his hands together and smoothed his beard. He looked ready to get down to business.

"Well, I figger you might wonder what we're doing over here so early like."

"That crossed my mind," Millie said.

"Well, we got a long day planned and wanted to get an early start. So's here we are."

Millie nodded, content to wait for the rest of the explanation.

"I caught those rascals that stole your backpack," Minnesota Mike said. "They was on the security camera. Samuel helped me learn how to use that thing. I remembered what young Tyler said about them threatening to turn over the trailers and I figgered they's probably the same fellers."

Emmett munched on a muffin, nodding his head as Minnesota talked.

"So's yesterday after you folks left I went and picked up Emmett—now that I knowed where he was—and brought him back here to help me ID those characters."

"Yep," Emmett said, "they're the ones that were giving me trouble. That's why I decided to up and take off."

"Well, doncha know, we called in Deputy Black. He found so many warrants out for those fellers, we won't be having any trouble for quite some time."

"They took my map and pictures of the ship," Millie said.

"Now that's a crying shame," Minnesota Mike said, "I knowed how much you had yer heart set on finding that ship."

"Did you know I've been looking too?" Emmett didn't wait for her to answer. "Me and my good buddy Gerard, we go out once or twice a month and hunt."

"Have you ever found anything?" Millie asked.

"Not much to speak of," Emmett said. "But we have a lot of fun looking."

"Now, hold on there, Emmett," Minnesota Mike said. "Doncha know, it ain't polite not to be honest with this little gal."

Chapter 70

Jeremiah

So I finally meet the mysterious missing Emmett. But did it have to be at the crack of dawn?

Samuel and I helped Millie with her bulky cast and crutches up into the front seat of Dad's truck, then we hopped in the back so we could all follow Minnesota Mike and Emmett over to the Ridge Riders Lodge. I still didn't understand why it had to be so early in the morning, but since this is getting us out of morning chores, it's fine with me.

Millie said Emmett discovered something interesting in the desert and Minnesota is taking us out to see it. I sure hope it has something to do with the lost ship for Millie's sake. But for my sake, although I would never admit it to her, I'm glad the map and pictures are gone. I'd be happy if I never had to hear about a lost ship in the desert again.

Dad cinched down the ice chest behind the back seat and said goodbye. Soon we were once again sailing along in the desert. Millie's crutches bounced around where she held them in the front passenger seat, and I noticed Minnesota Mike didn't drive as fast as usual. Thank you Millie for having a broken leg and cheating us out of a fast run in the buggy.

There was a chill in the early morning springtime air, and I was glad for a jacket and gloves. I looked over at Samuel and noticed that ever since yesterday he was a different guy. More relaxed and happy. I guess knowing he was going to live with Minnesota Mike was a big relief to him. I never asked him why h\he wanted to leave, but I was pretty sure it had a lot to do with my sister. Someday I'd have to ask him about his mom, too. He never talked about her long illness or death. And I didn't know how to bring it up.

An hour later, Minnesota pulled the buggy up on the outskirts of a huge body of water. I'd heard about this sea in the desert, but we'd never been over this way yet. I wondered if this was Emmett's big discovery.

"What are we doing here?" Millie said when Mike shut off the engine.

So much for thinking this was the discovery.

"Well, little missy," Minnesota said, "I figgered if we're looking for a lost ship we oughta start where the water is and go south from here. Didn't those papers say something about a flood from the gulf sending waters up this way? That ship coulda sailed up those waters, then got stranded when the flood receded."

"I thought we were going to look at something Emmett discovered." I was ready to give up on this ship business.

"We'll get to that, but I figgered while we're out fer the day, let's give this a shot." He started up the engine. At least this was interesting. I'd never explored this part of the desert before.

"Keep yer eye out for that ship of yours, little missy."

I couldn't see her expression from the back seat, but hopefully she was happy we were out looking.

Mike gradually increased power, unlike his usual stomping on the accelerator, and turned south. The ground was rough, and soon he dropped into a deep wash, with four or five foot dirt walls on either side. Water had rushed through here at some point.

We traversed the winding wash for about a half hour, then popped up the side wall, nearly straight up. I held back a gasp, wondering if we were going to flip backwards. Minnesota gassed it at just the right time and we bounced over the top onto more rugged desert terrain.

Ahead, just on the other side of an unused old asphalt road, we could see an unkempt large structure, and what looked like a stable.

"Are those camels?" Samuel turned toward me, while pointing in the direction I was looking.

"Sure looks like it to me."

"Camels!" Millie yelled so loud we could hear over the engine. "Can we stop and pet them?"

Minnesota Mike didn't respond, but slowed the buggy down as we got closer. He pulled up next to a faded sign. Millie was already pulling off her helmet and probably didn't notice what the sign said.

"Ya see that sign there, little missy," Minnesota Mike got her attention.

"Ships in the Desert Haven," my sister read out loud.

CHAPTER 71

Millie

"Is this some kind of joke? Who put that sign there?"
"Ain't no joke at all," Minnesota said, removing his helmet. He rolled the buggy in closer to the stables, then shut off the engine.

An older man strolled out to greet them, his hand held up to his forehead, shielding his eyes from the early morning sun. He peered into the buggy. "What can I do for you folks?"

"Emmett sent us here," Minnesota Mike said as everyone climbed out of the buggy.

"Can I pet your camels?" Millie asked.

"Sure can." The man's threadbare shirt had the name "Lyle" embroidered on it. "You can even take them home with you."

"Don't tell her that," Jeremiah said, "that's what she'll want to do."

They all moved over to the fence. Lyle pulled a couple of carrots from a feedbag hanging on the fence. "Here you go." He handed them to Millie. "They'll like this."

"Why do you call this place 'Ships of the Desert'?" Samuel asked.

"It's a nickname for camels. Because of their ability to transport heavy loads across the desert."

"We were out searching for a lost ship, when we found you," Millie turned from the camels to face Lyle. "But I was hoping to find an actual ship, not some camels called ships."

Lyle's eyes brightened. He looked at Millie with the hint of a smile. "You don't say?"

"Have you heard of the lost ship?"

He nodded.

"My nutty sister here believes the legend."

"My great grandpa, 16 times over, sailed aboard the lost ship."

Jeremiah stopped laughing and joined the others, staring wide eyed at Lyle. Even Millie looked stunned.

"Are you kidding me?" she said. "You're related to someone who was on the ship? So you know where the ship is? Is there really treasure on it?"

"Hold on there, now." The old man laughed. "You sure know how to fire off the questions."

"I'm just really curious about the lost ship. I want to find it."

"Curiosity killed the cat, don't you know?" Lyle pointed to her leg. "Is that what got you that broken leg?"

Millie looked sheepish. "You could say that."

Lyle held out a couple of carrots for the camels to nibble, then brushed his hands together and looked around the group.

"Come with me," he said. "I'll show you something."

Chapter 72

Jeremiah

Inside the run-down building, Lyle led us to a small room he called his office. A wooden box sat on a dusty desk in the middle of the room. Lyle reached into his pocket and retrieved a key. Slipping it into a small padlock on the front of the box, he turned the key, then lifted the lid. He removed a small leather journal covered with dust that had seeped through the cracks.

Lyle opened to the first page and read aloud.

The memories of my ancestor, my many times over great grandfather, a pearl diver for Captain Alvarez de Cordone.

I felt goosebumps rise on the back of my neck and wondered if my sister did as well. Had we really stumbled upon someone connected to the mysterious ship?

"Did you write that journal?" Millie asked.

Lyle held the journal close to his chest. "No, not I." He

once again opened the small book. "My great-great-grandfather wrote these words that have been passed down through the generations."

He continued to read.

I was hired, along with many other pearl divers, to sail with the captain along the coast of Mexico. We sailed into the gulf of California, farther north than we had ever been before, finding more oysters than we could imagine.

Lyle stopped reading and looked around at all of us.

"What happened then?" I felt like Millie. No patience to wait until he resumed on his own.

Lyle flipped over a few pages and continued.

A great earthquake came, cutting off the sea we harbored in from the ocean we had sailed from. We found no way out and waters receded until it beached our ship. We gathered the supplies and pearls we could carry and hiked for months over the desert until other ships rescued us.

Millie nodded to Samuel at the mention of pearls. "Tell him about yours," she whispered.

Samuel shook his head, accompanied by a look that shut Millie down. I wondered why he didn't want Lyle to know about the pearls he found.

"Have you searched for the ship yourself?" Lyle looked up when I asked, then closed the journal and placed it back in the locked box.

"So," he turned to Minnesota Mike. "Are you interested in taking the camels?"

Millie, Samuel, and I exchanged glances.

It seemed everyone was keeping secrets.

Chapter 73

Millie

"Well, I was praying for the good Lord to send someone my way that can take my last two camels." Lyle looked toward Minnesota as the group headed back to the stables.

Millie's heart beat hard and her thoughts were racing, trying to come up with ways she could talk her parents into letting her have these camels.

"What are you and these camels doing out here, anyway?" Minnesota asked.

"Well, many years ago, before they built the big highway," he pointed to the dilapidated asphalt road nearby, "this used to be the main thoroughfare. We were swamped with tourists and travelers. We had a full crew and a couple dozen camels."

Lyle pointed behind him. "That building was a beauty when it was first built. We had camel souvenirs and books. We sold sandwiches and drinks." His eyes lit up as he remembered the good days. "Everything died out when the traffic diverted to the new highway. I had to let all the employees go."

"What happened to the rest of the camels?"

"A few died, the others I was able to sell or give away."

Millie looked over at Minnesota Mike. "I want these camels."

"You think Dad's going to let you bring home some camels?" Jeremiah asked.

Millie started to fire off a strong retort, but bit her tongue, remembering her newfound goal to get along with others.

"Well, I'll tell you what," Lyle said, "you'd be doing me and the boys a great service, if you took them."

"So you really want to give them up?" Samuel asked.

"I don't have a choice," Lyle said. "I got some business I need to tend to and where I'm going, I can't take the camels. I need to clear out the warehouse behind this building. Got some important stuff I got to get moved."

"Where are you going?"

"Well, young lady," Lyle said. "You ask a lot of questions, but right now the only question that matters is, will any of you give these boys a home?"

Chapter 74

Jeremiah

"I have to talk Mom and Dad into letting us take them," Millie insisted.

"Millie, Dad and Mom aren't going to let you have a couple of camels."

"I think they will." That's the last thing I expected to hear Minnesota Mike say.

"Are you kidding me?" I stared, dumbfounded, at M&M.

"Let's say, not just do I think they will, I know they will. Me and Emmett already done talked to them about it."

My sister threw her arms around Minnesota Mike, her crutches falling to the ground.

"Whoa there, missy, you and me both are gonna fall down here." M&M struggled to balance both himself and the weight of my sister leaning against him.

"Emmett told me he'd pray right along with me that God would send someone to give the camels a home," Lyle said. "I sure am glad that guy stumbled on my place a few days ago."

"You mean you didn't know Emmett before that?" I asked.

"No, never seen the man in my life," Lyle said. "He and a friend were out searching for the lost ship when they ran across my place."

"It's just like my mom told me when I found your family before she died," Samuel said. "All things work together for good to those who love the Lord."

"Romans 8:28," Millie said. "That was one of my memory verses when I first moved in with Dad and Mom."

"I guess we better get home and start building a camel barn." I looked straight at my sister. "I don't mind telling you, I'm glad the hunt for the ship that's nothing more than a phantom is over."

Chapter 75

Millie

"You never told me where you got those pearls," Millie said when they took a break from building the stable.

Jeremiah and her dad were working on the barn, while she and Samuel finished up the stable. Minnesota Mike had dropped Samuel off early that morning to help with the camel facilities.

"Did you think I found the ship?" Samuel smiled. Millie felt ashamed realizing Samuel smiled a lot more now that he was living with Minnesota Mike at the Ridge Riders Lodge.

"I absolutely did," Millie said. "And I was angry that you were keeping it a secret."

Samuel nodded. "I shouldn't have done that." He brushed the dirt off his hands, then reached for the glass of lemonade her mom had brought out. "I admit at first that's what I wanted you to think."

"Why?"

He took a long swig of the lemonade. "Just did."

Millie groaned. "So where did they come from?"

"They were my mom's. I took apart her pearl necklace and sprinkled the dirt on them so it looked like I found them."

"Wow." Millie stared at him. "I can't believe you did that."

"Neither can I."

"Do you want them back, something to remember your mom by?"

Samuel patted his chest. "I have her here, many memories." He smiled. "You keep them, she would have liked you."

Millie took a drink of her lemonade and munched on a cookie, admiring the work they'd all done, thankful for how this adventure was turning out.

"So, what were you looking at in the binoculars that day? We thought you spotted the ship."

"I'm pretty good at fooling you then. Is that what you're saying?"

Millie laughed. "Well, much as I hate to admit it, I guess you are."

Samuel laughed so loud, her dad and Jeremiah looked over. "Hey you two," Jeremiah said. "You don't look like you're working very hard."

"We're on a break," Millie yelled back. Then turned back to Samuel, "Well?"

"I wasn't looking at anything, just trying to fool you."

Millie punched him in the arm. "So since you're being honest, now you can tell me why you wanted to move in with Minnesota instead of living here. It was because of me, wasn't it?"

Samuel picked up his tools and moved toward the partially built stable fencing. "You might say that."

"I knew it," Millie said. "I'm sorry I was so mean to you."

"It wasn't that so much," he said as he hoisted up another plank for the fence.

"What then?"

Samuel looked right at her. "Because I don't want you for a sister."

"What's that supposed to mean?" Millie was stumped at that response.

"Think about it." Samuel smiled, then returned to his work.

Chapter 76

Jeremiah

"What's that box you're carrying?"

Caleb struggled up the path toward the house, holding a wooden box that looked a lot like the one we'd seen in Lyle's office last month.

"I found it down by the gate." He dropped it at my feet on the front porch. "It's got your name on it and Millie's too."

Millie was at the stables tending to the camels, so I peeled open the envelope taped to the top of the box. Inside was the little key Lyle used to open the lock.

"Did you see anyone leave this?" I stood and looked in the direction of the front gate. No cars could be seen or heard on the dirt road leading to our property.

"No, sir!" Caleb shook his head back and forth. "I just found it sitting there and thought it looked like a treasure box."

Caleb watched as I unlocked the box and lifted out the journal. He leaned over to peer inside, then shook his head again. "That's no treasure! Just a dumb book to read."

I could see Millie working with Mía in the stables, probably teaching her how to take care of our new pets, so I plopped down on the porch and began flipping through the journal. I couldn't believe Lyle was giving this to us.

Some pages were bent and torn, the writing smeared and hard to read. There would be time later to read it word for word. Now I skimmed through it until I got to the last few pages.

Here the ink looked fresher, the handwriting different. My heart beat hard as I read the words under a journal entry dated a few days earlier.

The mission is accomplished and the last of the camels have a home. They truly were ships of the desert over the years as they helped me travel the land and recover pieces of the ship my ancestor once sailed on hundreds of years ago. The mast and the cross pieces are safely transported to my new home and all that remains of the so-called lost ship is buried under the new highway, never again to be disturbed by treasure hunters.

I dropped the journal back into the box and latched the padlock.

Millie approached as I stood to head toward the stables.

"Wow, what happened to you," she said. "You look like you've seen a ghost."

"I think I have. A ghost ship."

"What are you talking about?"

I pointed to the box on the porch. "You're never going to believe it."

As I walked away, I remembered Millie had never doubted that there was a ship while we were searching.

I turned back. "On the other hand, you probably won't be surprised at all."

Acknowledgements

My goal is to tell a story that's fun and exciting, one that leaves the reader wondering what's coming next. But I've discovered that I also tuck some sadness into the MotoMysteries books since we've all been through sad times. Maybe not the very same sadness, but we each know what it's like to struggle.

I'm not sure I could write this series without the input of our granddaughter Summer, age 14. She is the first reader and an enthusiastic encourager. My Aunt Jana, who is close enough in age to be a sister, is the second reader who patiently answers what feels like hundreds of questions I text to her about each project, the main one being "Should I really keep doing this?"

And finally, my husband Steve, who painstakingly reads every word in the MotoMysteries books, editing out unnecessary words and providing feedback and input. In *Phantom Ship in the Desert* he helped me uncover the mystery of the lost ship, when I couldn't quite figure out what was happening.

Lastly, I give all praise to God, the Creator, for blessing us with creative abilities and for His wondrous gift of salvation and abundant life.

Will you help promote MotoMysteries with a review of *MotoMysteries Collection: Books One to Three?*

Online reviews play a big role in the success of a book. Many readers choose what book to order based on what reviewers have to say. If you could take a few minutes and give an honest review at one or all of the following websites, I'd be very grateful.

Amazon.com
BookBub.com
Goodreads.com

Thank you and thanks for coming along on Jeremiah and Millie's adventures!

Sherri Kukla

Sherri Kukla
sherrikukla@gmail.com

P.S. Would you like to send me an email after you leave a review? I'd love to hear from you and to go on-line and read the review!

ABOUT THE AUTHOR
Sherri Kukla and her husband Steve are the publishers of *S&S Off Road Magazine* and the founders and directors of Thundering Trails off road camp for kids. They reside in the off road community of Ocotillo Wells CA with their teenage granddaughter and a dozen or so motorcycles, surrounded by coyotes, snakes, rabbits and other desert critters.

Have you read these MotoMysteries books?

Book 1 – The Skeleton and the Lantern
Book 2 - Ghost Lights of Dry Brook
Book 3 - Phantom Ship in the Desert
Book 4 - Harbor Point Haunt (Fall 2021)

The Christmas Miracle
A Christmas Mini-Mystery

Available in print and ebook on Amazon

www.sherrikukla.com
www.facebook.com/motomysteries

If you or someone you know ever have thoughts of giving up on life, *please reach out to someone*:
Friends
Parents
Counselors
Teachers
Pastors
Suicide Hotlines like the ones listed below

Sadness doesn't last forever, and suicide is a permanent solution that can never be undone.

National Suicide Prevention Lifeline
1-800-273-TALK
1-800-273-8255

Jason Foundation
Call the hotline above
or text **JASON** to **741741**
www.jasonfoundation.com

Made in the USA
Las Vegas, NV
15 April 2022